Sodomy's Solicitations

In the series *Sexuality Studies*,
edited by Janice M. Irvine and Regina Kunzel

ALSO IN THIS SERIES:

Joseph J. Fischel

Sodomy's Solicitations

A Right to Queerness

TEMPLE UNIVERSITY PRESS

Philadelphia • *Rome* • *Tokyo*

TEMPLE UNIVERSITY PRESS
Philadelphia, Pennsylvania 19122
tupress.temple.edu

Library of Congress Cataloging-in-Publication Data

Names: Fischel, Joseph J., author.
Title: Sodomy's solicitations : a right to queerness / Joseph J. Fischel.
Other titles: Sexuality studies.
Description: Philadelphia : Temple University Press, 2025. | Series:
    Sexuality studies | Includes bibliographical references and index. |
    Summary: "This book advances a queer politics that backgrounds
    nonnormative identities and foregrounds instead the state's deployment
    of sex to govern"— Provided by publisher.
Identifiers: LCCN 2025002622 (print) | LCCN 2025002623 (ebook) | ISBN
    9781439915844 (cloth) | ISBN 9781439915851 (paperback) | ISBN
    9781439915868 (pdf)
Subjects: LCSH: Sexual rights—Louisiana. | Sex and law—Louisiana. | Sex
    crimes—Law and legislation—Louisiana. | Sodomy—Law and
    legislation—Louisiana. | Sex offenders—Legal status, laws,
    etc.—Louisiana. | Sex work—Law and legislation—Louisiana. | Queer
    theory.
Classification: LCC HQ65.5.L8 F57 2025 (print) | LCC HQ65.5.L8 (ebook) |
    DDC 323.3/2609763—dc23/eng/20250331
LC record available at https://lccn.loc.gov/2025002622
LC ebook record available at https://lccn.loc.gov/2025002623

The manufacturer's authorized representative in the EU for product safety is
Temple University Rome, Via di San Sebastianello, 16, 00187 Rome RM, Italy
(https://rome.temple.edu/).
tempress@temple.edu

Contents

Acknowledgments

This book and I were in an on-again, off-again love affair for over a decade, so the people, animals, and places to whom I owe gratitude is sizeable. As for the animals, I am thinking mostly of my truest, toothless companion, pup Abby B. Ginsburg, but also the pigs, goats, cows, and chickens who patiently entertained me and my friend and coauthor Gabe Rosenberg. The start and finish of writing this book coincided with the start and finish of my marriage to Igor de Souza, whom I love truly. I will forever cherish Igor's intellectual, emotional, and gustatory support.

I am beyond grateful for the opportunities I was given to workshop *Sodomy's Solicitations* at several universities and academic conferences. The book benefited profoundly from these encounters.

The seedlings of this project were cultivated by fabulous friends and mentors in and around the 2011–2012 Pembroke Center for Teaching and Research on Women at Brown University, among them Cal Biruk, Denise Davis, Poulomi Saha, Suzanne Stewart-Steinberg, Elizabeth Weed, and Debbie Weinstein. I received some of the hardest and most necessary challenges to the book's preliminary arguments at the *Sex and Justice* conference held at the University of Michigan in 2012. Thank you to the organizers, Scott De Orio, David Halperin, and Trevor Hoppe, and thank you for pushing back, Alexis Agathocleous and Deon Haywood.

For permitting me to think aloud about sex in public, infinite thanks to Jane Ward for hosting my visit to University of California, Riverside; to Sina Kramer, Andrew Dilts, Mairead Sullivan, and their students at Loyola

Marymount University; to Michael Dango and Erin Spampinato for the exhilarating panel they organized on "Theorizing Rape and Aesthetics" at the 2021 American Comparative Literature Association conference; and to Mary Anne Case for inviting me to the Regulation of Family, Sex, and Gender Workshop at the University of Chicago Law School—I am especially indebted to Deborah Tuerkheimer and Alex Boni-Saenz for their smart interventions.

For a while, the third chapter was traveling under the obnoxious talk title "Gay Rights for Cows?" The chapter was enriched by engagement from magnanimous scholars, including Joel Burges, Tanya Bakhmetyeva, Kristin Doughty, and their students at the 2021 Rainbow Lecture at the University of Rochester; and Mel Chen, Lori Gruen, Leslie Salzinger, and several others at the "Theorizing Sexual Violence" speaker series hosted by Gender and Women's Studies at UC Berkeley in 2021.

The third chapter's coauthor, Gabe Rosenberg, and his partner, Harris Solomon, are two of my best friends and fiercest intellectual comrades. I was scarily sick for many weeks in the summer of 2022 and it is little exaggeration to say they were lifesaving.

My theorizing, evidencing, and ultimately advocating for a constitutional right to sex work benefited from the wisdom of Reva Siegel at Yale Law School, from the insights of Jill Weinberg and Michal Buchhandler-Raphael at the Law and Society Association conference in 2023, and from the superb labor of former-student-turned-research-assistant Anna Lipin, who was essential to building my archive and investigating relevant case law.

In the spring of 2023, I was honored to deliver the Mary Edwards Memorial Lecture at SUNY Purchase, care of Samuel Galloway and Shaka McGlotten, where I ultracondensed, and with only partial success, the entirety of this book's arguments into a fifty-minute talk (my mother would tell you it was an hour). So thanks to Samuel, Shaka, and the audience—including my sweet, game-for-nerds boyfriend Jack Goldman—for bearing with me. The coda of the book formalizes some of the ideas that percolated in the talk.

I lived in New Orleans in the spring months of 2012, 2016, and 2019 to conduct interviews and archival research for *Sodomy's Solicitations*; during my last stay, I volunteered for the American Civil Liberties Union of Louisiana. I made lifelong friends like Menaka Phillips, Chris Sullivan, and Rebecca Robinson, who were unbeatable tour guides, encyclopedic of so much New Orleans. And my research benefited from the generosity of activists, archivists, librarians, reporters, politicians, and (yes, even) police officers: Wendi Cooper, Matt Hindman, Michael Merricks, Kayla Mulford, Jim Mustian, Patricia Smith, Greg Osborn at the New Orleans Public Library, Connie Phelps at the Earl K. Long Library, and Devan

Wilkinson and Krystal Dean at the Louisiana House of Representatives Administrative Services. Thank you to Becky Atencio and her colleagues in Gender and Sexuality Studies at Tulane University for providing me a visiting scholarship to ease my research endeavors. I am profoundly indebted to the women and men registered as sex offenders in Louisiana who graciously agreed to be interviewed despite the overwhelming hardships in their lives.

I have been lucky to have critical, caring interlocutors in Bill Araiza, Lauren Berlant, Brenda Cossman, Diana Kim, Sina Kramer, Adam McGee, Joe Rollins, Joan Tronto, Charles Upchurch, and the editors at *The Feminist Wire*. The manuscript went through an exacting workshop with brilliant feminist scholars Jennifer Nash, Robyn Wiegman, and Linda Zerilli.

My colleagues at Yale University have been supportive in every possible way, and I am privileged to work and learn with them. Thank you, Crystal Feimster (and the supercharged students in our seminar on New Orleans), Rod Ferguson, Inderpal Grewal, Scott Herring, Greta Toe Pick LaFleur, Caleb Knapp, Reg Kunzel, Dara Strolovitch, Linn Tonstad, Gerald Torres, Deb Vargas, Kalindi Vora, and Gideon Yaffe. Administrators Moe Gardner, Ellen Cupo, and Christina Wethington are the best—facilitative, good-humored, and kind.

I am tremendously appreciative to the Fund for Lesbian and Gay Studies and the A. Whitney Griswold Faculty Research Fund at Yale, both of which provided necessary financial support for the project.

Matt Nadel briefly served as a formal research assistant for the book, but his influence reaches well past the job description. Matt and I are collaborators, comrades, even cocurators; and we became close friends through our shared commitment to supporting a social justice movement in New Orleans. I thank him for his diligence, tenacity, and creativity.

Together, Matt's documentary and my book accelerated our efforts to dismantle—by reform, repeal, or lawsuit—a discriminatory Louisiana sex law (much more on this in Chapter 1). Thank you to the attorneys and activists who continue to push the campaign forward: Nora Ahmed, Bruce Hamilton, and the American Civil Liberties Union (ACLU) of Louisiana; Syrita Steib and Operation Restoration; and Suzanne Hazeldean and her students at the LGBTQ Advocacy Clinic at Brooklyn Law School. Deepest admiration for Wendi Cooper, who leads the charge.

As research assistant, Kate Brennan stewarded the (long) last lap of this endeavor. She is phenomenal—a spectacular editor, supremely skilled researcher, and overall unparalleled interlocutor. I could not have finished this project without her.

Shaun Vigil is a merciful yet masterful editor, to whom I am much obliged for his guidance and encouragement.

An earlier and too jargoned version of Chapter 1 was originally published in a 2013 issue of *differences: A Journal of Feminist Cultural Studies*; highly truncated and unelaborated versions of Chapters 2 and 5 were published in separate articles in the *Boston Review* in June 2021 and February 2022, respectively. Finally, ideas and arguments and a few passages from an article I wrote for the *Journal of Homosexuality* in 2017 are scattered throughout the manuscript, mainly in the Introduction's gloss on the historical multipurpose of antisodomy laws in the United States. All the material published here has been significantly renovated from its earlier iterations. Thank you to the aforementioned journals for permitting reprints.

Triangles are the strongest shape, according to some engineers on the internet (and to Freud). I'm not sure what that means, but over the past many years, enduring the unendurable, my mother, sister, and I have become each other's closest friends, bullshit-checkers, and trusted counsel. I love them to infinity and I respect them even more. The book is dedicated to Shelley and Eliana Fischel.

Sodomy's Solicitations

Introduction

Sex Offenders, Exhibitionists, and Zoophiles?

The Radical Potential of Queer Politics

In late summer of 2023, my boyfriend and I traveled to New Orleans together to party at Southern Decadence, the city's yearly gay—increasingly queer— celebration featuring dances, street fairs, drag brunches, and a culminating parade in the French Quarter. We went to Decadence in part to celebrate my submitting this manuscript to Temple University Press. We went in part because we are queers who enjoy queer spaces, sweaty dancing, sex parties, and wearing silly, shiny outfits. And we went finally because this is a book about New Orleans, sodomy and sodomy law, and the ways we might accommodate, rather than criminalize, a public sexual culture—so it felt professionally irresponsible (really) that I had not yet been to Decadence.

Late one night, we poured out of a leather bar onto the streets of the Marigny, joined by hundreds of other men, many of whom were sporting just jockstraps in the sticky summer air. Men offered one another friendly and more-than-friendly caresses. The following day, people of all genders and in all varieties of fabulous dress and raunchy undress paraded through the Quarter, pasties abounding.

Stationed outside the leather bar that night as well as along the parade route the next afternoon were officers of the New Orleans Police Department

---

Portions of this chapter previously appeared as Joseph J. Fischel, "Sodomy's Penumbra," *Journal of Homosexuality*, 64 (14), p.2030–2056, doi: https://doi-org/10.1080/00918369 .2017.1293403. © 2017 Taylor & Francis, reprinted by permission of the publisher (Taylor & Francis Ltd, http://www.tandfonline.com).

(NOPD), unbothered by the butts and breasts; evidently, none of this was new to them. In both scenes the NOPD officers were hands-off, even a little bored, monitoring crowds and occasionally redirecting foot traffic.

Behold a queer regulatory state in action! At the leather bar and on the parade route, what struck me was how sex and sexuality were so clearly culturally, politically, and phenomenologically special for us participants compared to how unspecial displays of sex and sexuality were for the police, state actors not historically known for their tranquil approach to nonnormative sex and sexualities; that is, to queerness.

Might these (non)encounters serve as political metaphors? How might we scale up a sexual politics that de-exceptionalizes sex when it comes to policing and criminal justice while also countenancing the specialness of sex in so many people's lives, livelihoods, and subcultural consciousness? Herewith, what is pretty much the same question now posed in the vernacular of contemporary, United Statesean political discourse:

What if we politicized sex without the conceptual precondition of identity? What might sexual justice politics look like if it were not so anchored in identity and identitarianism, and if sexual justice politics were not brokered—entirely—on women's and LGBT equality?[1]

Sodomy's Solicitations: A Right to Queerness advises a "break from,"[2] but not wholesale rejection of, identitarian-based approaches to sexual justice, opting instead for what I term *paraidentitarianism*. Paraidentitarianism is a mouthful of a neologism, but the term gestures toward a politics of social transformation that recognizes patterned injuries against identity groups—so mine is not an *anti*-identitarian project—without confining the analyses of and remedies for those injuries to identity formations alone. We are not all women, gays, Jews, or Black people (reader: I will come out as two of four), but we are all sodomites or could be.[3] For now, "sodomite" refers to any person who performs, might perform, wishes to perform, or is presumed to perform nonprocreative sex acts, typically but not exclusively oral and anal sex, and typically but not exclusively with other humans.[4]

You might not have expected that last paragraph to land where it did, but *Sodomy's Solicitations* advances a queer politics calibrated to challenging those state practices and political discourses that exceptionalize sex and sexualize subjects to legitimate forms of governance that superordinate some populations and subordinate others. Those others that may or may not be the "usual suspects": racial and religious minorities, women, and LGBT folks, among others. To pay political heed to that universality—we are all sodomites or could be—need not require the erasure of marginalized groups but might instead draw necessary attention to social asymmetries. Whose rights to sex, sexuality, gender diversity, and intimate association—what

I will later detail as *rights to queerness*—are relatively unencumbered and whose rights are systemically denied, denigrated, or delimited? To theorize and politicize a right to queerness across rather than within identity formations is to reconstruct, with English professor Madhavi Menon, a "universalism [that] insists on straddling, on standing athwart ontological categories that divide up the world and the people in it"; a "universalism [that] names the impossibility of having any particular assume ontological wholeness."[5]

The next section of this introduction is an interlocution of political scientist Cathy Cohen's field-forming article for gender and sexuality studies, "Punks, Bulldaggers, and Welfare Queens: The Radical Potential of Queer Politics?" Cohen's signature essay motivates the paraidentitarian politics of sexual justice I theorize throughout this book.[6] The section concludes with a few reflections on how this project fits alongside queer studies now as well as a short explanation of the book's subtitle, *A Right to Queerness*.

The following two sections provide a nascent, abbreviated, extremely partial, paraidentitarian political theory of sodomy and a nascent, abbreviated, extremely partial, paraidentitarian historiography of U.S. antisodomy law, respectively. My turn to sodomy and to antisodomy law is what propels, normatively and retrospectively, the Introduction's opening provocation (what if we politicized sex without the precondition of identity?), and so these sections on sodomy's political theory and antisodomy law's historiography set the backdrop for three twenty-first-century contestations over sodomy that this book spends most of its pages limning for their queer potential. I then offer an outline of the chapters and the coda. As these contestations over sodomy are all sited in or near New Orleans, I conclude by answering the (not-quite-right) question, *Why New Orleans?*

Paraidentitarianism

The title of this introduction, "Sex Offenders, Exhibitionists, and Zoophiles? The Radical Potential of Queer Politics," evidently riffs off Cohen's "Punks, Bulldaggers, and Welfare Queens: The Radical Potential of Queer Politics?" My conception of paraidentitarianism, and with it a paraidentitarian politics of sexual justice, springs directly from my long engagement with Cohen's magnificent text (and indirectly from many others, among them Hortense Spillers's "Mama's Baby, Papa's Maybe," and Spillers's neologism, "pornotroping").[7] The political and normative tensions in "Punks," first published in 1999, and the amplification of those tensions in a 2019 retrospective symposium around the essay,[8] put into focus the queer politics proposed in this book, a politics distilled yet distinguished from Cohen's coalitional vision. Let me adumbrate, if a bit cheekily, Cohen's and my differences by reference to our respective titles. Cohen imagines a coalitional politics among "punks, bulldaggers, and welfare queens," metonymic figures for those citizens disadvantaged by multiple, intersecting layers of oppression, foremost racism.[9] Cohen placed her titular question mark at the end of the subheading ("The Radical Potential of Queer Politics?"), betraying a skepticism that queer politics could ever fully deliver on a promise of collective justice for punks, bulldaggers, and welfare queens, whom Cohen later renames as "Black women, Black poor people, Black trans and gender-nonconforming folk, and Black gay, lesbian, and queer folks."[10] My question mark comes after my "bad queers"—the "sex offenders" whom you will meet in the first chapter, the exhibitionists conjured by religious conservatives in the second chapter, and the "zoophiles"[11] imagined by liberal legislators in the third—to signal that I am not actually proposing such a coalition of the purportedly monstrous. For me, these figures are constructed by and emblematic of state policies, laws, and political discourses that exceptionalize sex or sexualize subjects to legitimate oppressive, unjust, cruel, reactionary, or just stupid governance. And so the radical potential of queer politics—sans question mark—is neither to transvalue this or that despised group nor to create coalitions among minoritized identities, as important as those goals must be, but to call out and resist state action and political discourse that deploy sex to curtail freedom and flourishing, and not just human freedom and flourishing. So that's the nutshell version and vision of a paraidentitarian sexual politics, to which I now add some dimension.

Cohen's "Punks" was addressed to an emergent, irreverent, anti-assimilationist, HIV/AIDS-focused sexual politics of the 1990s, self-designated as "queer." The politics, often associated with the organization AIDS Coalition to Unleash Power (ACT UP), eschewed the mainstream U.S. LGBT movement's strategies for inclusion and nondiscrimination, opting instead for unconventional, confrontational, creative modes of protest against the material and symbolic privations of what queer studies scholars Lauren Berlant and Michael Warner defined as *heteronormativity*: "institutions, structures of understanding, and practical orientations that make heterosexuality seem not only coherent—that is, organized as a sexuality—but also privileged."[12]

This quick rendition of *queer politics v. LGBT politics* is so simplified as to be silly, but as Cohen's foil (which is not to say it is an inaccurate foil), the point is that queer politics, unlike an LGBT politics of assimilative inclusion into "dominant norms,"[13] promised to re-norm a world for more sexual freedom, gender diversity, and intimate pluralism. Importantly for Cohen, too, that universalist commitment to sexual and gender flourishing entailed with it an ostensibly left worldview that was concomitantly anticapitalist, antiracist, and feminist.[14]

On my reading of "Punks," Cohen then levels two criticisms at queer politics so defined, both criticisms contouring the paraidentitarian sexual politics on offer here. I consider these two criticisms in reverse order as Cohen presents them.

In the latter half of her essay, Cohen takes queer politics to task for not countenancing and so not considering as political allies those "heterosexuals on the (out)side of heteronormativity," namely, populations whose "nonnormative heterosexuality has been controlled and regulated through the state and systems of marginalization."[15] This was and continues to be a mind-blowing intervention for queer thought and activism. The state, state policies, and political discourses "queer" some straight folks, insofar as their (hetero)sexuality is rendered deviant, dangerous, or pathologized.[16] Cohen's historical examples are of (mostly) Black people in the United States: state prohibitions on marriage between enslaved persons; prohibitions on interracial marriage; the political demonization of the racialized "welfare queen" as unmarried, promiscuous, and reproductively and parentally unfit; and state practices of "prosecuting pregnant women for using drugs" or "forced sterilization of Puerto Rican and Native American women."[17] Cohen marshals these examples "to remind us of the numerous ways that sexuality and sexual deviance from a prescribed norm have been used to demonize and to oppress various segments of the population, even some classified under the label 'heterosexual.'"[18]

For me and for *Sodomy's Solicitations*, this criticism of Cohen's is what rectifies and radicalizes a queer politics: a politics challenging the state's use and abuse of sex to render populations denigrated, dangerous, or disposable.[19] This is a queer politics that would "designat[e] sexuality and struggles against sexual normalization as central to the politics of all marginal communities."[20] As Cohen's later reflections on "Punks" accentuate, if Black people who are viciously killed by police officers are "queer," this is not

> because of their sexual practice, identity, or performance but because they, as well as other young and poor folks of color, operate in the world as queer subjects: the targets of racial normalizing projects intent on pathologizing them across the dimensions of race, class, gender, and sexuality, simultaneously making them into deviants while normalizing their degradation and marginalization until it becomes what we expect—the norm—until it becomes something that we no longer pay attention to.[21]

In Cohen's most powerful criticism, Black people and other racial minorities are the populations paradigmatically queered by the state and U.S. political discourses, but that fact is an historical contingency. Statutory and political discourses may very well exceptionalize sex in ways that do not denigrate racial minority populations but that are nonetheless unjust; or the state and political discourses may sexualize and thereby subordinate populations that are not necessarily racial minorities.

Yet Cohen's earlier criticism of queer politics in "Punks" cuts more intersectional and identitarian (despite her claiming otherwise),[22] which allows me to define and defend, by contrast, the *para* of paraidentitarianism. Bluntly, Cohen calls out queer activists and queer political movements for trivializing or ignoring issues of racism, class inequality, and sexism. In this line of criticism, Cohen demands not that queer politics resist the state's deployment of sex, but that it embrace a "left intersectional analysis" attuned to white, class, and male privilege.[23] As she reflects in 2019, "Politicized identity is radical in the sense that those who embrace the identity of queer also often articulate an anti-capitalist, feminist, and nonnormative politics, committed to fighting with and struggling for those who are most marginal in our communities and the larger society."[24]

I am going to suggest that a queer politics calibrated to the statutory and political discursive deployment of sex, and a queer politics calibrated to challenging oppressions along multiple axes of race, class, and gender ("struggling for those . . . most marginal") are not fully compatible; and I am going to make the further, perhaps uncouth suggestion that queer politics, if it is *queer*, should harness its energies toward the first objective, not the second, as necessary and critical and urgent as anti-Blackness, misogyny, homophobia, and transphobia are in our historical present. This suggestion is not to disregard minoritized groups; to the contrary, there are a plethora of coalitional, solidaristic movements attuned to oppressed identities. However, not all identities are oppressed via *sex* or *sexualization*. But *queer* names, or from my perspective should name, processes that are in some sense nonnormatively *sexual* or at least proximate to the nonnormatively sexual; like Melani McAlister, "I'll go out on a limb and say that I think queering needs to be about sex."[25] Absent from our contemporary political moment is a movement against the state's use of sex to marginalize and minoritize populations, a phenomenon tracked—in one state, over one decade, and around one body of law—across this book. If queer politics as such must always and only be about sexism, racism, classism, homophobia, and their intersections, then queer politics will overlook how and when the state and political discourses deploy sex and sexualize subjects in ways that are not immediately or most pressingly identitarian. But what makes paraidentitarianism *para* is this: often, but not always, statutory and political discursive deployments of sex do marginalize or dehumanize already vulnerable, minority populations, as Cohen (and Hortense Spillers) so powerfully shows. The sexualization of Black mothers as "welfare queens" is the primary case in point. Frequently cited, Cohen laments that 1990s queer activism "has come dangerously close to a single oppression model," wherein the danger of a single-axis politics of sexuality is a conservative blindness to the comparative privilege of some (indexically white, male, and wealthy) queers and the comparative disadvantage of some (indexically Black, poor, and female) heterosexuals.[26] But singling out sex, or sex as a "single-axis" of progressive politics, only tilts conservative if politics is honed to groups rather than to state power. To single out the state's singularizing of sex is queer indeed, and potentially foregrounds some of the most insidious ways religious, racial, gender, and sexual minorities are pervasively demeaned and disenfranchised. So, unlike other left political analyses that glibly write off identitarian concerns as siloizing, balkanizing, epiphenomenal, liberal, or whatever, a paraidentitarian politics of sexual justice is cognizant that state sexualization and sex exceptionalism disparately impact vulnerable, minority populations. That's just not all state sexualization and sex exceptionalism do and do wrong.

This book and its paraidentitarian queer politics labor to stick with the sex, or the "politics of sex itself," as David Halperin puts it, for "the politics of sex cannot be reduced to the politics of identity."[27] In queer studies, there is not as much cersis on sex—political, literary, sociological, anthropological, discursive—as one might think.

Despite several wayward paths, sex is not the direction queer studies has traveled since the early 1990s. Since then, identity and identitarianism have hardened rather than released their hold on gender and sexuality scholarship. Rather, and under the sign of sexuality/queer studies, we encounter important, sometimes groundbreaking research on the proliferation of non- or quasi-LGBT and nonbinary identities;[28] and on the ways sexual identity intersects with other social axes of inequality like race, nation, or disability.[29] "Queer" has come to signify reporting on secondarily or exponentially marginalized sexual minorities, as the QTPOC (queer and trans people of color) abbreviation suggests, as does the recent multitude of texts on queer and transgender prison populations.[30] Alternatively, queer analyses that took flight from identity also took flight from sex more or less altogether, concentrating theory onto affect, kinship, friendship, ecology[31] . . . or even larger, world-making abstractions: "What does queer studies have to say about empire, globalization, neoliberalism, sovereignty, and terrorism?" asked well-known sexuality scholars for a state-of-the-interdiscipline issue of the journal *Social Text* in 2005. "What does queer studies tell us about immigration, citizenship, prisons, welfare, mourning, and human rights?"[32] Where went the sex?[33]

The laws, enforcement patterns, legislative reforms, and activisms I explore in this book ramify across identitarian registers, fueled in whole or in part by gay-affirmative, transgender-affirmative, homophobic, or transphobic energies. But there is more to say than that, and investigating the non- or paraidentitarian consequences of sex law and legal reforms potentially yields important returns for expanding our political imaginary around sex and sexual justice. Toward that end, *Sodomy's Solicitations* finds cross-disciplinary compatriots in Jennifer Evans's effort to "rediscover and redeploy the radical potential of queer as a politics, analytics, and way of life," by "account[ing] for unanticipated alliances, bad gays, monstrous others, and imperfect heroes" in postwar Germany;[34] in Charles Upchurch's investigation of mid-nineteenth-century campaigns to end the death penalty for sodomy in Britain, which concludes: "If we keep the focus on issues of sexuality, especially as they intersect with issues of race, class, and gender, and make the subject the discovery of how issues played out in politics to create ethical subjects, more ethical social interactions, and greater justice, this might open avenues to a queer analysis focused on issues of power, rather than issues of identity";[35] in Stefan Vogler's proposal that "we should reconceptualize sexuality . . . not merely as an identity but as a technology that can powerfully shape the world";[36] and finally, if more remotely, in Avgi Saketopoulou and Ann Pellegrini's insistence "that gender, *all gender*, is both delightfully stranger *and* more savagely violent than our theories can imagine," for gender, according to the psychoanalyst scholars, far from innate and static, accrues through social, familial, and sexual encounters and traumas.[37]

Yet despite my proposition that sex is underattended in queer studies, I am less inclined than Oliver Davis and Tim Dean to conclude that "queer studies hate[s] sex." The scholars rhetorize the assertion as a titular question—"Does Queer Studies Hate Sex?"—but their answer is yes.[38] Davis and Dean proffer psychoanalytic, political, and academic-professional reasons for why queer studies has allegedly come to hate sex, but pertinent for this introduction and my intervention more generally is their provocation that gender, but especially race, racism, and racial difference, edged out sex in queer theorizing. Race and gender, contend Davis and Dean, are "categories with which the neoliberal university . . . is considerably more comfortable";[39] "[t]hinking instead [of sex] about race and gender enhances academics' political credibility and institutional authority";[40] in their "quest for social justice," queer scholars came to truck in the juridical idiom of racial justice over and against sex.[41] On the authors' account, Kimberlé Crenshaw's notion of intersectionality overran queer studies, whereby *sex* was reduced to *gender*, and "issues of race" were "prioritize[d],"[42] in part because race, like gender, can be comprehended through "identity categories" whereas sex is "other-dimensional" to identity and so less assimilable for politically progressive scholarship.[43]

Sodomy's Solicitations is clearly influenced by Davis and Dean's indictment of queer studies. My hesitation to sign onto their polemic though is due not only to the scholarship just cited (Evans, Upchurch, Vogler, Saketopoulou, and Pellegrini) but also and more so on account of the scholarship archived in my second chapter as "Black and Brown Pleasure Studies," which collates a variety of texts, notably uncited in Davis's and Dean's *Hatred of Sex*, that theorize sex in methodologically diverse, unabashedly explicit, often hedonically calibrated ways. For just a few titles, consider: Jennifer Nash's "Black Anality" and her monograph, *The Black Body in Ecstasy: Reading Race, Reading Pornography*; Amber Musser's *Sensual Excess: Queer Femininity and Brown Jouissance*; Ariane Cruz's *The Color of Kink: Black Women, BDSM, and Pornography*; Mireille Miller-Young's *A Taste for Brown Sugar: Black Women in Pornography*; Angela Jones's *Camming: Money, Power, and Pleasure in the Sex Work Industry*; and Deb Vargas's "Ruminations on *Lo Sucio* as a Latino Queer Analytic."[44] Some of this scholarship is discussed in more detail in Chapter 2, but none of the texts referenced here jettison sex to vault race; to the contrary, they theorize how racialized subjects enjoy, navigate, monetize, resignify, or are otherwise interpellated through sex and sexuality.

One can only conclude that queer studies hates sex if texts like the aforementioned are neglected or miscategorized as not-queer studies, which would be an embarrassing jurisdictional error. While sex is neither trivialized (as not as serious as race) and by no means "eclipse[d] from intellectual consciousness"[45] in this scholarship, in all or nearly all of the texts, race, racial difference, anti-Blackness, and/or white supremacy are either diacritic or atmospheric, which just means that some of the best contemporary humanistic and social theoretic work in and around sex collocates in queer studies, ethnic studies, and Black studies.[46] On this point, I reiterate my pivot from Cohen's "Punks": *Sodomy's Solicitations* sticks with sex and with sex's governance to explore the consequences of state practices and political discourses that sexualize and sex-exceptionalize, consequences that are too often but not always racialized; consequences that sometimes exceed or are even obscured by the identitarian terms more readily at liberals' and progressives' disposal.

But if queer studies does not hate sex, it does hate the state, especially the United States and Israel.[47] Or less hyperbolically, scholarship in queer studies is generally antistatist; the political calls therein tend more toward the abolitionist than reformist or legislative (my colleague in the interdiscipline gently chides this intellectual tendency as Queers Against Speedbumps). *Sodomy's Solicitations* has no special (unrequited) love for the state, either; most of the proposals herein are to repeal sex laws rather than to revise them, although I put forward a few ideas for reforming indecent exposure laws, and Gabriel Rosenberg and I suggest better regulatory directions for protecting and promoting nonhuman animal welfare. Still, that I insist (reforming) state sex laws and policies matter for nonnormative lives, relationships, and intimacies positions this book to the side of influential work in queer studies (and Black studies[48]) that renders engagement with the state as complicit or worse.

And yet the sodomitical episodes contained in these pages, the paraidentitarian sexual politics derived from them, and what I think is best termed *a right to queerness* for which those politics must be waged, demonstrate that we can neither refuse the state's regulatory regimes nor should we. Might we imagine a queerer regulatory regime instead of fantasizing a stateless world cleansed of *-isms*? What would that queer regulatory regime look like? *Sodomy's Solicitations'* constellation of negative rights and (mostly speculated upon) positive rights, and its criticisms of state sexualization and state sex exceptionalism, tend toward a right to queerness.

In truth, I landed on the book's subtitle after reading a parenthetical dismissal of such a right in the preface to Lee Edelman's *Bad Education: Why Queer Theory Teaches Us Nothing* (2022). Edelman's write-off of the right to queerness is symptomatic of a broader left-academic, structuralist indictment of the (U.S.) state as, at its unchangeable core, anti-Black, anti-queer, and antitrans (it has become less fashionable to condemn the state as male and patriarchal, but the later critiques are cut from the same cloth as dominance feminism).[49] Like me, Edelman understands "queerness" to "signif[y] diacritically in relation to a norm," an abstraction that "implies a disturbance of order, a nonconformity to prevailing logic or law, a glitch in the function of meaning."[50] Under this nonidentitarian meaning, *queerness* aptly describes persons sexed by the state and political discourses as sex offenders, exhibitionists, and zoophiles, wherein queerness is neither an ontological truth of persons nor an appellation for their sexual identities, but rather designates discursive processes of stratification through sexualization (see, as earlier in this section, Cohen's presumptively heterosexual "welfare queens").

But then Edelman takes another step in his repositioning of *queerness* that strikes me as defeatist. According to Edelman, queerness as social negativity, meaninglessness, and nullification is always and only antagonistic to politics as such, for queerness undermines totalization, coherence, and idealization that politics, perhaps especially progressive politics, demands. "*Bad Education* questions the recuperative possibility of progressive politics, including the progressive politics that represents itself as queer," writes Edelman, for even queer progressive politics necessarily depends on exclusion—and the exclusion is the structural position named "queer[,] or, for that matter, Blackness, woman, trans*, incest, 'sex.'"[51] Edelman's primary, metonymic exhibit for queer progressive politics' operative exclusions is

Bostock v. Clayton County, the 2020 U.S. Supreme Court decision holding that workplace discrimination against gay and transgender employees qualifies as unlawful sex discrimination. Of the opinion, Edelman is unforgiving—and here we come upon the fateful, fatalist parenthetical:

> *Bostock v. Clayton County* did not and could not advance "queer" rights. In extending employment protections to persons who are "homosexual or transgender," it merely continued the juridical dissociation of those categories from queerness. . . . *Bostock* . . . said nothing about a right to queerness *(whatever that would mean)* but could only contribute to the normalization of "homosexual or transgender" persons.[52]

"Whatever that would mean" is Edelman's way of saying a right to queerness cannot mean anything, because queerness is the catachrestic placeholder for the abjection against which all rights may be constituted and then conferred. These structural claims and their concomitant chain of equivalences seduce left-leaning students, especially after years of pandemic privations and right-wing ascendance, but they offer a tendentious vision of "politics": if one defines (progressive) politics as negation then all politics negates. Queer progressivism is conflated with liberal legalism, which is then conflated with LGBT-rights litigation through the narrowest possible reading of *Bostock*. Most legal commentators agree that *Bostock* protections extend not just to gays and transgender people but to a wider array of nonnormative gender identities, gender expressions, and sexualities.[53] If that is right, it becomes harder to claim that all *Bostock* is good for is normalizing gays and transgender people, and that it normalizes subjects *against* queerness, if queerness means something between positivized identity forms and pure negation, say, something like gender, sexual, and intimate pluralism. *Bostock* should also protect intersex folks, bisexuals, and gender-nonconforming and nonbinary workers from employment discrimination, to which Edelman might reply that these are simply cosmetic inclusions to the normalizing regime, except that cannot be the whole story. *Intersex*, *nonconforming*, and *nonbinary* signify beyond or beside taxonomic identity to anatomical, stylistic, and aesthetic configurations of gender and sexuality, that is, to "queer" bodies and behaviors that resist normalization and assimilation. That one cannot be fired from their job, say, for having top surgery, or for wearing a dress to work if they have a penis, does not mean those people are now "normalized." It just means they might get to keep their jobs.[54]

If a right to queerness is defined as *a right to sexual freedom, sexual welfare, and gender expansiveness far less policed by the state (or employers), a right not-so-tethered to and nonsynonymous with "L," "G," "B," and "T" rights*, then a right to queerness is not meaningless. And queerness is not "incompatible with . . . progressivism," if progressivism is not as beholden to pregiven sexual identities and subjects as Edelman assumes. "Queerness, if it is to have any political resonance," illuminates José Muñoz, "needs to be more than an identitarian marker and to articulate a forward-dawning futurity."[55] What might that future look like, statutorily speaking? The progressive, paraidentitarian, queer politics I outline in the chapters that follow advocate for, among other things: the abolition of sex offender registry and notification systems (Chapter 1); a (qualified but nevertheless expansive) right to public nudity and public sexual activity, a right anchored against the state's historical, phobic sexualization of racial minorities and queers (Chapter 2); the abolition of antibestiality statutes, the abolition of industrial agricultural practices, and material provisions to better protect and promote nonhuman animal pleasures (Chapter 3); a right to commercial sex, sodomitical or otherwise (Chapters 4 and 5); and a robust civics and sexuality education for young people to become queerer, more resilient political agents (Coda). Mine is less a queer politics honed to "affording the shelter of meaningful being to those living negated identities,"[56] than to gender freedom, sexual freedom, and freedom from sexualization. At the risk of sounding righteous—but I think not hopelessly "liberal humanist"[57]—a right to queerness, far from a performative contradiction, is a political imperative for sexual justice.

To propose some initial ways we might politicize sex without the precondition of identity, I examine contemporary state and political discursive practices of sexualization and sex exceptionalism. And while the scope may at first appear exceedingly narrow, this book focuses exclusively on the life and afterlives of twenty-first-century Louisiana antisodomy laws. Tracking three political episodes in and around such laws, I analyze the paraidentitarian, queer sexual politics we might glean from them if identity claims did not so saturate our cultural landscape. Before outlining the sodomitical episodes in Louisiana, and before addressing the question, *Why New Orleans?*, I provide some political theoretic and historiographic scaffolding for why I turn to sodomy and antisodomy law to build out a paraidentitarian politics of sexual justice. The following two sections are by no means a serious history of sodomy and antisodomy regulations—to crib from Cohen, "as a political scientist a little history is all I can offer."[58] Rather, these sections offer some historical, normative, and political theoretic coordinates for the ensuing arguments of the book.

A Political Theory of Sodomy, or Notes toward
a Sodomitical Contract

Carole Pateman's *The Sexual Contract* and Charles Mills's *The Racial Contract* were gauntlet-thrown, field-forming confrontations for contemporary political thought.[59] Feminist political theorists and philosophers of race and inequality have devoted a great deal of ink to these texts, and Pateman and Mills themselves have served as interlocutors for one another to tease apart the similarities and differences in their interventions.[60] I call upon these late twentieth-century texts not to offer another close, comparative reading of them, but because their theories of group-based subordination at a general level of abstraction—namely, that those gendered "women" and those racialized as "nonwhite" subtend invidious fictions of democratic equality—have had enduring influence over what Robyn Wiegman calls "identity knowledges."[61] Indeed, one way to partially genealogize left-academic narratives of the Other as a gendered and racialized container for and displacement of all kinds of affects, appetites, labors, and irrationalities that would otherwise mark the unmarked but tacitly white-and-male category of "citizen," "person," or "human" is through Mills's racial contract and Pateman's sexual contract.[62]

For both Mills and Pateman, key to the story of freedom and political equality embedded in the social contract—where unmarked "persons" mythically band together to contract out political authority, rather than submit by divine right (or by force) to queens or kings—is philosophers', colonists', and slaveholders' discursive offloading of carnality, unruliness, heteronomy, and hedonism onto women and nonwhite others.[63] Philosopher Sina Kramer richly theorizes these political epistemological operations as "constitutive exclusion."[64]

Constitutive exclusion, or offloading, permits the fiction of white men as temperate: deliberative contractors governed by reason. (That offloading, as described by Pateman and Mills, appears equivocal in the case of women [just white women, for Mills] but unequivocal in the case of nonwhite men.)[65] Schematically and overstated, the fiction of white men as deliberative, rational, and reasonable demands a correlating fiction of women and nonwhite people as impulsive, appetitive, and libidinal.[66]

We can think of "offloading" as a two-step process: first, the discursive construction of the remainder (sexuality, carnality, unruliness, appetite);[67] second, the discursive relocation of the remainder onto others.

But what if the second step did not automatically flow from the first? What if carnality/appetite/desire were "contractually" avowed? What if the hedonic were rendered elemental to, rather than corrosive of, political alliances? What if excess, pleasure-seeking, unruliness and, attendantly, the will-to-*not*-procreate were enfolded back into the political body and all its citizens, rather than ejected and then projected onto others? Projection fails or is incompletable, I am submitting, because regardless of our racial classification, gender identification, or sexual orientation, we all have mouths and anuses. To put this in less corporeal, more political theoretic terms: antisodomy law and its proponents locate unruliness, excess, and hedonism within, not below or beyond, political personhood. While jurists and preachers have long seen the libertinism metaphorized by sodomy as a profound problem for political order, I wish to recast sodomy and its associated specters as an alternative ground for coalition. Sodomy and its specters accelerate a "reconstitution of politics and the terms of political agency that would no longer operate by means of [constitutive exclusion]."[68]

Sodomy—or the anxiogenic amorphousness of "sodomy"[69]—provides a conceptual locus for retrieving, as Mills puts it, "contract idea's radical egalitarian potential."[70] Mine is a call neither for a deracinated liberal humanism nor a socialism cleansed of cultural difference, but a more modest one suggesting that there is potential for alliance to be found not just in our abjected or otherwise othered identities, however intersectional, but across them, through our sodomitical acts.[71] Here, I mean "sodomitical" in its most inclusive connotation: not merely as a descriptor for anal sex between men, but as a referent for all kinds of relational and sexual practices that have augured social disorder, avarice, unproductivity, and perversions or inversions of "natural" hierarchies, according to authorities secular or spiritual.[72]

Across British, colonial, and U.S. law, antisodomy statues have long traveled under the sign "crime against nature," etymologically rooted in antiquity and influentially described as such by William Blackstone (in English) and Immanuel Kant (in Latin).[73] (Louisiana enacted its sodomy law, prohibiting "unnatural carnal copulation" between men and between men and animals, in 1805, shortly after the Louisiana Purchase. For but a brief period, sodomy thus was permitted under American rule, until the Territory adopted English common law into its criminal code and with it a mandatory life sentence for sodomitical sex, understood then as penile penetration of an animal or another man's anus.)

But what does it mean for "crime" to be "against nature," or "unnatural" when a "crime" is always already part of a conventionalist order? There are no "crimes" if there is no polity and the polity itself, in the liberal imaginary, is contracted *against nature*, against the state of nature. If the very idea of political rule premised on voluntary agreement ejects us from nature, what should it matter to law or to legislators if citizens commit sodomy?

One easy and historically available answer is that a crime against nature is a crime against God, against the divine command to be fruitful and multiply: *Do not spill your seed unless it is for baby-making*, in which case seed is not spilled so much as properly funneled.[74] Yet in U.S. sex law as well as in other jurisdictions, ejaculation was made explicitly unnecessary as an element of sodomy, one of several data points that suggests that the contravention of the divine procreative mandate is not all that makes a "crime against nature" against nature.[75]

What is so persistently *contra naturam* about sodomitical sex is that it figures men, and occasionally women, as appetitive, hedonistic, governed by passion, and uncontrolled by powers of rationality and reason.[76] Absent the alibi of procreation, sodomitical sex has historically been conceived as orgiastic, violent, or both. In some parts of the world today, and in some parts of the United States, the meaning of sodomy—hedonic violence or violent hedonism—has been positively inverted, what Lee Edelman would call "positivized," into identity: sodomy represents consensual sex par excellence, and its personage, the gay man, has ascended as the exemplary agent of sexual freedom, a model citizen whose sex is governed not by family, obligation, baby-making, or subordination, but by powers of deliberation and self-determination.[77] In the parlance of Mills's metacontract theory, (white) gay men are "full persons and full contractors" in the polity, not despite but because of their sexuality.[78] The late modern liberal story of the cultural transformation of gays and lesbians from dangerous to dignified is one of successful social movement, cosmopolitan tolerance, and Ellen DeGeneres. But if we travel back in time, prior to homosexual identity and just prior to liberalism and the inauguration of modern contract theory—to Puritan New England, for starters—we can retrieve a more expansive political valence for what we might term the sodomitical contract.

Michael Warner offers an illuminative account of Sodom as a central, recurring political metaphor underwriting Puritan migration to the New England colonies in the 1600s.[79] Warner shows how Puritan clergy and preachers emigrating to New England figured England and the English Church as Sodom, unruly and sinful, corrupt and in social decline. In Puritan writings and jeremiads, "the fable of Sodom represented, in a way no other image could, an entire society open to discipline and in need of saving."[80] As Warner documents, such deployments of "Sodom" had less to do with anal sex between men per se than with "unmanaged and unofficial sex" as threatening the social and "spiritual order."[81] Still, the "anathematized sexuality of Sodom was . . . never quite irrelevant, only held in reserve as an ambiguous referent," a referent that Puritan leaders soon drew upon to warn of societal decline in the emergent colonies.[82]

John Winthrop and John Cotton, along with several lesser-known Puritan leaders, saw in sodomy not the problem of a despised sexual subclass but the problem of "nonreproductive erotics"[83] devolving their own community into "a degenerate and onanistic New English Sodom."[84] Puritans railed against "an interpenetration between Sodom and Canaan," that Canaan could become Sodom, that New England could degenerate into England, because the colonists—needless but necessary to say, white men—are so easily tempted by flesh, carnality, and wickedness.[85] Borders between persons and places, and between righteousness and sin, are all too penetrable; compare this metastasizing carnality with sexual difference as prefigured by Pateman or racial difference as historical yet determinative by Mills.[86]

Warner makes two other pertinent observations. First, he catalogues the many "city-on-a-hill theme" sermons and pamphlets that repeatedly reference Sodom; the writings suggest that "New England's nervousness" about the sodomitical was anchored in concern that the people as a collective, rather than the individual sinner, would be perceived as, and divinely punished for, their excessive, exceptional filthiness.[87]

Second, Warner ties Puritan fixations with Sodom and sodomy to the erotically charged attachments among male colonists that energized their covenant with one another and with God. While "Puritans were anything but voluntarists at the level of the individual," clarifies Warner, "at the level of the social . . . covenant theory pioneered the legitimacy of elective ties modeled in contract relations," contract relations best exemplified by the "private bonds of fraternal men."[88] John Winthrop describes his subservience to Christ and his friendships with men in sensual, corporeal, even lustful terms. He idealizes brotherly affection as "creat[ing] the very bonds of the social by acting as a force of desire."[89]

To wit: the desire between men that facilitates the social body looks awfully similar to the desire between men that ends civilization. Warner proposes that the "violence of that contradiction was unleashed on the bodies of William Plain [convicted for sodomy] and others like him."[90] For Pateman, modernity's transition from paternal right to fraternal right was and is lubricated by the continuous subordination of women, now under the alibi of voluntary agreement. For Warner, though, fraternity as elective affinity always poses the risk of erotic affinity because what drives affinity as "elective" is desire, as opposed to natural order or hierarchy. If the shift from status-based hierarchy to a contract among equals demanded relocating lower status elsewhere, say onto women and nonwhite peoples, the shift from status to contract, adumbrated and emblematized in the "'inadvertent' liberalism"[91] of American Puritanism, also telegraphs the world-creating, world-destroying power of white men's choices to intimately affiliate with one another.

And yet must the covenanters, seekers of intimacy beyond the bond of family, only and always be white men? If "the conventions of male friendship took on different meanings in this changing context, as a system of status-based personal service gave way to systems of voluntary and contractual association," then the voluntarism of sodomy itself, combined with its ever-expanding (that is, until the mid-twentieth-century)[92] definitional contours in law, puncture "male [white] friendship" as the outer bound of political community.[93] What Warner sees, or what Warner sees Winthrop seeing, is neither a community of men banding together for sex (what would be pro-logue for a gay rights, identitarian story) nor a community of men banding together for self-rule (what would be prologue for the social, sexual, and racial contracts, along with their collateral offloading), but men realizing possibilities of freedom through, not against, erotic association, and that is the prologue for radically egalitarian political community, an embrace of excess.[94]

"As a paradigm for social bonds in general," then, "nonreproductive erotics unmoored from natural hierarchy" launches a political moder-nity—our own—that feigns egalitarianism.[95] But those nonreproductive erotics could very well herald the radical egalitarianism Mills envisions in a contractarianism cleansed of white supremacy, the radical egalitarianism Pateman envisions beyond contractarianism's horizon of super- and subor-dinate relations.[96]

Consider the following examples, drawn from wildly different places and times, that similarly gloss sodomy and sodomitical relations between men as challenges to the political status quo:

1. Historian Alan Bray, whom Warner cites, proposes that in Eliza-bethan England erotic relations between men were publicly con-demned, "stigmatized as sodomitical," only when they appeared to cut across and therefore threaten status relations; affective attachments "among gentlemen," on the other hand, refastened rather than dissolved "class and rank hierarchies."[97]

2. Classicist Zachary Herz, revisiting the infamous 1990s historico-legal debates over Plato's views about homosexuality, observes that in Plato's *Laws*, while Plato indeed decries sex between men and sex between women as "contrary to nature," the histori-cal and textual evidence suggests that Plato's condemnation is highly specified to "tyrannicide borne of homoerotics."[98] Echoing Thucydides, Plato's caution is that those in same-sex bonds, en-slaved to pleasure, are easily impelled to act courageously yet also recklessly. Men's love for one another, hedonic and abounding, tends toward political alliance, defiance, and revolution. "Elite homosociality" rivals the allegiance demanded by the state.[99] Plato's warning attests to, in the words of Christopher Chitty,

"the ancient association of same-sex eroticism with the hatred of tyranny, which had become a commonplace by the time of Aristotle."[100]

3. In his delightful if devastating account of sodomy proscriptions in fifteenth-century Florence, historian Michael Rocke suggests that such proscriptions were both inconsistent and overdetermined, but their codification and enforcement were fueled by concerns about population growth, normative masculinity, and sexual violence perpetrated against young boys. Yet Rocke describes a secondary set of anxieties too: "Evidently it was feared—perhaps with good reason—that politically active sodomites might constitute a sort of conspiratorial support network."[101] Even as the infamous priest Bernardino of Siena warned his audience that "young males lost all sense of reason because of their sexual lust,"[102] he also warned, all but contradictorily, that "one cohesive element of group loyalties in factions . . . was partisans' common homoerotic interests."[103]

4. Wedding together the examples of men's potentially revolutionary, sodomitical relations from antiquity (Herz) to Renaissance Florence (Rocke), Christopher Chitty comments that "throughout Machiavelli's discussions of conspiracies in *Discourses on Livy*, he returns to examples from antiquity to explicitly connect the sources of conspiracy against princes with political instabilities generated by the play of same-sex desire across hierarchies of age and status."[104] Obliquely commenting upon "Lorenzo de' Medici's campaign against sodomy," Chitty avers that "Machiavelli offers a historically new thought about cultures of male violence and sodomy in the time-honored guise of commentary on antiquity, *singling out this passion as threatening to the foundations of modern political power, as intimately bound up with hatred of tyrants and love of freedom*."[105]

Whether the sodomites are New England Puritans, Elizabethan Englishmen, Renaissance Florentines, or ancient Greeks, in these historical examples we see, first, that hedonic excess is assigned not to demonized others but is perceived instead as a powerful, psychical element of men in the ruling class. Second (and contra Kant, for whom sex undoes reason),[106] such unbounded eros does not incapacitate men from contracts and politics but instead recapacitates them, vitalizing new alliances against the powerful.[107] Of course, for Plato, Bernardino, Machiavelli, and John Winthrop, political community that coalesces through, or that may implode under, nonreproductive erotic affiliation and proliferating pleasures—what I am short-handing as "sodomitical"—is a Big Problem. But the sodomitical contract is a Big Problem because it sources collective resistance. How might the notion of a sodomitical contract, a collective organized through and not against the hedonic, inform a left political imaginary attentive but not reducible to identitarian injury?[108]

The sodomitical contract is a political theoretic rider, if you will, to the sexual and racial contracts, a rider that invites coalition anchored in nonnormative sex and its exceptionalizing surveillance. However, as the sodomitical episodes in this book will soon reveal, it is not precisely the ecstasy or affinity that the Puritan or Florentine sodomites delighted in through oral and anal sex that I wish to politicize, but rather a contiguous right to sexual and gender self-determination relatively free from policing: a right to queerness.

A Truncated Historiography of Antisodomy Law, or Finding Fellatio

Among feminist and antiracist political theorists like Pateman and Mills, rape law is often marshaled to metaphorize and magnify the problem of liberal consensus.[109] What appears to contemporary liberals as a law that defends the rights-bearing subject from sexual violence has been exposed as an integral instrument of patriarchy and racial hierarchy. From an un-intersectional (male) antiracist perspective, U.S. rape law and its enforcement historically function to demonize and criminalize Black men. From an un-intersectional (white) feminist perspective, U.S. rape law and its enforcement historically function to legitimize white men's "ordinary" sexual violence against women as part of everyday heterosexual relations. From an intersectional perspective, the injurious experiences of women of color drop out entirely from both dominant antiracist and feminist glosses on both rape and rape law.[110] But shared across all three perspectives is that a law nominally preventing sexual violence has functioned to install racialized, Black-and-white, gendered relations of inequality. As historian Emily Owens summarizes, "reading rape law in both black and white explains the sexual opportunism of white men's law, through which they created expansive sexual permissions for themselves."[111] Rape law, we have come to learn, is identitarian all the way down.

What if we additionally looked to *antisodomy law*, and not only rape law, as a departure point for sexual justice politics? An inversion to rape law's signification by left theory, what appears to contemporary liberals as a law that codifies and perpetuates homophobia in fact has a much longer history as a measure against sexual violence, particularly the sexual victimization of boys.[112] Meanwhile, in both colonial and U.S. contexts, antisodomy law has also been deployed discriminatorily against all sorts of marginalized groups: gay and queer boys and men; Indian, Asian, and Asian American men; Jewish men and men of Mediterranean backgrounds.[113] As far as I know, the sodomitical episode that comprises the first chapter of this book is the only instance of antisodomy law ever being used to target Black women. By taking a break from rape law (or rape law's left historiography), we can read antisodomy statutes as sex laws that are more serpentine than "adamantine,"[114] commingling regulatory concentration on same-sex sex, sexual violence, and sexualized others. Antisodomy law impels—or could— a coalition of marginalized groups against the state's regime of sexual normativity *du jour* and *de jure*.

As a prologue for a book "about" twenty-first-century Louisiana antisodomy law (but really this is a book about reconceptualizing queer politics), I surveyed the state's multipurpose of its antisodomy laws from the turn of the twentieth century up to the present, primarily by reading the available district, appellate, and state supreme court sodomy cases.[115] I contextualized the Louisiana-based research with supplementary "sodomitical" data from Georgia and from secondary sources on the history of antisodomy law codification and enforcement patterns in the United States.[116] My findings—published elsewhere[117] and here synopsized—complicate or corroborate three dominant, identitarian glosses on the history of antisodomy laws: first, that antisodomy law reflected and reiterated heretofore unwavering homophobia, animus largely directed at gay men and male anal sex;[118] second, that for most of its career, sodomy law enforcement targeted sexual violence and sexual abuse against children, mainly boys.[119] In this account, sodomy law reaches assaultive sex against men and boys that rape and statutory rape law, both historically requiring female victims and male perpetrators, failed to cover; third, that sodomy law reaches assaultive sex against women and girls that does not register as assaultive-enough to qualify as "rape" by judges and juries.[120] In the first narrative, sodomy law is homophobic; in the second, sodomy law is a corrective to the gender-specificity of traditional rape law; in the third, sodomy law is a corrective to the "problem" of women's credibility and to masculinist notions of resistance and force.

The first story of modern sodomy law—as always and forever phobic—is wrong, or grossly overstated, despite the gay animus that underlines episodic enforcement.[121]

The other two sodomy stories both pivot on protection: protection of boys or protection of girls and women. Although these two accounts are more historically substantiated and specified than the first, they too overlook or at least underplay sodomy law's multiple meanings and consequences, meanings and consequences not captured by an identitarian analytic.

Historians have shown that sodomy law in the nineteenth century usually targeted violence against boys, whereas over the course of the twentieth century sodomy law increasingly, if not consistently, was enforced against gay men. This account is accurate, but potentially glosses over how antisodomy laws continued to be deployed against perpetrators of sexual violence well into the twentieth and even early twenty-first centuries, sexual violence that was directed at not just boys but girls too.

For example, of the sixty-four sodomy cases heard by the Louisiana Supreme Court from 1957 to 2005, fifty-two defendants were charged with aggravated crime against nature. "Aggravated" entails, inter alia, use of force and/or age differences where the victim is under seventeen and the defendant is more than three years older than the victim.[122] Nine cases from this period include charges of "solicitation" or otherwise involve sex workers. This leaves but three cases involving nonaggravated, nonsolicitous charges—the paradigmatic but unlikely case of (gay) consenting adults having sex in private. In these state supreme court cases of aggravated crime against nature, where the sex of the victim is stated, the female to male victim ratio is 2:1. This ratio, combined with legal scholar William Eskridge's nationwide data on antisodomy law,[123] further complicates conclusions that, in the twentieth century, sodomy prosecutions either reflected homophobia and/or protected exclusively boy victims.

The gloss on sodomy as a solution to the problem of juries' and judges' disbelieving girls and women—a thesis championed by philosopher Lynne Huffer—is creative and appealing but largely incorrect.[124] Huffer's argument more or less is that "simple sodomy"—unforced, noncommercial oral and anal sex—functions as a failsafe to the problem of disbelieving sexually assaulted women. Juries may doubt (his) force or (her) resistance, but if oral or anal sex occurred, then therewith a (strict liability) conviction.

Huffer's account is convincing because it conforms to feminist fundamentals: sexual violence against women and girls is disbelieved; rape law fails women; rape trials revictimize victims. But the account—as dramatization of a pattern—is misleading. As data from Louisiana, Georgia (Huffer's sodomitical site),[125] and across the country reveal, this is not quite how antisodomy prosecutions proceed, for in nearly all criminal cases documented defendants are charged with "aggravated" or "forcible" sodomy, which in most instances requires proof of force and nonconsent—that is to say the charge of *aggravated* sodomy or *aggravated* crime against nature does not bypass questions of (his) intent, (her) resistance, and (her) credibility.

Beyond a critique of extant accounts, what my earlier research contributed to sodomy historiography is this: The not-so-hidden component of our national, late twentieth-century sodomy (law) story is more, well, sodomitical than identitarian, more about sex and its competing social definitions than about gender or sexuality and their compulsory normativity. Antisodomy law, in addition to being unevenly homophobic and protective, reflects (and codifies) our cultural pluripotence around oral sex, mainly fellatio.

In the 180 Louisiana state appellate rulings involving antisodomy indictments from 1980–2005, there is not one case involving simple anal sex (although there is one instance of an undercover police officer arresting a man for attempting noncommercial oral sex).[126] Indeed, at least 176 of the 180 crime against nature cases (98 percent) involve charges of forcible oral sex (and/or oral sex committed with a minor), nearly all of which document allegations of forcible fellatio. Of those cases, 156 state the sex of the victim(s), 138 of which include a female victim (88 percent). At least forty-seven of these 138 cases involve girl victims under eighteen (34 percent).

My suspicion is that forced or unwanted fellatio is a persistent pattern across all U.S. sodomy cases heard between *Bowers v. Hardwick*, the 1986 Supreme Court case holding antisodomy laws constitutional, and *Lawrence v. Texas*, the 2003 Supreme Court case overturning *Bowers*.[127] Indeed, 40 percent of those cases involve forced sex between different-sex adults and another 55 percent involve sexual conduct between adults and children.[128]

How might we begin to theorize the rise of forcible fellatio under antisodomy law? I offer just two hypotheses that, while speculative, should at least serve to supplement the historical accounts canvassed earlier and to set the stage for the more prescriptive analyses to follow.

Fellatio, historical: At common law, oral sex was not criminalized under crime against nature statutes. Fellatio was enfolded into sodomy law primarily in the early 1900s (by judicial interpretation or legislative reform), in part because of the creation of public parks and restrooms that, as Eskridge hilariously puts it, "fueled an explosion of fellatio" among men. Around the same time, women sex workers also helped popularize oral sex;[129] fellatio did not risk pregnancy, and the service fetched a higher fee as wives apparently did not want to fellate. Some states later proscribed cunnilingus, but cunnilingus never attracted anything like the legislative or judicial handwringing as fellatio. According to Eskridge, "sodomy arrests skyrocketed" in the early decades of the twentieth century because of the statutory envelopment of fellatio as a crime against nature.[130]

Although drafted amid a fellatio free-for-all and enforced largely against nominally consenting adults, the law later targeted forced oral sex between adults and oral sex between adults and children. What may have fueled proscription in the early 1900s were public fears of both the sexualization and homosexualization of urban space: moral decline signaled and solidified by the casualization of nonprocreative, nonmarital sex acts. I wonder if, in the long shadow of the sexual revolution and the Stonewall riots, oral sex appeared again on the statutory radar in part because of renewed, abiding national ambivalence over fellatio.

A national joke since at least the 1998 Clinton-Lewinsky affair, the blow-job has a longer history signifying the casualization of sex and so-called hookup culture while also symbolizing men's presumptive sex right and sense of sexual entitlement. Might the way fellatio is perceived as both banal and sex-lite, while at once carrying residues of kink, crudeness, and objectification, contribute to its ongoing legal and cultural classification as not quite sexual intercourse but not merely sexual contact—something else, something sodomitical? There is a publicness and class dimension to oral sex, too—the go-to for quick sexual trysts in parks or street alleys, evident from the 1900s until today—that may also send fellatio into statutory isolation.

What about the forcible component of almost all appellate adult sodomy cases in the later stages of U.S. antisodomy law's career?[131] When Louisiana legislators amended its rape law to include forced anal sex, they sought for "the crime of rape to be defined on both heterosexual and homosexual terms," while redefining "heterosexual rape" as "any sexual penetration, vaginal or anal" of a woman without lawful consent.[132] One might think the revision simply reflects gay animus, but this seems unlikely. The bill was drafted in the middle of rape law reform across the country that, inter alia, specified degrees of sexual assault (often reserving the severest penalties for forced penetrative vaginal or anal sex), gender-neutralized victims and defendants, relaxed resistance requirements, and eliminated or scaled-back marital exemptions. The legal meaning of "rape" was at the time undergoing a national sea change, from a gendered property violation against a father or husband to a gender-neutral rights violation against a victim. Meanwhile, boys were increasingly recognized as victims of sexual assault and gays were increasingly, post-Stonewall, recognized as a social class. Combined, the historical conditions were ripe for anal sex to become sex and forced anal sex to become rape.[133] If homosexuals have "sex" and boys are "raped," then what gets penetrated? An analogical-anatomical episteme combined with the primacy of penetration—in a word, heteronormativity—point toward the anus. The admission of anal sex as sex—in law (e.g., Louisiana) and life—leaves one human hole remaining for abominableness or unnaturalness: the mouth.

Oral sex is not as easily assimilated under a heterosexual or homosexual register and, likewise, when forced, more resistant to classification as rape: if oral sex is not sex, can it be rape? What, then, is oral sex? A 1978 case of the Louisiana Supreme Court held that, to qualify as a crime against nature, unnatural anal copulation requires penetration, whereas unnatural oral copulation merely requires oral-genital contact.[134] So: the mouth is unlike an anus; an anus is like a vagina; a vagina requires penetration for sex. But if sex requires penetration and oral sex need not require penetration, then oral sex is not exactly sex. But it is "against nature."[135]

Fellatio, semantic: The singular unnaturalness of and ambivalence surrounding oral sex finds linguistic evidence in the Louisiana state appellate cases as well. In case after case, the facts are narrated in some variation of the following linguistic pattern: "after performing oral sex and while still armed with the razor, defendant raped her";[136] "He forced the victim to perform oral sex again and attempted penetration two or three more times";[137] "The gunman and the other two remaining men took turns raping the other woman. She was also forced to engage in oral sex";[138] "Thereafter the defendant, while in various rooms of the mobile home vaginally raped the victim seven times, anally raped her two times and forced her to commit two acts of fellatio upon him."[139] In a final and stunning example of rape's "grammar":[140] "defendant forced her head down in his lap and ordered her to commit an act of oral sex on him, threatening to rape her if she 'didn't do the job good.'"[141] In a queerer, less genitalized imaginary, this last sentence might read: he threatened to sexually assault her by sexually assaulting her.

The grammar in this judicial lexicon would be torturous were it not commonsensical in our cultural lexicon. Whereas women "are raped," as are vaginas and anuses, no such straightforward grammatical construction exists for forcible oral sex or mouths. Indeed, in one of the appellate cases, the judge substitutes what would be the more syntactically consistence "orally raped her two times" for the wordy but more digestible "forced her to commit two acts of fellatio upon him." We see in these appellate sodomy decisions passive subjects coupled with active infinitives: she is forced to engage; she is forced to perform. Is she a performing agent or a forced victim? And if she is both, does that tell us something about the sodomitical quality of oral sex?

This linguistic incommensurateness signals the improbability of representing, in law, oral sex as sex and thus forcible oral sex as rape. If our identitarian imaginary is no longer firmly gendered when it comes to sex, it still hinges on an active/passive binary. "Man fucks woman; subject verb object."[142] We "know" what this means. Man fucks man. We "know" too what this means. Vaginas and anuses—in sex—receive. They do not act, perform, or penetrate. Mouths are (fictively) murkier. A mouth, unlike the anus or vagina, is our expressivist source of autonomy. If the rectum is a grave where, via sex, our selves shatter, mouths are cradles where, via speech, selves assemble.[143] Sex, where we become undone, cannot (not should not) take place at the mouth, where we become. This commingling of activity and passivity is strange, unsettling, against nature.[144]

Analogous to the perennial question of lesbian sex (for what do women do without a penis?), but in a nonidentitarian register, is oral sex's undecidability between activity and passivity. The active/passive grammar in the appellate rulings mirrors the active/passive ambivalence elemental to the phantasm of oral sex. Is the receiver of oral sex the agent or patient? Is the giver passive or active? These questions are rhetorical; they are, as a matter of law, representationally undecidable. Or rather: the active/passive binary is always already available to representational capture for vaginal and anal sex (the law may not know a power bottom when it sees one). This is untrue of fellatio and forcible fellatio, remaindering oral sex to the realm of the sodomitical.

I theorize neither fellatio nor its proscription much in the proceeding pages, even as it is the most frequently performed and politicized sexual act in the chapters ahead; neither "gay" nor "straight," it is policed oral sex or its solicitation that turns so many of the women and men in this book into criminals. Rather, I have summarized my earlier historical investigations here to foreground the kinds of questions about and possibilities for sexual justice that antisodomy laws potentially telegraph, questions and possibilities undetectable under an identitarian radar.

Sodomy's Solicitations

Each of the first three chapters of *Sodomy's Solicitations* tracks a different, twenty-first-century political contestation in the life and afterlives of Louisiana's antisodomy laws. Collectively, these chapters scrutinize what I shorthand as "sodomitical episodes," chronologized from 2007ish–present-ish, to contrast the extant, identitarian narrative of each episode alongside paraidentitarian amendments or alternatives. The identitarian read of each chapter tends toward the descriptive, the paraidentitarian read tends toward the prescriptive. To mix metaphors, readers might imagine the identity-based politics, knowledges, and modes of thought circulating around each episode as the proscenia of a theater, delimiting what takes place onstage. The paraidentitarian interventions of each chapter are not teardowns of our ideological proscenia (that's a mouthful), so much as invitations for renovation. How might we expand the terrain of our sexual justice politics, for whom, and for what purposes? How might these sodomitical episodes be renarrated or reinterpreted to yield a sexual politics that protects and promotes queerness—a pluralism of gender identities and styles, sexual expressions, and intimate associations—including and beyond taxonomized (L, G, B, T . . .) identity? In Judith Butler's idiom, *Sodomy's Solicitations* queries the political configurations "that produce the ontological horizon within which state coercion appears necessary and justified."[145]

All three sodomitical episodes occurred in Louisiana, but the nascent, paraidentitarian sexual politics I glean from them extend outward, or so is my hope.

Sodomitical Episode 1, Chapter 1 (2007ish–Presentish)

The first sodomitical episode is the most intricate of the three, involving a large cast of stakeholders, changing political, legislative, and litigation objectives, and an epilogue-in-progress as of this writing. The grievance at the center of the episode, simplified, is this: until 2012, the state required nearly nine hundred people, overwhelmingly low-income Black women, to register as sex offenders; and they were required to do so for—indexically and allegedly—offering blowjobs for money to undercover police officers.[146]

Louisiana is the only state in the union that makes soliciting oral and anal sex for money its own unique crime. The commercial sodomy law, titled Crime Against Nature by Solicitation (CANS) proscribes the offering of oral and anal sex for money, whereas the state's Prostitution law prohibits that same conduct but additionally prohibits the performance or offering of vaginal sex for money. The sodomitical conduct criminalized across these two laws is identical; the difference was in the penalties. A person convicted for CANS faced harsher penalties—steeper fines and longer prison sentences—than someone convicted for Prostitution. Moreover, and more politicized, a CANS conviction triggered onerous, ostracizing, and stigmatizing sex offender registry requirements, requirements to be detailed in the first chapter, while a Prostitution conviction has never required sex offender registration.

A few years after Hurricane Katrina and the state and federal governments' lethally appalling response to the storm, the New Orleans–based organization Women With A Vision (WWAV) led a multipronged, spectacularly successful campaign against the CANS law's harsh penalties, penalties disparately impacting Black women, trans and cis, and queer Black men. WWAV spurred legislative reforms to prospectively equalize the CANS penalties, garnered national media attention to the discriminatory law, and helped put together a lawsuit that removed hundreds of people convicted of CANS from the sex offender registry.[147] In 2023, about a decade after the lawsuit, the *New Yorker* released the documentary *CANS Can't Stand*, which chronicles WWAV's campaign and spotlights two Black transgender women who were part of that campaign and who continue to fight against the ongoing discriminatory consequences of the commercial sodomy law that they and too many others endure.[148]

In Chapter 1, I canvas this sodomitical episode to illustrate two ways identitarianism winnowed and may continue to winnow the anti-CANS campaign's sexual politics. I then offer two normative abstractions, *fairness* and *debility*, that point toward a more capacious vision of sexual justice.

You might be thinking to yourself, *is this white gay man (me) seriously going to criticize a political campaign, now led by Black transgender women, for being too identitarian?! How annoyingly, obtusely, and typically "queer."* So I will spell out the critique a little more here, even if repeated in the first chapter, to withstand the charge of white gay obtuseness. My efforts undoubtedly fall short.

After the storm, the CANS law was politicized as a homophobic relic redeployed against Black women and Black LGBT people. In the 2020s, and partially as a result of the *New Yorker* documentary, CANS was subsequently repoliticized as a law that "criminalizes Black trans women."[149] My own research revealed that the law was first put on the books in the early 1980s to target young men of color selling sex in the French Quarter. My first identitarian-skeptical concern, though, is not, chiefly, that focalizing one vulnerable population as the "true" victims of the law neglects other targets, but rather that the focus on discrete identities overlooks how the state deploys (sodomitical) sex to flexibly discriminate across minoritized populations. Likewise, the media's more recent, myopic focus on Black trans women as the exclusive victims of CANS potentially undercuts coalition among gender and sexual minoritized groups and those who would support them. As political scientist Paisley Currah comments about dominant cultural representations of antitrans violence, "the continuities between trans women and cis women drop out of the picture, and that inhibits our ability to develop effective responses." Currah avers, "there's nothing wrong with using a trans vs. cis frame to show that trans people are more likely to be victims of violence. But violence against trans women should also be seen as driven by misogyny."[150]

My second identitarian-skeptical concern strikes deeper. I show how the legislative, litigation, and grassroots efforts to declassify persons convicted of CANS as sex offenders were largely mobilized by a more invidious identity formation: the mythic, monstrous figure of the predatory, recidivistic sex offender. Metonymically: the child rapist. The multipronged campaign waged to declassify sex workers as sex offenders discursively depended upon distancing sex workers from the "true" predator, the child rapist, as if that villainous figure is the appropriately, justly registered sex offender by the state. The chapter does not seek sympathy for people who perpetrate sexual violence; instead, I contend that sex offender registry and notification systems are an ineffective and antifeminist metastasis of the carceral state.[151] So too, because those systems are *their own form of sexual violence*, insofar as they transform singular acts into despised, sexualized identities, a queer paraidentitarian political project should reject them as regressive nonsolutions for making communities safer.

In the last third of the chapter, I propose that we might look to *fairness* and *debility* as orienting abstractions for sexual justice. Many if not all of the sex offenders I interviewed for this chapter mentioned "fairness" or its cognates, and I reconcile their ordinary use of the term with its more technical usage in liberal political theory, namely Rawlsian political theory, to see if fairness so reconstructed might portend a more forgiving, more ecological sexual politics. Pivoting off several vulnerability and disability theorists, I draw on a notion of debility as the *state imposition of vulnerability* to provide conceptual architecture for a sexual politics honed more to marginalizing state practices of sexualization and less to marginalized sexual identities.

Sodomitical Episode 2, Chapter 2 (2013–2015)

Chapter 2 is a defense of sex in public, neither polemic nor pastoral, against the braided threats of gayness, intergenerationality, and incest.

A year after the success of the CANS campaign in New Orleans, a sodomitical scandal erupted in Baton Rouge. A local news report exposed that officers of the East Baton Rouge Sherriff's Office were arresting men for "attempted sodomy" at cruising sites in the city's public parks, even though the state's antisodomy law (that is, a law criminalizing *noncommercial* sodomy: blowjobs and butt sex) was rendered unconstitutional a decade earlier by the landmark Supreme Court ruling, *Lawrence v. Texas*. The district attorney appropriately tossed the arrests but that came late for the indignities (and jail time) suffered by the men. In any case, the arrests and the embarrassing national attention they drew led a Democratic state representative to propose a bill that would repeal Louisiana's antisodomy law.[152] The bill failed stunningly, the opposition mobilized mainly by a powerful, conservative Christian lobbying group falsely claiming that the repeal of the law would sexually endanger children. Adding fuel to the phobic fire, religious leaders and police officers claimed that the city parks were no longer safe spaces for children because men were indiscriminately having sex with one another in them.

The identitarian account of this episode would be, and was, that every single aspect of it is painfully homophobic, and that would be, and was, accurate. But while the arrests of the men, the failure of the antisodomy bill, and the child sex panic are manifestly antigay, they are latently erotophobic too, driven by the presumption that sex in public, or that a public culture of sex, will endanger children, the family, and society. So the second chapter asks instead, *What if it had been true? What if men were having sex with other men in public? When and why is sex in public wrong, and when might it be right and good?*

This chapter runs on a long counterfactual then, despite all the warnings I received back in graduate school against utilizing counterfactuals. This counterfactual, though, has the dubious privilege of standing as a truth claim for those who espoused it: namely, that there really were men fucking men in public parks in Baton Rouge, and so brazenly that (presumptively straight?) parents could not bring their (presumptively straight? Protostraight?) children there.

To tease out the counterfactual (men having sex with men in front of children) and the moral or legal violations to which it may or may not give rise, I look to liberal or liberalish legal theory on indecent exposure, queer scholarship on sex public, what Black feminist scholar Jennifer Nash helped me constellate as an archive of Black and Brown Pleasure Studies, and less methodically to my own "sex in public" at a well-known gay beach. The punchline: nearly all sex and nudity performed in public, however we define "public," should not be legally actionable, and the public sex that is violative is violative not because it is public but because it is assaultive or assault-like, and so sexual autonomy-infringing (for example, a man masturbating *at* you on a bus, or a Zoom bomber doing the same online). Studies in Black and Brown Pleasure accentuate that what state actors have perceived and then criminalized as "sex in public" is too often an upshot of racist, phobic sexualization, and so the brief for sex in public is at once a brief against phobic sexualization.

The chapter concludes with some meditations on incest, incest taboos, and civilizational demise. The conceit is that what might affront many of us about sex in public (or its phantasmatic possibility) is its unconscious connotation with incestuous disorder. That the incest palimpsest of public sex might make such conduct especially discomfiting to witness does not mean it should be illegal—but it might explain why sex in public is almost never "sex" and never really in "public."

Sodomitical Episode 3, Chapter 3 (2018)

Coauthored with gender studies professor Gabriel Rosenberg, Chapter 3 examines what is likely the strangest (as of yet) episode in the apparently eternal afterlife of Louisiana's sodomy law. In the summer of 2018, having endured over two hundred years in statute, the Louisiana Legislature struck the bestiality ("with an animal") element of its criminal sodomy statute, enacting in its place a new and gradated catalogue of sexual abuse offenses against animals. As elaborated upon in the chapter, two aspects of this episode are the launchpad for paraidentitarian critique.

First, several Republican state representatives opposed the new slate of animal sexual abuse statutes, for they feared that excising bestial sex from the antisodomy statute would make it more vulnerable to constitutional attack. More precisely, the law—prohibiting sodomy between humans—was already found unconstitutional under *Lawrence*, as mentioned earlier. The opposing representatives wanted to keep the bestial sex close, statutorily speaking, to the gay sex, so proscribing the latter could remain on the books. The homophobia of Republican state representatives outweighed their sympathies for sexually abused animals—this is the discursively dominant, identitarian gloss of the episode.[153]

Second, though, Louisiana's animal sexual abuse law, like antibestiality laws in almost all other states, include exemptions for agricultural, husbandry, and veterinary practices, exemptions that throw into relief just how little we or the state care about animal abuse and killing, let alone animal (sexual) welfare. Rather, we endorse a great deal of animal (sexual) suffering insofar as that suffering generates profit, labor markets, and food. Modeled on child pornography and child molestation laws, the animal sexual abuse statute does not in fact target such abuse but rather presumptively predatory, indexically male desire. Here, the identity formation of the bestialist or zoophile obscures and thereby legitimates a trillion-dollar market anchored in animal suffering.

Continuing to think sex without identity, or sex "without the subject,"[154] Rosenberg and I ponder what kinds of polices, institutional norms, and cultural practices might be activated to facilitate the kind of (sexual) welfare that twenty-first-century animal sexual abuse laws promise but cannot deliver. Human-animal sexual contact occurs thousands of times a day for the production and consumption of meat. So we have a lot of "sex" with animals. Is any interspecies sexual contact just, and if so, what would make it just? Elsewhere I have argued that "consent" or its absence is a readily available and all but useless metric to ethically gauge our relations with nonhuman animals.[155] Here, and facilitated by our interviews with a few Louisiana farmers, we soften the sendup of consent and propose additional normative principles and moral considerations that might direct our thinking about and interacting with animals. Such an inquiry may appear unnecessary or even farcical, but we insist that in the absence of more ecological thought on sex (within or across species), liberal, identitarian accounts of sexuality and sexual politics risk being just as phobic as the more explicitly sex-negative accounts from the right. In the final pages we propose technologized meat, or meat without death and suffering, as a dialectic, plenitudinous possibility for the proliferation of inter- and intraspecies pleasures. The theorizing that gets us there is the same theorizing the queries if the "vegetarian," too, as an identity formation, unnecessarily delimits our ethical obligations for nonhuman animal welfare, sexual, reproductive, or otherwise.

The last two chapters shift gears, analytically and rhetorically, from the prior three. Styled somewhere between legal briefs and law journal articles (but not as boring as that sounds, I hope), Chapters 4 and 5 build out arguments, respectively, that the CANS law in Louisiana and antiprostitution laws in the United States more generally are unconstitutional. Animus-soaked both in its codification and its enforcement patterns, Crime Against Nature by Solicitation violates the equal protection guarantees of the federal and Louisiana state constitutions. Laws categorically proscribing commercial sex (antiprostitution statutes), meanwhile, are deprivations of liberty offensive to the Due Process Clause of the Fourteenth Amendment of the U.S. Constitution.

It is supremely unlikely although not altogether impossible that the constitutional cases I advance against CANS and antiprostitution laws would ever prove victorious in U.S. courts of law (but for what it is worth, the case against CANS is stronger than the case against antiprostitution laws, so if one of these arguments were to be successful I would place my bets on the former—if CANS has not yet been repealed by the Louisiana Legislature).[156] Why then go through the trouble of writing these last chapters, and more importantly, why should you go through the trouble of reading them?

Collectively, the chapters press for and so discursively scaffold negative rights to sexual freedoms—what we might call noninterference rights to queerness—with attendant injunctions against the state's surveilling and policing nonnormative, gender, sexual, and racial minority subjects. The arguments of these chapters depend on neither the presumptive specialness of sex nor the presumptive fixity, innateness, or solidity of sexual identities, and so they model strategies of litigation that supplement or at least syncopate with a paraidentitarian politics that champions relatively unpoliced gender and sexual pluralism.

Chapter 4 demonstrates that CANS is arbitrary, redundant, and saturated by animus. I survey both the legislative history of Louisiana's commercial sodomy law as well as several state appellate and state supreme court cases in which the constitutionality of CANS or CANS's penalties were challenged by plaintiffs.

The legislative history of CANS reveals that the law was enacted solely for the purpose of punishing young men sex workers more harshly than punishing women sex workers. Against this background, legislative reforms in the 2010s to equalize CANS's penalties with those for Prostitution are testament to legislators' recognition that the law is and has always been impermissibly prejudicial. Over its ugly career, CANS has been used to disproportionately target young men perceived to be gay, Black cisgender women, and Black transgender women. Steeped in animus, the law's codification and enforcement violate constitutional equal protection guarantees, an argument substantiated by extrapolating from what legal scholar Dale Carpenter calls the "quadrilogy" of Supreme Court cases establishing animus-based legislation to be constitutionally impermissible.[157] Importantly, my anti-animus approach does not depend on showing that harms were incurred by a singular, discrete, nonintersectional, politically powerless group, like "Blacks," "gays," or "transgender women." Just as the previous chapters turn greater analytic attention to the state's deployment of sex than to sexual identities per se, so here the point is that CANS allowed, in fact encouraged, state actors to flexibly denigrate varying and overlapping populations by associating them with sodomitical sex acts (that the population discriminatorily victimized by CANS changes over time does not preclude a plaintiff from one or another denigrated group to file suit).

I rehearse state-level constitutional challenges to CANS to show, in short, how state courts have erred, either by misunderstanding the CANS statute and ignoring (or flatly denying) its political history or by proffering justifications for CANS's harsh penalties that no longer pass constitutional muster (for example, "public morals" as grounds to punish the offering of oral sex for money with longer prison sentences than the offering of vaginal sex for money). Any "good reason" for criminalizing commercial sex (oral, anal, or vaginal)—for example, maintaining public health or preventing violence against women—is already met by the state's prohibition against commercial oral, anal, and vaginal sex under its Prostitution statute. And yet, those good reasons are not so good after all, which brings us to Chapter 5, laying out the constitutional case for a right to sex work.

The potentially sex-regressive cul-de-sac of Chapter 4 is that, by suggesting that Louisiana's Prostitution statute makes CANS not only redundant (for the same conduct is criminalized) but thereby unconstitutional (for the redundancy evidences impermissible bias), I come close to legitimating antiprostitution laws. But these laws also fall afoul of our Constitution, or so I submit. The first two-thirds of the chapter propose that a line of case law establishing constitutional rights to contraception, abortion, sodomitical sex, and interracial and same-sex marriage ought to shield commercial sex from criminalization. I show too that the three arguments lower courts have so far marshaled to slice out sex work from constitutional protection—alleging that sex work 1) is necessarily public, 2) is definitionally nonintimate, and/or 3) creates social problems—are facetious, ideologically driven, and incompatible with prior case law.

If the first two-thirds of the chapter locate a right to sex work in a *right to sex*, the last third offers an alternative constitutional anchor in a *right to work*. This part of the chapter is motivated by *Dobbs v. Jackson Women's Health Organization*, the infamous 2022 U.S. Supreme Court decision overturning what was a half-century-established constitutional right to terminate one's pregnancy.[158] While many commentators have lamented that the *Dobbs* opinion opens the door to abrogating the aforementioned rights (to contraception, sodomitical sex, and so on), my contiguous point is that the judiciary now seems more reluctant than ever to broaden a right to sexual freedom, let alone to encompass commercial sex. If that is correct, then *a right to work* might be a more promising constitutional path for repealing antiprostitution laws since such an occupational right, as I recount, has a formidable history in case law and appeals to conservative jurists. But let's be candid: an asserted occupational right to sex work will likely be laughed out of court too (and has been),[159] so my interventions in this chapter and the preceding one are designed less to convince judges than to expose how sex is exceptionalized when it comes to morality (CANS) and trivialized when it comes to employment (prostitution). I catalogue and contest the damage that exceptionalism and trivialization do to all kinds of minoritized, nonnormative subjects.

Combined, these last two chapters make the rather simple point that nobody should go to prison for sucking dick. To put that more formally: regardless of our gender, sexual, and racial identifications, a right to sexual self-determination—let's call it a right to sodomy or queerness—should not be so breezily abrogated when it is paid for, publicly solicited, or even "publicly" performed.[160]

Children—but more often the symbolic Child[161]—travel across, are in fact elemental to, the sodomitical episodes I chronicle and critique, although they are under- or untheorized in the chapters themselves. Given the political atmosphere in which this book is being completed, wherein many state legislatures are unconscionably criminalizing gender affirming healthcare for children in the name of protecting them, prohibiting some girls from playing sports with other girls, undermining girls', women's, and other pregnable people's autonomy and civic participation by fetishizing the fetus, and outlawing "sexual" (read gay and trans friendly) speech from public schools while deputizing parents and school boards to ban Black- and queer-affirmative books, the book concludes with a coda that I playfully if provocatively title "Sodomy's Solicitations: Children's Edition." The coda circles back through the sodomitical episodes to foreground the ways children and/or the Child function in these political contestations, tracking how and for what purposes the children and the Child are weaponized, fetishized, eroticized, or otherwise mobilized by political campaigns, pundits, and state actors. Building upon scholarship in legal theory and cultural studies attuned to the potential political and sexual agency of children, I propose in the coda that if we are to advance a paraidentitarian politics of sexual justice above and beyond putting out culture war fires ignited by the Right, we must commit to championing both the queerness of children and children's right to queerness. I suggest, perhaps counterintuitively, that such a commitment demands engendering children's collective political agency more so than their individual sexual or gendered agency.

New Orleans: American Sodom, Modern Sodom, Perfect Sodom

I lived in New Orleans during the spring semesters of 2012, 2016, and 2019, in the Marigny, Bywater, and Uptown neighborhoods, respectively, and visited for shorter stints in between and after. Over the years, I interviewed sex offenders, police officers, politicians, city officials, farmers, community organizers, and civil rights leaders. I spent a good deal of time in legal archives in New Orleans and Baton Rouge, reading through the sodomy cases heard by the Louisiana State Supreme Court and the Criminal District Court of Orleans Parish. But I spent a much greater deal of time sitting on top of my bed in my shotgun on Desire Street, reviewing hundreds of Louisiana appellate sodomy cases made available by LexisNexis. I volunteered for the ACLU of Louisiana, writing up a report for the organization on the relationship between the NOPD and the city's LGBT community. I walked in and sometimes costumed for dozens of parades, ate way too much jambalaya, listened to bogglingly talented musicians, and got appropriately blitzed for Mardi Gras. Like so many others I fell in love with the city, which means I do not always like it.

I am not an anthropologist nor are the findings herein ethnographic. There are no representative samples of populations. The n is small whatever the dataset. And while my research visits were centered in New Orleans, and while New Orleans–based lawmakers, activists, and political events are critical for the project, the project is also "sited" in Baton Rouge parks, in the state legislature, in judicial opinions and legal theory, in a beach on Cape Cod, Massachusetts, in and around queer studies, and in longer histories of racialized sexuality in the South. On this last topic, I must confess that the structure of this project—analyzing contemporary antisodomy laws and reconstructing their politicizations—did not allow me to foreground excellent scholarship on the mobilizations and manipulations of enslaved, formerly enslaved, and free persons' sex and sexuality in colonial,[162] antebellum,[163] and postbellum[164] New Orleans and the American South as much as I would have liked.

Yet, this project is embedded in New Orleans and Louisiana, even as I hope its findings and arguments are generalizable. So why is the project sited in the city?

For three reasons at least. Preliminarily, because of my earlier work on the politics of sexual consent and on sex offender registration and notification laws, I was fascinated by the strategies and rhetoric of the masterfully coordinated campaign to remove sex workers from the Louisiana Sex Offender and Child Predator Registry.

Second, because as the explosion of scholarship on New Orleans after Hurricane Katrina attests, New Orleans is the exceptional case and the most representative.[165] New Orleans is positively unlike any other city in the United States when it comes to cuisine, architecture, and cultural production, and disturbingly archetypal when it comes to racial inequalities, neoliberalized social services, privatization, gang and drug violence, and police corruption and misconduct (although the NOPD has improved considerably in recent years). The city is obscenely rich and shockingly poor, sometimes impenetrably insular but necessarily touristic, racially diverse but with recent and seismic shifts in its demography.[166] Heavily marketed as a harmonious "cultural gumbo" by its tourist companies, the moniker belies the deepening divides and residential segregation of the city.[167] Such contradictions are perfectly metaphorized in Mardi Gras, the let-it-all-hang-out, citywide celebration that is marred by white supremacy and red hot intra- and interracial conflict.[168]

Louisiana is the only state to single out the solicitation of sodomy for criminalization, most convictions for which occur in New Orleans, even as New Orleans is so famous for readily satisfying touristic gratifications, sexual, sodomitical, alcoholic, and otherwise. During Southern Decadence, as I mentioned in the Introduction's opening vignette, men parade outside wearing jockstraps and chest harnesses with nonchalance,[169] nonchalance that led one transgender women of color I interviewed, previously convicted of CANS, to question her very membership in the LGBT community (she, after all, was arrested by an undercover officer for allegedly soliciting sex). Indeed, based on my research and volunteer work, it seems that two of the groups I interviewed, (mainly) white gay men and young transgender people of color, live in wholly separate New Orleanian universes, making the phrase "LGBT community" hard to say with a straight face.

In any case, these contradictions to which I but briefly gesture—outlier but representative, culturally mosaic but increasingly siloized, permissive but policed, insular but touristic, exotic but Americana—are the right ones to site this study, which tracks the life and afterlife of exceptional, outlier sodomy laws in order to read off their more universal ramifications for our conceptions of sex and sexual violence and for the normative parameters of our sexual politics. New Orleans is known just as notoriously for its social differences (e.g., Spanish, French, American, Creole, freeperson, slave, Haitian, local, tourist, Black, white, Vietnamese, Latinx) and allegiances (e.g., Krewes) as it is for its rather postidentitarian if utopic motto, *laissez les bon temps rouler*. It is alongside and against the competing truths of this city that I theorize the interplay between the identitarian, paraidentitarian, and nonidentitarian ramifications of sodomy law.

Finally, while San Francisco might be a close contender,[170] no American city is more frequently compared to Sodom, the biblical city destroyed by God's wrath for its denizens' avarice and rapacity (and from which of course we inherit the term *sodomy*)[171] than New Orleans.

The author of an 1856 travelogue, appalled that Christian men would attend a "masked ball" on "every Sabbath," referred to New Orleans as a "perfect Sodom."[172] An 1826 travelogue relayed: "this place has more than once been called the modern Sodom."[173] Indeed, the city's association with Sodom derives in no small part from its antebellum proliferation of brothels; simultaneously, its "presence of a large black population reinforced New Orleans's reputation for sexual depravity."[174] In 1893, a New Orleans newspaper decried the city for housing "the crimes of Sodom and Gomorrah" in its caption accompanying a photograph of two women holding one another (Figure I.1).[175]

Unsurprisingly albeit horrendously, many right-wing groups hailed New Orleans a contemporary, American Sodom in the cataclysmic devastation following Hurricane Katrina (devastation, it bears repeating, that resulted primarily from rising waters that breached the poorly maintained levees several hours after the storm hit the city, and secondarily from mismanaged city, state, and federal emergency responses).[176]

The connection I want to draw here is deeper than a coincidence of terms. New Orleans is in fact a hotbed of all that conduct historically associated with Sodom and sodomy: luxury, gluttony, indulgence, pride, social disorder, purposeless (nonprocreative) sex.[177] What if, though, our fleshy excesses, our purposeless yet criminalized sex, indeed the whole parade of horribles that *sodomia* alternately describes or invites, served as common denominator of our sexual politics rather than as its destroyer at "the end of the world"?[178]

GOOD GOD!
The Crimes of Sodom and Gomorrah Discounted.

Figure I.1 Front page of *The Mascot*, October 21, 1893. Howard-Tilton Memorial Library, Tulane University. *(Thanks to Joseph Roach for providing the image, printed in his* Cities of the Dead: Circum-Atlantic Performance.*)*

1

Sodomy's Solicitations

Toward a Paraidentitarian Politics of Sexual Justice

"Everybody is a sex offender in one shape or form."[1]

Introduction

In June 2013, the state of Louisiana declassified around nine hundred people as sex offenders, three-quarters of whom were women and nearly four-fifths of whom were Black.[2] Among the most powerful consequences of declassification, symbolically and materially, was the removal of the citizens' names, addresses, criminal convictions, and pictures from the state Sex Offender and Child Predator Registry (LSOCPR) website, its grid of visuality like an uncanny dating app. So too, "SEX OFFENDER" would no longer be printed in orange block letters on the indexically Black women citizens' driver's licenses and other forms of state identification (Figure 1.1).

How did hundreds of Louisianan women end up as sex offenders and why were they removed from the registry?

Louisiana has two laws that criminalize commercial sex. "Prostitution" proscribes the offering and performance of vaginal, oral, and anal sex for money.[3] "Crime Against Nature by Solicitation" (CANS) proscribes the offering of oral and anal sex for money.[4] "Crime against nature" is from the Latinate-derived *contra natura*, adopted in many criminal codes to refer to sodomy, although historically "it was employed by theologians, inquisitors,

A previous version of this chapter appeared as Joseph Fischel, "Against Nature, against Consent: A Sexual Politics of Debility," *differences: A Journal of Feminist Cultural Studies*, 1 May 2013; 24 (1): 55–103. doi: https://doi-org/10.1215/10407391-2140591. © 2013 by Brown University and *differences: A Journal of Feminist Cultural Studies*. Reprinted by permission of Duke University Press.

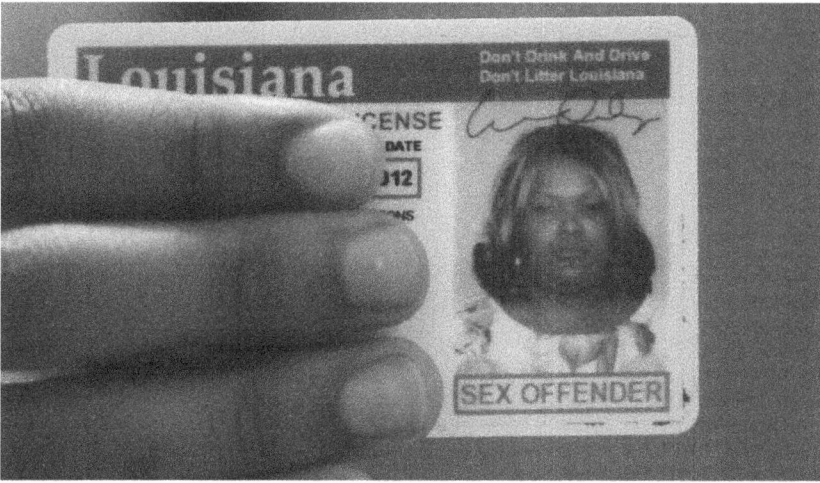

Figure 1.1 In Louisiana, "sex offender" is printed in block letters on state identification cards of registered sex offenders. Driver's license featured in *CANS Can't Stand* (2020). *(Still from* CANS Can't Stand *by Matt Nadel and Megan Plotka.)*

and criminal authorities as a marker of difference that attained meaning through non-procreative acts such as autoeroticism, same-sex sexuality, and bestiality."[5] In twentieth- and twenty-first-century Louisiana, though, CANS is specifically a no-sodomy-for-sale law; and even more precisely, in practice CANS is a no-blowjob-offer-to-an-undercover-officer law—the NOPD "would send out 'blowjob patrols'" to bank CANS arrests.[6] In any case, Prostitution and CANS laws criminalize the same exact kinds of commercial sex, but Prostitution additionally penalizes "p in vg," as Jonah Hill's character in *Superbad* memorably calls it.[7] Enacted in 1982, the CANS law was a felony for most of its career and carried far more severe penalties for conviction than Prostitution, a misdemeanor. From 1992 to 2011, a CANS conviction additionally triggered state sex offender registration and notification requirements.[8] These requirements, onerous beyond the publication of personal information on the state's sex offender website and the sex offender label printed on state identification cards, will be discussed later in the chapter. Police officers and prosecutors had total discretion whether to charge sex workers (or people whom officers alleged to be engaged in sex work) with Prostitution or CANS. As a result, in Louisiana and unlike any other state in the union, hundreds of women were registered as sex offenders. Until 2013, roughly 40 percent of sex offenders from New Orleans were registered on the LSOCPR site because of CANS convictions.[9]

Activists in New Orleans agree that CANS enforcement and registration amped up after Hurricane Katrina in 2005.[10] In 2007, the issue was brought to the attention of Women With A Vision (WWAV), a well-known and widely respected New Orleans advocacy group for marginalized women lead by Deon Haywood.[11] Under Haywood's direction, WWAV coordinated with other local and national activist groups to launch the coalitional NO Justice Project in 2008, designed to end the harsher penalties for CANS convictions, especially CANS's sex offender registration and notification requirements.[12] WWAV and the NO Justice Project were spectacularly successful in their objectives. In 2010 and 2011, Louisiana state legislators equalized CANS penalties to those of Prostitution and declassified CANS as a registerable sex offense.[13] These reforms did not apply retroactively, however, so WWAV assembled a team of civil rights attorneys to file a lawsuit on behalf of people previously convicted of CANS who were on the registry. The federal lawsuit of nine anonymous petitioners challenged the constitutionality of CANS's harsher penalties and its registration and notification requirements on equal protection grounds.[14] The equal protection claim was straightforwardly premised on the fact that Prostitution and CANS criminalize identical conduct but with decidedly different consequences for the convicted. At the end of March 2012, Judge Martin Feldman of the U.S. District Court for the Eastern District of Louisiana ruled in *Doe v. Jindal* that the harsher CANS penalties and registration requirements were unconstitutional. To classify CANS as a registerable sex offense but not Prostitution "is not rationally related to achieving any legitimate state interest."[15] A few months later, the attorneys from the Center for Constitutional Rights (CCR) and other civil rights organizations filed a class action complaint requesting that not only their plaintiffs but also hundreds more convicted of CANS be removed from the LSOCPR.[16] The case settled in June 2013, when Louisiana finally obliged the declassification demand.

In sum, WWAV led a victorious, multipronged, legislative, litigation, and grassroots campaign, a campaign that relieved suffering and realized justice for citizens, mainly Black women, who were forced to register as sex offenders, typically for offering or allegedly offering oral sex for money to undercover officers.[17]

What do we lose when we win? And must winning always entail loss?

In what follows I critique identitarian modes of thought, praxis, and discourse that cabined and continue to cabin the force of the coalitional sexual justice politics launched by the social movement challenging CANS, the first of three "sodomitical episodes" as I reference them in the Introduction to the book. I offer critique more so than criticism; I profoundly admire the activists, organizers, and attorneys who challenged the CANS statute's harsher penalties and who continue to combat the law's ongoing inequities. Indeed, over the past few years I have worked with a coalition of activists, filmmakers, law students, lawyers, politicians, and lobbyists to repeal the

CANS law outright (remember, CANS is still on the books even though its penalties have been equalized to those of Prostitution) as well as to expunge CANS convictions from people's criminal records.[18] In my crosshairs are not particular political or legal actors involved in the ongoing CANS campaign. Rather, I want to show how sexual identitarianism saturates our political imaginary, even or especially our progressive political imaginary, and at a high price. In that sense, while the CANS sodomitical episode is the chapter's point of departure, I hope the arguments herein helpfully extend outward for how we think about and advocate for sexual justice.

There are two ways identitarianism structures and winnows the CANS campaigns of the recent past (2008–2013) and present (2020s). The first way, explicitly avowed by anti-CANS stakeholders and their supporters, foregrounds minoritized subjects targeted by the law: namely, as we will soon see, "Black trans women," "Black women," and "LGBTQ people of color." I will point to some collateral in framing CANS as, for example, "a law that criminalizes Black trans women,"[19] but for the most part it is the second mode of identitarianism, not morally positivized but nevertheless mobilized, that undercuts a broader attack on the state's ineffective, antifeminist, hypercarceral, and perverse apparatus for regulating sex and sexual violence. On this read, the identity figure or phantasm structuring political thought and practice is the "sex offender," along with its—*his*, really—contemporary cultural equivalences: "sex predator," "child rapist," "pedophile." My earlier writing on this Louisianan sodomitical episode homed in on the sex offender's normative antithesis, the "consenting adult," as a mobilizing, moralizing political figure for the CANS campaign and litigation.[20] Upon revisiting the scene, I think it is more precisely the figure of the sex offender, whom we might perceive as the constitutive Other of the consenting adult, that contours yet cabins progressive (and conservative) sexual politics, in Louisiana but well beyond.

The first, briefest part of the chapter tracks the first mode of identitarianism and its possible ramifications; the second part tracks the second mode and its probable ramifications.

The third part, initiating from interviews I conducted with New Orleans–based sex offenders, legislators, and community organizers, gestures toward two normative abstractions that might anchor a paraidentitarian, coalitional politics of sexual justice, un- or less beholden to sympathetic subjects and attuned to sexualized state violence. This part proposes to supplant, partially and provisionally, the seductive figures of the minoritized sexual subject (i.e., Black trans women, sex workers) and the monstrous sex offender (i.e., pedophile) with comparatively unsexy elucidations of *fairness* and *debility* as abstractions for progressive, paraidentitarian, sexual— or we might call them sodomitical—politics. Taking fairness and debility seriously, I suggest, rightly extends our political sympathies and energies without triggering, as much, quarantining moralism. "Fairness" was an oft-repeated appeal of the registered sex offenders I interviewed in New Orleans, and the invocation of fairness directs us to an ongoing paradox of fairness and punishment foregrounded in liberal political theory. That paradox is not resolved but exposited as it clarifies the treacherousness of embracing fairness as a political idiom, an embrace I ambivalently endorse. Building upon philosopher John Rawls's and his critics' glosses on fairness and punishment, I ask if fairness might be more promisingly resignified through conversations with those sexed and penalized by the state. Lastly, I define and defend debility as a useful concept for advancing and extending sexual politics; not incidentally, a turn to debility hedges against the more serious problems a turn to fairness might otherwise transmit. This last part engages scholarship on vulnerability and state redress to distinguish and defend debility as an organizing principle of a more ecological and less individualizing politics of sexual justice.

Across this chapter and alongside the scholarship of Black Studies professor Terrance Wooten, I am asking how we might repurpose progressive sexual politics if "sexuality" were perceived not, in the first instance, as "sexual identity—when someone *becomes* LGBTQ or articulates their LGBTQ identity," but rather as a "category of analysis" elemental to the statutory and cultural "management of deviance and difference."[21]

Sympathetic Subjects, or the Sexual Identities We Like

Let us begin at the end, or an epilogue that may be prologue, of the CANS campaign. In 2022, Matt Nadel and Megan Plotka released their short and now award-winning documentary, *CANS Can't Stand*.[22] The documentary chronicles Wendi Cooper (Figure 1.2), a "woman of trans experience," as she beautifully describes herself, who has been a leading organizer drawing attention to CANS and its discriminatory enforcement against and impact on Black transgender women. Cooper was one of the plaintiffs in *Doe v. Jindal*, the district court decision holding CANS's harsher penalties and sex offender regulatory requirements unconstitutional. Today—and this is why the film may now function as prologue—Cooper continues to fight against the statute and its disparate, stigmatizing ramifications (for example, CANS convictions remain on some people's criminal records whereas a Prostitution conviction would not). While Cooper and her good friend Milan Nicole Sherry (Figure 1.3), the other Black transgender activist the film spotlights, emphasize the antitrans policing and prosecution enabled by the CANS law, both organizers also explain that CANS has been deployed against all sorts of sex workers, cis women, and queer folks more generally.[23]

Figure 1.2 Community organizer Wendi Cooper featured in *CANS Can't Stand* (2020). *(Still from* CANS Can't Stand *by Matt Nadel and Megan Plotka.)*

Figure 1.3 Community organizer Milan Sherry featured in *CANS Can't Stand* (2020). *(Still from* CANS Can't Stand *by Matt Nadel and Megan Plotka.)*

However, when the documentary was picked up for distribution by the *New Yorker* in 2023, the news magazine added its own subtitle to the documentary: *CANS Can't Stand: Liberation for Black Trans Women.* Undoubtedly well intentioned, the *New Yorker*'s subtitle circumscribes the political agitations of Cooper and her comrades, as if those agitations are for Black trans women and Black trans women alone. The magazine's tagline (and its write-up generally[24]) for the documentary similarly identitarianizes, if you will, the film and the politics it records: "A group of Black trans women fight to repeal a law used to target queer locals."[25] The tagline is true but myopic, for CANS has a much longer enforcement history against *not-so-queer* locals too, mainly straight-identified women. A spring 2023 episode of the American Civil Liberties Union's podcast, "At Liberty," featuring Cooper and Sherry, praises *CANS Can't Stand* and its lead subjects for raising political awareness against anti-Black, antitrans discrimination. The podcast and its host double down on the identarian posture and, well, get things wrong. Click-bait titled "This Law Criminalizes Black Trans Women," the ACLU should know better: the law criminalizes blowjobs and butt sex for cash (conduct), not status (Black transness), notwithstanding the police's use and abuse of CANS to go after women for "walking while trans."[26] The podcast host explains, mistakenly, that the law was "specifically designed to target queer people, especially Black trans women."[27] In the documentary itself, Sherry supposes a similar origin story for CANS: "it was put on the books to criminalize same-gender loving individuals."[28]

But from my research conducted in the 2010s I was surprised to discover that the law was enacted in 1982 by the Louisiana Legislature in the hopes of stymieing racial minority boys and young men selling sex in the French Quarter.[29] We do not know how these boys and men understood their sexual orientations—maybe they were "same-gender loving," but maybe not. In any case, the legislature enacted harsher penalties for CANS than those for Prostitution in the hopes that they could slap the boys with longer prison time and heavier fines before they smarted to the law.[30] Additionally, the legislature enacted CANS because state representatives thought the Prostitution law would not reach the conduct in question since they, the state representatives, assumed the Prostitution law only applied to women—that is, only "women" could be prostitutes—but this was in error, since the Prostitution law had been gender-neutralized years before, the word "woman" having been substituted for "person."[31] In other words, the state representatives thought they needed CANS in order to criminalize the offerings of young male sex workers but the Prostitution law already did so. This misperception had devastating consequences undetectable under an identitarian register intersectionally calibrated to Black trans women alone, which as I have mentioned is not precisely Cooper's or Sherry's calibration but rather the *New Yorker*'s and the ACLU's. So the law was codified to penalize young brown and Black men, and because the law criminalized the *same* conduct as Prostitution, and because CANS does not target "same-gender loving individuals," but rather blowjobs and butt sex, *cis* women could be targeted by the commercial sex law too, and they were, making up the lion's share of convictions and sex offender registrations. By far, cis women constituted the largest population of the hundreds of sex offenders who were registered for their CANS convictions.[32]

As I write this in 2023, it is more than politically understandable why the *New Yorker* and the ACLU frame both the CANS political contestations and the documentary about CANS as exclusively orbiting Black trans women. We are living through a tidal wave of regressive, horrific antitrans legislation across the United States, and Black trans women continue to be murdered in this country at appalling rates.[33] Indeed, the ACLU released the podcast episode to "celebrate International Transgender Day of Visibility."[34]

The exclusive focus on Black trans women, though, may inadvertently play into the balkanizing discourse of "gender critical feminists" and other phobic pundits who segregate out and discredit some women from other women. It seems to me that we are in an urgent moment to press what cis women, trans women, and gay men (or men who have sex with men) share rather than what differentiates them, in this instance: discriminatory policing, draconian penalties for sex work, and pervasive debility from sex offender registration requirements. A lesser but still identitarian-skeptical concern of this chapter is that the exclusive, siloizing focus on Black trans women overlooks how the CANS law has been mobilized across an array of minoritized, vulnerable populations. For example, it is quite likely that some of the boys targeted by the enactment of CANS in 1982 were later persecuted under the same law, but as older, transgender women, in the mid-aughts. Political campaigns that over-index identity categories potentially undercount not only the people outside such categories but also those folks who slide across them. This complaint may appear to give *all lives matter* vibes, but the point is less about recognition—determining which gender and sexual minorities suffered when—than about tracking and challenging the state's deployment of sex to surveil, contain, and control its citizens.

Back in 2008–2013, the NO Justice project to declassify CANS as a registerable sex offense focused, rhetorically and politically, more broadly on Black women and LGBTQ people of color impacted by the law.[35] But here too we see some limits to identitarian frames. In their write up of the campaign, activist and scholar Laura McTighe and WWAV executive director Deon Haywood genealogize the CANS statute within the long history of "policing black womanhood," a manifestation of "the system of modern state racism [that] crystallized under Jim Crow."[36] From this perspective, "CANS was but one tool being used to control nearly every aspect of Black women's lives."[37] McTighe and Haywood take umbrage too with what they allege to be a "pinkwashed," gay historiographic version of CANS and its discontents peddled by journalistic accounts that "reframed [CANS] as a threat to lesbian, gay, bisexual, transgender, and queer (LGBTQ) rights."[38] For McTighe and Haywood, CANS is rightly an identity story, then, but one about Black women and Black feminist activism, not about LGBTQ people as a class. An attorney on the *Jindal* case, Andrea Ritchie, narrated CANS similarly if more inclusively, as "a powerful tool of racialized policing of gender and sexuality in Louisiana."[39] Ritchie too criticizes "previous efforts to challenge this law which focused only on LGB people," although she provides no citation for those prior struggles. In any case, Ritchie lauds WWAV and NO Justice for "centering the experiences and voices of women of color, and highlighting the shared experiences of policing and punishment among poor Black women and poor and homeless LGBTQ people of color."[40]

McTighe, Haywood, and Richie's accounts of CANS and the campaigns against it are more accurate because they are more expansive than the *New Yorker*'s and ACLU's pedestaling of Black trans women. Historical accuracy is not exactly my beef, though, nor is it particularly relevant for my analysis that about 20 percent of CANS sex offender were not Black and about 25 percent were men (although this last statistic is perhaps unnecessarily muted by feminist scholars Susan Dewey's and Tonia St. Germain's political diagnosis that "the New Orleans criminal justice system used the CANS legislation to deliberately target African American women and transgender individuals").[41] Rather, what drops out from all of these identity stories—is CANS about the men it was designed to prosecute and persecute? Is CANS about the mainly cis women that ended up on the registry? Is CANS about the Black trans women whom the law disparately impacts and who lead the campaign against the law today?—is, again, the way *sex* has been policed and politicized to flexibly discriminate against all these social groups and more. By sticking with the sex, we can better perceive that it is the policing of blow jobs for cash, not the policing of any particular identity category, that has allowed CANS to devastate so many different kinds of people: boys, men, cis women, and trans women—most, but not all, of whom are Black and economically disadvantaged. Whereas philosopher Michel Foucault and later Jonathan Goldberg instructed that antisodomy laws of the past were purposefully vague, capturing all kinds of nonnormative sexual conduct ("sodomy—that utterly confused category"[42]), it is the relentless specificity of Louisiana's CANS law that has allowed its reach to metastasize across vulnerable, overlapping populations.[43] From the vantage point of *sex*, we need not insist on swapping out one identity story with a better one. We can instead contest the state's variable deployment of sex to make deviance and deviants. Ritchie extols WWAV's and NO Justice's campaign for "challeng[ing] the criminalization of all sexualities deemed to be 'deviant,'"[44] but as the next section illustrates that is not quite right, for the identitarianism driving the CANS campaign relocated deviance elsewhere,[45] onto the "true sex offender":[46] the pedophile, the child rapist, those villainous sexual identities we loathe and need.

The Political Perversity of the Sex Offender, or the Sexual Villains We Loathe and Need[47]

In the ACLU podcast, Cooper says, "I feel like I shouldn't have been a sex offender in the first place."[48] A motivating grievance of the documentary, *CANS Can't Stand*, one of its key political complaints, is captured by Cooper too: "When you're labeled as a sex offender, it's like this modern-day scarlet letter, right?"[49]

But who "should be a sex offender in the first place"? Who, if anyone, deserves the scarlet letter and its collateral hardships?

Nobody, because the sex offender registry is a failed system for remedying sexual violence.

Louisiana's sex offender regulatory regime is like the regimes of other states, if extreme. Louisianan sex offenders must periodically check in with local authorities. Their travel is severely restricted, their access to the internet often limited,[50] and some are prohibited from living within measured radii of institutions like schools, parks, libraries, and recreation centers.[51] Sex offenders are prohibited from an assortment of occupations, among them operating a taxi. In Louisiana, in the event of hurricanes and other environmental emergencies, there is a separate evacuation system for sex offenders.[52] All Louisiana sex offenders are forbidden to wear masks on public holidays, notably Halloween and Mardi Gras.[53] (The no-mask law was a recurring point of frustration throughout my interviews with sex offenders, mostly on account of its symbolic, stigmatic force.)

For over fifteen years, and in concert with other feminist, queer, antiracist, and prison abolitionist scholars, I have strenuously opposed state and federal sex offender regulatory regimes,[54] and we have taken our cue in large part from survivors of sexual violence, and parents of victims of sexual violence, who have resisted sex offender registries and who have posed alternative, restorative, and rehabilitative justice models for preventing and remedying sexual violence.[55] And so before critiquing some ways the "sex offender"—as an identity formation—cabins progressive sexual politics, I offer a brief primer on why the U.S. sex offender regime (registration, notification, residency restrictions, GPS-tracking, and so on) are *ineffective* and *antifeminist*; how the regulatory regime extends *carcerality* beyond prison walls as a nonsolution for social problems; and, most pertinent for this chapter, how sex offender registry and notification systems comprise their own form of *state-sponsored sexual violence*. I provide the primer because if our federal and state sex offender regulatory systems effectively reduced sexual violence then it might not matter, or might not matter as much, that the figure of the "sex offender" ideologically and materially circumscribes our visions, politics, and practices of sexual justice.

Ineffective: Collectively, U.S. sex offender regulatory regimes fail to make communities safer from sexual violence. No research study has ever concluded that our dominant sex offender policies, such as sex offender websites and residency restrictions, effectively remedy sexual violence.[56] These systems are ineffective, and sometimes counterproductive, in part because they are designed to deter a bogeyman, the relentless-recidivist stranger-predator. The Louisiana Legislature, like other state legislatures, reiterates fictions of sex offense and sex offenders as rationales for its registry systems:

> The legislature finds that sex offenders, sexually violent predators, and child predators often pose a high risk of engaging in sex offense and crimes against victims who are minors even after being released from incarceration or commitment and that protection of the public from sex offenders, sexually violent predators, and child predators is of paramount government interest.[57]

Given the expansiveness of what counts as a registerable sex offense (from voyeurism to kidnapping to "pornography involving juveniles," etc.), the legislative assertion of high risk of reengagement is incoherent. Given, too, that most sex offenders are first time offenders, and that the great majority of sex offenders are not reconvicted for other sex offenses, it seems safe to say that the legislative findings are not founded on much. Nevertheless, the information is presented as authoritative, despite what we know from decades upon decades of research: sex offenders have some of the lowest rates of recidivism of all people convicted of crimes, and most offenders are acquaintances, intimate partners, or family members of the victim.[58]

Antifeminist: And so what makes sex offender regulator regimes antifeminist is, among other reasons, their political focus away from the family and gender norms as site and source of sexual violence and onto the fiction—a highly productive fiction—of the sex predator. Historian Linda Gordon states the problem plainly and powerfully: "Without a feminist analysis, evidence of child sexual abuse means that danger lies in sex perverts, in public spaces, in unsupervised girls, in sexually assertive girls. . . . [C]hild sexual abuse without feminist interpretation supplies evidence and arguments for constricting and disempowering children."[59] Gordon's comment predates, but presciently, the contemporary sex offender registry system. The registry's focus on the stranger-pervert places danger outside the patriarchal home rather than within it, as if perpetrators of sexual violence are not typically fathers, stepfathers, mother's boyfriends, uncles, husbands, intimate partners, family friends, police officers, and prison guards, but sicko men in white vans. Danger so mislocated, the solution is equally misguided and antifeminist: keep children—especially girls—home, off the internet and social media, away from sexual information and education.

Political scientist Rose Corrigan updates Gordon's observation to directly indict the registry:

[Sex offender registration and notification] laws represent a significant ideological attack on feminist reforms that broadened understandings and applications of sex offense statutes. These . . . policies and practice[s] have serious counter-productive effects on the ability of the criminal justice system to identify and prosecute sex offenders.[60]

The difference between rapists and other men is that rapists get caught, to paraphrase feminist legal scholar Catharine MacKinnon.[61] That position is less nuanced than either Corrigan's or Gordon's, but these feminists' collective intervention elucidates that the registry constructs both sexual violence and its perpetrators as exceptional and aberrant rather than all too ordinary, inextricable from gendered norms and gendered inequality. It is that ordinariness, that inextricability of sexual violence from gender as we know it, that led Gordon to advise the following recommendation, over thirty years ago:

Probably the most important single contribution to the prevention of incest would be the strengthening of mothers. By increasing their ability to support themselves and raising their social and psychological self-esteem, allowing them to choose independence if that is necessary to protect themselves and their daughters, men's sexual exploitation could be checked.[62]

Along with Gordon's call to financially empower mothers, we ought to add some of the recommendations feminist abolitionist author Judith Levine and education and gender studies professor Erica Meiners put forward for preventing sexual violence: abolish sex offender registries and sex offender civil commitment programs; "invest in radical and free sex education"; support young people's sexual agency and decision-making; turn toward community models of restorative and transformative justice to resolve conflicts and heal harm; facilitate "mutual aid and care" through a "robust welfare state," not a carceral one; dismantle prisons, and not only because they are the site of so much (sexual) violence.[63]

Carcerality: As it stands, though, the sex offender as a legal category, social construction, and identity formation legitimates and extends carceral governance as a nonsolution to social problems. Sex offenders have now become a bedrock for what Foucault called the "carceral archipelago,"[64] redefined by contemporary scholars as "a set of interconnected carceral spaces and practices, including prisons, police, detention centers, segregated cities, reservations and enclosures."[65] Historian Paul Renfro, surveying the explosion of sex offender regulatory requirements since the 1990s, argues that the requirements "are fueling mass incarceration while doing little to actually help survivors. . . . Only by dismantling the registry and, in its stead, assembling a more equitable, less punitive society . . . can we actually end the phenomena of sexual harm."[66] Meanwhile, according to Levine and Meiners, "people with sex-related convictions constitute one of the fastest-growing populations among the 2.3 million people locked in US prisons, jails, and detention facilities."[67] Along with Renfro, law professor Eric Janus, and sociologist Roger Lancaster, Levine and Meiners caution that the registry as a model of carcerality has infiltrated and intensified our criminal justice system: "The logic and technologies of the registries serve as a beta test for a vast 'prison without walls,' with electronic ankle bracelets, surveillance cameras, and tens of thousands of collateral consequences fencing in everyone convicted of a felony."[68] (An important historical amendment to the critique of late modern, technologized carcerality, Black feminist scholar Sarah Haley spotlights how, in Jim Crow Georgia, forced domestic labor for paroled Black women prisoners extended "the carceral state's reach beyond the discrete institution of the prison.")[69]

When social and sexual justice advocates call for abolishing mass incarceration or defunding the police, we are often met with the objection, "but what about the child rapist?" This question operationalizes what English professor Gillian Harkins calls the "pedophilic function." An "adaptive and expansive threat," the virtual pedophile "can never be fully contained."[70] At the turn of the twenty-first century, as a confluence of geopolitical, digital, and aesthetic transformations, Harkins argues that the pedophile morphed into a "threat [that] existed in all bodies and spaces, rationalizing a shift from targeted policing to total surveillance as the charge for sexual security . . . [his] threatening potentiality expands processes of securitization."[71] And so the very question, *What about the child rapist?*, and its underpinning logic are part of what keeps mass incarceration and carceral systems more broadly in place. The idea of the "pedophile," symbolically fungible with the "sex offender," functions to legitimate prison, policing, surveillance, and securitization as the American way of life.

State-sponsored sexual violence: Perhaps provocatively, I want to propose that the sex offender regime is itself a form of state-sponsored sexual violence against citizens, for it exceptionalizes sex to make "personages," *really bad* personages, whose identities are defined by their offense.[72] We do not do this with other offenders. Bank robbers are not understood to bank robberists, and to call people who commit drug offenses "drug offenders" now seems retrograde.[73] Generalizing the point to all incarcerated or otherwise criminalized persons, civil rights activist and law professor Michelle Alexander writes, "there are many things that are difficult to manage during this period of our nation's history; avoiding terms that reduce people to prison labels is not one of them."[74]

The *identity* function encourages us to think of people who commit sex offenses as "sex offenders," as a sexually aberrant, subhuman species, when in fact, "no single factor or cause of sexual offending has yet been identified. Research suggests that a combination of factors likely contribute to sex offending behavior," among them: childhood victimization, neglect and abuse; "self-regulation and impulse control problems"; mental illness; and drugs and alcohol.[75] The comparatively low recidivism rates of people who commit rape and sexual assault combined with the literature attesting to an array of etiologies for those who commit such acts undermines, or should, the sex offender as a kind of person, and sex offending as an identitarian truth of a person.

When Cooper and too many others convicted of CANS report that police officers sexually assaulted them,[76] we must reckon with the fact that these citizens may in part be seen by state officers as "rapable" because the state itself has registered them, literally and figuratively,[77] as sexual deviants. Like those officers, the registry itself perpetrates state-sponsored sexual violence. Among his interviews with eighteen homeless Black male sex offenders in Maryland, Terrance Wooten reports that "[s]ix of the men . . . shared stories of being assaulted in a shelter once others found out they were sex offenders."[78] State sexualization, the statutory conversion of persons into sex offenders, breeds civil violence.

According to the complaints filed in the *Jindal* case against CANS's sex offender registry requirements, as well as a scathing 2011 Department of Justice (DOJ) report on NOPD's endemic civil rights violations, trans women of color were routinely charged with CANS by virtue of their being on the street, whether or not they were soliciting sex work.[79] When the state sexualizes a class of women by posting identifying information and their conviction histories online, when the state turns the women into image-objects for widespread consumption and transmutes them from persons to pixels, the state is acting as the sex offender it imagines itself preempting. When the targeted objects are "predators" rather than "prostitutes," is the upshot any different (Figure 1.4)? And insofar as "Black men are more likely to receive longer sentencing terms and higher penalties for sex crimes and thus are more likely to be on the sex offender registry than white men," state sexual violence is racialized sexual violence, too.[80]

	131		LLOYD ▓▓▓▓ Level: Tier 2	▓▓SAINT CLAUDE AVE	NEW ORLEANS
	132		Sidney ▓▓▓▓ Level: Tier 3	▓▓GRAVIER ST	NEW ORLEANS
	133	Non-Compliant	WILLIAM ▓▓▓ Level: Tier 3	▓▓CAMP ST	NEW ORLEANS
	134		CLEVELAND ▓▓▓ Level: Tier 3	▓▓PALM ST	NEW ORLEANS
	135		DAVID▓▓▓▓ Level: Tier 3	▓▓▓DOROTHEA ST	NEW ORLEANS
	136		JAVAHN▓▓▓ Level: Tier 2	▓▓HUNTLEE DR	NEW ORLEANS
	137		Bradley ▓▓ Level: Tier 3	▓▓▓▓LOYOLA AVE	NEW ORLEANS
	138		EMMANUEL▓▓▓ Level: Tier 3	▓▓DOROTHEA ST	NEW ORLEANS
	139		Eugene▓▓▓▓ Level: Tier 2	▓▓CLEMATIS ST	NEW ORLEANS
	140		RUSSELL ▓▓▓ Level: Tier 3	▓▓▓DOWNMAN RD	NEW ORLEANS
	141		TEDDY▓▓▓ Level: Tier 1	▓▓SUMNER ST	NEW ORLEANS
	142		VINCENT▓▓▓ Level: Tier 3	▓▓▓▓▓ (RAYBURN CORRECTIONAL CENTER)	NEW ORLEANS
	143		MIKE▓▓▓▓ Level: Tier 1	▓▓▓▓ (LA STATE PEN)	NEW ORLEANS

Figure 1.4 Screengrab from the Louisiana State Police, State Sex Offender and Child Predator Registry Site.

Let me be as clear as possible that a right to queerness—the subtitle of this book substantivized in the Introduction—does not entail a right to sexually molest children or sexually harass and assault others. But a right to queerness encourages us to challenge a sex offense regulatory regime that sexualizes its citizens, fails to redress sexual violence, and powers up the carceral machine.

What I observed from my research into the CANS contestations was the way the litigation, legislative, and grassroots strategies to declassify the (mainly) women registered as sex offenders for CANS convictions rested, in part or in whole, implicitly and sometimes explicitly, on the idea that these women are not rapists, not pedophiles, "not the predators that are after our children. They are innocent parties sometimes in, in this situation as well," as Louisiana state representative Charmaine Marchand-Stiaes put it when defending her bill to declassify CANS as a registerable sex offense.[81] In other words, these women are not the sexual monsters properly designated by the state as sex offenders.

Consider first my interviews, conducted primarily in 2012 with some follow-ups in 2016 and 2019. I interviewed four women registered as sex offenders for their CANS conviction, about a dozen men registered as sex offenders for non-CANS convictions (e.g., possession of child pornography, sexual assault), as well as attorneys, community organizers, and an NOPD sex crime detective involved in the CANS declassification campaign. As one community organizer put it, reflecting the sentiment of most of my interviewees, "Look, if you rape a child, it need[s] to be branded across you damn forehead . . . there are no exceptions. . . . I don't want to hear it, there's nothing you can tell me."[82]

Nearly all the interviewees agreed that there should be a sex offender registry but that they themselves should not be on it. Lucy thought repeat CANS or Prostitution offenders should have to register but not that she herself, who was falsely charged, should. Two other women said they should not have to register since they are not dangerous, but that rapists and child predators must. Kathy was visibly offended by my asking why "those people" should be required to register.[83]

When I asked the men convicted for crimes involving force, minors, and so on, they too, for the most part, insisted that they were "victims of circumstance," that they were not threats to public safety, but that dangerous people should be monitored by the state upon release and subject to registration and notification requirements. When I asked if or why some people should be on the sex offender registry, two offenders immediately spoke of their children. One woman warned, "If somebody did something like that to my daughter, I'd probably be in jail for murder . . . so yeah I think those people deserve to be there. But I wasn't hurting anybody, you know?"[84] Andy, a white man in his sixties convicted of possession of child pornography, keeps newspaper clippings of the "true sex offenders," who he says should "yes, absolutely" be on the registry. "That's a wolf! . . . I'm in the same boat with a rapist child rapist predator!" he decried, his syntax mirroring cultural presumptions of compulsive recidivism.[85]

These gestures of disaffiliation might qualify as what political scientist Cathy Cohen calls "secondary marginalization," except here what is at stake is not only the purification of the minority group from polluting liabilities but also the refusal of state-assigned membership: I am not what you call me, but those people are.[86]

While most of my interviewees held similar beliefs about the sex offender registry (right for thee but not for me), there was a minority of alternative or ambivalent viewpoints that foreground and foreshadow a less-identitarian sexual justice politics. Evan, a young white man, said that, before he was convicted, he thought to himself, "Fuck sex offenders." But after having been found guilty of attempted carnal knowledge of a juvenile, he changed his mind: "Humility . . . kinda took over." Although he said that child predators and rapists should be required to register, he also thought that too expansive a registry is counterproductive for identifying real threats (this comment reiterates a pervasive argument found in scholarship on and activism against sex offender registries).[87] A Ron Paul supporter, he added, "The state is the big enemy here," and discussed U.S. mass incarceration and the War on Drugs as main engines of national violence.[88] Ken, a white man in his forties, did not see how the registries worked to make communities safer and proposed instead that education and community programs might be better methods of sexual violence prevention.[89] Phillip, a Black man in his fifties, did not support sex offender registration either, but his opposition was not politicized like Ken's or Evan's. He was morose. The various conditions of registration had all but extinguished his hope for a decently livable life. Depressed, his opposition to registration seemed to reflect frustrations with the state's continued debilitation of his life opportunities fourteen years after his prison release.[90]

What I am pressing upon is not that some of these interviewees are right and some are wrong, nor is my intention to make light of the fear and atmospheric punitiveness that I take to be undergirding most interviewees' sense that sex offender registries are necessary and good even if they overreach and underperform. I am suggesting that my interviewees' responses capture a pervasive cultural logic, an invidious mode of identitarianism, one that concentrates sexual monstrosity and violence into the fiction of the relentlessly recidivistic stranger-pedophile. While that identity fiction has traveled under different appellations ("white slavers, sexual delinquents, and sexual psychopaths"[91]) at different points in time and for different disciplinary purposes, today the fiction is located under the statutory sign of the "sex offender." The identitarian fiction of the sex offender as a summary source of sexual violence inflected not only my interviewees' responses but also the CANS grassroots campaign, media coverage, and litigation strategy.

As part of WWAV's declassification campaign, executive director Deon Haywood opined, "many of these women are survivors of rape and domestic violence themselves, many have struggled with addiction and poverty, yet they are *being treated as predators*."[92] Who, if anyone, should be treated as a predator, and for what purpose?

The NO Justice Policy Brief, "Just a Talking Crime," pull quotes a woman convicted of CANS who pleads, "I was raped and used many times myself, and I never hurt anyone—why am I on the registry as a sex offender?"[93] Another woman's pull quote reads, "there are children getting raped every day, but you want to go after me, and go after the transexuals out there. It just vex my spirit."[94] The implication, not so implied, is that child rapists and others who hurt people should be registered as sex offenders, and that such registration is both warranted and just.

Taking its cue from the NO Justice Project, the New Orleans *Times-Picayune*, like many other local and national news outlets, extended its sympathy to those convicted of CANS as (the kinds of) people wrongly classified as sex offenders. As an editorial penned during the declassification campaign relayed:

> Such offenders are not predators. They are not drug addicts desperately seeking money for their next fix. They [sex workers, or those otherwise convicted of CANS] should be punished, but they should not be forced to spend the next 15 years labeled a sex offender.[95]

Let me put a few rhetorical questions to the editors that might direct our present inquiry: why should sex workers "be punished" at all (see Chapter 5)? Should anyone be labeled as a sex offender for fifteen years? For life? Might cognizing people who commit sexual violence as "predators" circularly justify the registry (Harkins's "pedophilic function")? What if sex offender registration and notification requirements, in Louisiana as everywhere else, do not make citizens safer from sexual violence? (Not to mention: is criminal punishment the best policy for "drug addicts"?)

In its *Doe v. Jindal* brief filed on behalf of nine plaintiffs who were registered as sex offenders because of their CANS convictions, the CCR emphasizes—the phrase is repeated eleven times—that CANS is the only registerable offense that does not involve "force, coercion, use of a weapon, lack of consent, or a minor victim."[96] The brief stipulates that

> [p]laintiffs pose no danger to anyone. They have not been convicted of any criminal offense involving force, use of a weapon, coercion,

lack of consent, or a victim who is a minor. They pose no threat of predation, violence, or danger to children. *Thus,* the mandate that they be subject to the harsh requirements of the sex offender registry law is unjustifiable and unconstitutional.[97]

The powerful if unfortunate implication is that sex offender registration requirements are justifiable, or at least constitutionally legitimate, for everyone else whose crimes entail what the state defines[98] as "force, coercion," and so on. I expressed this apprehension about the litigation strategy in an article published in 2013, to which Alexis Agathocleous, who was then the CCR's attorney for *Jindal,* responded that my interpretation "reveal[ed] a fundamental misunderstanding of the equal protection theory in this case."[99] That theory—simple, brilliant, and effective—was that if CANS and Prostitution criminalize identical conduct (soliciting oral and anal sex for money), then the penalties ought to be identical; harsher penalties for the former violate the equal protection guarantee of the Fourteenth Amendment of the U.S. Constitution. In other words, the legal strategy did not rest on whether the criminalized conduct involved force, coercion, weapons, or a minor; it rested on the fact of identical conduct being penalized unequally by the state. But then why repeat, eleven times, that CANS is the only sex offense in Louisiana that does not involve "force, coercion . . ."? Why the "thus," predicating the unjustifiability of the sex offender requirements on the proposition that the plaintiffs are not child rapists (the formula is repeated later in the Complaint: "Where [CANS] involves no minor victim . . . or lack of consent. . . . Defendants are *thus* violating Plaintiffs' right[s] . . . in violation of . . . the United States Constitution")?[100] We all know why, which is to say my critique was never a criticism of the *Jindal* lawyers or the *Jindal* lawsuit so much as an effort to make manifest the normative, juridical, and psychical work the "sex offender" does for all of us, and not just judges: the gothic character partitions the world. On one side are sympathetic subjects who deserve constitutional protections; on the other, predatory perverts who deserve more than they could ever get. In *Jindal,* Justice Feldman opines:

> It seems clear and the Court stresses that no Equal Protection claim would exist here if the Louisiana legislature had determined that sex offender registration would be mandated for *all* individuals who are convicted of performing oral or anal sex for money.[101]

The Louisiana Legislature could have responded to the asymmetrical penalties for Prostitution and CANS by also making Prostitution a registerable sex offense, and this would have neutralized the equal protection challenge. Imagine, though, if the conduct in question was not commercial sex but possession of child pornography. Imagine further a scenario in which two separate laws criminalized possession but only one law triggered sex offender registration and notification requirements. Forgive the extended counterfactual, but there is simply no way such a law would launch a grass-roots social movement, and it is unlikely a civil rights organization would take the case. Unquestionably, a state legislature would ratchet up the "lax" child pornography law to mandate sex offender registration. I am not carrying the flag for child pornographers. I am contending that the social and juridical movement against CANS, like many a movement for sexual justice, is not merely a formal Aristotelian one of treating like cases alike, but substantively dependent on a dominant, dangerously wrong, antifeminist cultural conception of the sex offender as a taxonomic type: a kind of perverted parallel to "lesbian" or "gay," the sex offender as an exhaustive repository for recidivistic, predatory sexual violence, barely controllable by the registry.

The CCR's lawyer, Agathocleous, "oppose[s]" "sex offender registration schemes," contending that "arguably . . . the [CANS] litigation actually opens up space for future challenges to other sex offender registries rather than shutting them down."[102] Unfortunately, though, during and after the CANS contestations and litigation, Louisiana intensified and broadened its sex offender regulatory regime. Herewith, a few examples with occasional side commentary:

- Beginning in 2008, and to come into compliance with federal standards set by the Adam Walsh Act, Louisiana expanded the definitions of, and increased the registration and notification requirements for, sex offenses. Among other notable amendments: registration terms were extended for every type of offense and retroactively applied; life registration requirements were retroactively imposed for those offenses redefined as "aggravated" (aggravated sex crimes include various degrees of [non-sexual] kidnapping); juveniles fourteen years old and over are mandated to register for certain crimes.[103]
- Also in 2008, then-Governor Bobby Jindal signed a bill permitting judges to require chemical castration for a first-time offense of aggravated rape, aggravated incest, and the like (as mentioned earlier, the state legislature went even further in 2024, greenlighting surgical castration for child sex offenders). Jindal defended the law proudly: "I am glad we have taken such strong measures in Louisiana to put a stop to these monsters' brutal acts."[104] Jindal has flipped causality: it is the political construction of the sex offender as a monster that permits or even demands he be castrated.

- In June 2012, the legislature passed a law requiring convicted sex offenders and child predators to declare their status on their Facebook and other social media pages, along with identifying information such as their home address. This law was passed only after an earlier law instituting a blanket ban on sex offenders from visiting any social media sites was ruled unconstitutional. The law's author, State Representative Jeff Thompson, said he proposed the bill "because we've got a lot of people out there that use the Internet to troll to hunt children," although there is little evidence for this assertion and plenty to the contrary.[105] As is well known but rarely influential on a policy level, most perpetrators of sexual violence do not use the Internet to groom or recruit.[106]
- In January 2013, Louisiana placed severe restrictions on public library use for anyone convicted of a sex offense involving a victim thirteen years old or younger. Offenders may visit the library in strictly limited time periods of the day. They cannot "loiter within 1,000 feet of public library property," and they are prohibited from employment with public libraries.[107]
- In June 2018, the legislature enacted an expansive animal sexual abuse law (see Chapter 3). Persons convicted of animal sexual abuse—which includes possessing bestial pornography but excludes "artificial insemination of an animal for reproductive purposes [whose purposes?]"—must "undergo a psychological evaluation for sex offenders" and enter a sex offender treatment program once on parole. After a second conviction, animal sexual abusers must register as sex offenders.[108] State Senator Jean-Paul Morrell mobilizes and makes manifest the equivalencies that were never quite latent: "Strong punishment for this heinous act is important because the sexual abuse of animals is an indicator of other violent, predatory sex crimes, especially against children."[109] So much for the animals. But we must dispute these factoids: how many studies demonstrate that people who engage in sexual contact with animals are likely to commit "predatory sex crimes" against children? How many studies demonstrate that "strong punishment" against animal sexual abuse deters child sexual abuse?

The CANS contestations and litigation are not in any way responsible for the metastasis of the registry. But it is equally if painfully true that that the rhetoric from the CANS campaign and lawsuit—synopsized: *Don't treat sex workers like child molesters, treat child molesters like child molesters*—lubricates and legitimates the sex offender regime for unsympathetic subjects.[110]

And that regime fails to make communities safer from sexual violence, redirects social and political attention away from the most prevalent forms of sexual violence and misconduct, invests in carceral governance over social welfare, and sexualizes citizens into perverts.

Fairness, Debility, and Paraidentitarian Sexual Justice

In the remainder of this chapter, I elaborate on *fairness* and *debility*. The first term and its cognates were explicitly and repeatedly used by the registered sex offenders I interviewed, both those registered for CANS convictions and those registered for other convictions, and it is the offenders' own use of term that motivates my effort, I think only partially successful, to recuperate it. The second term, *debility*, I superimpose to describe a range of responses detailing the interviewees' lived experiences in the world of registration and postconviction. It will not surprise any reader that sex offenders feel they receive unfair treatment from the state and its functionaries, nor that they often feel debilitated by supervision and regulation. My solicitation is that we harness *fairness* and *debility* not simply to invoke charitable feeling but to develop a more just sexual politics.

Recuperating the Remainders: Fairness

For political philosopher John Rawls, "justice as fairness"—an idea he famously elaborated and revised over several volumes penned across three decades[111]—necessitates two principles that structure a minimally just society. The first is that all citizens are equally entitled to "a fully adequate scheme of equal basic liberties," like freedom of conscience, freedom of speech, and the right to vote. The second, more complicated principle structures how social and economic inequalities ought to be distributed. The second principle is itself two-pronged: the first prong, a kind of nondiscrimination clause with teeth, requires that "offices and positions [be] open to all under conditions of fair equality of opportunity"; the second prong stipulates that, should there be societal inequalities of goods, opportunities and resources, those inequalities "are to be to the greatest benefit of the least-advantaged members of society"—what Rawls calls the "difference principle."[112]

The registered sex offenders I interviewed obviously did not reference "fairness" in its technical, Rawlsian sense, but the ordinary usage they deployed was not unrelated to "justice as fairness," either. Interviewees asked, rhetorically, if it is fair that they were treated as sick or dangerous; if it is fair that people convicted of Prostitution are not subject to the same requirements as those convicted of CANS; if it is fair that many of their registration requirements and durations were expanded and extended in

2008, years after their convictions; if it is fair that they had to pay court and registration fees when registration (and the label "sex offender" on their driver's licenses) prevents them from earning an income. "I don't think it's fair. . . . [L]et that be known," said Nicole, who was on the registry for over sixteen years for CANS. Regarding the different sanctions for Prostitution and CANS, Kathy commented, "That's a backwards law. . . . [I]t's not fair." Ken, a white man in his forties convicted in 2000 of indecent behavior with juveniles, opined, "We tend to make a big deal about sex offenders, but I mean, we could have some sort of a crime registry where everybody would be on it and then it would seem more fair."[113]

Insofar as their invocations of fairness connote related principles of equal treatment under law, due process of adjudication, uneven denials of opportunity, and debilitating economic disadvantage, the interviewees' grievances resonate with Rawls's own reconstruction of the term. Ken's comment, though—on fairness as potentially warranting a registry system for *all* persons convicted of crimes—concisely illustrates a pressing paradox of fairness when placed proximate to punishment. What does it mean to treat a "criminal," rather than a "law-abiding citizen," with fairness? If we were to surveil all criminals the way we currently surveil sex offenders, would such equal treatment be "fair"? My fieldwork in New Orleans encourages a response to the relative inattention to punitive practices by queer studies,[114] which, I hypothesize, rests on a certain dumbstruckness in the face of the criminal, especially the sexual criminal, a figure who performs the constitutive outside of consensus, a figure beyond palatable identity formations.

In what follows, I canvas a couple of interventions offered by political theorists who labor to think through the legitimacy or illegitimacy of state punitive practices under a Rawlsian imaginary and in a Rawlsian just society. This all might seem a bit in the theory-weeds, but my elucidation suggests that if we are to recuperate *fairness* for an ecological, paraidentitarian politics of sexual justice, we may have to jettison fairness's conventional, dyadic comparators (for example, should the state treat person A as it treats person B?) and instead turn our analytic and normative attention to the nonideal, unjust, and "unfair" state.

Political theorist Bonnie Honig observes that in John Rawls's model of justice, justice as fairness, criminals are *bad people.* Criminals are morally retrograde, and the ascription of moral badness is a constitutive, not severable, element of Rawlsian justice. Honig's argument proceeds as follows: the difficulty Rawls encounters with punishment is symptomatic of the larger problem of his approach/reproach to politics. In aiming for a tight, procedural, "expressivist" basic structure of society that manifests, structurally, a rational person's, which is every person's, ideal of justice, Rawls "seeks a reconciliation without remainders."[115] There are no persons or parts of the rational self that are not mirrored in the political apparatus (our divergent comprehensive doctrines of the good notwithstanding, as citizens' differing belief systems and ways of life are expected to be quietly contained under a universal procedural system agreeable to all). But there are always remainders. Since everyone should, could, and will agree to "justice as fairness" when veiled in the thought exercise of the original position—Rawls's moralized state of nature where "free and equal persons" deliberate principles for a just society—defection or partial compliance simply *is* criminality.[116] To defect is to not have rationally calculative power, thus the criminal is a type of person, a bad person—threat personified:

> [I]n the absence of systemic injustice, there is nothing that can account for criminal behavior; criminality must be a symptom of sheer perversity, orneriness, a tic of some kind, a defective character. Criminality, in short, must be an assault on the system from some outside, from some mysterious and terrifying state of nature: It must be sociopathic.[117]

For other figures in Rawls's schema—those with more or less natural talent, those with more or less earning power in a market system, and so on—"antecedent moral worth"[118] is, radically, "arbitrary" to justice.[119] However, moral desert "returns to haunt justice as fairness when Rawls himself reaches for antecedent moral worth (or unworthiness) to account for the presence of criminality in a just regime and to justify punishment."[120] Punishment, then, is administered to neutralize or hold at bay persons unreasonable in their nature. This would suggest the authorization for unleashing any and all state power, for the criminal is ontologically toxic to the well-ordered society. Now, perhaps Rawls's guarantee of basic rights and liberties in a liberal political regime, along with his fair equality of opportunity and difference principles, might hedge against more severe schemas of crime and punishment, but it is doubtful, precisely because the "criminal" is characterologically unable to appreciate liberty, order, and justice. To return to the sex offenders in New Orleans, "fairness" in reference to punishment is potentially a nonstarter. Fairness, to work, must be withheld from fairness's violators. This is the paradox of fairness and punishment.[121]

Honig offers a Nietzschean "counterwager."[122] "[T]he spectral power of the bad character is diminished somewhat," she supposes, "if we think of the criminal and the bad character as personifications of those aspects of the self that are resistant to the formation of responsible subjectivity."[123] If we incorporate "outlaw impulses" into our theorizing justice, we might arrive at more just regimes of punishment.[124] In a way, Honig's is a Rawlsian solution to Rawls's dilemma: tinker with the concept of the hypothetical citizen in the original position, and we will arrive at a better elsewhere. I will return circuitously to the limitation of this necessary corrective through reading another, comparatively "more" Rawlsian approach to the political practice of punishment.

Political theorist Corey Brettschneider hopes to derive a proportionate, democratic theory of punishment from a Rawlsian thought experiment. Brettschneider's recuperative effort initially seems to offer persons convicted of crimes more latitude than Rawls's *Theory of Justice*. However, Brettschneider's impasses are productively revealing, suggesting that if we are ever to approximate a theory of fair punishment, we must ultimately depart from ideal theory and its modal, model citizens; we must begin our theoretic appraisals in conversation with the punished—sex offenders in New Orleans, for instance—and move outward and upward.

Brettschneider begins from a simple and compelling premise: in constructing our theory of punishments, we should approach criminals as *citizens* rather than as *persons*.[125] The criminal-as-citizen is party to the political community, which Brettschneider dubs "democratic contractualism."[126] As democratic contractualism requires justification for all forms of coercion, punishment is no exception.[127] Echoing Rawls's discussion of reasonability and social cooperation in his *Political Liberalism*, Brettschneider contends that punishments must be reasonably agreeable to those who would be punished.[128] As Brettschneider points out, criminals do not have to actually agree to their punishments for them to be justified, but punishments must be of the sort that could be acceptably imposed.[129] The democratic contractualist view of punishment does not eject the criminal from the polity, like Hobbes's view does or Rawls's might.[130] The criminal would agreeably forfeit some rights for the stability of democratic community but not all rights sans self-preservation.[131] Creatively, Brettschneider's argument opposes capital punishment in all circumstances: for a person to reasonably accept punishment as a citizen, the person must be alive.[132]

What becomes ever more apparent in this reconstructed Rawlsian account, however, is the way criminality, in a theory-first, practice-second order of operation, is always an indelible feature of some persons. Or, to resonate the point in this chapter's lexicon: these theories of punishment quietly presume reasonability or, antipodally, criminality as function and feature of *identities*. For (Honig's) Rawls, partial compliance to the social order—any criminal act—betrays constitutive unreasonableness. For Brettschneider, one who commits crimes may still be amenable to reason, but the fact of the crime remains a fact about the person and never a fact about political structure. He writes, "[W]hen it comes to criminal punishment, this task [of justification] is complicated by the fact that *actual* criminals punished by the state often do not accept the core values of democracy."[133] In the absence of empirical evidence, the "actuality" of the assertion is impelled only and unsuccessfully by the theoretical apparatus. What should we, democratic contractualists, do with the remainders? Brettschneider's supposition that "any reasonable citizen would recognize that convicted murderers must forfeit some rights of citizens in a scheme of democratic contractual justification" is surely illocutionary.[134] Mens rea must be presumed in this theory and presumed really bad: there is no conceptual room to consider the potentially plural circumstances leading to a homicide. Tellingly and presciently, the problem is most acute when Brettschneider contrasts his theory with retributivist accounts via the example of the *child molester* (among my research participants, Eric, Ken, and Evan would qualify as "child molesters"). He argues that the advocate of retributivism cannot explain why the state, but not a fellow prison inmate, should have the right to kill the molester, as either way, "the child molester receive[s] what he 'deserves,' since we have stipulated that the appropriate punishment is death."[135] Moral desert, he concludes, cannot be the political justification for punishment because anyone can exact desert. While Brettschneider opposes capital punishment, the child molester is primed as the character who does *morally* deserve death, but moral desert is untenably justificatory for politics. He contends that retributivism "risk[s] privileging one particular viewpoint over other reasonable viewpoints held by citizens of a polity"; some may believe the child molester deserves only excommunication, chemical castration, or a long prison sentence, but not death.[136] Left unquestioned in the democratic contractualist and retributivist model alike is that the child molester is a type. All viewpoints agree, there is a kind of person that is a child molester; the punitive question is what to do with him. Nowhere might we ask why acts are determinative of moral identities, whether punishment is best comprehended as practices against types of persons (molesters, criminals) or patterns of behavior, and whether, even, forfeiture of rights should be the question of first priority.[137]

Eric, Ken, Nicole, Patrick, Kathy: these are not bad persons, they are not beasts. A theory of fairness proximate to punishment cannot begin at ideal theory, which is not to indict ideal theory tout court.[138] But because crimes are committed for a whole variety of reasons, almost none of which have to do with the pathological predation of persons; because some crimes should not be crimes; because people are not always already reason machines, unfailingly equipped with moral powers; because sometimes people make mistakes, are led astray, get drunk and angry, get high and impulsive, and have been abused and neglected, a theory of fair punishment must be ironed out in the unjust, carceral world we inhabit. To do otherwise necessitates suturing partial compliance to bad personhood, which cannot be a model for fair punishment. In Brettschneider's case, individualized criminality (in ideal theory) is wedded and naturalized to extant forms of punishment (in practice), so that the fairness of imprisonment and voter disenfranchisement is evaluated only according to scope (for example, *What is the right amount of caging?*) and not in kind (for example, *Is imprisonment fair?*).[139]

What difference does sex make? In these theoretic glosses on punishment and proportionality, sex drops out of the picture. Yet it is not incidental that Brettschneider's example par excellence of the bad criminal is the child molester. Even if Honig's reading of Rawls or my reading of Brettschneider is ungenerous—if state punishment is not entirely pegged to bad character, or if it is but checked by democratic rights—the sex criminal may yet be perceived as a toxic excess, an ineliminable source of danger and cause of terrible injury. In that case, proportionality would provide no haven. Political theorist Keally McBride, engaging with Aristotle, Grotius, Hobbes, and Locke, among others, observes no such paradox of punishment and fairness among these thinkers. To the contrary, "[F]or both Grotius and Locke, the ability to punish guaranteed the presence of consent as opposed to coercion."[140] This is because punishment presupposes a social contract that recognizes the necessity of ceding punishment power to the sovereign—for restoration of rights, for purposes of deterrence, and so on, but ultimately for proportionately rebalancing political order. However, McBride also astutely observes that "what transforms punishment into an injustice is perception," and so, too, the converse: perception normalizes injustices into what we call punishments.[141] If the sex criminal is currently (if episodically),[142] popularly, and politically perceived as a relentlessly recidivistic, intemperate, predatory body, then the ratcheting up of sex offender regulations and ever-increasing methods of surveillance and requirements of public notice are not excessive, unjust, or unconstitutional but perfectly proportionate. Endless punishment might always fit the sex crime.[143]

Honig asks us to introduce "outlaw impulses" into the psychical structure of subjects in the original position, which, like Brettschneider's approach, may well mitigate punitive practices. Yet, no matter how we construct the political subject prior to state-building, ideal-theorizing of punishment must assume subjects who are noncompliant to an otherwise just system. As such, whether we occasionally misbehave (Honig) or whether we hold onto powers of reason even as we commit crimes (Brettschneider), in these framings the political system itself is never the problem; the problem is, rather, those persons who reside in it. In order to assess how existing states punish people, whether those punishments are fair or unfair, conducive or anathema to a democratic polity, we cannot only work backward from competing conceptions of the morally deserving or undeserving person but must, rather, investigate actual forms of contemporary punitive practice. The CANS episode, then, invites questions like: why does the state designate sexual infractions as uniquely heinous? Do sex offenders deserve particu-laristic treatment? Are regimes of registration, notification, and (generally, nontherapeutic, nonrehabilitative) supervision fair if they fail to deliver a sexually safer world?

These questions are unanswerable from the political theoretic stand-point of the idealized reasonable person called upon to measure fairness in relation to partially reasonable persons. Perhaps one alternative (conse-quentialist, ecological, and paraidentitarian) metric for punitive fairness is to ask what punishment does rather than to whom it is done. What do sex offender registration and requirements do—to perpetrators, for victims, or for the reduction of sexual violence? Might it be politically useful to call these requirements unfair because the burdens they place on people, on their abilities to find jobs and maintain family relations or to live with a sense of social or financial stability, are not offset by any measurable improvement in the sexual or social welfare of the jurisdiction? That kind of calculation cannot be articulated within a model of fairness either blind to patterns of inequality or keyed only to degrees of human rationality. Honig's conclud-ing caution that punishment "is not something that we ever get right" makes the same point.[144] Because noncompliance always entails interrogating both the actions of the noncompliant person and the political economic system to which she or he is not complying, assessing the fairness of punishment can only be resolved through ongoing engagement and never through per-manent codification.

As admonition, this subsection concludes dismally, with the kickback of hegemony. Patrick, a Black man in his mid-forties, was convicted in 1998 of second-degree kidnapping. A drug deal went sour, and while carrying a gun he coerced a woman to retrieve his money. The woman was under eighteen years old. Only in 2008 was his crime redefined as a sex offense (as Louisiana redrafted their sex offense laws to come into compliance with the Adam Walsh Act), subjecting him to the full battery of sex offender regis-tration requirements. "They retroact this law back from 2008"; retroactivity was Patrick's idiom of unfairness.[145] Ken, convicted of indecent behavior with juveniles in 2000, was originally mandated to register for ten years. In 2008, he was told he would have to register for yet another seven years. Devastatingly for Patrick and Ken, the central reason registration require-ments have withstood constitutional challenges (Fourteenth Amendment due process, Eighth Amendment cruel and unusual punishment, double jeopardy, and ex post facto [retroactive application of punishment]) is because the laws are designated *regulatory* rather than *punitive*. Earlier, I slid from the term "punishment" to "punitive practice" as a way to straddle the following tension: it is precisely by not being "punishment" that the state's scheme operates punitively.[146] Constitutionality and fairness, of course, are not synonyms. We must then say that while it could be constitutional to level up penalties for everyone—for example, and as we saw Judge Feldman explain, Louisiana might have cleared the CANS equal protection challenge had the state required persons convicted of Prostitution to register as sex offenders, too—leveling up carcerality is doubtlessly unfair: ineffective, socially and economically devastating, exponentially injurious to already vulnerable populations.

Recuperating the Remainders: Debility

Michelle Alexander's *The New Jim Crow: Mass Incarceration in the Age of Colorblindness* makes the case that the U.S. criminal justice system instantiates racial hierarchy not simply in enforcement but, more invidiously, by design.[147] She catalogs phenomena that resonate strikingly with both (indexical) gay experience and my discussions with sex offenders, describing the terrible anxiety ex-offenders face "coming out" to their family, neighbors, and potential employers about their status. Like the sex offenders with whom I spoke, and like the historical testimony of queers, ex-offenders are burdened by isolation, self-hate, fear of outing, and what Erving Goffman calls "stigma management."[148] The reproduction of systemic injustice, Alexander argues, depends more on the "prison label" than the "prison time."[149] Both labeled, sex offenders and ex-offenders face social isolation and often find it nearly impossible to secure employment or stable housing. Both groups too are inundated with fees owed to the criminal justice system (court fees, registration fees, probation fees, fees for flyers and newspaper ads).

Extant literature suggest that the predicaments of the sex offender are not collapsible into those of the ex-offender, and that sex offenders indeed face particular impediments as a class. But I want to argue that as a point of departure for imagining sexual justice and solidarity, we would do better to think about debility, about the shared experiences of those bodies debilitated by the state, rather than posit the sex offender as an exceptional case or a particularly weighted symbolic form. The sex criminal may have a particular (but not altogether discrete) discursive life compared to other criminal characters, but that need not determine our political imaginings. In this sense, my critique synchronizes with Alexander's updated reflections on the role of "violent" crime in fueling U.S. systems of mass incarceration, in and beyond prison walls. Responding in part to critics that challenged her earlier, political emphasis on nonviolent crimes, Alexander insists that, while she still holds the War on Drugs primarily responsible for late modern, racialized, mass incarceration in the United States, "we will never close prisons on a large scale in this country, or drastically reduce the prison population, if we do not change the way we view and respond to violent crime."[150] That "virtually no one commits violence without first surviving it," and that "inflicting violence and suffering upon people in order to teach them that violence is wrong . . . is a doomed strategy" buttresses the urgency for theorizing and resisting *debility*, for taking stock of and then dismantling "punishment bureaucracies [that] perpetuate the harms of crime and violence."[151] Alexander de-exceptionalizes the "violent criminal" as I hope to de-exceptionalize the "sex offender," pointing instead to debility as a shared experience of persons victimized by state violence and state sexual violence.

By debility, I am thinking about the multifarious, statutorily imposed ways the registered sex offenders I talked with are deprived of a shot at not only the good life but even a livable life. Undirected despair, even more than directed anger, coursed through many of my conversations with interviewees. Debilitations, in these instances, arose not from the excess, harassment, or vigilantism often featured in progressive literature on sex offenders[152] but from impersonal administration and regulatory law: "organized violence perpetrated by our own government."[153] Andy and his wife will likely be forced to relocate on account of residency restrictions, leaving their extended family and network of friends. Phillip told me the state forbids him from visiting his grandchildren (he was convicted of forcible rape nearly three decades ago as of this writing). If Eric visits his mother for more than five days at a time, she will have to register her house as a sex offender residence. Both Phillip and Patrick have all but given up on finding jobs: employers "looking at me like, we'll call you back later." Unsurprisingly, people registered as sex offenders for CANS conviction report the same employment frustrations: "The minute they find out I'm a registered sex offender, they tell me, 'no thank you,' or [that] they'll call me back, or they'll get back with me, and they never do."[154] We should be cognizant that the sex offender regulatory system debilitates all its registrants—nearly all of whom have already served a prison sentence—from civic and economic participation, whether they were convicted of CANS or sexual assault, whether they are sympathetic subjects or unsympathetic, whether they are the sexual identities that progressives champion ("transgender") or the ones they despise ("child pornographer"). Almost all offenders discussed the crippling costs registration entails; self-paid flyers and newspaper ads are "kind of expensive when you don't have a job."[155] (Resistances should not be underplayed: one offender scratches "sex offender" off their driver's license, and another photocopies the license while covering the label.) These predicaments may or may not engender sympathy, but they should spur politics. I am not advocating an antistatist position, where queer legal thinking too often finds itself.[156] Sometimes and for good reasons we may want the state to debilitate its offenders, whether they are sex offenders, other criminals, white nationalists, or corporations. The intervention point for political theorizing, though, might be to deliberate over which practices of debilitation are just, which debilitations promote livable lives and sexual/social flourishing. Perhaps our analyses might begin by interrogating a notion of just or fair debilitations, rather than putting forward types of persons, specified identities, to be privileged above debility.

I flesh out what I mean by debility—and why I think it may be a generative departure point for political praxis—by thinking alongside and against prominent scholars who argue for some form of social justice politics of debility or vulnerability, namely, Jasbir Puar, Martha Nussbaum, and Martha Fineman.[157] There are certainly several points of contact between the argument I am delineating and disability studies scholarship more broadly: for example, the historical intimacy between dominant notions of disability, feeblemindedness, and racialized criminality; the gendered and sexed demarcations of and stereotyped associations with ability and disability; and, most obviously, the central function of the state in determinations of who is and is not disabled, and who is and is not a sex offender.[158] I allude to these connections in the ensuing consideration of Puar's, Nussbaum's, and Fineman's interventions, but only insofar as these connections clarify the definition of debility I am proposing, as well as its normative function in advancing a paraidentitarian politics of sexual justice, a politics not so beholden to the identity forms of the sympathetic subject and the dangerous predator.

Gender studies scholar Jasbir Puar argues for a deployment of debility that resists the identitarian currents of "disability" and disability studies. My understanding of debility as a political tool builds on and departs from Puar's. Among her objectives, and following other scholars, Puar posits "debility" as a diagnostic to measure how "populations are constructed through prevailing ideas of variability and risk."[159] I understand her to be suggesting that, as opposed to meanings of disability that locate inadequacy in the individual or the "fit" between the individual and the social structure, debility both broadens and deepens our perspective.[160] Debility offers a reading of relations between normativity, risk, and management both on subindividual, genetic planes and on macroscopic planes of global populations. Interested in "more diffuse networks of control," Puar interrogates how parts of persons or whole populations are rendered debilitated and interrogates too the governance that debility invites.[161] Puar is in part building off and in part criticizing[162] the "social model" of disability that aims to remedy not the apparently biological impairments of the body but the social structures that disable participation.[163] However, like critical disability theorists, Puar resists reifying impairment as either prediscursive or prior to institutions of power. And since she levels her critique at the management and containment of populations, her theorization of debility is decidedly inappropriable for the claiming of rights, in contrast to the "social model" of disability.[164] What Puar's politics would demand, however, is somewhat unclear (although in her *Right to Maim*, Puar is unwavering that an end to Israel's occupation of Palestine is necessary to relieve "the ongoing bodily debilitation of the Palestinian people").[165]

Insofar as Puar's debility schema is scalar, it is productively appropriable for the analysis of sex offense and sex offender regulation, as is her identification of regimes of governance that construct, penalize, and profit from debility, "a practice of rendering populations available for statistically likely injury."[166] Although envisioning debility in relation to its many manufacturers is critically important, Puar's agents of debilitation (not the objects of debility) are so ubiquitous as to make critical traction potentially untenable. For her, "capital machinations," "colonial and postcolonial violence, labor migrations, economic exploitation . . . , the interventions of western biomedicine," and "neoliberal regimes of biocapital" are all responsible for the biopoweristic, unjust distributions of debility.[167] There is little political foothold in this tidal wave of debilitation, which is why her solution of a "praxis" of "conviviality" feels incomplete. She describes conviviality as an "ethical orientation," wherein

> bodies . . . come together and dissipate through intensifications and vulnerabilities, insistently rendering bare the instability of the divisions between capacity-endowed and debility-laden bodies. . . . [T]he challenge before us is how to craft convivial political praxis that does not demand a continual reinvestment in its form and content, its genesis or its outcome, the literalism of its object [or] the direction of its drive.[168]

Puar's analysis helpfully illustrates the way debility incapacitates bodies and populations, but the specific function of the state in the manufacturing of such debility risks dissolving under a laundry list of bad neoliberal governances. As such, with a sometimes targetless target, Puar's politics of conviviality risks apoliticism. Although she takes directionality, object orientation, and investment in continuity to be anathema to a coalitional politics (of debility), I take them to be the sine qua non of political work.

Martha Fineman's "The Vulnerable Subject: Anchoring Equality in the Human Condition" and Martha Nussbaum's *Frontiers of Justice: Disability, Nationality, Species Membership* bring the state back in, each imagining legal and political institutions keyed to the universal condition of human vulnerability. Fineman wants her reconstructed notion of vulnerability to stretch past the "prototypical examples" of prisoners, children, and the elderly, to cover the ineliminable vulnerable conditions of all humanity.[169] Nussbaum wants her notion of vulnerability to stretch past particular bodies rendered disabled and to cover the dynamic neediness and dependency of humans as they travel through the life cycle.[170] Neither Fineman nor Nussbaum wish to flatten all differences among populations, proposing that political institutions will be more just to the extent that they accommodate vulnerabilities shared across populations, rather than distinct to them. Nussbaum's *capabilities approach* is a model of social justice explicitly contrasted to Rawls's *justice as fairness*. The fact that some humans require extreme care or are above-average dependent is Nussbaum's critical inroad into Rawls's entire theoretical apparatus. The requirements of justice to the disabled, whether physical or mental, cannot be derived from 1) the conception of the person as autonomous and rational;[171] 2) well-being indexed through material distribution alone;[172] or 3) a notion of collective enterprise based purely on mutual advantage among equals.[173] Therefore, because such a scheme is at best inattentive but more likely hostile to the disabled, Nussbaum jettisons *justice as fairness* while nonetheless keeping the Rawlsian direction of theorizing and Rawls's commitment to consensus. Like Honig, Nussbaum interjects a different kind of person in the original position, one who is or at some point will be needy and dependent. The objective of political institutions and distribution mechanisms is no longer to stabilize mutual advantage but to guarantee a set of enumerated human capabilities that realize our common human dignity.[174] Nussbaum's just society is more robust that Rawls's (which itself is orders of magnitude more democratic and egalitarian than, say, the United States). Nussbaum's capabilities approach ensures substantial provisions for human (and nonhuman) welfare across several institutional dimensions; such provisions democratize responsibilities for vulnerability.

Martha Fineman worries that Nussbaum's model veers toward the eugenicist, as it is grounded in a predetermination of what counts as human worth and the minimal capabilities that are human worth's prerequisites.[175] Nonetheless, Fineman too wants to substitute the vulnerable subject for the autonomous subject as our referent for modeling social justice. For Fineman, vulnerability is "universal and constant, inherent in the human condition."[176] If we think about persons as always susceptible to injury and misfortune, then we must demand a state that provides far more resources to its citizens, one that narrows the gap between privilege and disadvantage in order to equalize people's "resilience" in the face of constant vulnerability.[177] This move is a criticism at once of the noninterfering state and of the merely formal equality it supposedly guarantees.[178] Fineman's intervention, like Puar's, is a critique of identity politics:

The vulnerability paradigm calls on courts to look beyond the identity of the disadvantaged developed over the past few decades under a discrimination paradigm. While the old identity categories—gender, race, sexuality, and so on—should not be totally removed from consideration, we must reframe our concerns in order to reveal and address things about the organization of society that are otherwise missed.[179]

Vulnerability analysis for Fineman is squarely about substantive equality and state structure, whereas antidiscrimination analysis is attentive mainly to formal equality and particularistic maltreatment.

While both Nussbaum and Fineman, like Judith Butler[180] and Bryan Turner,[181] acknowledge that political institutions may aggravate vulnerability, neither pays adequate attention to the ways institutions make vulnerability, or what I am calling debility.[182] Combining the insights of Puar, Fineman, and Nussbaum with the experiences of my interviewees, I propose that we tentatively define debility as *the state imposition of vulnerability*. This definition shifts emphasis from ontological vulnerability to politically enforced vulnerability, with the Puaresque advantage of not conflating vulnerability and minoritized identities. However, by looking first at state debility rather than to the universal truth of human vulnerability, we might not discard identity-based analyses as quickly as Fineman might like us to. Quite often, the distributions of debility redound along minoritized identity lines: historically, state practices of debility disparately impact, intentionally or not, women and minority racial and religious groups.[183] In this sense, a politics of sexual debility is contiguous with and supplemental to, but never a full replacement for, redressing identity-based inequalities.

There are two prongs built into my provisional definition of debility as the state imposition of vulnerability.[184] On the one hand, debility may refer to the ways the state makes certain persons or groups more likely than others to be hindered by nonstate actors, for example, more vulnerable to discriminatory employment or housing practices. On the other hand, debility may refer to state impositions themselves, that is, to the material, psychic, spatial, and other hindrances the state brings to bear on the (sex) offender. Prison is the ubiquitous, contemporary, racialized example of debility.[185] This two-pronged definition aligns with scholarly reconstructions of vulnerability and with the corporeal and socioeconomic experiences of my interviewees. Fineman defines vulnerability as both a universal condition of humanity—a kind of ontic predisposition to hazard, contingency, and so on—and an enumerable consequence of catastrophes, institutional arrangements, and economic/political orderings.[186] Law professor Ani Satz, applying Fineman's vulnerability thesis to disability accommodations and the law, reconceives vulnerability to describe the greater impairments disabled people may face as a class, as well as the ways disabled people may be categorically more susceptible to impairment (Satz's text amends Fineman's, recognizing the identitarian basis of the harms some groups face while also illustrating the ways vulnerability and disability extend themselves beyond protected classes).[187]

The sex offenders with whom I spoke suffered both from increased risk of impairments as a result of state notification and registration requirements and from actual, additional impairments as a result of those requirements (of course, exposure to interference can be a form of interference). The orange block print of "sex offender" on their driver's licenses made it virtually impossible for many registered offenders to find adequate employment, even though the state does not forbid them from pursuing an occupation altogether. Moreover, many if not all the interviewees had virtually no social network or community. Andy and Ken had their spouses for support, and Kathy, Lucy, and Nicole had their husbands or boyfriends, but most offenders were and felt alone. "[Sex offender requirements] destroyed my family," reported Kathy.[188] A few offenders moved to the outskirts of the parish to avoid potential harassment. Two relayed psychological breakdowns on account of registration and its entailments, and some had medical problems like diabetes, amplified by lack of employment. All were despondent, save one. In these cases, the state did not make registered offenders lonely, precarious, sad, or unhealthy, but the state aggravated their circumstances. In other situations, the state directly impedes people's flourishing: by restricting travel to friends and family, by mandating episodic check-ins with probation officers, by requiring offenders to pay court fees and fees to publicize their identifying information to the community, by delimiting their use of the internet and other communication technologies.

Expanding a working concept of debility to incorporate the ways subjects are made both vulnerable and susceptible to vulnerability by the state does not rid the term of two other complications, one conceptual, the other normative. Filtered through the lens of the social model of disability (and its third-wave critics),[189] debility defined as the state imposition of vulnerability may run into a reductio problem. Discerning which disabilities are not statutorily imposed becomes potentially confounding; we might see practices of debility everywhere. If the levies in Louisiana gave way during Hurricane Katrina because the state failed to maintain them, has the state imposed vulnerability?[190] If the state provides public transportation that is not wheelchair accessible, has it imposed vulnerability? Does not income tax impose vulnerability? This list could be endless, and a lot rests on how we define *imposition* and *vulnerability*, not to mention *state*. In any case, the indeterminacy could make for a political nonstarter. What I want to elevate, though, in ruminating on debility as a recurring feature of the lives of the sex offenders I interviewed, is first, how the state debilitates and sexes its subjects, or debilitates its subjects by sexing them (through the registration, notification, and labeling of, and the special requirements particular to, the sex offender) and second, how state practices of seemingly nonsexed debility (incarceration or residency restrictions, for example) inhibit intimate and sexual flourishing.

Currently, as with the CANS episode in New Orleans, our progressive sexual politics centers on the sympathetic subject—say the sex worker, trans woman, or homosexual—and moves outward to demand that political institutions defend or at least not encroach upon their rights and behaviors. This political orientation moralizes the consenting adult as a sexual orientation, as I have argued previously.[191] Sex workers required to register as sex offender for their CANS convictions were "not involved in anything other than consent," explained Bill Quigley, another attorney representing the plaintiffs in *Jindal*.[192] But suppose we look first to political institutions. In the case of sex offenders, including but not limited to those convicted of CANS, the state debilitates its subjects by sexing them. Whether or not such forms of sexed debilitations are just, effective, or conducive to sexual flourishing and/or to the minimization of sexual violence cannot rest squarely on the presumptive good personhood (sex worker) or bad personhood (child molester) of the debilitated. The deservingness, undeservingness, quantity, and quality of statutorily imposed vulnerability should be measured neither to the sexual identities we champion nor to the sexual identities we condemn.[193] This segues to a second, more normative challenge to the prospect of debility: should we not care more about the victims of sex offenders than sex offenders as victims of the state?

Sexual injury is specific; it is different from other forms of injury. It is or can be especially grievous, and for the purposes of this rather ungenealogical chapter, I am not asking why that is so or whether it might be an alterable fact of late modernity.[194] We cannot seriously or sympathetically take heed of the state's debilitation of its sex offenders without noticing the more obvious exploitation of vulnerability: those registered as sex offenders often harm those—women, minors—most vulnerable. Some sex offenders debilitate, too, even as we know that most perpetrators of sexual violence, abuse, harassment, and misconduct will never be statutorily designated "sex offenders."[195] In a democratic state that allocates risk and provides social safety, it seems nearly incontrovertible and unremarkable that the state should restrain those who do or would (sexually) injure. The political question posed by sex offense is not whither state debilitation but what kind of debilitation and why? This latter question, I have been insisting, is nearly written off the table by reigning juridical, legislative, and even sexual progressive constructions of the sex offender as always already unredeemable, recidivistic, morally retrograde—the anti-identity of sexual identities.

A definition of debility that specifies the state does not discount other institutions that debilitate or administrate debility: pharmaceuticals, colonialism, or heterosexuality, for example.[196] Rather, it suggests that there are analytic and practical reasons to hold these phenomena apart. One of those reasons, though, is not, contra Foucault, to reintroduce state sovereignty or juridical power as the premiere object of critical analysis as against disciplinary institutions or biopolitical capital. Rather, the point is to recall that the state and its impositions matter profoundly—spatially, temporally, financially, and so forth—in the realization or debilitation of our social and sexual lives. Theorizing dimensions of debility is intended not to invoke sympathy but to invoke political judgments that are otherwise sidelined when we default to the presumptive goodness of minoritized sexual subjects and the presumptive badness of the rest. Our political affiliations and sexual justice imaginings should not come to a full stop at the paradigmatic liberal subject—say, the good gay—of civil rights discourse.[197]

Toward what does a sexual politics of debility gesture? Such a politics would resist the automatic, statutory conversion of sex acts—albeit nonnormative, all too normative, or assaultive—into despised identities. A sexual politics of debility would call for the abolition of sex offender registries to de-exceptionalize the sex offender, to align his (and her) indexical experiences with populations and tribulations of ex-offenders. To pursue this reorientation epistemically and politically, we ought to recognize as well the ways incarceration infects a variety of intimacies, debilitates kinship arrangements,[198] quietly[199] or deafeningly[200] exacerbates sexual violence, and increases rates of sexually transmitted infections.[201]

To centralize debilitated populations over the sexual minoritarian subject is not antistatist but calls for justifications of debilitation. To refuse all forms of state debility is impractical and indefensible. But our first appraisals of debility ought to be anchored in suspicion (a fine distinction from paranoia, but a distinction with a difference), a suspicion that should travel to other spheres of sex and gender regulation. Under this purview, we might reject proposals for antibullying and hate crime legislation, for enhanced sentencing penalties for bias crimes. Such a rejection does not callously dismiss the vulnerable but opens a wider space for alternative policies promoting safety and gender/sexual expression. For we know that the groups whose own social and intimate lives suffer most under penalty enhancement provisions are those already hyperneglected or hyperregulated by the state.[202] Indeed, a dilemma faces trans prison activism analogous to the dilemma posed by moral cum political hierarchies of sex offenders:

> [B]uilding arguments about trans people as "innocent victims" while other prisoners are cast as dangerous and deserving of detention only undermines the power of a shared resistance strategy that sees imprisonment as a violent, dangerous tactic for everybody it touches.

The construction of trans-segregated prison facilities under the pretext of protection runs the danger of debility: "We know that if they build it, they will fill it, and getting trans people out of prison is the only real way to address the safety issues that trans prisoners face."[203] In a similarly paraidentitarian register, political science professor Paisley Currah cautions against transphobia as the ur-explanatory variable for trans imprisonment in the United States:

> [I]t's not just that Black trans feminine individuals are much more likely to spend time in jail or prison than white trans feminine individuals. It's that in the United States there is a close relationship between white supremacy and mass incarceration, and, more recently, between the economic dislocations of recent decades and prison.[204]

Debility exhorts us to perceive state action and inaction that impose vulnerability in and across populations. And it is not just that antecedently minoritized populations are debilitated by the state ("Black trans feminine individuals"); populations are minoritized and sexualized by debility ("sex offenders").

Moving from the worlds of Fineman and Nussbaum, in which institutions are designed to accommodate varying degrees of vulnerability, I have suggested reversing our political theoretic direction by interrogating when and why state institutions debilitate, when they should, and for what purposes. Similarly, such a political project scrutinizes the processes more than the products of debility; it is concerned less with resignifying or valuing up disabled/debilitated/nonnormative subjects than with intervening upon state impositions of vulnerability. If progressive sexual politics entails, minimally, institutions that defend and promote pluralistic intimate relations, security from sexual violence, provisions to ensure safer sex and safer sexual communities, and access to sexual education, then we might judge the debilitation of sexual/political subjects by the degree to which such debilitation realizes these stated objectives (or others—this list is fallible, revisable, and certainly not exhaustive). On this mapping, in the face of sex offenders and sex offenses, progressive sexual justice politics might deprioritize securing civil rights and reprioritize advocating a minimal material threshold for social and sexual welfare. Sexual and gender violence prevention organizations like Stop It Now!, the Sexual Violence Prevention Program of the Minnesota Department of Health, INCITE!, and the Association for the Treatment and Prevention of Sexual Abuse (ATSA) target sexual violence as a preventable but epidemic problem of public health. (Law professor Leigh Goodmark similarly encourages us, for policy purposes, to comprehend intimate partner violence as a problem of not only public health but also community cohesion, economic inequality, and human rights.[205]) For these organizations, sexual violence is manageable or even eliminable not (exclusively) by punitively debilitating convicted offenders. Rather, they advocate building sexually safe environments through reconciliation processes and rehabilitation programs, safer sex and sexual violence prevention education, community actions and public awareness campaigns, the sharing of accountability across communities, and the identification and containment of societal variables that probabilistically catalyze sexually aggressive behavior. My bid is that entertaining fairness and debility might, like these organizations, engender more capacious political solidarities and effectuate foreclosures that do not redound to those vulnerable subjects already penally or politically displaced.

Michel Foucault was skeptical of "vulnerability" and "vulnerable populations" as rationales for governance.[206] Yet it seems to me that those of us committed to sexual justice face a pressing double challenge: first, to discriminate between those forms of vulnerability that require state correctives, those forms of vulnerability manufactured in the interests of gendered, capitalist, or otherwise regressive normativity, and those forms of vulnerability produced or amplified by the state, which I have called debility; while, second, to remain critically cognizant that such distinctions are always fictions. The objective is not to discover the "truly" vulnerable subject or population as opposed to the merely discursively vulnerable, but to consider how vulnerabilities are politically distributed and produced, and to advocate ways they might be distributed or produced otherwise, in order to achieve more socially and sexually just outcomes.

2

Sodomite Pride!

What Is Right and Wrong about Sex in Public?

I n 2014, then-Louisiana State Representative Patricia Smith proposed a bill that would have removed Louisiana's antisodomy law from the state's criminal code.[1] The bill would not have repealed the state's anomalous Crime Against Nature by Solicitation (CANS) law, considered in the previous chapter, but instead would have repealed Crime Against Nature sans solicitation (CAN), what courts and prosecutors call "simple sodomy," or consensual oral and anal sex.[2] One need not be an expert on constitutional law to smell something funky. Why would Pat Smith need to propose such a bill in 2014, eleven years after the Supreme Court held antisodomy laws unconstitutional?[3] Because in 2013 it was revealed by a local news investigation that the East Baton Rouge Sherriff's Office had been going undercover to park cruising sites for at least the prior two years to arrest men for attempted (noncommercial, nonaggravated) sodomy (Figure 2.1).[4] The arrests were later thrown out by the district attorney since CAN was no longer good law. Then, one year after Representative Smith proposed her bill, Baton Rouge police arrested two men for allegedly having sex in a car; here too, a district judge threw out the charges.[5]

Patricia Smith's bill was defeated by a 2–1 margin in the state assembly. Let that sink in: in Louisiana, as this chapter goes to press in 2024, the state criminalizes adults of whatever genders to engage in consensual oral

A previous version of this chapter appeared as Joseph J. Fischel, "Keep Pride Nude." *Boston Review*, June 23, 2021, https://bostonreview.net/articles/keep-pride-nude/.

or anal sex.[6] Opposition to the bill was primarily driven by the conservative Christian group Louisiana Family Forum (LFF), who warned that should the sodomy law be repealed, predators would have easier access to children. The East Baton Rouge Sherriff, and later religious leaders and legislators, claimed that children were witnessing or could potentially witness gay sex in parks, and that families could no longer bring their children to parks because of all the gay sex taking place there. As a Baptist leader bemoaned, "it's virtually impossible for parents to allow our children to spend any time unsupervised in our city parks because of the prevalence of this kind of conduct [anal and oral sex between men]."[7]

None of this was true. Not a single arrest was prompted by either an underage complaining witness or her parents. No parents reported that their children had seen any sex in public nor were there any reports that parents were hesitant to bring their children to the parks because of said gay sex. Rather, "[c]ops would sit in public parks in unmarked cars, propositioning [men] for sex, then when the men agreed, the police would arrest them for attempted crimes against nature."[8] In an incident of what should be catalogued as unconscionable state violence,

> an East Baton Rouge Parish sheriff's deputy propositioned a 65-year-old man he met in a public park, asking him to join him for "some drinks and some fun" back at [the] undercover officer's apartment. The man followed the deputy home, and, upon entering it, was handcuffed and booked on a single count of "attempted crime against nature."[9]

The men looking for sex with other men in Baton Rouge parks were not humping in front of any children. They were cruising just as their gay elders had done before them: at night, discretely, in tenebrous areas, deliberately distanced from anyone, young or old, who might object.[10] And they were arrested.

The identitarian response to these political contestations would go like this: the evocation of children forced to witness gay sex was homophobically deployed to quash the antisodomy law repeal bill; the arrests of men soliciting other men for sex in the park under the state's archaic antisodomy law was doubly homophobic (antigay police enforcing an antigay law). All such claims to the political accomplishments of homophobia would be true, even if it might be more precise to say the antisodomy law is discriminatorily enforced rather than discriminatorily designed.[11]

This chapter asks instead, in a not-so-identitarian register: *What if it had been true? What if children were watching (gay) sex in the parks? When is sex in public wrong, if ever, and why? And when might sex in public be right and good?*

Earlier in 2014, before Smith's bill was roundly defeated, Louisiana legislators voted to repeal the state's "incest" statute, relocating the proscribed conduct under its sodomy law, probably to shield the sodomy law from constitutional attack (or to shield the law from Smith's legislative attack).[12] We could ask similar questions about incest as about sex in public: *What is incest, why is it wrong when it is, and what should we do about it?*[13] Here though, in the conclusion of the chapter and accompanied chiefly by Judith Butler, I will interpret the legislative subsumption of "incest" under "crime against nature," or the transmutation of incest into sodomy and sodomy into incest, as much more than a tactical maneuver. Read psychoanalytically if paranoically, I propose that sodomy and public sex indeed connote incest, not only but especially in the conservative mind. And even if in our collective unconscious the "incest" connoted is consanguineous sexual relations, it nevertheless persists, theorizes Lee Edelman, as "an indeterminate figure for the threat of indetermination."[14] That is, if public sex signifies incest, such signification travels below and beyond mere (?!) sexual reconfiguration, "gestur[ing] toward something unspeakable because fundamentally unknowable: incest as the nondifferentiation prior to articulated speech and thought."[15] The symbolic equation might be: public sex = incest = indeterminacy, nondifferentiation, meaninglessness, civilizational demise. The equation telegraphs the chapter's concluding thesis at the cost of overstating it. In any case, if public sex is incest-signifying, that does not make it actionably wrongful; but it does make such sex distinctively disturbing, repelling and alluring, psychically disorienting, and, finally, politically potent from a paraidentitarian perspective.

I enumerate here six questions that strike me as necessary for any serious or seriously queer investigation about the rightness and wrongness of sex in public:

1. What is sex?
2. What is public?
3. When, if ever, are certain kinds of sex in certain publics wrongful, or right and good?
4. Why? What makes the sex wrongful, or right and good?
5. If certain kinds of sex in certain kinds of public are wrongful, what is to be done?
6. What does sex in public have to do with sexual violence?

My subsequent speculations and provocations draw upon, inter alia: my reading of liberal and liberalish legal theory on indecent exposure and indecent exposure law (for it is indecent exposure laws and the like, and not antisodomy laws, that more properly—as in within constitutional limits—bear on public sex practices); queer scholarship that rezones sex into public spheres; Black and Brown feminist and feminist-adjacent scholarship that reclaims nonnormative pleasures under conditions of white supremacy; something like informed queer intuition; and my own "sex in public," dutifully sanitized. And I hope to show that the sort of bourgeois sanitization of my own sex in public is neither irredeemably sex negative nor erotophobic but rather a matter of respect, which is distinguishable from respectability. Some sex in some publics is more rude than transgressive, or assaultive.

I have so far adumbrated that when sex in public is affronting (but not wrongful), it might either be because it is incest-signifying or rude, and not principally because such displays are witnessed nonconsensually, displays that we legally term under "indecent exposure," the broader category of "disorderly conduct," and the like ("obscenity" in Louisiana). By the end of this chapter, though, I will speculate that part of what makes some sex in some publics rude is in fact that the sex is incest-signifying, thus collapsing the rudeness prong into the motherfucking prong. In other words, such sex is rude—and distinctively rude from other visual distractions—because, at the level of the unconscious, it alerts us to too much possibility, desublimated. Sex that signifies incest signifies the end of civilization, a devolution not "against nature" but consumed by it. When the Louisiana Legislature reclassified incest as sodomy, a "crime against nature," it unwittingly betrayed a truth that public sex, gay sex, and incest collectively reveal: we humans are unruly, excessive, and hedonic creatures, whose unruliness, excess, and hedonism are contained not by our "nature" but by norms and laws.

But back to the six questions. I do not answer any of them comprehensively (although I get pretty close with the fifth, which is the easiest to dispense with, the least conceptually interesting, and the most politically urgent). The questions and my varyingly insufficient responses to them map the field of investigation for the chapter's subtitular challenge (*What is right and wrong about sex in public?*) and its titular exhortation (*Sodomite pride!*). The first two:

1. What is sex?
2. What is public?

Let us take as contestable preliminaries that there are many publics and that that there are a variety of individual, relational, genital, and nongenital acts that qualify as sex, and that however you or I answer these first two questions, the answers are avowedly contextual, contingent, constructed, and nonontological. As we will see, erotic vomiting can bid for "public sex" too. I rehearse neither the literature that degenitalizes sex (hailing principally from disability studies and queer studies[16]) nor the literature that retheorizes and denaturalizes publics,[17] as I think the rather simple point for our purposes is that "sex in public," along with "public nudity" (often a synecdoche for sex in public in popular discourse) are not singular things, but we will temporarily imagine them to be for analytic and political traction. *Sex* and *public* thus pluralized, discursively drenched if not saturated, the remaining four questions are:

3. When, if ever, are certain kinds of sex in certain publics wrongful, or right and good?
4. Why? What makes the sex wrongful, or right and good?
5. If certain kinds of sex in certain kinds of public are wrongful, what is to be done?
6. What does sex in public have to do with sexual violence?

Considerations of the third and fourth questions comprise the core of this chapter's case for a paraidentitarian, public sexual culture. Those considerations are scaffolded, though, by an analytic and political sensitivity toward penalty (question 5) and violence (question 6), so I foreground those questions now and then mostly set them aside.

If Certain Kinds of Sex in Certain Kinds of Public Are Wrongful, What Is to Be Done?

As for penalty, criminal punishment is rarely, and probably never, an appropriate remedy for (any kind of) sex in (any kind of) public. And it is not just feminist and queer thinkers who think so. Here is what three influential liberal and liberalish legal thinkers have to say about the penalties for indecent exposure and similar offenses.

Legal philosopher Joel Feinberg opines:

Even if there must be defined crimes with specified penalties for purely offensive conduct [among which Feinberg includes "open lewdness"], however, the penalties should be light ones: more often fines than imprisonment, but when imprisonment, it should be measured in days rather than months or years.[18]

And here is famously hard-to-pin-down-ideologically Judge Richard Posner, whose view on pornography has more wide-ranging application to public nudity, strip teases, and the like:

The resources that our society is willing to devote to law enforcement are limited [are they?!] in relation to the amount of violence and other serious lawlessness against which they are deployed. We should not dissipate them in efforts—which are bound to fail—to suppress activities that may be as harmless as witchcraft or heresy.[19]

A more recent gloss forms Stuart Green's "unified liberal theory" for adjudicating the rightness and wrongness of sex laws:

> But more often than in the case of the voyeur, the exhibitionist will be exercising a right that is owed a significant deference. Sometimes that right will be a specifically sexual one. Other times, it may be more generally expressive, political or artistic. Thus, even more than in the case of voyeurism, the criminalization of exhibitionism is likely to present substantial moral and legal conflicts.[20]

Green concludes his study of indecent exposure measuredly: "out on the public street, the criminal law should not intervene unless the brightest of bright lines is crossed."[21]

Later, I will revisit Posner's, Feinberg's, and Green's reflections on obscenity and public indecency to distinguish public sex that is affronting from public sex that is actionably wrongful (question 4), but the point for now is that these three thinkers remind us, and from not especially leftist points of view, that we should be extremely reluctant to punish behavior that others claim to find upsetting or yucky but not injurious. And these scholars' reflections caution that social opprobrium and moral disgust are each as flimsy a foundation for criminalization as they are historically appealing.

What Does Sex in Public Have to Do with Sexual Violence?

I approach this sixth question rather circuitously by way of commercial sex, but my reason for doing so should soon be made clear. Louisiana's CANS law, criminalizing commercial anal and oral sex, was held constitutional by the state's Supreme Court in 2005 because it purportedly proscribes sex "in public."[22] In other words, what distinguishes CANS (the focal point of the prior chapter) from CAN (the focal point of this one) is the "S," solicitation, which shields the law from *Lawrence v. Texas*'s lance.[23] *Lawrence* drew a hard line in the sand (that is, hard for Justice Kennedy, all but vanishing for Justice Scalia,[24] and I still think Justice Scalia was right[25]): "The present case does not involve minors," opined the Court, " . . . [i]t does not involve public conduct *or* prostitution."[26] But the disjunctive "or" betrays the Court's equivalence, which is that prostitution just is public conduct; that is why many courts have subsequently held that prostitution is constitutionally unprotected from criminalization.[27]

So what does all this have to do with public sex and/as sexual violence? In a post-*Lawrence* world, the most rational-sounding rational basis (or in less legalistic but more winky terms, the most reasonable reason) for proscribing sex work is, among a few distant contenders: the prevention of (sexual) *violence* against, and (sexualized) subordination of, women.[28] While many sex worker rights activists and scholars have countered that criminalizing sex work aggravates rather than ameliorates violence against women (a contention endorsed in the fifth chapter), I would ask instead, resuscitating feminist theorist Catharine MacKinnon's earlier critique of heterosexuality,[29] why we think sex *without* money is liberty-enhancing rather than equality-thwarting. After a lecture MacKinnon gave at the University of Chicago in 2011, a student pressed her on a claim she made about the trauma of sex work. The student pointed out to MacKinnon that a study from Australia suggested no variance between the mental health of sex workers and "the general population." "I am also not here to defend what happens to women every day of the week," MacKinnon shot back.[30] If the rational basis for antiprostitution laws is the prevention of *violence* against women, then we might just want to outlaw hetero sex tout court.

I am mostly joking, but the necessary caveat to the liberal legal scholars' stance that sex in public should rarely if ever be penalized let alone criminalized must be that sex itself can be cleanly demarcated from sexual assault; if sex cannot be, then the sixth question, *What does sex in public have to do with sexual violence?*, has renewed ethical import. What I am getting at (again, circuitously but I hope compellingly) is that if prostitution is impermissible because it is "public," then the best argument, in turn, for why "public sex" is impermissible would no longer be that it is either amoral or icky but that *sex itself* constitutes or heralds violence.

This is a relatively new supposition raised against public sex[31] and yet it seems pressing in a political climate in which the paradigm of public indecency is less the homeless or drunk man urinating on the street corner than the subway flasher, pornographic Zoom bomber, or, for that matter, the invidious right-wing fiction of the kindergarten teacher who cannot help but speechify sex to his charges. Can we really say the jerking off Zoom bomber is "merely" masturbating in public, like a man masturbating at night in an alley? The shift in what is saliently, publicly indecent is overdetermined; no doubt, #MeToo and the Jeffrey Toobin-esque virtual mishaps of the COVID-19 pandemic are partial explanatory variables, as is the right's reignited culture war to legitimate authoritarianism and to assuage while amplifying white left-behindism.[32] Certainly, the Tennessee law that potentially criminalizes drag shows "on public property and in places where they could be watched by minors" was mobilized by fear that such shows are "sexual" and that such sexuality is not just gross but violative.[33] (Against those claiming the law criminalizes only obscene performances, rather than all drag shows, viewable to minors, I would pose an iteration of the indecorous question that opens the chapter: what if a child sees a striptease?[34] It is unquestionably more likely for a child to be shot by a gun than traumatized by a thong. "What's the leading cause of death amongst children in this country? And I'm going to give you a hint. It's not drag show readings to children."[35])

Today, liberals, leftists, and maybe even some conservatives tend to agree, if unarticulated as such, that the core wrong of rape is a violation of another's sexual autonomy, another's right to codetermine her sexual relationships.[36] The emphasis is on constraints against, or the extinguishing of, choice, rather than the imposition or threat of force. For most liberal legal theorists, and for some feminist legal theorists, violations of autonomy are read off the refusal or nonperformance of consent.

In which case, might sex or even nudity in public be rape aestheticized? Other people's sexual activity to which onlookers have not consented? The problem of "public sex acts" would then be, as philosopher Martha Nussbaum maintains, "that they take place in the presence of people who have not consented to witness them."[37] Indeed, consent is Nussbaum's core normative guardrail to defend gay men's public sexual activity: she carries the constitutional flag for public sex when "there is no unwilling imposition on nonconsenting parties."[38] This, then, would distinguish the indecent Zoom bomber from the unwitnessed man in the alley.

Nussbaum's position, hinging on consent, cannot be totally right, and if it is at all right, the supposition would have to meet at least two objections. First, most versions of sexual autonomy normatively rely upon "the bodily integrity of the individual. Autonomy . . . is not only mental and intellectual, not only the capacity for meaningful, unconstrained choice. It is also physical, the separateness of the corporeal person."[39] For your sexual autonomy to be violated, your body, and not just your senses (visual or aural), has to be nonconsensually intruded upon. (But maybe bodies should no longer matter in this way, especially now that so much sex and intimacy is on, with, in, and potentially reconstituted by screens?[40]) Second, we run into a *reductio ad absurdum*. I did not consent to watching a bar fight between two other people, but I cannot claim I have been assaulted by witnessing their fight. Moreover, I am far more offended by a Proud Boys demonstration than by witnessing, say, a straight couple having sex on the subway. But then should we permit the couple to have sex on the subway? On a crowded subway? On a crowded subway in front of children? I will later flesh out the argument that one's sexual autonomy may be violated by public sex, and in a similar way that one's sexual autonomy is violated by a pornographic Zoom bomber or by a sexual harasser: when the perpetrator intends a sex act *at* a nonconsenting person, under conditions in which it is unreasonable for the perpetrator to assume the sex act would be welcomed (or alternatively, under conditions in which it is unreasonable that the witness be expected to assume the risk of another's exposure). For now, let us point out that the consent argument collapses the imposition of unwanted sex with the imposition of unwillingly *seeing* sex. The argument from (non)consent also potentially overextends to criminalizing or otherwise prohibiting all kinds of horrible, offensive, racist, misogynist, and phobic expressions that negatively impact many of us more so than witnessing sex. And that we consent to see some things, like a violent movie or football game, does not necessarily inoculate us from experiencing deep hurt, even trauma, at what we see. Summarily, I worry that Nussbaum's argument from consent, while politically expedient to protect gays as a class, dissolves the problem worth tackling: whether or not and under what conditions witnessing sex (or whatever) is injurious, let alone actionably so.

In the mid-2010s, I organized a symposium at my university featuring four well-known gender studies scholars. The lecture hall was filled with, among others, many of my undergraduate students. As part of his presentation on Blackness and love, a scholar screened, unannounced, a brief clip of a Black man stroking his erect penis in a bathtub. I freaked out, expecting Title IX complaints to arrive imminently. Nothing happened. I would have gone to the mat, and still would, on behalf of my colleague's academic freedom. First, because I doubt the clip, in this situation, should qualify as a "sex act" directed *at* others; and second, because even if the clip were a "sex act," it would not be unreasonable for the scholar to assume it would be (intellectually) welcome in a queer studies conference.

But was it a good idea to show the clip? Is the clip *sex*? I don't think so, although I am not certain. What if the scholar had exposed his penis, unmediated by a screen, to the audience? If we assume an unannounced (re)presentation of a Black man's erect penis to be threatening, is it because we are antisex, antisexual violence, heteronormative, or racist? Finally, I thought the video and its purpose might have been better thematized into the scholar's talk, which suggests that if there was a problem with screening the penis, that problem was aesthetic, not assaultive.

The scholar did not rape the audience, even figuratively. And yet, there is something intuitively appealing about recognizing that a problem with sex in public might be a rights-violation of some kind, especially in a world stratified by sex and other inequalities, our world. I will return to this intuition after constellating our analytic terrain by way of some kissers in South Africa, some vomiters in New York City, scholarship Black feminist scholar Jennifer Nash has helped me constellate as Black and Brown Pleasure Studies, and my sexual escapades along our national seashore. The South African kissers and the New York City vomiters act as prolegomena, priming us to think with more precision and less moralizing baggage about the commingling of 1) minoritized public sexual culture and 2) the phobic sexualization of minorities that Black and Brown Pleasure Studies so expansively foregrounds. My time at the beach, then, personalizes and performs "sex in public" for the reader, but extolling its gay subcultural virtues (among them, that a penis paraded in public is not necessarily violent and can even be charming) over its libidinal delights.

When, If Ever, Are Certain Kinds of Sex in Certain Publics Wrongful, or Right and Good?

Kissing in South Africa: Legal scholar Katherine Franke would like us to sodomize in public.[41] Not really, but she penned one of the first and best queer commentaries on *Lawrence v. Texas*, the 2003 U.S. Supreme Court case referenced earlier that held state antisodomy laws unconstitutional. Justice Kennedy superprivatized privacy rights, Franke criticizes, cabining consensual, noncommercial, adult-only, freedom-to-fuck in the no-longer-just-marital bedroom. Franke proposes that we look to South Africa for a better way to strike down sodomy laws, on grounds of equality and dignity.[42] In the South African case, the presiding Justice, Justice Ackermann, imagines the following scenario: at a "social gathering," a gay male couple, a lesbian couple, and a straight couple each make out. According to the South African Sexual Offenses Act, only the gay male couple would be guilty of a crime.[43] "What is remarkable about this hypothetical," comments Franke,

> is the degree to which its absurdity does not depend on a conception of privacy. The kiss is in public, in front of an audience, and is explicitly erotic in nature. It is the disparate legal treatment of similarly situated kissers that strikes Justice Ackermann as absurd and unfair, not the location in which the same-sex kissing takes place.[44]

All well and good, but I bet you can see where I am heading. What if, at the neighborhood barbeque, a man goes down on his husband, or his wife? For that is the equivalence Franke's appeal requires. I do not think we should incarcerate such a man, but I do think it is weird and rather unfair for the other BBQ attendees who were expecting potato salad, not cunnilingus. Moreover, I am skeptical that the world would be queerer, sex-positive, and better if we normalized neighborhood barbeque blowjobs. But maybe the most salient aspect of the reconstructed hypothetical is how remarkably unappealing it is to everyone, or at least to me: sex in *some* publics turns me on, but not at all this one, which then re-begs the question: what is a public, and might the distinctive features of an erotic public or a counterpublic—a bathhouse,[45] a nude beach, a park cruising spot—attenuate that public's claim to publicity? Is a public a public by virtue of its hetereogeneity, by the unpredictability of its inhabitants? Does the exhibitionist's libidinal charge of "getting caught" dissipate if she is? Having a tryst in an alley is hot in part because strangers might walk by; it is less hot when they actually do. And if it is hot *because* you are affronting someone else's sensibility, I think, at best, you are obnoxious. And yet, when I was in college, I drunkenly headed out one night to make out with my best friend Aaron at the fraternity DKE, purposely to offend heteronorms. I was punched in the face. I meant to be obnoxious, but in that instance my obnoxiousness was right and good and political and queer, or so 19-year-old me thought. I think 40-year-old me still thinks so, but of course we were making out with our clothes on, not fellating on the dance floor (and if we had been, I still should not have been punched). Let's countenance here an additional, provisional distinction between same-sex friends making out to unsettle suffocating heteronorms (and let's be honest, we were craving some attention from frat boys) versus a man jerking off *at* an unwilling subject, gratifying himself through her humiliation.

Vomiting in New York: Famously, or famously in my interdiscipline anyway, Michael Warner and Lauren Berlant close out their queer *cri de coeur*, "Sex in Public," with a scene of one man inducing a younger man to vomit, pushing milk and food down his throat, onstage, at a leather bar.[46] Just as Judith Butler's drag queen was never meant to be a figure of the radical gender vanguard,[47] Berlant and Warner are not advising public puking as an antidote to heteronormativity. But they recreate the public with their readers that the "tweaking and thwacking" generated with them.[48] A nonreproductive, nongenital erotics, Berlant and Warner's final act is neither "sex" nor "in public," but a plea to expansively reterritorialize both terms. The occasion occasions thinking about norms and rituals. When we go to a leather bar for its weekly, kinky talent show, is this not what we came for? To be shook and shocked? I would like to complement the notion of "derepression"[49] with "dedensitization." Opting in to eroticized dedensitization morally matters, though, as does the ability to opt out with relative ease. To be held as captive audience to public sex (or any nuisance, for that matter) shifts the normative terrain from queer world-building and toward offense or violation. On my plane home from Chicago, having just given a talk based on this chapter, I found myself seated between several women en route to a bachelorette party. For two and half hours, they yelled over me about the bride's destination wedding, the many chefs and bands hired for the affair, and the collective expectation that their boyfriends and husbands could not be relied upon to perform their assigned tasks. I will not pretend

I felt offended, let alone violated, but such compulsory aural heterosexuality made me question anew the fuss around kink at pride.[50] The parade attendee has easy exit options and closeable eyes. I was about 35,000 feet in the air with no headphones. Next time I'll pack proper prophylactics.

Black and Brown Pleasure Studies—Public sex, phobic sexualization: In *Wayward Lives, Beautiful Experiments*, Saidiya Hartman describes how, in New York City a century prior to Berlant and Warner's night out, "all the vice and untoward desires of the white world were channeled into the Negro quarter of the city."[51] At the turn of the twentieth century, Blacks were white folks' sex public. Black urban space authorized and provided an alibi for white carnality, so that even or especially white progressives "delighted in being lost in the sea of blackness."[52] "Privacy" was a privilege not afforded to Black people. "The hallways, bedroom, stoop, rooftop, airshaft and kitchenette provided the space of experiment" in the sex lives and relationships of Black city residents. Even the Black bedroom, as Hartman shows, was a "public" space, since "the police and the sociologists were there also, ready and waiting."[53]

Courts, legislatures, and police often have answered the question, *Who is guilty of lewd acts?* with, *A woman offering it for money, or the* kind *of woman who might.* "The mere willingness to have a good time with a stranger was sufficient evidence of wrongdoing," remarks Hartman, describing the hyperpoliced, surveilled lives and intimacies of young Black women at the turn of the twentieth century, not the twenty-first—right?[54]

Hartman dramatizes not only how young Black women and the queerly gendered of the industrialized city were rendered as *sex in public*, but also how the publicly mediated, unruly intimacies of Black women's lives were a mode of survival, a nascent politics of freedom. Hartman's recreation of young Black women's "wayward practices" inverts the question, *What is wrong with sex in public?*, into, *What is right, necessary, and antiracist about it?* Were it not for racial segregation, avers Hartman, the "promiscuity-sociality of the lower ranks might have sounded a whore's *Internationale*."[55] The criminalization and demonization of prostitution, vice, and public indecency ought to have laid the groundwork for a cross-racial, working-class, queer coalitional politics against the scapegoating and criminalizing of minority communities. White supremacy got in the way.

Hartman's *Lives* is part of a plethora of relatively recent Black and Brown feminist and feminist-adjacent literature that recenters and revalues pleasure, sensuality, and sexuality for Black and Brown lives, Black counterpublics,[56] and antiracist politics. Across an array of academic disciplines and subject matters, scholars including Jen Nash, Amber Musser, Ariane Cruz, Darieck Scott, Rod Ferguson, Mireille Miller-Young, LaMonda Horton-Stallings, and Deb Vargas labor to embrace the nonnormative erotics, genders, and sexualities historically ascribed to Black and Brown bodies.[57] Contemporary Black and Brown feminist thought, for the most part,[58] shelves respectability politics, asking instead what hedonic, more just world we might make together should we transvalue white supremacist denigrations of the supposed sexual and appetitive excess of Black and Brown communities.

I share but briefly a few examples of this scholarship—defining, defending, and complicating feminist and queer of color sexual publics—from a variety of textual, historical, and contemporary locations.

Consider first and most geographically germane, LaMonda Horton-Stallings's *A Dirty South Manifesto*, a genre-bending (despite its title) set of interventions on various twentieth- and twenty-first-century moral, cultural, and political contestations over minoritized Black genders and sexualities in the South, two contestations of which are sited in New Orleans.[59] Stallings starts from a familiar premise that "we must refuse a politics of respectability when issues of gender and sexuality are at stake," criticizing conservative as well as Black church leaders for moralizing against queer Black sexual expression (in the form of art, literature, and street protest) as impolitic, obscene, and dangerous.[60] Stallings recalls, for example, when Senator Jesse Helms attacked Audre Lorde and Minnie Bruce Pratt for being awarded creative writing fellowships from the National Endowment for the Arts. Lorde responded with her poem "JESSEHELMS," which referred to "jessehelms' come" as "knit[ting] moral fibre" that demonizes Black queer lives.[61] In part of the poem uncited by Stalling, Lorde admits, "even I'd like to hear you scream / ream out your pussy."[62] For Stallings, Lorde's response emblematizes a politics of resistance that presses back against, rather than capitulates to, moralizing authority. To put it in ahistorical and therefore more powerful terms, "women's sexual autonomy and public voice are always seen as a threat to white male supremacist patriarchy."[63]

Stallings is focused as equally on the politics of sexual expression as she is on a sexual politics of space and land, recuperating the purported *dirtiness* of racialized sexualities that has been and continues to be discursively weaponized to cleanse, clean up, or violently reterritorialize the commons. "I continue to advocate something that a moral revival will not do: reflecting upon obscenity of settler sexuality and settler colonial politics and reveling in and rolling around in the dirt to make new knowledge about gender and sexuality."[64] She continues:

> Contemporary modes of terror and violence visited upon sexual minoritarians too often mimic histories of settler colonial violence demonstrated in the administration of Indian removal in 1830, slavery, Reconstruction-era rape and lynching law, or police raids on LGBTQ venues in the McCarthy era.[65]

Now reconsider the arrests of men seeking out sex with other men in Baton Rouge parks; and reconsider, in New Orleans, the undercover stings, arrests, and subsequent sex offender registration of trans and cis women in New Orleans for offering commercial sex. "Land politics," explains Stallings, "dictate how institutions can carry out their missions, determine which institutions are worth state and national advocacy, and which communities' experiences of culture are worthy of institutional curation."[66] The Louisiana lawmakers who opposed the sodomy repeal bill lamented that they and other citizens could no longer bring their children to parks with all the gay sex taking place there. The question that has more or less structured this chapter has been, *Even if the gays were fucking always and everywhere in the park (they were not), so what?* But Stallings encourages us to think beside that question in order to ask another: why (white) heterosexual nuclear families with children should be more entitled to the public space of the park than the men who wish to have sex with other men there (or more accurately and less sensationally, *than the men who meet up with other men in the parks to have sex somewhere else, usually indoors).*[67] Children could play elsewhere. What we might really need to accommodate a public sexual culture are non-phobic zoning and utilization regulations, like "adult swim" at the municipal public pool. For example: *henceforth, 9pm–12am is gay cruising time in specified areas of this Baton Rouge park, so bring your kids before sunset and/ or to the family-focused areas (if you do not want your kid to see gay people, gay people talking, or, and far less likely, gay people having sex).*[68]

Stallings catalogues a 2018 issue of the lesbian journal *Sinister Wisdom*, "Conjuring New Orleans Dyke Bar Project," which "looks at artists, archivists, and community members creating performance art centered on the birth and death of lesbian dyke bars in New Orleans."[69] She summarizes the voices of the interviewees:

> [T]hese young people's inquiries exemplify why calls for lesbian spaces are not an should not be read as nostalgic, but instead should be read as advocating for a continuation of evolving lesbian imaginations for a new generation, some of whom may be gender-fluid.[70]

As Samuel Delaney influentially observed, space not only structures sexual experience and possibility but also cultivates unexpected desires, mobilizes new identity formations (the "gender-fluid"), and potentially softens the borders of gendered and sexual taxonomies.[71]

Like, Stallings, Deb Vargas transvalues the filthy and the dirty, or *lo sucio*, as part of her "queer Latino analytic." Vargas draws on the sounds and imagery, and the smells and temporality of, respectively, a Mexican music video and a shutdown Latino gay bar in San Francisco, to call upon "sensual refusals" of "sanitized citizenship."[72] Vargas locates, in the "unprof-itable bodies"[73] of Mexican teenage girls wasting time and partying, and in the enduring "stench of queer generations past,"[74] a ballast against not only the clean-up gentrification projects of neoliberal capitalism but also "homo-normative projects [that] similarly require the cleansing of nasty, filthy, and obscene sex *out of* queer sex and sexuality."[75] Vargas's argument is not just to carry a brief for the queerness of queers but to describe that queers' dis-avowal of queerness tends to implicate and then indict what Cathy Cohen specified as the "secondarily marginalized"[76]: racial minorities, the poor, the femme-gendered (like cis and trans sex workers). Also like Stallings, Vargas concentrates on public or semipublic space, on "reconfiguring spaces . . . for sustaining queer worlds within hetero- and homo-normativity's structural violence."[77] The promise of Vargas's "Latino queer analytic of *lo sucio*" is to

> offer a productive engagement with sites and performances of queer sex and sexuality that persistently violate, and at times, willfully fail to arrive to sexual intimacies produced through capital. *Sucia* gen-ders signal possibilities of a queer sustenance within rapidly aggres-sive moves to destroy alternative imaginaries of joy, intimacy, and care.[78]

Vargas's contemplations on the ways public expressions of Brown femme sexuality, through smells and tastes, singing and dancing, offer lifelines and community-making lines for queer racial minorities, calls back a similar defense of Brown counterpublic sexuality proffered a generation earlier by José Muñoz (whom Vargas cites).[79] I quote here at length from Joseph Osmundson's COVID-19-orbiting collection of essays on intimacy, virality, and care, for he writes eloquently on the public-claiming work of Muñoz and Audre Lorde both. Osmundson reflects upon both Muñoz's profile of Pedro Zamora, a Cuban American gay man living with HIV/AIDS who appeared on the first season of MTV's *The Real World*, and Audre Lorde's *Cancer Journals*:

> José Muñoz considered Pedro Zamora's decision to live his private life publicly on TV . . . , writing, "subjects like himself never have access to full privacy." Lorde, a self-described Black, feminist, les-bian, understood that publicly writing the full extent of her private illness was a radical breaking of the public/private binary, a binary that for her—as a queer Black person—had always been a lie. For queer people, as Muñoz writes, privacy is a recent and incomplete right. For Black People, the history of America is one without the possibility of private life: what right does property have to privacy?[80]

What Hartman demonstrates to her readers, though, is that privacy deprivations for Black people are not only a function of enslavement ("what right does property have . . . ?"), as if privacy were won with the Reconstruction Amendments, but also that such deprivations are dynamic, attendant to white policing and surveillance, including progressive-minded superintendence. In any case, what Osmundson alludes to, by way of Muñoz and Lorde, is that much of Black and Brown Pleasure Studies' criticism of the public/private divide for racialized queer sexualities does more than advocate for sexual publics, but presses upon hetero-, or perhaps now amato-,[81] normative whiteness that structures the binary, such that *public* and *private* are defined less by who does what *where* than *who* does what where. This insight in turn instructively helps us perceive a critical distinction between a paraidentitarian sexual politics and an anti- or nonidentitarian one. Under a nascent paraidentitarianism, we can and must launch a universalizing brief for sexual freedom while nevertheless remaining attentive both to the ways sexual freedom has been withheld from minoritized groups (public sexual culture) and to the ways sexualization has served to undercut minoritized groups' social standing, political agency, and material well-being (phobic sexualization).

And so a last example on the paraidentitarian point, one more generatively ambivalent than Stallings's and Vargas's (and Muñoz's and Osmundson's) transvaluations, comes from GerShun Avilez's *Black Sexual Freedom*.[82] Avilez's monograph tracks the many ways diasporic Black queer artists of the twentieth and twenty-first century "consistently and defiantly express desire and claim a freedom *within restriction*."[83] The prepositional phrase is key for Avilez, whose thesis is that "spatialized injury is a central component of Black queer experience through the diaspora."[84] Avilez, like the artists, essayists, and poets he draws upon, does not so much laud Black queer sexuality as he foregrounds how cultural producers envision temporary reprieves of Black queer freedom against the relentless imposition of vulnerability. Less fatalistic than Afropessimism, Avilez's persuasive point nonetheless is that when injury "encircl[es]" Black diasporic life, full throttle reclamation is both dangerous and impossible.[85] Because the "minority body" is under "near constant public attention," Avilez's surveyed cultural producers aspire not to *privacy*, so easily "invaded and circumscribed," but rather "they use art to create possibilities for *interiority*," which Avilez in turn defines as "spaces made possible through the imagination and artistic practice that elude [public] attention."[86] How the bid for *interiority* translates aesthetically: Avilez's poets, photographers, and writers are not interested in making their sex explicit, since Black bodies are too often forced into sexualized exposure; they effort to announce and celebrate nonnormative desire as provisional paths for freedom. The Black lesbian poet Pat Parker, for example, envisions "holding hands with my lover . . . / i can go to a public bathroom / & not be shrieked at by ladies."[87] When Avilez looks to an edited collection of prison art and writings from the 1980s, and a prison memoir from the early 2000s, he observes how the texts foreground same-sex desire, yearning, and longing, rather than sex itself, to withstand "the violent prison gaze" and "systematized visibility" of carcerality.[88] South African photographer Zanele Muholi chronicles the "quotidian lives" of "lesbians who have faced violence and discrimination," imaging women holding hands, hanging out, smoking pot, decidedly not fucking. "Muholi . . . show[s] us that which is obscured by our desire to know about and control female sexuality."[89] Ironically, Avilez's artists build public sexual culture by evading public sexualization. "Public sex"—in the form of intimate writing, yearning, expression—is a counterweight to state and extralegal surveillance. "Although the queer body is never able to escape institutional processes of exposure and the physical and psychological threats they pose," explains Avilez, "artists use desire to disrupt *enforced visibility* and assert autonomy."[90]

In this chapter's sodomitical scene, and recalling Stallings's resonant claim for queering space, the solicitation on offer from Avilez might be to reconceive Baton Rouge park sex (or the noncommercial solicitation for it) less in terms of a literal right to fuck than in terms of a collective if still amorphous "desire for spatial justice,"[91] a desire that manifests public space as no longer held hostage to the incessantly imagined injurability of the witnessing child. When men seek out other men in dark corners of public park for sexual encounters, they are creating a world alongside, and as respite from, propriety and proprietary sexuality. Under these lights, it is the *arresting police offers* who publicize the men's "public" sex, just as antitransgender "bathroom bills" publicly sexualize—and therefore endanger—women who want to pee.[92]

I have turned to Avilez because his thesis sounds promisingly with a politics of paraidentitarianism, a coalitional politics unbeholden to identity yet attentive to group-based asymmetries of maldistribution, violence, and misrecognition. For any subject, desire (and art) may forge a path through an environment of injury and threat, even as some subjects are structurally more prone to injury than others. Unlike my intervention, though, Avilez places his "emphasis on aesthetic redress in place of legal or political redress," for he cautions that conventional political redress may "reify the state," that is, legitimate the very institutions that condition, condone, or cause racialized injury.[93] Despite the risks, I want to marshal Avilez's nonstate project toward the project of thinking a better state, a state whose regulatory sex regime is principled on neither phobia nor innocence but on gender and sexual pluralism opposed to white supremacy. While Avilez's "artists offer queer subjects *aesthetic redress* or paths to freedom and pleasure that imagine ways through but that never fully move beyond threat," we must tend to the irrefusable juridical question: what forms of regulation best support, or least impede, erotic and aesthetic "paths to freedom and pleasure"?[94] If we imagine cruising sex as an aesthetic practice of queer freedom, and always also a plea for interiority under phobic strictures, how might we repeal, repurpose, or rewrite laws that potentially criminalize cruisers (like the attempted crime against nature or obscenity statutes in Louisiana) to instead democratize and pluralize sexual culture?

To reappraise sexualities maligned as exhibitionist, promiscuous, and pernicious—whether that "sexuality" takes the form of a New Orleanian sex worker, a kinky Pride parader, a trans woman walking, a Pakistani woman driving, or a Texan trying to get an abortion (*Roe*'s overturned privacy holding notwithstanding)[95]—is to build a culture of "public" sex that withstands righteous parochialism masquerading as family friendliness, and the paeans for the Child that are worse than worthless, as the Right issues fatwas against queer kids, which is to say most kids.[96] And if, as gender studies professor Rod Ferguson puts it, "racist practice articulates itself generally as gender and sexual regulation," then a powerful form of antiracism is to nurture minoritized sexuality, to reclaim what transnational feminist theorist Jacqui Alexander terms "erotic sovereignty" and what English professor Amber Musser prescribes as "sensual excess" against and within state and social regulation.[97] To defend the intimacies, sex practices, and sexualities of minoritized subjects from surveillance and sanction need not depend on naively reading subjective pleasure off individual experience, as if the sex worker's right to sex work, or the gay cruiser's right to cruise, is founded upon *liking it*. Instead, and put most generally, the archive of Black and Brown Pleasure Studies underscores communal resistance against, and creative resignifications of, coercive impositions of hetero and white supremacist norms on racial minority subjects. In that sense, the political reclamation on offer is possibly compatible with Emily Owens's sobering observation that searching for sexual pleasure—"outside of violence"—in the antebellum archival traces of enslaved women in and around New Orleans is likely a fool's errand.[98] "But," as Owens also reminds us, "the present is not the past."[99]

Boy Beach: Critical theorists are wary of "utopias" and the aspiration for them—homogenizing, naïve, impractical, and impracticable.[100] "Boy Beach" is my utopia notwithstanding, a gay beach on the coast of Provincetown, Massachusetts, where I work and play in the summer. Federally owned land, Herring Cove (colloquial: "Boy Beach," Figure 2.2) could not be any more "public." Yet, miles from heterosociality, naked and unbound, intimate and exposed, it could not be any more "private." Ninety-eight percent of its visitors, unscientifically speaking, are gay men, half of them fully nude. Here are the best days of my life: reading the Sunday *New York Times*, yoga in hot sand, wading into tide ponds with newly made friends, popping over the dunes for brief, beautiful, infrequently outstanding, sunscreen-scented sex. Almost always, an audience of excited, mostly tender mostly elders appear in a circle around the men-at-play (usually standard fare: hand jobs, blowjobs, anal sex for the douched and fearless). Here too, a private is partitioned in the public, or another public partitioned in the private. We play *over the dunes*, away from the main strip, I think, because we want the audience to want to be there; *over the dunes*, too, because sex out in the *open* open feels ostentatious rather than inviting, campy even, and campy is many fabulous things but not erotic. I am trying to theorize why some opens open to sex, and some do not or should not.

Occasionally, straight couples, out-of-towners, stumble onto Boy Beach. When the men see a woman, they instinctively cover themselves. I no longer do. I think it is sexist. What is more, to cover the penis is to assume the penis can never not be a weapon. On Boy Beach, penises are fun and funny, salty, shriveled from the freezing ocean. Less frequent than even women visitors are national park rangers, who issue citations to exposed fronts and backs. The citations deter nobody. When a ranger is spotted, one man will yell "ranger!" down the strip, triggering gay telephone as we scramble to cover ourselves with towels or T-shirts if our bathing suits are out of reach. I have not spoken at length with a ranger, but my sense is that they are not motivated by a phobic calling to extinguish vice. It's a respectable, reliable government job that you cannot phone in.

In his exquisitely written memoir-cum-eulogy of gay bars, Jeremy Lin wonders if sites for public gay sex have been gentrified out of transgressive possibility, now just another attraction for wealthy, mostly white gay tourists, part of a privatized, late modern urban landscape evermore inhospitable to the poor and working class.[101] Probably. At the same time, Lin also explains that when the United Kingdom decriminalized sex between men "within totally private spaces," the legislation (the Sexual Offences Act of 1967) legitimated and expanded the criminalization of more public, and so more heavily working-class, gay social and sexual spaces.[102] If public gay sex is neoliberalized for profit (the bathhouse as a slutty Starbucks), the decriminalization of private gay sex can serve to sanitize the commons, so choose your capitalist poison. The pressing political question, urged as we saw by Katherine Franke, is whether a right to sex anchored not in privacy but in equality might better offset normative collateral.[103]

Like Lin, Joe Osmundson, canvassing debates surrounding Truvada, the medication manufactured by Gilead that many gay men use to prevent HIV transmission (Truvada for preexposure prophylaxis, or PrEP), writes "PrEP, the argument goes, turns gay sex into a profitable (and therefore palatable) enterprise in the age of late capitalism, where everything is moral if it's making someone rich. Gay sex parties aren't sinful debauchery; they're added value for Gilead shareholders."[104] Of course, such parties are both profitable for the pharmaceutical and playful and pleasurable for gay men, since no nonnormative practices, sexual or social, are purified of contradiction. For me, quasi-public, promiscuous sex on the beach, in addition to being delightful, has cultivated an assortment of friendships, ranging in their intensities. The beach and its erotic adventures are an escape valve from the grind of endless work (and my work is not as monotonous as most), which probably also means these sorts of unentangled pleasures ensure the endlessness of work. Yet Boy Beach salves my temperament; and it replenishes my faith that other humans—even *men*—are capable of play and pleasure without predation.

Reflecting on my Boy Beach adventures after synopsizing some entries in Black and Brown Pleasure Studies, I do not make a false equivalence, as if Black lesbian artists in the United States South and I sit together on the vanguard of queer world-building. Instead, I am insisting on the political porosity between public sexual culture and phobic public sexualization; one is never disentangled from the other, but degrees of freedom matter. At the same time as Hartman's Black girls, women, and the queerly gendered were migrating *en masse* into northern cities, "*all* sex acts between men were considered public and illegal," writes Allan Bérubé, so "gay men were forced to become sexual outlaws. They became experts at stealing moments of privacy and at finding the cracks in society where they could meet and not get caught."[105] George Chauncey expands on the point: in 1920s and 1930s New York City,

> Gay men had to contend with the vigilante anti-gay violence as well as with the police. In response to this challenge, gay men devised a variety of tactics that allowed them to move freely about the city, to appropriate for themselves spaces that were not marked as gay, and to construct a gay city in the midst of, yet invisible to, the dominant city.[106]

Public sexual culture is forged against and sustained in the shadows of phobic sexualization.

In the sodomitical scene of this chapter—men looking for sex with other men in dark corners of Baton Rouge parks, and then being arrested—we witness the alchemy of public sexual culture and public sexualization. The common denominator across Hartman's subjects, Bérubé's, the men at the beach, and the criminalized sex workers of New Orleans discussed in the last chapter is not identity, however intersectionalized, nor subjective pleasure, but a wish to pursue, unpoliced, nonprocreative sex acts in informally partitioned zones of publicity.

Figure 2.1 Manchac Park, Louisiana, where undercover police officers met men and later arrested them for attempted crime against nature.

Figure 2.2 Sex in public? "Boy Beach," Provincetown, Massachusetts. *(Photograph by Emil Cohen)*

Note that my defense-in-progress of public sex does not depend, as does Nussbaum's, on cataloguing some "public" spaces as "private" to defend the sex that takes place there. Nussbaum points out that private facilities like gay bathhouses have been pretextually rendered "public" by courts and local officials in order to shut them down.[107] Nussbaum's argument from consent and her argument from privacy converge: bathhouse sex is permissible because it is shielded from a nonconsenting public, and that the bathhouse is shielded from others' view is testament to its relative privacy. The problem with Nussbaum's rezoning tactic is not simply that it leaves all that other "sex" rather[108] unattended—sex in the park or in the street alley—but the tactic reinscribes sex in such publics as presumptively suspect, injurious, criminalizable. Consider Justice Blackmun's quick dismissal of public sex from his dissent in *Bowers v. Hardwick*, the (subsequently reversed) Supreme Court case upholding the constitutionality of sodomy laws:

> Statutes banning public sexual activity are entirely consistent with protecting the individual's liberty interest in decisions concerning sexual relations: *the same recognition that those decisions are intensely private which justifies protecting them from governmental interference can justify protecting individuals from unwilling exposure to the sexual activities of others.*[109]

Bracketing the constitutional question, Blackmun's distinction is exactly why the *ethical* case for (public) sex must never rest either on valorizing choice or on rezoning institutions to be private. The sanctification of sex as, and because it is, "intensely private" is the normative and logical extension of Nussbaum's argument for "public" sex. "Burden[ing]" sex with an "excess of significance,"[110] insisting on sex's deep meaning and special dangers, both Blackmun's and Nussbaum's arguments sanitize sex from the world. If sex has such profound meaning for all of us, then each of us should be entitled to control not only when we have sex but also when we see it or anything proximate to it. Might the better argument for protecting public sex ride not on sex's purported profundity, but its comparative mundanity?[111]

The argument-in-progress here is to protect sex neither under the banner of privacy nor under the banner of gay personhood, as if gay sex is necessarily elemental to gay selves.[112] Rather, we should protect sex from being coercively conscripted, through penalty of criminalization, into normative whiteness and normative straightness, lest that sex demonstrably wrongs—harms or violates—others. The discursive terrain for public sex so relandscaped, the pertinent question for its accommodation is no longer what should count as private but what should count as wrongful, harmful, and violative.

What Makes Certain Kinds of Sex in Certain Kinds of Public Wrongful, or Right and Good?

Against the backdrop of what is right and good about sex in public, with political attentiveness to the ongoing definitional conundra of "sex" and "public," and with historical attentiveness to the public sexualization of minoritized groups and persons, what might we conclude about when certain kinds of sex in certain publics are wrongful? Let's circle back to our liberalish legal theorists of sexualized exposure before turning anew to germane Louisiana law. And the germane law here—to desist the made-up men from having made-up sex at parks in front of made-up children—would not actually have been the statute proscribing sodomy (CAN), as Louisiana lobbyists and legislators claimed, but rather the law criminalizing public sex and the public exposure of genitals.

In their considerations of public indecency and obscenity, Richard Posner, Joel Feinberg, and Stuart Green all arrive at the same conclusion: the problem is or should be wicked intent, not merely nonconsent. "The flasher thrusts his nudity on an unwilling stranger," as Posner instructively phrases it, intimating that public nudity is wrong when such nudity is rape-like or -lite ("thrusts").[113] The wrong of public indecency, on this account, is that the perpetrator holds others captive to his nudity or sex acts in order to gratify himself and subjugate the witness. Feinberg suggests that a critical determinant for whether a nuisance—anything from a neighbor's blaring heavy metal music to a passerby's farting—ought to be permissible or impermissible is *the motive of the defendant*, in particular its character as innocent or spiteful."[114] Feinberg proposes that a fruitful way to consider nuisance anew is to inquire about the boundaries marking the "private domains of persons." Breaching a person's boundaries "without his consent" is presumptively violative.[115] Importantly, the "private domains of persons" is context-dependent and may or may not map onto Schulhofer's "corporeal personhood," that is, bodily intrusion. But I do not think any of these scholars would claim that gay men having sex behind the bushes in a Baton Rouge park violates anyone's private domain of personhood, even a child's.

Two decisive questions for Green are, first, "whether the victim consented to or assumed the risk of witnessing the offender's conduct," and second, "whether the offender's conduct was intended to cause or recklessly caused significant disgust, shock, embarrassment, fear, or distress in the victim."[116] Green doubles down on bad intent harder than Posner or Feinberg; in fact, he chides Feinberg's nuisance guidelines for not being intent-centered enough. Echoing Posner, Green writes: "When A exposes himself to an unwilling B, he does more than merely preempt her attention; he infringes on her sexual autonomy. He enlists her, involuntarily, as a participant in his sexual life."[117] Notice that for Green, but unlike for Schulhofer, a person's sexual autonomy may be violated even when her body is not—but the threshold for that violation is very high. Green goes one step further, acknowledging that the "exhibitionist's act can have socially recognized value. . . . Even having sex in public can be a meaningful way of finding human connection and expanding one's erotic horizons."[118] Green's (indexically white?) exhibitionist is not Hartman's young Black urban laborer, who is not the man on the Boy Beach offering to suck on someone's penis; but for all three, sexual expression in whatever we mean by public is not a weapon but an invitation, analgesic, or ballast.

Green's "assumption of risk" clause is essential, even if it generates justifiable concern about who is anointed to assess someone else's risk assessment. Why? Because the arrests of the men in Baton Rouge parks are a late chapter in the too long history of police stings of gay space. If an undercover police officer heads to a park cruising spot at two in the morning and another man strokes his exposed, erect penis in the direction of the officer, the officer should not later be able to argue that his nonconsenting renders the exposure criminal. The officer assumed the risk. He went looking for that erect penis even if he did not consent to it.

When it comes to wrongful indecent exposure, I find myself in reluctant agreement with these three white liberal or liberalish guys, except I would more narrowly tailor the inculpating motivations than Green does: sometimes nudity and sex are performed in political protest to "shock,"[119] but intent to cause fear, distress, harm, or subordination, without the consent of the victim and when the victim has not "assumed the risk of witnessing the offender's conduct," seems to me violative of another's sexual autonomy and so actionably wrongful.

I agree reluctantly, though, because a Foucauldian at heart—or on this point, a Marxian, Nietzschean, Butlerian, and believer in the injustice termed institutional racism—I am allergic to bad intentions as an explanatory variable for nearly any social problem worth explaining. In the realm of sexual violence and sexual affrontingness, my reservation about the badness of bad men cuts second-wave feminist and what we might queer libertarian. Second wave: the rapist as a *bad man* cleanses ordinary masculinity of its misogynistic violence. I care less what about what was in Brock Turner's head, for a provocative example, than about 1) the gendered consequences of his actions and 2) the disconcerting but unsurprising possibility that if it had not been Brock Turner who sexually assaulted Chanel Miller it could have easily been another drunken frat brother.[120] And yet, queer libertarian: we should be extremely reluctant to punish sexual fantasies, even or especially the "bad" fantasies.[121] For another provocative example, when it comes to the men we have collectively determined are indeed the *really bad ones*, the child molesters and the pedophiles, I think that if the "child" in question is not a child but an adult decoy, an undercover police officer, or altogether nonexistent, the really bad man with really bad intentions has committed no crime at all, not even attempt.[122] I see no benefit, or no benefit worth the cost, of incarcerating men who fantasize about molesting a child but do not do so for all sorts of reasons, chief among them that there is no child to molest.

All this individualizing, localizing focus on nasty and lecherous men, though, could make one lose sight of the more sanguine correlate: the varieties of public sex practices that we might want to revalue, and that the aforementioned feminist and queer of color scholars have revalued, as benign, amusing, mildly to moderately inconvenient, or politically potent. We might then think about the wicked intent of the flasher as an exception to a norm of public sex accommodation. The Model Penal Code (MPC), a highly important, influential model of standardized penal law first drafted by legal scholars in the postwar period, comes close to that very position:

> A person commits a misdemeanor if, for the purpose of arousing or gratifying sexual desire of himself or of any person other than his spouse, he exposes his genitals under circumstances in which he knows his conduct is likely to cause affront or alarm.[123]

Notice the diminution and circumscription. First, the MPC categorizes indecent exposure as a misdemeanor, not a felony. Second, exposure will only be indecent, which is to say misdemeanant, if it is for getting off or getting someone else off—pranks, public urination, and wardrobe malfunctions will not cut it. Third, butts and boobs get a pass under the model statute, since genitals are definitionally limited to vulvas, clitorises, penises, and scrotums.[124] Fourth and most permissively, the *knowledge* requirement for the circumstantial element "likely to cause affront or alarm" provides significant shelter from liability, at least on its face, for the men playing in parks, beaches, and other cruising spots (still, I would substitute "affront" with "fear" or even "fear of sexual assault"). What makes a cruising spot fit for cruising is that sexual activity therein will *not* cause affront or alarm, but rather will cause tumescence. On the one hand, the circumstantial provision summons queer spaces and queer publics: anywhere you and your paramours are "aware"[125] that genital exposure is *un*likely to affront or alarm is a *safe space*, so to speak. On the other hand, if nakedness qua nakedness is presumptively affronting, then heteronormative jurisdictions and sensibilities may be a fait accompli and queer gerrymandering, so to speak, thereby made illicit. The circular problem is that, for instance, the public display of female breasts might desensitize, or de-"affront," the public to exposed female breasts, but those breasts cannot be so displayed as long as the public is considered always already "affrontable." Put in less Sisyphean terms, the political and cultural labor necessary to accommodate sex in public—although the aforementioned female breast example is best comprehended as a case for "sex equality" rather than a case for "public sex"[126]—cannot entail sex in public, at least at first, but rather queering collective sensibilities or colonizing straight space. Fifth and finally, the MPC statute makes no mention of zones of publicity or privacy. Inculpating circumstances could very well be a private dinner party late at night; exculpating circumstances could very well be Central Park in the middle of the day, provided you have located the right bush.

As Posner and Katharine Silbaugh documented over a generation ago, states' and municipalities' actual proscriptions against nudity, indecency, and public sex vary considerably, and most criminalize a broader range of conduct, and with weaker intent requirements, than the MPC.[127] One common statutory provision—found in Louisiana's "obscenity" law—is instructive for our thinking about the failed antisodomy law repeal bill in Louisiana, specifically, but also for our theorizing the objectionability of sex in public more generally. Let's call it the *child clause*.

Many states add an "in the presence of a child" provision to their criminal obscenity/public indecency statutes. The flavor of the child clauses suggests strict liability—whether one "knows" that he is "likely to cause affront or alarm" is likely immaterial if an actual minor is nearby. Consider the child clause of Louisiana's obscenity statute, which, not incidentally, makes moot all the performed anxiety among religious leaders and state officials that the repeal of the state's sodomy law would usher in an era of unrestrained gay sex across state parks (although such anxiety, however performed, could never be made moot by something like a fact):

> When a violation of [the obscenity statute] is with or *in the presence of an unmarried person under the age of seventeen years*, the offender shall be fined not more than ten thousand dollars *and* shall be imprisoned . . . for not less than two years nor more than five years, without benefit of parole, probation, or suspension of sentence.[128]

That is some harsh stuff. If someone "intentional[ly]" "expos[es]" her "pubic hair" or her "female breast nipples" (seriously) for the purposes of "arousing sexual desire," and a teenager walks by, she is in grave trouble.[129] Other violations of the statute, not involving minors, "receive benefit of parole, probations, or suspension of sentence." In the *absence* of a teenager, and upon first conviction for obscenity, the minimum-maximum ranges of fines and prison sentences are far less severe ($1,000 to $2,500 and six months to three years, respectively).[130] And the fine and imprisonment for obscene conduct not-near a child are *disjunctive*, but *conjunctive* for obscene conduct near one. To summarize: obscene conduct in the presence of a child receives a fine *and* a prison sentence with no avenues for leniency.

Let us assume having sex with a young child is not a good idea for a whole variety of reasons, incapacity to consent not being the best of them.[131] In Louisiana, having sex with anyone under seventeen is not a good idea either, if you are at least four years older than the teenager or you have not married her.[132] And we might surmise too that purposefully exposing your genitals to a(n unwilling?) teenager, or purposefully engaging in sexual contact in front of a(n unwilling?) teenager is also not a good idea, although in such instances what the child's young age might be a proxy for is the increased likelihood that she does not want to be there and cannot easily leave. But the question I keep skirting because it is never not dangerous to ask, let alone answer, is: *What is the presumptive harm or legal violation if a child happens upon a guy going down on another guy in a park?* It seems unlikely witnessing such an act invariably leads to trauma and irreparable sequelae. We are familiar with the potential consequences of "secondhand smoke on unwilling bystanders," but what are the consequences of second-hand sex?[133] Why is Nussbaum's defense of gay public sex qualified, conditioned even, by shielding such sex "especially from children"?[134] There are not too many studies out there on the effects of children's seeing public sex or nudity. Would such children necessarily or even likely feel violated, or are we feeling violated on their behalf? Might the child more likely be curious or embarrassed than traumatized or otherwise damaged? The assumption that witnessing a sex act harms the child is colored by the doxa that sex harms children, just like the assumption that because sex without consent is wrongful, so must be seeing sex (or nudity) without consent. In both cases, the slippage is understandable but unsupportable, lubricating punitive, panicked imaginaries, if not regressive state laws.

Stuart Green proposes, as already considered, that in cases where a witness has assumed the risk of indecent exposure, the exhibitionist should avoid liability. One of his examples is of special relevance: "if [the witness] attends a parade in the French Quarter of New Orleans on Mardi Gras, it is quite likely she will see people flashing and mooning."[135] In such an instance, argues Green, there is no legal wrong or there should not be. I am inclined to go one step further: if you bring your child to the Quarter on Mardi Gras, she might see boobs. I think the boob-shower has committed no legal wrong. As with Joel Feinberg's Nasty Bus: whether the other passengers in transit are sixteen, nineteen, or fifty should have little to no bearing on whether the obscene/offensive activity at issue should be considered tortious, criminal (rarely, but take Feinberg's "Story 7" and "Story

8" in which passengers sit beside you, eat "live insects, fish heads, and pick-led sex organs" of farm animals, puke [Story 7] or defecate [Story 8], and then consume their vomit or feces[136]), or just especially irksome. Let me be clear that I am not advocating the dissolution of all age distinctions in law and life. An ordinance that reduces vehicle speed limits around schools is sensible and none too phobic. Elsewhere I have argued that adolescents be recognized as a "separate sex class under law," for whom we should codify an affirmative consent standard[137] along with heightened restrictions on sex in vertical relationships of power.[138] But age distinctions are only and always proxies, sometimes good ones, sometimes less so, and I am unconvinced that age distinctions (and strict liability clauses) in indecent exposure law are a justifiable proxy for anything.

In our case, the festival might not be Mardi Gras but Southern Deca-dence, a many-decades-old raunchy gay festival in New Orleans, and the witness, a child, might observe men making out, grabbing each other's butts, or even stroking each other's cocks outside a gay leather bar. In this scenario, I think the best answer to the question *What is to be done?* is: if watching the exchange of hand jobs between men is not your or your child's thing, walk away from the gay leather bar. And "quite apart from the point that visual affronts are more easily avoided (we can shut our eyes more easily than our noses and ears)," reminds Feinberg, "the visual sense seems less vulnerable to affront than the others. . . . Eyesores, so called, are for the most part not as great nuisances as noisome stenches and loud or grating sounds."[139] (Although, as I will speculate in a moment, public sex absorbs our attention distinctly; generally, it is harder to avert our eyes from nudity or sex than from, say, an antichoice protester. Feinberg agrees: "part, but only part, of the explanation of that displeasure, no doubt rests on the fact that nudity and sex acts have an irresistible power to draw the eye and focus the thoughts on matters that are normally repressed." The question is: why?[140])

But what if it is your child's thing? A counterthesis: what concerns the conservative Louisiana state legislators who refused to repeal the sodomy law, and what concerns the conservative Christian lobbyists who lobby them, is not that their children might be averse to public gay sex but intrigued by it.[141] The "problem" with gay sex in (partitioned) publics is that it might model how to have gay sex. In which case, the progressive response to anti-sex alarmism should not be *Oh stop it, the gays aren't doing that anymore*, but rather, *Your kid* especially *might need to see some gay sex* (but really gay sociality).[142] And not because, finally, protogay kids ought to witness queer sex to realize their true gayness, but because public experiments in sex, nudity, and intimacy might relax, rather than rebind, our attachments to prescribed, preclusive sexual identity.[143]

Conclusion: Incest Palimpsest

In the same year the Louisiana Legislature voted to retain its unconstitutional sodomy law,[144] it also voted to recategorize incest as sodomy, a crime against nature (CAN), in its criminal code. I suggested at the beginning of this chapter that the legislative decision was likely a tactical one to reconstitutionalize CAN after *Lawrence* (2003), after the arrests of men looking for sex with other men in Baton Rouge parks (2013), and before an incoming bill to repeal the law (2014). Now, I take the occasion of bad faith lawmaking to propose that the lawmakers knew not what they did or did more than what they knew; or rather, that the specter of incestuous sex is indeed linked with sodomitical sex, and so too with public sex, but at the level of our collective unconscious. Such a hypothesis is frustratingly unfalsifiable and spectacularly speculative, but I hope to convince you anyway. That public sex recalls, unconsciously, incest, does not make it wrongful but rather distinctly distracting and discomfiting. At the same time, and also like some incestuous relations, public sex invites possibilities for newfound social and sexual affiliations in syncopation with the political paraidentitarianism I champion throughout this book.

In *Antigone's Claim*, Judith Butler reminds us that aversion to homosexuality, homosex, and queer family formations is proximate to, if not a manifestation of, the incest taboo:

> Consider that the horror of incest, the moral revulsion in compels in some, is not that far afield from the same horror and revulsion felt toward lesbian and gay sex, and it is not unrelated to the intense moral condemnation of voluntary single parenting, or gay parenting, or parenting arrangements with more than two adults involved. . . . These various modes in which the oedipal mandate fails to produce normative family all risk *entering into the metonymy of that moralized sexual horror that is perhaps most fundamentally associated with incest.*[145]

Butler dilutes these otherwise seismic claims with a bunch of qualifiers ("not that far afield," "not unrelated to," "risk entering into," "perhaps most fundamentally associated with"). Nevertheless, Butler draws out these chains of equivalence through their extensive consideration of Antigone's defiant decision to give a proper burial to her brother Polyneices despite Creon's royal decree against doing so. The relevant point for my purposes, and one Butler insists upon, is that Antigone's performance, in speech and conduct (and in speech as conduct) throws into crisis normative gender, sexuality, and kinship relations: "The insistence on *public* grieving is what moves her away from feminine gender into hubris, into that distinctively manly excess that makes the guards, the chorus, and Creon wonder: Who is the man here?"[146] In burying her brother who is also her nephew (for she is daughter and sister of Oedipus, as Polyneices is son and brother), her "performative repetition . . . reinstates kinship as a public scandal"[147] or "kinship trouble."[148] And yet Antigone troubles kinship, gender, and sexuality not only because Oedipus fucked his mother but also because

> in acting, as one who has no right to act, [Antigone] upsets the vocabulary of kinship that is a precondition of the human, implicitly raising the question for us of what those preconditions really must be. . . . Antigone is the occasion for a new field of the human, achieved through political catachresis, the one that happens when the less than human speaks as human, when gender is displaced, and kinship founders on its own founding laws.[149]

Readers familiar with Butler's earlier scholarship will sense the gay-and-lesbian-affirmative, protopolitics churning in the background of their gloss. If slightly tendentious, it is such a protopolitics I want to press upon in my brief for public sex, despite and because of its connotation of both incest and the incest taboo.

In acting out, acting publicly, manly, as a man, as sister/aunt yet political actor, Butler's Antigone is, at first, a threat to the order of things, symbolic and real: who rules and is ruled? Who belongs where, doing what, and with whom? Who is intelligibly gendered and politicized as "human?" Civilizational crisis adheres to the figure of Antigone, a crisis that (literally) derives from and devolves back into incestuous disorder: Antigone as *a threat to the order of things*. But Antigone is also, secondly, a promise for (without being an agent of[150]) alternative, more pluralistic, more forgiving, less panicked, less phobically organized sexual and intimate associations, associations that prefigure paraidentitarianism: Antigone as *a prologue for pluralistic intimate associations*. As with the figure of Antigone, so goes the public park sodomites of Baton Rouge, or more precisely the fantasy of them (not only) in the conservative mind.

A Threat to the Order of Things

Butler's meditation on Antigone, and on Antigone's fate as an invitation to theorize what "might be fatal for heterosexuality in its normative sense," recalls for Butler the "radical socialists" of the 1970s "who refused monogamy and family structure," but who then came to regret their wholesale rejection. "It seemed to me," writes Butler, that the [socialists'] turn to psychoanalysis, and, in particular, to Lacanian theory, was prompted in part by the realization by some of those socialists that there were some constraints on sexual practice that were necessary for psychic survival and that the utopian effort to nullify prohibitions often culminated in excruciating scenes of psychic pain.[151]

So Butler links the cursed fate of Antigone and, critically, Antigone's insistently *public* performance of troubled kinship, with a collective sense of social and psychic undoing, thousands of years later, among left intellectuals and activists. I am proposing that the figure and fantasy of the public sodomite, like the figure and fantasy of the "public woman" (Antigone, or sex workers in New Orleans), taps incestuous possibility in our collective unconscious, and so therefore triggers the fear of societal decline, implosion: a hedonic, violent, irresistible, unbearable, fatal fuckfest. Writing on French and U.S. cinema in the second half of the twentieth century, Damon Young arrives at the same point: "The intrusion of women's and queer sexualities into the public sphere also inspires converse fantasies of civilization's demise."[152]

If sublimation is the condition of possibility for civilization, sex in civilized and civilizing publics—a blowjob at the neighborhood barbecue, or "a man and woman locked in sexual embrace at high noon in Times Square"[153]—threatens to spiral us out of order, overpowering our capacities of cooperation and deliberation. Sex in public undoes the social contract or invites us to, undermining by metonymic association the tabooness of the taboo that compels exogamous, procreative social order. "Homosexuality in particular," avers Young,

> is conceived as privileging of individual pleasure over social responsibility. The discourse of the republican social contract pits the idea of a selfish individual seeking only his or her own gratification against the "public good," where the public corresponds to a social order taken to be founded on heterosexual filiation.[154]

That is, *exogamous* heterosexual filiation. In the context of the United States, we could also add *white*. Christina Sharpe shows both how racial "amalgamation" signifies unnatural sexuality but also how the incest taboo selectively operates under enslavement, so that white men's sexual violence against their Black daughters was not cognized as violation of kin but as continuation of property, a civilizational diacritic that haunts "postslavery" subjects and subjectivity.[155]

As we saw in the Introduction to this book, Oliver Davis and Tim Dean aver that sex tout court—and not just public sex, sodomitical sex, and commercial sex—"is a destabilizing force that tends to undo individual and social ordering."[156] Under Davis and Dean's psychoanalytic account, "sexual pleasure—specifically, its centrifugal propensity for unbinding—threatens my sense of myself as coherent being with secure boundaries."[157] The unbinding quality of sex is why we—and it's a universal *we* they posit—share, as their book title announces, a "hatred of sex." Sex disrupts or dissolves our otherwise fixed identities, secure attachments, and sense of group-belonging that give meaning to our lives and relationships.

Davis and Dean overstate both the power and hatred of sex. A lot of sex just isn't good enough to be hated. Sometimes sexual pleasure is not so centrifugal; it's just better than whatever else is on offer, like reading a student's paper or another Netflix show. But I draw upon Davis and Dean's insights because I think their thesis better applies to my case, sex in public, than to theirs, sex outright. And here I do not actually mean sex in public but rather the specter of it, in this instance conjured by Louisiana police officers, conservative lobbyists, and state representatives. The specter of sex in public is indeed unbinding, disorganizing, and centrifugal, inculcating civilizational meltdown, bodies and persons out of place. "Privates" in public erode social and hierarchical organization and community cohesion, tempting us toward an equalizing[158] animality—*you and me baby ain't nothing but mammals.*[159]

It seems noncoincidental that effigies[160] of children recur in public deliberations over sex in public—in Baton Rouge parks, on the streets of New Orleans, at LGBT Pride parades—as if sex in public (and its synecdoche, public nudity) will ultimately and inevitable regress into the violated child. And who will violate the child but the excitable parent protesting/projecting the child's violation?

If you are rolling your eyes, remember that we are talking about the unconscious, which might just make you roll your eyes harder. In any case, it is at last worth reconsidering, with Butler's Antigone in mind, Louisiana legislators' decision to absorb the crime of incest into the crime against *nature*. Psychoanalytically speaking, the legislators' decision is a mistake: incest and public sex are all too natural, a crime against *civilization*.

Let me offer one more political anecdote—one that also took place in Baton Rouge and also revolves around an unsuccessful legislative effort to decriminalize consensual sex practices—to shine light on the incest palimpsest of public sex.

In May 2021, the Administration of Criminal Justice Committee of the House of Representative of Louisiana heard over three hours of testimony, mostly in support of Representative Mandie Landry's bill to decriminalize all forms of consensual commercial sex in the state of Louisiana.[161] These hearings, remarkable for foregrounding so many voices of sex workers and sex worker organizers in official state proceedings, motivated the fifth chapter of this book, which builds out an argument for a constitutional right to prostitution. For now, I focus on a tiny but telling moment of the hearings, when Representative Marcus Anthony Bryant, a supporter of Landry's decriminalization bill, offered his closing comments.

After inquiring about under- or unremedied sexual violence against sex workers, Representative Bryant worries aloud about "the idea of women, um, being ok to sell their body [sic] and do this in the homes of *minor kids* . . . seems like it could be very unhealthy and problematic for us to go forward and legalize it and make that ok."[162] Representative Landry diplomatically explains to Representative Bryant (again, a *supporter* of the decriminalization bill) that sex work already takes place in people's homes and reassures him that she too would hope children are well cared for by "trusted adult[s]."[163] Now unsettled, Representative Bryant replies with threadbare coherence:

> For any parent or any person has a child—to see your father or your mother with a person that you know is not your family member and a person that you know is not your dad or your mom is traumatic in itself. No child wants their parent around anybody of the opposite sex [sic] going into a closed room and closing the door. My kids with their own mom don't want me locking the door. So let alone that is a traumatic experience and that does sit with a kid for a long period of time, when you see a child or your mom or dad with somebody of the opposite sex going into a locked room or door where they can't have access to that parent, that in itself is trauma.[164]

Representative Landry is speechless: "I, um, thanks, I don't, I don't know what to say to that."[165] Talk about a brush with the Real.

Representative Bryant has transformed a bill to decriminalize sex work and sex work solicitation into the primal scene, in which the child, now Bryant's, is traumatized by (the fantasy of) his parents, or one parent, violated by sex. Notice how the interchangeability of the parent's partner undermines Bryant's very point: whether the father fucks the sex worker (and the sex worker is always a "woman" for Bryant, despite Landry's gentle reminder that sex workers come in all genders) or fucks the other parent, there the child sits, equally sexually violated by violative sex just behind the closed door. In fact, for the child to be properly traumatized, the only necessary condition for her parent's partner is that she be of the "opposite" sex, mobilizing while naturalizing exogamous heterosexualization as the presumptive, exclusive resolution against the incest taboo.[166] But what exactly is predicatively traumatizing for the child (that is, to what does Bryant's repeated use of the demonstrative pronoun *that* refer)? Is it that the child knows that the parent is having sex? Is it that the child fantasizes that the parent is having sex? Or is it, finally, that the child "can't have access to that parent" for himself, as his own, the fantasy of the closed door the projection for where he wishes to be?

I am dwelling on Representative Bryant's child sex panic because it is instructively uncanny, absurd but familiar, like we knew the sexualized child was coming even though she has no place here, just as she arrived so unexpectedly, all too expectedly, to quash the antisodomy law repeal bill in 2014. Bryant's concern is that the sky may fall if we categorically decriminalize sex work, but the metaphor he reaches for is not the sky falling but the child violated, violated by his parent, by his parent's sexual decisions. For Bryant—and maybe for all of us—the normative out-of-placeness of the sex worker (and Antigone), her public sexuality and her sexualized personhood, call back incestuous disorder. She uproots the sexual, gendered, generational divisions of the private home that we lethally imagine to be otherwise safe for women and children. "The protected zone of the home is currently one of the riskiest places to have sex."[167] Despite hours of testimony from sex workers that criminalization endangers them, they are figured not as endangered but dangerous, and dangerous because incest-signifying. Overstated: all the slippery slopes lead here, gratuitous sexualities—for money, in the butt, in the bushes—sliding into incest, the taboo no longer taboo, sublimation desublimated, civilization game over.

While many gender studies and cultural studies scholars have demonstrated how the figure of the innocent child is mobilized for regressive, conservative, and phobic political projects, I am suggesting, by way of sex workers in New Orleans and sodomites in Baton Rouge, that the about-to-be-violated innocent child may also be put into discursive circulation as a displacement for and condensation of otherwise inarticulable incestuous desire. Public sex or its possibility activate the "moralized sexual horror" of incest, a horror manifested in yet mystified by the child, a horror that portends horrors, the end of everything good and right as we know it.[168] The specter of incest is evermore activated by arguments for gay rights and public sex lodged in *consent*—rather than, say, equality or anticarceral principles—as we might make horrible, horrifying choices. Calling out consent to incestuous relations as "problematic" does not necessarily make it so;[169] to the contrary, our very darkest fears of incest may be that we might choose it, not that we cannot.[170]

A Prologue for Pluralistic Intimate Associations

Butler has hope for Antigone yet, for her resuscitation in queer political imaginaries. By way of brief conclusion, I relay Butler's simple but smart final shave on *Antigone* and Antigone: if social and sexual organization are driven by the incest taboo, this does not necessarily mean that social and sexual organization must be so narrow, heterosexual, monogamous, and unforgiving, even if other, alternative, intimate kinship arrangements distinctively call back incest under present (or late 1990s?) cultural norms.[171] What, Butler is intimating, might be possibilities for sex, intimacy, and kinship in between motherfucking and father-killing, on the one hand, and exogamous, monogamous marriage, on the other? Butler's intimation recalls their earlier gloss on psychoanalytic accounts of incest, in which they point out that "the oedipal conflict presumes that heterosexual desire has already been *accomplished*. . . . [I]n this sense, the prohibition on incest presupposes the prohibition on homosexuality, for it presumes the heterosexualization of desire."[172]

Butler cannot help but be identitarian in *Antigone's Claim* and *The Psychic Life of Power* even as, in both texts, they make anti-identitarian gestures for us to rethink our sexual selves, not-so-defensively-taxonomized, and our relational selves, not-so-marital.[173] The charge of identitarianism is no dig: Butler is thinking through the psychic strongholds of pervasive, violent homophobia and how to release their grip, a scholarly effort as desperately needed, if not more so, in the 2020s United States as it was in the late 1990s.

On the other hand, the "public woman" and the public sodomite impel not only alternative arrangements of sex, intimacy, and kinship, but also an alternative possibility for sexual politics. I have separated, both analytically and textually, the sex workers of New Orleans (Chapter 1) from the public sodomites[174] of Baton Rouge (Chapter 2), and such separation makes sense for geographical, historical, political, and identitarian reasons. What is mystified, however, in accepting the journalistic and political terms on their face ("sex workers"; "gay men"), is the shared experiences among these groups, namely, as citizen-targets of state violence, and citizen-targets of state *sexual* violence, for *soliciting or performing oral and anal sex in nominally public spaces.* When police officers sexually assault women made vulnerable by their CANS convictions, or police arrest and humiliate men seeking out other men in the park, or even when legislators refuse to decriminalize oral and anal sex—thus endangering sex workers, queers, and queer sex workers alike—we ought to comprehend these episodes as state-sanctioned sexual violence.[175] What might a responsive sodomitical politics, organized around orality and anality, look like? I am suggesting that it might in part be identity formations and identitarianism, along with the normative domestication of sexuality, that inhibits us from developing and then defending a public sexual culture, a sexual culture anchored not in our intersectional differences but in our sodomitical sameness.[176]

In surveying the public sexual culture of nineteenth-century Paris, historian Andrew Israel Ross "trace[s] how certain categories—the female prostitute, the male homosexual, the 'normal' Parisian—remained rather murky when approached through an analysis of space." Ross "argue[s] that urban space brought the three groups together without necessarily defining them as different from one another. *Sexual identity thus fails to capture the significance of their encounters*."[177] Later in the monograph, Ross makes the rather startling claim that "the female prostitute enabled the eventual emergence of the homosexual."[178] He proposes that the same state surveillance and regulatory mechanisms that propelled "the apparent coherence of the category of the prostitute," when applied to men who had sex with men, helped create the category of the male pederast, or the homosexual. Where once men who had sex with men were not seen as types of persons or a sexual subclass, police and other authorities' treatment of women who sold sex as irredeemably *prostitutes* carried over to their approach of male pederasty. The solidification of the (male) homosexual as an identity form was propelled by policing that "increasingly focused on maintaining order on the streets."[179] The model for regulating men who had sex with men was the regulation of women who sold sex. Oversimplified, the latter became "prostitutes," the former "homosexuals."

I doubt social identities can be volitionally unmade, but they can be de- or repoliticized. I would like to reverse engineer the historical process Ross spells out for us. In nineteenth-century Paris, public nonnormative sex acts were policed into nonnormative sexual identities. In twenty-first-century New Orleans and Baton Rouge, nonnormative sexual identities were policed because of their attendant nonnormative public sex acts. I started this chapter by supposing that the identitarian response to the charge that men were having sex with each other indiscriminately in parks (a charge designed to defeat the antisodomy decriminalization bill) would be: *lies! homophobia!* And the anti- or at least nonidentitarian thesis that took up the bulk of this chapter, in scattershot form, was to canvas what exactly is wrong or right about indiscriminate sex in parks, or public sex. The utopian, paraidentitarian parting shot I want to end with is this: imagine a politico-sexual alliance calibrated not only to LGB or T but also to unpoliced oral and anal sex, which is to say sexual freedom by way of accommodating public sexual culture (without accommodating wicked men in trench coats). There would surely be a lot more people under our tent.

And not just people. As we will see in the next chapter, an act-focused, ecological, and paraidentitarian commitment to sexual welfare traverses the species divide, too. In the next sodomitical episode from Louisiana, lawmakers relocate bestial sex out of its antisodomy statute and into a free-standing animal sexual abuse law. Ironically, the legislative reform authorizes mass-scale sexualized violence against nonhuman animals, violence blinkered from view by the identitarian personages of the homosexual, the homophobe, the sex predator, the bestialist, and the vegetarian.

3

Hot Dog Sex

Animal Welfare and the Failure of Bestiality Law

With Gabriel N. Rosenberg

In the spring of 2018, when a Louisiana state senator proposed a bill to criminalize "animal sexual abuse," the senator's conservative colleagues accused him and his cosponsors of surreptitiously supporting gay rights.[1] If that sounds confusing yet offensive, you are correct.

What happened? How did identitarian, homophobic feeling creep into legislative debate and popular discussion regarding animal sexual abuse? And is homophobia the only form of identitarianism that misguides our thinking about animal sexual welfare? Short answer: no. As we will show in the following pages, the identitarian specters of the zoophile, the bestialist, the homosexual, and even the vegetarian undercut our ethical assessment of, and legal regulations regarding, animals' suffering and pleasure.

More provocatively, we show that Louisiana's animal sexual abuse law, like similar statutes enacted in the late twentieth and early twenty-first century across the country, exhort the very abuse they proscribe, a cruel irony buttressed and mystified by identitarianism.[2]

Most provocatively, we conclude the chapter by arguing that eating meat might very well be the centerpiece of an ethical program that defends and promotes animal pleasures. Eating meat, that is, but not eating animals.

Let us step back from our preliminary proclamations. In the preceding two chapters, as in the preceding two decades, we have seen that Louisiana's liberal lawmakers and progressive organizers targeted the state's sodomy statutes for criminalizing socially marginal, sexual minority subjects, namely trans and cis women of color sex workers and gay men. Whether successful (the declassification of CANS as a registerable sex offense) or not (the repeal of CAN), these reform efforts were formally identitarian: a point of sustained critique but not wholesale indictment. Across both movements, organizers, attorneys, and state representatives evidenced how seemingly act-based, gender-neutral sex laws denigrated racial minority women and gay men. And in both cases, sodomy laws were faulted for overreaching, for doing too much, for perpetuating phobia under pretexts of social preservation and harm prevention.

In this chapter, liberal lawmakers take aim at sodomy statutes for underperforming, for doing too little, and for neglecting sexual victims. In this sodomitical episode, though, the imagined sexual victims—here victimized by law's absence—are not boys and girls (Introduction), women (Chapter 1), or gays (Chapter 2), but dogs, cats, goats, and horses.

The following section explains why, in Louisiana, the case against animal sexual abuse seemed to be a case for gay rights. We detail the Louisiana legislative reform to synopsize our sodomitical defense of animal (sexual) welfare before schematizing the remaining sections of the chapter.

Gay Rights, Animal Rights, Animal Wrongs

Four years after the failed effort to repeal Louisiana's CAN law, legislators had more success defending the sexual rights of animals than homosexuals; briefly and risibly, the increasing social acceptance of the latter jeopardized protections for the former.

In the spring of 2018, then-state senator J. P. Morrell, in coordination with the Louisiana Humane Society, proposed to replace the four words in Louisiana's CAN law proscribing bestial sex—"or with an animal"—with a freestanding "animal sexual abuse" statute.[3] The CAN language was unspecified and sparse, inapplicable to an array of sexualized horribles people might commit against animals; lawmakers and lobbyists seemed chiefly concerned about the production, distribution, and possession of, as well as profiteering from, human-animal pornography.

Ten conservative state senators, however, voted against Morrell's proposed bill. They charged that the excision of the bestial language from CAN was a covert maneuver to undermine the law's constitutionality.[4] The theory was: Morrell and his colleagues, gay rights supporters, were pulling the "animal" from CAN so that that the law would criminalize only the "unnatural copulation of a human being with another of the same sex or opposite sex," thereby making it unavoidably unconstitutional in light of Lawrence.[5] In truth, CAN was already unconstitutional; the excision of "or with an animal" would render CAN baldly unconstitutional. It appears conservative senators perceived the legislative reform as a follow-up attack from the failure of the sodomy repeal in 2014. One senator called Morrell's bill a "Trojan horse to delete the sodomy law," and for good measure warned that "this bill was written because the far left wants to undermine our other laws [CAN] that protect family and traditional values that the people of Louisiana hold dear."[6] Gene Mills, president of the powerful LFF, clarified that although bestiality "destroys a human soul," he and LFF principally oppose the animal sexual abuse bill for it severs, statutorily and symbolically, bestial sex from gay sex.[7] For Mills and for LFF, bestial sex and gay sex equally endanger the community and its moral order, and for the same reasons. To put this as unequivocally as possible: homophobia mobilized opponents, who re-identitarianized CAN (for remember, CAN criminalized unnatural copulation across all sexes) as state-sanctioned antigay animus, animus they wished to preserve over and against the sexualized suffering of animals.[8]

"God forbid you vote against this bill. Good luck explaining it," Senator Morrell chided his colleagues.[9] The conservative senator holdouts were indeed roundly panned in local and national press.[10] The bill made its way through both houses of the Louisiana State Legislature and Governor John Bel Edwards signed it into law.[11]

To say the new animal sexual abuse law is expansive is an understatement; its relentless specificity about the things one cannot do to or with an animal takes vengeance on the presumptively paltry protections of CAN.[12] We will not enumerate all the law's interdictions and penalties but will highlight instead the provisions that foreground our thesis: that the liberal position, as codified, is as identitarian, phobic, and futile as the conservative position. The conservatives, at least, avow their phobia.

We point to five provisions of the animal sexual abuse statute to evidence that the law is regressive. Under the pretext of protecting animals, the law instead focuses upon the desires and fantasies that emanate from presumptively wicked, perverted men. Rerouting attention onto a sexual identity, the unnamed bestialist, distracts from, but more insidiously legitimates, the lion's share (pun intended) of abuse against animals' bodies, genitals included.[13]

First, the law criminalizes all human "sexual contact" with animals. Sexual contact is broadly defined to include any permutation of genital-anus-mouth interaction across the species divide; a human touching an animal's genitals or anus with any part of their body; and the insertion of any human body part or instrument into an animal's anus or vaginal opening. What makes such contact "sexual" is that it is performed "for the purpose of sexual arousal or sexual gratification, abuse, or financial gain."[14] We realize readers may not care much about the plight of those caught it the law's dragnet, but at least take stock of the diverse population you will find there, uniformly punished: the man who tops the horse; the man topped by the horse; the teenager whose dog licks his peanut-butter-covered testicles; the woman who fellates a bull calf for a pornographic video; a woman who rubs her clitoris while she rubs her cat's vagina; a man who kills a chicken while penetrating its cloaca. The law is a blunt instrument but need not be this blunt. The common denominator across these hypothetical acts is not animal suffering or abuse, but rather that a human derives pleasure from them. It is unseemly human pleasure that drives criminalization.

Second, the law criminalizes "filming, distributing, or possessing pornographic images" of human-animal sexual contact.[15] Again, we are not suggesting you should be friends with a person who does such things, but ponder whether the teenager who has downloaded a video of horses penetrating men's anuses should be thrown into prison. If a stallion is unbothered topping a human, indeed likely enjoys it, it seems all but certain the stallion is not revictimized by the recording, let alone the downloading. This section of the law likely violates the First Amendment too, collapsing ugly expression into injurious conduct.[16] That the law is unconstitutional tells us nothing about whether the provision is morally right or wrong, but the criminalization of bestial pornography, especially possession, hints that the legislators' and activists' motivations may not be explained in full by concern for animal welfare.

The hint that the law's target is bad men rather than animal suffering is borne out by a third provision, that perpetrators convicted of animal sexual abuse are forbidden to be around all other animals and must undergo sex offender treatment.[17] Indeed, mirroring the sex offender regulatory requirement that those convicted of child molestation cannot reside near children, this law runs on a similar assumption about perverse desire as indiscriminate, recidivistic, and uncontrollable. But why would a teenager who downloaded a clip of a horse topping a man also want to fuck his family's parakeet? Mandated sex offender treatment assigns disparate acts to a singular identity with a singular psychology: a bestialist who is disturbed and disturbing, a man we imagine as morally, specially beneath us, his sexual relations with animals wholly unentangled with, and so not implicating, our own cuddly affections.[18]

Fourth, the law stipulates that animal refers to "any nonhuman creature, whether alive or dead."[19] What possible reason is there for criminal law to intervene upon a person who penetrates a dead chicken with his penis before he eats it, our disgust notwithstanding?[20] Which is worse, from the chicken's perspective, getting fucked or killed and eaten? And if the law permits you to eat only the cows with whom you have not had sex, well, the cows might very well have preferred foreplay before slaughter. We assume the "alive or dead" clause was inserted to cover cases where it is factually unclear whether the human perpetrator engaged in sexual contact with the animal before or after he killed it. But if the perpetrator killed the animal while penetrating it, the conduct is surely proscribed under the state's animal cruelty laws, which we turn to anon.[21] If the perpetrator penetrated the animal after killing it, that is weird, but seems to us no more criminally actionable—*as a form of sexual assault*—than penetrating a tube sock.[22]

Fifth and finally—and this is the crown hypocrisy, the law's Pyrrhic provision—the animal sexual abuse statute exempts several forms of conduct from its reach, pertinently "artificial insemination of an animal for reproductive purposes" and "accepted animal husbandry practices, including grooming, raising, breeding, or assisting with the birthing process of animals."[23] These exemptions are ubiquitous across state bestiality laws, and they are or should be astonishing. For the exemptions license the coerced breeding practices, the forced inseminations and castrations, that are at the core of factory farming, and the mass-scale suffering and misery factory farming exacts from livestock. Criminalizing bad men and bad desire while condoning modern breeding practices means we can have our meat and fuck it too. We would venture that the great majority of human-animal genital conduct, probably in the ballpark of 90–99 percent, occurs for the human production and human consumption of meat. And we would estimate that 100 percent of human-animal genital conduct that takes place in the context of industrial agricultural operations is unwanted by the animal (or at any rate, whatever animals might want or not want is wholly irrelevant to the factory farm). This law—RS 14:89.3—promotes the abuse and exploitative use of animals' genitals for human pleasure: meat-eating.

As the debate around and codification of the state's bestiality law illustrates, sexual identity figured front and center for both sides: conservative lawmakers imagined an emancipated homosexual tearing apart the heterosocial fabric; liberal lawmakers imagined the criminalized bestialist, or bestialist pornographer, whose desires, pleasures, and profits would be quashed by law. Neither position substantively realizes animal welfare. We contend that a sodomitical (act-based), hedonic (pleasure-focused) approach better guarantees well-being within and across species divides. And we think that a sodomitical, hedonic approach best fulfills the ethical, not moralistic, motivation behind the animal sexual abuse law: to free animals from human maltreatment and to ensure them prosperous, pleasurable lives. The next part of this chapter historicizes the emergence of bestiality laws in the United States over the past several decades, before we extend our preliminary criticisms of such laws into a disputation of the philosophy animating them. We then briefly explore, and then (nonpolemically) refuse, *consent* as an ethical metric for adjudicating sex between humans and animals, since consent has such magnetizing, normative force for liberals, animal rights activists, and animal rights theorists. The final two sections, drawing upon our interviews with farmers, scholarship on animal welfare, and technological transformations in meat production, articulate a sodomitical, hedonic defense for multispecies flourishing and for the proliferation of pleasures.

Against "Interspecies Sexual Assault"

The transformation of Louisiana's criminal proscription of human sex with animals parallels national trends. Since the Colonial period, most states criminalized human sex with animals through the same statutes that criminalized other nonprocreative sex acts: antisodomy statutes. However, moved by pressure from legal reformers, activists, and the medical community to decriminalize consensual same-sex intimacy, many states repealed those laws beginning in the 1960s. Prosecutors, politicians, and journalists were sometimes surprised to learn, when encountering sensational bestial acts, that sex with animals was no longer illegal in their states, and that a confirmed bestialist might get off.[24]

In the 1980s, some legislators sought to recriminalize sex with animals. These efforts encountered resistance from farmers, veterinarians, and animal breeders, who worried that their regular commercial activities, most notably artificial insemination, would be made illegal. As a result, several of the antibestiality proposals failed. In the 1990s, as Wayne Pacelle, the former president and CEO of the Humane Society of the United States (HSUS) explained, the HSUS began "methodically going state by state to close the gaps in the legal framework."[25] Legislators thus crafted statutes that explicitly and categorically exempted animal husbandry and veterinary medicine. These statutes often won the support of agricultural interests, and the novel alliance of the Humane Society and the farm lobby propelled new laws onto the books, sometimes referred to as "animal sexual assault" or "animal sexual abuse" statutes.[26] In 1990, sex with animals was legal in most U.S. states. As of this writing, forty-eight states have statutes criminalizing bestiality, and there are active campaigns to criminalize it in the two recalcitrant states. Nearly all the new statutes have included the explicit and categorical exemptions for animal husbandry.[27]

The criminologist Piers Beirne offers the most extensive defense of these laws. In his 1997 article, "Rethinking Bestiality: Towards a Concept of Interspecies Sexual Assault," Beirne argues for the adoption of such laws based on three commitments.[28] First, Beirne suggests that old laws (antisodomy statutes) were based in anthropocentrism and that a perspective cleansed of speciesism must recognize animals as victims of sexual violence. Second, animal sexual victimhood is guaranteed by the inability of animals to consent, which renders sex with them categorically harmful and assaultive. Third, the exceptional character of *sexual* harm warrants state intervention.[29] Beirne also pins much or most of "interspecies sexual assault" on "malicious masculinity."[30]

We agree that some men (and occasionally people of other genders) get off on the pain and suffering of animals, and we agree with Beirne, like Carol Adams, that the conduct of such cruel bestialists can reinforce both the speciesist domination of animals and the patriarchal domination of women.[31] Where we disagree with Beirne is almost everywhere else.

Beirne's scholarship on animal sexual abuse offers a philosophical underpinning for the spate of U.S. bestiality laws enacted in the early twenty-first century. Beirne himself gave public testimony to the Maine legislature in support of such a law.[32] Beirne's arguments are influential and misguided, so we take a few moments here to refute them. His proscriptions mirror and more dangerously mobilize not-so-veiled disgust that undermines an honest, queerer account of animal sexual welfare. Beirne's arguments against interspecies sexual assault subscribe to an identitarian logic that excludes an act-based analysis of human-animal sexual conduct, the absence of which makes any ethical assessment of interspecies relationships inadequate from the outset. In turn, Beirne's identitarianism devolves into the very anthropocentrism he aimed to avoid, redirecting our attention away from animals and back onto (presumptively perverted) humans. Toggling between identitarianism and anthropocentrism, Beirne's "interspecies sexual assault" unintentionally legitimates humans' domination and exploitation of animals.

Identitarianism: Beirne buttresses his case against interspecies sexual assault in opposition to a foil: the "pseudo-liberal stance of tolerance fashionable today."[33] In later writing, the pro-bestiality "stance" ballooned into a "pseudo-liberal agenda" that accepts bestiality as "a legitimate orientation that has been consciously chosen and practiced by a few individuals in all societies since the dawn of time."[34] Needless to say, references to an actually existing pro-bestiality movement are in short supply. It is nonetheless crucial for Beirne's case that he imagines such a movement, committed to the "normalization of bestiality as a form of sexual diversity," a form heretofore socially denigrated like, but just as morally respectable as, "gays, lesbians, and other sexual orientations."[35] Conjuring his opponents as vulgar liberal identitarians vying to recognize bestialists with another stripe on the rainbow flag, Beirne effectively frames the question of human-animal genital contact as identitarian all the way down, so that he concerns himself centrally with the bestialist, as a type of person, rather than bestial acts, and the pleasures and pains to which they may give rise. Even as he catalogues "immensely varied" conduct—horses fellated by women,[36] a dog's nipples sucked by a girl,[37] a milked cow,[38] a donkey topped by a young man,[39] Beirne concedes that he does not know what to do with these acts, or how they ought to be ethically parsed. Having defined interspecies sexual assault as "*all* sexual advances by humans to animals," he at once qualifies that "such a principle clearly has inherent problems which I cannot pretend to know how to solve."[40] So unsolvable, Beirne substitutes a finer-tuned consideration of the acts themselves—which surely must be the most important consideration from the animal's perspective—with a four-part typology of people who commit such acts, reinstalling the anthropocentrism he set out to refuse.[41]

Anthropocentrism: Beirne tells us his is an argument against bestiality that will shed archaic, Judeo-Christian, anthropocentric ways of thinking: that sex with animals is wrong because man contravenes divine order, pollutes Nature, downgrades his species-superiority, and might produce "monstrous offspring."[42] Instead, Beirne wants to focus our attention on the sexual abuse suffered by animals, except then he enumerates instead four kinds of bestialists with varying degrees of malevolent intent: the "sexually fixated" zoophile; the man who commodifies the animal for pornographic profit; the experimenting farm boy; and the cruel sadist.[43] Beirne's first anthropocentric move is to turn the gravamen of bestiality back onto human intent emanating from, as Foucault memorably calls them, personages.[44]

Beirne's second anthropocentric move is to collapse distinctions among nonhuman animals, rendering them all, categorically and completely, "beings without an effective voice."[45] In turn, all "human-animal sex" (which seems to be any genital contact between humans and animals, if arousing for the human; although here too Beirne is inconsistent[46]) necessarily "involves coercion[,] . . . produces pain and suffering, and violates the rights of another being."[47] As Sunaura Taylor reminds us, it is the insistence on animals' voicelessness that robs them of their voice, such that we refuse to recognize rather obvious signs of pleasure, satisfaction, pain, or fear because of our affective, political attachments to their helplessness.[48] Beirne perpetuates the human dominion he decries. This is nowhere more apparent than when Beirne surmises that bored-looking horses and cows being fondled by humans are, in actuality, probably disassociating from the trauma of the sex, "a coping strategy for numbing the pain inflicted on them";[49] or psychologizes that a tumescent orangutan who humps a woman likely does so because of prior sexual abuse.[50] These animals are made voiceless so Beirne can assign them the voices he wants, human-sounding, sounding-in-pain.

Beirne's third anthropocentric move is the transposition of human sexual exceptionalism onto other species, as if sexual injury is injurious to animals in the same way it is to us. In the early 1980s, Catharine MacKinnon provocatively and persuasively suggested that rape law's emphasis on penile penetration is epistemically patriarchal.[51] Penetration with a penis might not be the severest form of sexual injury for the woman. Beirne follows MacKinnon's lead, advising that interspecies sexual assault statutes expand definitions of the crime beyond penile penetration into all forms of sexual contact.[52] But this substitutes patriarchy with anthropocentrism, defining what is sexual and sexually injurious for the animal on human terms. Likewise, Beirne's sexual exceptionalism directs him to nonconsent, applying a standard for permissible human-human sexual contact to human-nonhuman animal genital contact. Indeed, not just "consent" but "sexual" itself is anthropocentric, if applied categorically. Is licking peanut butter off human genitals sexual for the dog? Does it make a difference to the cow, phenomenologically, which of her orifices the farm boy penetrates, and whether the farm boy uses his hand or his penis?

Contradictions: Consent at his normative disposal, Beirne proclaims that "bestiality involves sexual coercion because animals are incapable of genuinely saying 'yes' or 'no' to humans in forms that we can readily understand."[53] But no sooner does Beirne make nonconsent the criterion for abuse before abandoning it for intent: "how do we establish a general rule for identifying actions that are physically identical to those defined as interspecies sexual assault but which have a different intent?"[54] But why must we search for that general rule, teasing out intents, if Beirne has already established that animals cannot consent to sexual relations with humans, whatever intent the human possesses? Intent allows milking cows to get a pass, but why? This is not reconcilable with the declaration that nonhuman animals can, under no circumstances, proffer "genuine consent" to genital contact.[55]

While Beirne's anthropocentrism directs him to consent, Beirne's identitarianism directs him to intent, relocating the wrong of interspecies sexual assault away from coercion and onto bad persons; otherwise, we would have to criminalize milking cows, or imprison Beirne's colleague for her "innocent and affectionate suckling" of her dog's nipples when she, the colleague, was a young girl.[56] We cannot have it both ways—or rather we can, which is why twenty-first-century antibestiality laws are disastrous for animals, and all but undetectably, for the laws' moral force appears both obvious and unquestionable.

An interdiction that pivots on nonconsent must cash out at abolition: no milking cows, owning cats and dogs, breeding livestock, eating meat, or zoos.[57] Nor will a "best interest" exemption do much exempting. If animals are as voiceless as Beirne supposes, how would we know their best interests? It may be in the mare's interest not to be nipped, kicked, and penetrated by the stallion, but surely any intervention on the mare's behalf reinstates the sort of human dominion that Beirne and like-minded activists wish to dispel.[58]

Yet an interdiction that pivots on intent cashes out at our unconscionable status quo, with minor corrections (if major criminalization) on the margin: punishing wicked men for getting off on genital contact with animals or punishing wicked men for filming genital contact with animals so other men can get off. But genital contact with animals for food and profit—again, what must account for nearly the entire universe of our sexual use of animals—is untouched, nay authorized, by the interdiction on intent. This is why the Maine statute for which Beirne provided testimony contains the exemption that nearly all state antibestiality laws, Louisiana included, adopt in similar or identical form: bestiality "may not be construed to prohibit normal and accepted practices of animal husbandry."[59] (Note that if a People for the Ethical Treatment of Animals [PETA] activist were to "videotape a person engaging in a sexual act with an animal," say a forced impregnation of a sow, she could be prosecuted for bestiality, but not the principal perpetrator.[60])

We briefly made the point about the cruelty of the agricultural exemption earlier, but here we want to emphasize that the exemption is not coincidental to, but mandated by, Beirne's argument. For his rhetorical gestures to nonconsent and bad intent imagine a sexually coercive scenario analogous to the scenarios of our human world: sexual assault against an unwilling woman or an incapable child. By hovering over nonconsent and malevolence, Beirne invites us to mistakenly see the paradigmatic problem of bestial sex in parallel terms: private and dyadic, coercive and mean, a bad man gratifying himself from sex unwanted by his partner, albeit a boy, woman, or hen. Once that image is in place, the false equivalence makes itself: "human-animal sex is a harm (animal sexual assault) that is wrong for the same reasons as is inter-human assault."[61] The parenthetical does too much work, collapsing human-animal sex into animal sexual assault in order to make what will now be the uncontroversial claim that assault across species is wrong for the same reasons as assault within one. The double equivalence (sex with animals = sexual assault against animals = sexual assault against humans) slides into place only because readers are already primed to know what we see: men fucking chickens, women stepping on kittens. In the parlance of the bestiality statute, these sorts of scenes are abnormal and unacceptable, intent looks pretty ugly, and we can more-than-plausibly read unwillingness off the shrieking kitten.

But the bad, perverted intent threshold writes off "normal and accepted practices of animal husbandry" as, well, normal and accepted. If "interspecies sexual assault" were to have any normative value, would it not be to puncture our sense of the normal and accepted, the everyday breeding practices that inflict horrific suffering upon nonhuman animals? Yet since farmers and agricultural workers are breeding and penetrating animals not for their own "sexual gratification," interspecies sexual assault lets them off the hook.[62]

The nonconsent threshold is both underinclusive and overinclusive. Underinclusive, for the dyadic relation it invokes—an individual man abusing his goat like his child or his wife—redirects our attention away from large-scale breeding practices of agricultural production, practices which can be atrocious for the animals whether or not farmers and laborers get off performing them. One might rejoin that these factory farm animals do not consent to their (sexual) use either, but we are suggesting that the consent imaginary, liberal and individualistic, reorients us to the dyad, to a bad man and his abused pet rather than to an ethically indefensible industry, and to entire political economies anchored in human and nonhuman animal suffering and subordination.[63] The nonconsent threshold is overinclusive too, for once that abusive, dyadic image saturates our thinking about, politicking for, and regulation of animal sexual welfare, the dog licking her owner's testicles is as morally abhorrent as the owner forcibly penetrating the dog. We will tell ourselves this is because dogs cannot consent, but as Beirne's exception for cow-milking makes clear, the wrong loops back to bad personhood and ugly intent.

In any case, what we are left with, and what Beirne leaves us with, is this: laws that punish men for getting their testicles licked by dogs under the pretense of nonconsent (which provides a translucent cover for bad intent), while the same laws permit—promote—wide scale human-animal genital contact under the pretense of benign intent, or profit motive. The scale of political economy absents consent from ethical relevance. "This is interesting," observes gender studies professor Kathy Rudy, for

[h]umans can kill animals, force them to breed with each other . . . and cut them open for science, and for the most part, the humans who perform those acts can be thought of as normal, functioning members of society. Yet having sex with animals remains almost unspeakably anathema.[64]

Professor Beirne, a key advocate of twenty-first-century animal sexual abuse laws, and Senator Morrell, the sponsor of Louisiana's version, in fact both avow that atypical human sexual behavior, rather than animal suffering, directs their joint project. For Beirne states decisively "that human-animal sex is a harm (animal sexual assault) that is wrong . . . whether or not it involves cruelty, [and] it should not be tolerated."[65] Morrell, in defense of his bill, alerted his fellow senators of a now infamous 2009 case from New Jersey, in which a judge dismissed animal cruelty charges against a former police officer who possessed videos of calves fellating him.[66] The judge explained that he did not condone the man's behavior, but that it did not reach the "torment" threshold as required by the state's animal cruelty law.[67] In any case, the cop received a thirty-year prison sentence for sexually abusing three girls,[68] New Jersey enacted an antibestiality law in response to the case (with an "accepted animal husbandry" exemption that winnows its force to a virtue-signal),[69] and the judge was forced into early retirement, largely because of the dismissal.[70] Good thing we're tenured.

Like New Jersey and all other states, Louisiana criminalizes animal cruelty, defined by an array of verbs, among them "torment," "impound," "mistreat," "beat," "injure," and "abandon."[71] Like animal sexual abuse statutes, the exemptions built into animal cruelty laws guarantee the continuity and profitability of animal suffering.[72] Regardless—and here we take the position Peter Singer approached but abandoned[73]—we believe animal cruelty laws properly cover all the conduct that ought to be actionable under animal sexual abuse laws. Or to put this another way: we find it disturbing that the police officer coaxed calves to blow him. But he should be in prison (if anyone should), and he is, not for having oral sex with cows or recording it, but for molesting children.

Consent Complications

We intimated in the previous section that *consent* is mostly unhelpful for elaborating our ethical responsibilities toward animals and their welfare. Yet we are unwilling to dismiss consent entirely.

For many liberals—our colleagues and our students, lawmakers and animal rights activists—consent is the intuitive moral abstraction to proscribe sex with nonhuman animals. The deceptively simple calculation: nonhuman animals cannot consent, ergo we cannot have sex with them.

Fischel has argued against consent as an adjudicative metric for our sexual and nonsexual relationship with animals:

> Consent is undeniably a human construct in relation to human transactions under conditions of human cognition. . . . [C]onsent, conceptually, presupposes a combination of expression, information, reason, and reflection that is unavailable to nonhuman animals. It is this combination that differentiates consent from simple expressions of want or manifestations of an urge, like a dog pawing its owner to be taken out or fed (internal citations omitted).[74]

Fischel's perspective inverts the zoophilic one as synopsized by Rudy:

> [I]n loving relationships, zoophilists suggest, animals can experience such a robust subjectivity that they not only give consent to sexual

acts, they also can initiate those acts, communicate their desires for specific kinds of pleasure, and even opt out of sex if they so choose.[75]

We think it makes more sense to say that, like a young child, an animal may initiate, ask for, and refuse sexual activity, but still not be considered capable of proffering or withholding "consent."

We still think—but with less conviction—that consent is or should be inapplicable in gauging our conduct toward animals, but we would like to augment this categorical criticism in three ways that direct our present argument.

First, there is anthropocentric hubris in gerrymandering consent for ourselves alone, especially given how contested the concept is just within our species. Nods to the varieties of animal intelligence notwithstanding, those nods patronize when we presumptively withhold consent capacities to nonhumans on the bases of "reason," "information," "reflection," and so forth. In other words, we are saying, *You animals may be smart, but c'mon, we are still smarter than you*, and that prior installs the very relations of, and rationales for, our domination, exploitation, and willful imposition of suffering upon animals. "We must first of all not weigh reason like a flag of separateness."[76]

In the past several decades, ethologists, primatologists, biologists, and philosophers have gone to great lengths to show the complexity of animal thought and feeling. Animals suffer; some experience pleasure, seeking out pleasure for pleasure's, and not procreation's, sake.[77] Animals may grieve the loss of offspring, mates, or friends, within and across species.[78] Some demonstrate not only the capacity for cooperation but something like a moral commitment to it.[79] Some animals empathize with others; some manifest a sense of fairness and justice, ostracizing or otherwise penalizing fellow creatures for failing to properly share resources or act reciprocally.[80] These discoveries of animal cognition and emotion are typically put to the task of either illustrating the evolutionary prologues of human beliefs and behaviors or, and often to the contrary, cataloguing the distinctive moral and phenomenological lifeworlds of animals, lifeworlds that may warrant their dispensation from human cruelties. For example, if a mouse violently reacts to her cagemate being injected with burning acid, should such evidence of empathy proscribe injecting mice with burning acid?[81] Our point is not that a particular emotion or mode of cognition warrants particular ethical engagement, but that human humility and openness toward the plurality of nonhuman emotional and cognitive capacities would caution against prematurely writing off any metric, consent included, as always already ethically unavailable.

Evidence of nonhuman animal consent, or something proximate, comes from our nonsexual encounters with them. In a famous study from 2003, Frans De Waal and Sarah Brosnan offered cucumbers and grapes to capuchin monkeys if they retrieved a rock for the researcher.[82] Capuchins favor grapes over cucumbers—who doesn't?—and while the monkeys were content to be rewarded cucumbers for the task, when one saw another receive a grape instead she grew outraged by the favoritism. She chucked her cucumber back at the researcher, banged on her cage, and inspected her barter rock to see if it was defective. The study, follow-up studies with monkeys and other animals, and the subsequent press coverage synopsize that several species comprehend and are affronted by inequity; by a principle of fairness, the capuchin is entitled to the grape like her cagemate.[83] What if, though— and we are not primatologists—the capuchin study and subsequent studies demonstrate not only a sense of fairness but also sense of betrayal, a sense that an unspoken agreement, an agreement tokened by exchange, was contravened?[84]

Nietzsche taught us that only humans are promise-makers, but if monkeys object to promise-breakers, might they be consenting or nonconsenting subjects, too?[85]

In *Entangled Empathy*, philosopher Lori Gruen recounts her experience bringing a children's book to her chimpanzee friend, Sarah. Another chimp snatched the book away from her, and a third chimp snatched it back from the second, returning it to Sarah.[86] So with the grapes, this might be a story about fairness traveling across species divides. It might also be a story about what us humans call bystander intervention. Sarah's prized object was taken from her, unwillingly; a fellow chimpanzee brought Sarah's (Professor Gruen's) possession back to her. Did the bystander have a sense of unwanted, unconsented-to trespass? How would we know?

Nietzsche told us that "dogs believe in thieves and ghosts."[87] Consider the epistemic arrogance to call dogs liars. Consider too, and contiguously, the story and study of a dog who had an anticipatory, possibly telepathic sense of when his owner was returning home.[88] To suppose dogs hold paranormal capacities does not mean, by some odd syllogism, that they are capable of proffering or withholding consent. Instead, we want to suggest it is hubristic to categorically deny this or that capacity from nonhuman animals, and that the denial seems to be more in the service of legitimating human superordination than in the service of facilitating animal welfare. Contiguously and no less invidiously, the unreasoning inferiority of animals posited in contradistinction to consenting humans often facilitates denying full humanity to other *humans*. Identifying so many not-quite-fully-humans, distinguished by race, sex, class, religion, ability, and so on for superintendence, and sometimes for murderous removal, has been a crucial element of what poet and theorist Sylvia Wynter calls the "genre" of "Man": the limitation of the political and social prerogatives of full humanity only to the narrow coordinates of white, Euro-American, capitalist modernity.[89] Our hesitation about dismissing consent prematurely derives less from an affection for the juridical construct itself and more from a curiosity about the rich cognitive lifeworlds that consent-championing aims, clumsily at best, to approximate. Following Black feminist theorist Zakiyyah Iman Jackson's exploration of diasporic African aesthetic reworkings of animality, we propose that imaginatively engaging animal sexual lifeworlds, even if short of codifying animals' sexual agency through law, may help unwind the animal/human binary without, as Jackson also cautions, flattening differences among humans to a derivative function of that very binary.[90]

Second, insofar as the consent criticism repartitions the world along the animal/human binary, it prematurely collapses ethicality along that binary too, as if consent is the right metric for sex when it comes to us humans, and as if there is some singular alternative for the rest of the animal kingdom. Binaries are not wrong by virtue of their being binary, but binary thinking can be lazy. Most likely, the principles that underwrite our (sexual) ethics with animals will vary across, and maybe even within, species, conditioned too by our existing, historically emplotted relations with them. Our obligations to livestock differ from our obligations to companionate animals which differ from animals in the "wild" or in the dumpster around the corner from our home.[91] All this, layered under the ethical obligations that may arise from the degree to which such distinctions—livestock, companionate, wild—are resultant from and contoured by human activity.[92] All this, layered over the ethical obligations that may arise from differences within those very distinctions. A pet goldfish and a pet Chihuahua are both pets; but a Chihuahua, we think, likely needs considerably more attention, supervision, and engagement for her to live a fully flourishing, properly hedonic Chihuahua life.[93]

Finally, to say consent is inadequate at best or inapplicable at worst to gauge our ethical, sexual relations with animals is to say what we are against, a sin for which lefty academics habitually get dinged. So consent (or capitalism or liberalism or multiculturalism or feminism or rights or whatever) is flawed—then what should take its place? See point 2: no singular abstraction ought to govern our encounter with fellow creatures (or humans; see also the Trolley Problem). Nevertheless—and while we will go to the mat for the criticality of the critic—we do, in the pages that follow, want to propose what a better, more pleasurable world might look like for human-animal relations, and some initial ways to get there. What are the salvageable sentiments behind the enactment of Louisiana's animal sexual abuse law, or what sentiments might be reconstructed and repurposed, to deliver a promise that the law at once announces and extinguishes?

While we are less sure about the outright denial of consenting/contract-ing/promising capacities to each and every nonhuman animal of each and every species, we remain skeptical if not cynical that nonhuman animals have a "sexuality" even as they engage in all kinds of nonprocreative, rec-reational, pleasure-purposed, same-sex, poly, allo-, and autosexual activity. By "sexuality" we mean a sense of a sexual identity as special and severable from other parts of the self, and under which sexual desires (and aversions) are burdened with significance over and beyond their object.[94] While "as many as three-quarters of all [Japanese Macaque] females actively seek sexual interactions while they are pregnant," it seems unlikely those mon-keys take pride in, or have a second-order identitarian attachment to, their predilections, or that the other quarter of the female monkeys cognize themselves as a sexual minority subculture.[95] To put this differently: while cases of homosexual sex abound in the animal kingdom, homophobia does not. Or to put this differently still: what difference does it make to a kitten if she is slapped by a human hand or by a human penis? When a farmer sticks his hand inside a pregnant cow to check on the development of the fetus, it is uncomfortable for the cow; but it is not, we suspect, violative in what we think of as a sexual way.[96] In 2016, PETA was pilloried for its advertise-ment comparing sexual violence against women with the "forcible artificial insemination" of livestock. The comparison trivializes women's sexual-ized injury, as critics agreed, but it also both under- and overdescribes the experience for animals. Artificially inseminated cows and pigs neither need nor seek out rape counseling services, nor do they organize Take Back the Night marches to reclaim their subjectivity and sexual agency. But artificial insemination may nevertheless be uncomfortable, painful, or even excruciating.[97]

"Piggy Desires": Hedonic Lives of Small Farm Livestock

"What could it mean to love animals?" asks Kathy Rudy. Rudy takes the human-animal relation to queer theoretically question, among other abstractions, the self-evidential meaning of "sex."[98] We mostly defer the conundrum of what sex is, but we nevertheless wonder what ethical animal sexual contact might look like. So we talked to some farmers.

We were interested in learning from small, avowedly welfare-centered farmers because we wanted to see how they square an ethical commitment to the well-being of farm animals with the economic need to breed them. What kinds of trade-offs exist between those two desires? We doubt large conventional farms could offer much insight into governing animal sex well.[99] Most conventional farms systematically subordinate welfare to prof-itability; they treat animals abysmally and everyone knows it. By contrast, the small farmers we interviewed distinguish themselves from conventional meat producers by financially investing in animal welfare and by making visible their efforts to like-minded consumers. We do not presume that these farmers were right about everything or that they were ethical merely by virtue of being farmers (elsewhere Rosenberg has questioned social deference to agrarianism).[100] Still, we can think of no group of people who must navigate the trade-offs of the overlap between sexual ethics and animal welfare more frequently than small, welfare-centered farmers. A more poetic, challenging version of the trade-off question again comes from Rudy: "Can you love someone and still kill her?"[101] Or yet: can we befriend the animals we breed?[102]

To begin answering something like these questions, we interviewed five farmers on three small farms, all within a two-hour drive of New Orleans (Figure 3.1). We pseudonymize the farmers, for we worry that a Google search linking their names to two lefty professors questioning the utility and ethicality of bestiality laws might jeopardize the farmers' reputations and livelihoods. We have extracted some principles from those conversations that they—and now we—find useful for theorizing animal sexual welfare. In order of precedence, they are *empathetic speciesism*, *particularity*, *capacities*, and *autonomy*.

Figure 3.1 Happy-looking pigs, among them co-author Rosenberg, on a small farm outside New Orleans.

Caleb, a native Louisianan, attended Louisiana State University in the early 2000s, where he enrolled in a food policy course that ignited his interest in sustainable farming. Learning about the havoc industrial agriculture wreaks on soil, the environment, population health, and animal welfare, Caleb purchased farmland in 2010, dropped out of LSU to enroll in an intensive farming program in New England, and began farming in earnest in 2013. Notably, Caleb told us that his commitment to animal welfare is an outgrowth of his commitment to environmental regeneration. Caleb raises cows, hogs, and chickens, brings the hogs and cows to a processing unit for slaughter (he and his staff kill the chickens on site), and sells meat through a butcher shop he opened a few years ago and directly to consumers. Caleb's farm was the largest of the three we visited. On Caleb's golf cart cruising through meadows and pastures, we observed hogs and cattle roaming freely; they appeared healthy and, if you will forgive the anthropocentrism, happy.[103]

Andy and Sue met at a bar in Louisiana and soon discovered a shared passion for aquaponics and raising the animals they eat. After Andy's service in the navy, the couple initially settled in Fort Wayne, Indiana, but sought a more rural life for themselves and their two daughters, away from "all the soccer mommies," as Sue put it.[104] So they relocated to a small town in Louisiana, but too close to an industrial pig farm. The smell was horrible and they would encounter "piles of dead pigs" next to their property.[105] They moved again to yet another farm town but the stench and conditions of the industrial farm had strengthened their resolve to raise their own animals, to give them better lives and more humane deaths. Their own pigs, they figured, would taste better too. Andy and Sue now raise, breed, and slaughter cows, ducks, chickens, goats, and pigs. Andy occasionally posts YouTube videos of operations on the farm, or of newly built constructions like coops and dens that make life more pleasant for their nonhuman dependents.

Like Andy and Sue, Frank and Kim's coupling together preceded their farming together. Frank is from rural Louisiana, where as a teenager he worked jobs composting and spreading manure. Kim was raised near soy and corn farms in Wisconsin. In 2009, Kim traveled to New Orleans to assist in post-Katrina reconstruction projects. She first met Frank at his gardening store where she went to buy compost and worms. Together, Frank and Kim purchased farmland and in 2014 they opened a small nursery where they sell meat, eggs, vegetables, and other products from their farm and neighboring farms. Of all our interviewees, Frank and Kim were the most politically conscious about their farming. Frank describes Michael Pollan's *The Omnivore's Dilemma* as his "gateway drug," and both Frank and Kim are impelled to till land and steward animals regeneratively, with great attention to avoiding pollutants and unnecessary hormones.[106] Kim expressed ethical concern for their animals' welfare per se, whereas Frank conceded that his concern was motivated more by self-interest. He wants (and wants to sell) meat that tastes good, that is not riddled with hormones, or that is too fatty.[107]

The farmers operated from a perspective we call *empathetic speciesism*.[108] They made extensive efforts to understand the world from the perspective of their livestock. But the farmers did not question the structural forces and cognitive differences that superordinated their judgments. Instead, they sounded superordination in the language of "stewardship." Superordination (we might say "human privilege") gave the farmers an ethical responsibility to govern their animals well, to provide them with the things that made their lives worth living, and to protect them from harm and suffering. Good farm governance requires balancing competing interests. All of the farmers fenced their livestock. After all, a cow might wander onto a road looking for new tender grasses. The differing cognitive capacities generally captured by "species" generates ethical responsibility for the farmers. If the farmer dismisses speciative difference—for example, if a farmer treats the cow's judgments as equal to her own—that farmer will be ethically negligent and the cow could be hit by a truck. "Freedom and autonomy for animals," we are averring, and in agreement with philosopher Martha Nussbaum, "are not incompatible with intelligent human stewardship."[109]

The farmers treated speciative categories with warranted ambivalence. The category of species could tell them some important things, but not everything. The farmers recognized the obvious anatomical, behavioral, and cognitive differences not only between themselves and their livestock but, importantly, also among pigs, chickens, goats, and cows. For example, we asked Caleb to explain what he saw as the key differences between "pig society" and "cow society," and he comfortably generalized along those speciative lines. If left to their own devices, he suggested, pigs would not get much done. They were often more creative than cows, but they were also lazier and individualistic. Cows were capable of more complex organization and problem-solving. He gave the example of a fence separating a hungry herd from fresh grass. One cow alone would not have much of a solution, but the herd would work together to knock over the fence.[110] Yet "there is no one way to be chimpanzee or goat or chicken, just as there is no one way to be human."[111] Andy and Sue agree that animals of the same species share ways of being in the world—they "communicate" and "organize" differently—but they also emphasize that individual animals' behavior varies dramatically, in ways that matter. They have personalities, habits, moods, and predilections that are distinct and defined. Sue mused about their "Queen Bee" goat named Missy. Missy "is determined to be in charge" and will frequently reestablish caprine social order by butting the other goats' heads. Because she has the horns, she wins.[112]

Particularity is our simple term for farmers' attention to differences across and within species. As a farmer obtains a more granular appreciation for what makes life worth living to a particular animal, she is better positioned to evaluate an animal's interests and to maximize its welfare. If *empathetic speciesism* hinges on a human/animal binary (humans are uniquely and unavoidably superordinated both on and off farms), *particularity* reveals that the dyad both obscures and clarifies by summoning a phantasmic abstraction, "the animal."[113] To our farmers, there was no such thing as an "animal" perspective; there were the perspectives of the different animals on the farm. These perspectives were informed but not exhausted by speciative difference. Just as important were individual differences in behavior and preference, and the farmers uniformly tackled this empirically. They paid attention to the moods and habits of particular animals, and abstracted lessons about both the species and individuals residing on their farms. They governed their farms on the basis of an empirical reconstruction of those affective states: "a happy cow is a quiet cow," explained Sue, but chickens express preferences more diversely.[114] Some chickens become skittish when upset, Sue further observed, but one hen would climb into her daughters' laps whenever it was distressed. "Animals are speaking all the time about what they want and what they don't want," as Nussbaum puts it. Just as we "don't have to wait until [children and people with cognitive disabilities] can speak fluent English or whatever language" before we listen to and respect them, "[w]e should be doing the same for animals."[115] Caleb praised the work of the animal scientist Temple Grandin, who famously designed "humane" industrial slaughter protocols based on theories of animal cognition.[116] Caleb was agnostic about the underlying theories, but he noted that if one does not follow Grandin's guidelines, "it doesn't work as smoothly."[117]

Our interviewees' articulations of animal welfare imbricated with scale. If welfare depends on assessing the affective states of particular animals, it would be impossible for large farms to operate ethically. For Caleb, welfare encompasses attention to the preferences of individual animals, but it also resolved to broader ecological patterns: if the farm had a healthy and sustainable ecology, Caleb presumed it also served animal welfare unless he had evidence to the contrary. By contrast, Andy and Sue, owners of the smallest farm, were the most particularistic in their assessments. Regardless, for all the farmers, considerations of individual welfare always acted as a brake on market logic. Meats might be fungible commodities, but animals are not. Caleb, for example, was palpably upset when he recounted the treatment his pigs received at a slaughterhouse where "the quality of give-a-shitness was just not there."[118] The slaughterhouse held the pigs in terrible conditions for days before finally killing them, and Caleb swore off ever having his animals slaughtered there again.

Both *particularity* and *empathetic speciesism* were important for how farmers governed the sexual welfare of their livestock, but those normative commitments work at cross-purposes, generating unavoidable contradiction. In keeping with a general ethic of stewardship, the farmers place a premium on their livestock pursuing their "natural" desires. As Kim put it, the question they ask themselves is "Are we letting them, like, fulfill their piggy desires?"[119] In such remarks, the farmers naturalize their animals' desires, perhaps inadvisably so. Modern livestock are the product of millennia of selective breeding, undoubtedly shaping their preferences and desires. And the farmers were also cognizant that left to their own "nature," animals breed badly: Andy and Sue's line breeding program permits bovine incest between fathers and daughters but forbids it between mothers and sons, on the assumption that the latter may result in defective calves.

This tension was no more apparent than in the vexed problem of chicken sex. Both Andy and Sue and Frank and Kim reported that roosters tend to fuck too rough. "Some of them aren't real good at it," remarked Andy.[120] The roosters frequently injure the hens, leaving them distressed with featherless patches, and they fight each other for mating access, sometimes to the death. Frank and Kim pondered ridding their farm of roosters entirely. Some of their roosters are so brutal that the older hens run from them. "A lot of animal sex is very rapey," said Kim.[121] These "natural" patterns of chicken sex might not be the ethical problem of the farmers if the chickens lived away from humans in a pristine forest, but Frank and Kim noted that the layout of the farm exacerbates sexual violence. In a forest, hens could flee from violent roosters. In a barn, hens are trapped. Rather than banishing roosters from the farm, Frank and Kim carefully observe the relative sexual aggressiveness of their roosters and keep and breed only roosters that are gentler sex partners. If a rooster "behave[d] like a proper rooster," he could stay on the farm.[122] Kim was unbothered by the contradiction of this superintendence: they were breeding for qualities they liked in animals so that the animals could live their animalness as fully as possible.

We see here the braided if conflicted values of *empathetic speciesism* and *particularity*. Ungoverned chicken sex poses a threat to the well-being of the hens and will interfere with the hens' abilities to flourish. Since the farmers have literally constructed the social world the hens inhabit, they feel ethically obligated to intervene upon rough, assaultive-looking sex. Their interventions are both made possible and demanded by speciative superordination, yet are tempered by empirical particularity: which roosters fuck nice? Selective breeding is sometimes criticized as the terminally anthropocentric commodification of animals—animal reproduction, bodies, and even desires are reformatted for human purposes[123]—but

Frank and Kim illustrate how the selection in selective breeding can also be ethically calibrated around the flourishing and well-being of governed animals.[124]

We have deferred two important questions: what is animal flourishing and how does it relate to sex? We turn to the third principle, *capacities*. We invoke philosopher Martha Nussbaum's capabilities approach and observe that, within the constraints of the farm, the farmers do their best to provide their livestock with an environment and opportunities to flourish in keeping with their species-specific capacities.[125] All of the farmers expressed an ethical investment in the positive affective states of their animals: happiness, comfort, pleasure, and fulfillment.[126] And they sometimes regarded access to sex as linked to, if not determinative of, those positive affective states. Andy and Sue prefer not to castrate their male swine. They believe it is both needlessly painful and "disrespectful" to the animal.[127] By contrast, Andy reluctantly castrated a calf, reasoning that an aggressive bull would threaten the safety of humans and other animals.[128] Similarly, Kim says that their pigs "want to have sex with each other." For some of the sows this is partially about "maternal instinct," but this desire for sex cannot be reduced to reproductive impulses.[129] As Frank notes, when boars and sows are separated, the boars will begin "humping each other," an observation that tracks with the ethological literature's vast documentation of same-sex, pleasure-oriented, and nonprocreative sex acts among animals.[130] Caleb, however, was indifferent to animal sexuality. Although his livestock were dtf (down to fuck), he plainly stated he did not pay much attention to their sexual preferences.

Caleb's nonchalant attitude about animal sex was representative of the fact that the farmers (and their animals) were not sexual exceptionalists. To the extent that they thought about sexual welfare, it was always within the context of a holistic account of capacities for pleasure and well-being. Yes, Frank and Kim's pigs "want[ed] to have sex with each other," but the pigs also wanted mud, shade, and feed. Sex was not freighted with the same "excess of significance" many humans attach to it.[131] That the boars humped each other in the absence of the sows probably did not offer any pigs (or farmers) insight into the deeper truths of their selves. Nor did sexual harm consequently carry more gravity than other harms the animals might encounter. In this sense, the farmers regarded animal sex like animal death: human preoccupation with slaughter seems to be as much about animal suffering as it is a projection of human existential dread. "I don't think length of life is commensurate with good life or bad life," explained Kim. Sex and death were part of good and bad lives both, but "making sure they have the best life possible," as Andy put it, meant the farmers needed to guard themselves from imposing their own anxieties onto their animals.[132]

Providing their livestock with "good life" runs the risk of heavy-handed paternalism or impractical micromanagement. To guard against either, we have suggested heeling *empathetic speciesism* with *particularity*. We would fortify those traits further with a principle of last resort: *autonomy*. The farmers governed their farms in accordance with the belief that, all other things being equal, individual animals were best situated to decide for themselves how to flourish and live well. This belief was made manifest by what the farmers both said and did. They all conveyed aspirations that their chickens, pigs, cows, and goats enjoy the fullest expression of their chicken-, pig-, cow-, and goat-selves. And unlike conventional farms, our interviewees did not confine their animals in cages, pens, or stalls. Andy and Sue may have restricted where their pigs could roam (recall the problem of livestock, roads, and trucks), but within that fenced space the pigs were free to roam where they liked.[133] The same held true of Caleb, Frank, and Kim. All of the farms featured structures that constrained choices and possible behavior, and the farmers sometimes directly coerced their livestock. But the over-whelming majority of decisions, if not always the most consequential deci-sions, were being made by animals themselves: Which grass to eat? When to roll in the mud? And, indeed, with whom to have sex?

Certainly, the limits of superintendence are practical. One or two farm-ers micromanaging dozens or hundreds of animals is not an option. But that limit is also normative and epistemological. Could a farmer know which patch of grass was most appealing to a cow? Even if a farmer could develop some relevant expertise—and even then we would rank her beneath all bovine authority on the matter—she could only do so by watching and interpreting how cows engage their world. To build serious expertise about the things that make life worth living to a cow, one needs to observe cows' judgments and behaviors. The five farmers presumed that where superin-tendence was not necessary, it was best to leave the animals to their own devices—to let them pursue their own "piggy desires."

Conclusion: Sex without Sexuality, Meat without Animals

Writing by vegans and animal liberationists on the question of eating meat has the virtue of ethical clarity: don't.[134]

A hurdle for this argument, likely insurmountable, is that billions of people enjoy—profoundly—animal flesh. Exponentially more humans are pleasured by meat than by sex. A significant subset of human meat-eaters may concede that pigs deserve moral consideration and concede further that they cannot square that consideration with eating bacon. But bacon is delicious. Kant worried that sex overpowers our capacity to reason; he should have been more concerned with bacon.[135] Abstention—vegetarianism or veganism—pits logical argument against, for many, visceral, irrefusable pleasure.

Queers and those who study them are familiar with the fact that knowing a desire is dangerous, harm-inducing, or otherwise bad is insufficient to dispel it. People pursue sexual pleasures despite the fact that they are told by others (and may themselves believe) that the pleasures they seek are unpleasant, abnormal, immoral, unnatural, gross, repugnant, and injurious. Agency and choice structure desire but do not exhaustively govern it. Desires are dynamic, open to reflection, intention, and mediation. Experiencing new pleasure may generate new desire (rather than pleasure always following the leash of desire), a point of not-so-celebrated agreement among queer scholars and homophobes.[136] In *Not Gay*, Jane Ward issues a delightful queer polemic on choice and desire:

> [W]hen straight women, several minutes into a rant about their husbands or boyfriends, gesture at alliance with me by bemoaning their presumably unchangeable heterosexuality with a dramatic sigh: "Oh I wish I could be a lesbian. I'd probably be a lot happier." ... [W]hat I would like to say in response is ... that I signed on to, and cultivated queerness in my life ... that if you think you would be happier as a dyke you could and should be one.[137]

As you can cultivate vegetarianism, so you can cultivate queerness.

"Cultivating" is more labor-intensive than choosing. Just because you can bend your desire does not make it easy. You may need to structure your entire life around a project of cultivating queerness (or vegetarianism), allowing it to guide your work, sex, community, friendships, politics, recreation, and values. And still, that may not be enough. This is one reason why identitarian logic holds power over queers, whose very name signals a dismissal of identitarian constraint. Identity disciplines, and one needs discipline to cultivate queer (or vegetarian) desires in a world arranged to deny them.

Let's take vegetarian and vegetarianism out of parentheses. Sociologists who study vegetarianism as a social phenomenon conceptualize it as an identity structure.[138] Vegetarians often have a strongly felt sense of self defined by their nonrelationship to meat, such that eating meat not only represents an injury to animals but also a betrayal of truth. We might get bogged down in the same questions of ontogeny that haunt human sexual identity (does eating a vegetarian diet reorient pleasure away from meat or does not liking meat make one more likely to become a vegetarian?), but regardless, vegetarians may think of themselves as *a kind of person*, self-disciplined in accordance. As Jane Ward toils to cultivate queerness in her life, we expect many if not most vegetarians toil to cultivate vegetarianism in theirs.

We do not ridicule vegetarians' identitarian attachments, but one point of this chapter, like this book more generally, is to ask what possibilities identitarian logic crowds out. Identitarianism, whether sexual or dietetic, too often devolves to a focus on the self; *empathetic speciesism* pays more attention to our reconstructions of animal experience. Expending energy on personal dietetics may make a vegetarian's pleasures less dependent on the exploitation of animals, but what will it do for animals if it does not also substantially transform other people's desires and pleasures? Vegetarian counterpublics are limited if their response to the pleasures of meat is denial. We challenge the identitarian assumption that there is a one-to-one match between the kind of person who cares about animals and the kind of person who does not eat meat.

Our first objection: there are a variety of ethical relations to animals that cannot be resolved by diet. Is it worth your time to ponder whether you should remove your dog's ovaries and uterus, or your dog's testicles, if you have already forcibly impregnated your cow, shot her in the back of the head, and eaten her body? Pondering how you treat your dog, an immediate dependent, may guide good ethical habits for how you treat your spouse, neighbor, or a stranger on the street. Yet the reduction of animal ethics to eating meat shields spaying and castration of companionate animals—forced human-animal genital contact, let us remember—from our purview (most Americans are unlikely to eat their pet dogs).[139] Conversely, and as the Louisiana animal sexual abuse law reveals, if meat-eaters presume that their ethics permit meat-eating, then "animal welfare" is all but hollowed out of meaning. Moreover, the Manichean framing of vegetarianism as an ethic—you are either the kind of person who eats meat or you are not—means that meat-eaters may see little use in distinguishing between farms where animals endure constant suffering and those where farmers make efforts to ensure the welfare, including sexual welfare, of their livestock.[140] Declaring all meat is murder and all breeding is rape (or "reproductive slavery"[141]) shores up ethical sensibilities that subtend a vegetarian or vegan identity, but the declarations strikingly dismiss animal experiences. It may not matter to a vegetarian how an animal is bred—that it is bred is the ethical wrong—but it most certainly matters to the animal.

Our second objection circles back to pleasures of the appetite, now moralized. For the joy of bacon is a twofold obstacle for animal welfare: first, because pleasures pummel reason; but second, because we scholars of the sodomitical prima facie think pleasures make lives worth living. Whatever meat's nutritional value, its centrality in the American diet is not merely functional. Many people enjoy the experience of eating meat. They like the taste, texture, and scent of a steak. Their mouths water for a hamburger. Sometimes we eat for a reason. But sometimes we eat to get away from reason, "a kind of rest for the exhausted self, an interruption of being good, conscious and intentional that feels like a relief."[142] Sometimes we eat for a reason only to find visceral unreason interrupting. Anyone who has ever tried to eat a salad while the person sitting across from them is chomping on a fried chicken sandwich already knows this. The smell of the chicken sandwich summons the memory of its flavor: the scent pulls us into a state of inconvenient desire, a desire that may drain whatever pleasure we were deriving from the salad as well as weaken our resolve to eat better. "Knowledge is not really power where the appetites are concerned."[143]

Meat-eating is tied up in potent sense-memories. And it is also one of the ways that people access the experiences of comfort, belonging, community, intimacy, and commensality:

> Meat is embedded in our culture and personal histories in ways that matter too much, from the Thanksgiving turkey to the ballpark hot dog. Meat comes with uniquely wonderful smells and tastes, with satisfactions that can almost feel like home itself. And what, if not the feeling of home, is essential?[144]

Animal liberationists run headfirst into such carnal pleasures as a practical obstacle, but we propose such pleasures are an ethical challenge, too. What is the moral value of the pleasure we obtain from eating meat? Does the intensity of that pleasure matter? The standard animal liberationist take on these pleasures, much like what some communists claimed of homosexuality, is that they are either a product of false consciousness[145] or morally unserious in the face of suffering.[146] To our ears this sounds like unattractive asceticism, an ethical calculus that shores up vegetarians as kinds of people and obscures needed ethical reflection on the kinds of acts that realize animal well-being. The "vegetarian" is a coordinating "personage," like the bestialist, that routes ethical reflection through identities that are defined by how individuals feel about animals (apathy, love, lust, etc.): once again, we are judging desires rather than acts and their attending pleasures and pains.

An ethical calculus that incorporates pleasure need not necessarily side in favor of meat-eating, yet we want to free the calculation of utility from the notion that there are only two different kinds of people: those who care about animals and those who do not, and that from each identity we can distinguish good desires from bad ones. What if there was a way to affirm and even embrace the moral value of the pleasure some people derive from eating meat while also defending the welfare of animals? Eating meat and animal well-being need not be zero-sum. One promising path out of that tangle is cellular agriculture, a potential "Hegelian solution" that overcomes the "tragic conflict" between bacon's yumminess (and all other meat-based pleasures) and animals' pain.[147]

Cellular agriculture proponents would like to create ways to cultivate synthetic meat without the need to raise and kill animals. Using a variety of biotechnologies, cell culturing, and tissue bioengineering, cellular agriculture will synthesize tissues that are functionally indistinguishable from meat. In short, advocates and scientists of cellular agriculture want to grow your cheeseburger in a vat (Figure 3.2). Current results have been uneven but encouraging. So far, the expense would place the product far outside the price range of everyone but the rich, and the fabrication procedure still depends upon proteins and acids extracted from cattle. These technical challenges are not trivial but are also probably solvable. The upside of successful cellular agriculture would be astounding. It would mean a marked reduction in the suffering of livestock and the multiplication of the pleasures of meat.[148]

Advocacy for cellular agriculture, including our own, must take stock of the political economy of seed biotechnology. The current intellectual property regime ensures that liberatory agricultural technologies are more expensive and less available than they might otherwise be, and they foster pernicious relations of dependency between farmers in the global South and farmers and agribusinesses in the global North.[149] If cellular agriculture is structured along similar lines, cultured meat will be produced by firms controlled by Euro-American interests and exported to consumers in the rest of the world. Small farmers throughout Africa and South America will continue to make meat the old-fashioned, low capital-intensity way: breeding, raising, and slaughtering animals. The solution, already grasped by organizations like New Harvest and the Good Food Institute, is to socialize meat culturing infrastructures as much as possible and to ensure that the technology is open-access.[150]

Rather than renouncing the pleasures of meat and driving meat-lovers from our ethical camp, we suggest that vegetarians and other animal-loving folks should consider the expansion of carnal pleasures to be fertile grounds for alliance. Vegetarians, vegans, animal-lovers, bacon scarfers, and steak cravers might unite to expand access to the pleasures of meat through cellular agriculture. Such an alliance could better attend to the capacious flourishing of meat-eating humans and a vast population of animals.

This alliance would offer several advantages:

It would be democratically hedonic:[151] vegetarians and meat-eaters collaborating to proliferate pleasures for themselves and for animals, pleasures unshared phenomenologically but agreed upon politically.

Figure 3.2 Cultured meat: the promise of human pleasure without animal suffering. (*Photograph courtesy of Mosa Meat*)

The alliance would shift politics from identitarian dietetics and disgust to social transformation. For example, the success of cultured meat depends upon activists' attention to both the livelihoods of small farmers in Paraguay and intellectual property law in the United States.

Such an alliance on behalf of animal welfare distinguishes, as we have noted, that welfare from meat, a wedge that frees us to ask questions about human-animal relations that are grayer than the relation between the butcher and the hog. If you kill or eat pigs, you may have a difficult time addressing with any rigor or consistency the question of whether it is permissible to have a dog lick peanut butter off a penis. That the question is less weighty is the point: what a dreary, useless task ethics will be if it only addresses extreme suffering. When sex between humans and animals is wrongful, what is wrong about it is best addressed through existing animal cruelty statutes. Fucking a chicken to death is wrong because it causes the chicken to suffer and irreparably damages its ability to flourish in the world. The United States criminalizes far too much conduct and incarcerates far too many people.[152] We see no good reason why conduct not injurious to animals should be criminalized.

The Peanut Butter Problem is not much of one.[153] There may be many good reasons to avoid having a dog lick peanut butter from your testicles. We doubt the wisdom of allowing a dog's hungry jaws near your genitals. But the idea that this scenario victimizes Fido is farcical. Dogs love peanut butter. Assumptions about *what sex is* and *how sex is exceptional* ought to be checked by *empathetic speciesism* and *particularity.* And following our *capacities* consideration, we will go a step further: pleasuring your dog is morally good. It may not warrant converting your genitals into a buffet, but your ethical relation to your dog is not exhausted by harm reduction; it must also grapple with provisions for pleasure and play.[154]

We emphasize preventing pain and providing pleasure, but "cruelty" may miss the mark as the relevant criterion for prohibition. "Cruelty" hinges on human intent, and, in this sense, it is incompatible with *empathetic speciesism.* This focus on intent hollows out animal cruelty laws' empathetic pretenses, making human motive rather than animal experience the gravamen. Such statutes qualify cruelty as "needless" or "gratuitous," provide defenses rooted in the "standards" of industries that are harmful to animals, and feature the same categorical exemptions for industrial agriculture we find in bestiality statutes.[155] A prohibition on cruelty so riddled with loopholes not only sanctions and normalizes animal suffering but also fosters *apathetic speciesism.*

For the promotion of animal welfare, we endorse legal protections rooted in our best, studied approximation and reconstruction of the subjective experience of animals. Such legal protections would be calibrated to the consequences of human conduct toward animals rather than to (cruel) intent or to identity ("homosexual" in the conservative mind; "bestialist" in the liberal one). For example, it may be advisable to categorically prohibit penetrative sex upon many animals since, after all, there is no safe way for a human to fuck a finch (for the finch). But we see no reason to treat a human rubbing a cat's genitals or a dog penetrating a human with the same presumptive caution. Similarly, the varying capacities of different kinds of animals, including variations among individuals within a species, warrants whatever particularity criminal law can afford. The human/animal binary erases meaningful differences of experience, injury, and pleasure.

Evidently if unexpectedly, our proposals have little to do with bestial sex. Sure, *Broad City*'s Ilana Wexler is correct when she insists that it is ethically better for a horse to fuck a man than a man to fuck a horse.[156] But who cares? Flippant yet right, it is the assumptions guiding Ilana's analysis that we have championed. Extant statutes about animal welfare, sexual and otherwise, assuage human guilt and punish socially stigmatized desire. They offer animals little protection, let alone pleasure. From the horse's perspective, as Ilana suggests, it matters quite a bit that the horse, not the human, is doing the fucking.[157] We think these ethical distinctions matter, not just for law making, but also for the practical ethics that inform our everyday relations with animals.

By selectively breeding animals, humans have shaped their personalities, desires, and preferences. Similarly, under the conditions of asymmetric power that characterize domestication, humans can (and sometimes do) train domestic animals to be active participants in sex. Those are exercises of power intended to shape and condition an animal's responses for human gratification. Such practices of animal socialization and sexualization are probably incompatible with *empathetic speciesism*; they weaken animal *autonomy*; and they have a dubious relationship to capacious animal flourishing. Now eliminate sexual exceptionalism. Consider caging, muzzling, shocking, docking, spaying, castrating, and euthanizing—practices far more common and less stigmatized than sex-grooming, but all of which should be equally ethically suspect, absent mitigating circumstances. Did you muzzle your dog to allow it to flourish or for your convenience? Did you dock its ears for your own aesthetic preference?[158]

It will require a dramatic reorganization of human society to consistently protect the interests, capacities, and pleasures of animals. A hedonic ethos need not pivot on sex—indeed, our caution against sexual exceptionalism leads us far from sex—but nor will it be indifferent to the sexual. Obviations of animal pleasure and reductions of animal sexuality to reproductive function is the bad fruit of an instrumentalizing anthropocentrism. Animals have complex interior lives characterized by rich and varied sensations and emotions. The same anthropocentrism that reduces animals to machines permits us to systematically disregard their suffering. Recognizing and valuing animal pleasure better clarifies why harming animals is wrong: such harms unduly contain or extinguish opportunities for joy, play, and pleasure.[159] Eliminating industrial agricultural breeding and slaughtering practices, embracing the particularities and capacities of nonhuman animals, scrutinizing our routine behavior toward companionate animals, and technologizing meat without death realize cross-species pleasures that animal sexual abuse laws, like Louisiana's, vanquish.

4

CANS and Social Equality

The last chapter journeyed across the species divide to theorize nonhuman animal flourishing alongside and against the forces of identitarianism, erotophobia, and sex law. The next two chapters and the coda return us to humans, specifically sex workers and children, to theorize on their civil and social freedom—what I shorthanded in the Introduction as a *right to queerness*—alongside and against those very same forces.

I. CANS Is Unconstitutional

Louisiana Revised Statute 14:89.2, Crime Against Nature by Solicitation, violates the equal protection guarantees of the Fourteenth Amendment of the U.S. Constitution and of Article I, Section 3 of the Louisiana Constitution. The law serves no conceivable rational purpose; its codification and selective enforcement are animus-based.

Crime Against Nature by Solicitation (CANS) is arbitrary and redundant, for it criminalized the exact sexual conduct that was already criminalized under La. R.S. 14:82, Prostitution. Prostitution and CANS both proscribe the solicitation of oral and anal sex for money; Prostitution additionally criminalizes the solicitation of vaginal sex for money.

Until 2010, a first conviction for CANS carried far more severe penalties than Prostitution, a reflection of the Legislature's moral disapproval of sexual conduct associated with homosexuality. Such moral disapproval (for example, that anal sex is "loathsome and disgusting," as the Louisiana

Supreme Court once opined[1]) is now considered an illegitimate, unconstitutional basis for state action that regulates the sexual lives and relationships of its citizens. If there are legitimate, nonmoralizing, government objectives for criminalizing commercial sexual conduct—for example, deterring trafficking, maintaining public health, protecting vulnerable populations from violence, protesting the commodification of sex—those objectives are already met by the Prostitution statute.[2]

While overlapping statutory provisions do not by themselves render such provisions unconstitutional, persons convicted of CANS are and continue to be purposelessly demeaned and humiliated by the law. The Louisiana Legislature's equalization of penalties for CANS and Prostitution in 2010 and 2011, along with a 2012 federal court's ruling that the sex offender registration and notification requirements triggered by a CANS conviction violate equal protection, both respond to—without ultimately resolving— the demeaning, humiliating legacy of CANS itself, a statute that is and has always been unnecessary and unnecessarily discriminatory.

CANS is arbitrary and redundant but it is also tainted by animus; the redundancy of the law speaks to the animus that drove its enactment. The legislative motive behind the 1982 CANS provision to the state sodomy law, as the Louisiana House Criminal Justice Committee record shows, was, chiefly, hostility toward gay men, specifically toward young gay male prostitutes. More recently, CANS has been unequally enforced against, and has disproportionately impacted, transgender women.[3] The gay male teenage sex workers in the 1980s, and the transgender women sex workers in the 1990s and 2000s, could have and should have been prosecuted under Prostitution, not CANS. In its prejudicial codification and in its discriminatory enforcement, CANS reflects a "bare congressional desire to harm a politically unpopular group," the gay and transgender community.[4] Bearing no legitimate government purpose, CANS offends the equal protection guarantees of the state and federal constitutions.

The following two parts of this chapter overview, respectively, the legislative (II) and case history (III) of La R.S. 14:89.2, Crime Against Nature by Solicitation. Section IV demonstrates that CANS does not survive rational basis scrutiny. Section V demonstrates that CANS is tainted by animus.

II. CANS's Legislative History

Louisiana has criminalized "crime against nature" since 1805, although the conduct that qualifies as "unnatural copulation" under the law has changed over time, by both legislative acts and judicial interpretation. Across its history, the Louisiana crime against nature statute has applied, facially, to particular sex acts (e.g., oral and anal sex) rather than to same-sex sexual activity. Additionally, in the nineteenth and twentieth centuries, the crime against nature statute was mainly enforced against perpetrators of sexual violence by men against boys and girls. In the last quarter of the twentieth century, the majority of crime against nature cases heard by Louisiana appellate courts involve allegations of men forcing women or girls to perform oral sex.[5]

In 1982, though, the Legislature attached a separate but severable "by solicitation" provision to the crime against nature statute. The law was intended to target consensual, commercial sex between men, not sexual violence. And while Crime Against Nature by Solicitation, like simple Crime Against Nature, was facially gender-neutral, it was enacted as a corrective to what was alleged to be the gender-specificity of the state's Prostitution law. The Legislature enacted CANS because of what state representatives saw as a growing social problem in the French Quarter of New Orleans: male prostitution. Further, representatives appeared to believe that the state's Prostitution statute only applied to women prostitutes, thus handicapping the NOPD from deterring commercial sex between men.[6] Importantly, and as will be elaborated in Section IV, that belief was mistaken: the Louisiana Legislature had already gender-neutralized its Prostitution statute in 1977 (replacing the word "woman" with "person") on account of an earlier but similar concern over male prostitution in New Orleans.[7] In any case, the Legislature enacted harsher penalties for CANS than Prostitution. A person convicted of Prostitution for the first time "shall be fined not more than five hundred dollars or be imprisoned for not more than six months."[8] A first-time conviction of CANS was, until 2010, "punishable by a term of imprisonment of up to five years, with or without hard labor, and/or a fine of not more than $2,000.00."[9]

In 1992, the Louisiana Legislature enacted its first law mandating the registration of persons convicted of specifically enumerated sex offenses and offenses against minor victims. The law and its subsequent amendments require, inter alia, wide dissemination of offenders' biographical information and conviction history as well as offenders' periodic registration with authorities. From 1992 until 2010, a first conviction for CANS was a registerable sex offense. A conviction for Prostitution is not and never has been a registerable sex offense.[10]

Recognizing that the penalties for CANS and Prostitution were arbitrarily different and so prone to discriminatory enforcement and prosecution, the Legislature equalized the punishments for first time convictions of both crimes.[11] In turn, only a second CANS conviction would trigger sex offender registration and notification requirements. In 2011, furthering its effort to eliminate disparate treatment under law, the Legislature equalized all penalties for Prostitution and CANS convictions, and removed CANS from the list of sex offenses triggering registration and notification requirements.[12]

The more recent legislative history of CANS (2010–2011) reflects representatives' awareness that the enactment of, more severe penalties for, and sex offender registration and notification requirements triggered by CANS (and not Prostitution) were rooted in prejudice toward sex acts "associated with the lesbian, gay, bisexual and transgender community."[13] Serving no rational purpose, CANS nevertheless remains a crime and continues to demean and humiliate, under color of law, transgender women, cisgender women, and gay men. Disproportionately, too, most persons convicted of CANS are Black. As the conclusion to Section V explains, that there are multiple, overlapping, vulnerable populations targeted by CANS's animus-soaked codification and CANS's animus-soaked enforcement patterns, and that the populations targeted have changed over time should not rescue the law from an equal protection attack.

III. CANS's Case History

Since its enactment in 1982 by the Louisiana Legislature, CANS has survived all but one of several constitutional attacks, among them void for vagueness, overbreadth, freedom of speech, cruel and unusual punishment, rights to privacy and due process, and equal protection. The equal protection challenges are the most pertinent for this chapter.

In *State v. Ryans*,[14] defendant argued principally that the penalties for CANS conviction are disproportionate and excessive, comparing the penalties to those for a Prostitution conviction. In *State v. Baxley*,[15] defendant argued that CANS unconstitutionally discriminated against homosexuals. In the trial decisions consolidated under *State v. Smith*,[16] defendants argued that the difference in penalties between CANS and Prostitution, La. R.S. 14:82, violated equal protection guarantees of state and federal constitutions. In *State v. Thomas*,[17] while the defendant challenged the constitutionality of CANS in light of substantive liberty interests to sexual decision-making as stipulated in *Lawrence v. Texas*,[18] the state supreme court also addressed the question of differential punishments. Most recently, *Doe v. Jindal*[19] held that the sex offender registration and notification requirements attendant to CANS violated the Equal Protection Clause of the Fourteenth Amendment of the U.S. Constitution. Through the settlement *Doe v. Caldwell*,[20] nearly all persons convicted of CANS were removed from the Louisiana State Sex Offender and Child Predator Registry and relieved of additional sex state offender registration and notification requirements.

This section rehearses and responds to the pertinent holdings of *Ryans*, *Baxley*, *Smith*, *Thomas*, *Jindal*, and *Caldwell*, to provide initial evidence that CANS serves no legitimate government purpose (Section IV) and is tainted by animus (Section V).

Ryans *(1987)*

The state appellate court rejected defendant's assertion that the penalties for CANS were unconstitutionally excessive because they were disproportionate to the penalties for Prostitution. Conceiving both crimes as "offenses of sexual immorality," the court nevertheless held that "today's society is much more affronted by" CANS than by Prostitution.[21] The harsher penalty "reveals that a crime against nature is considered a more serious offense than is prostitution," a more serious violation of "public morals."[22]

The penalties for CANS and Prostitution have now been equalized. Nevertheless, *Ryans* reveals that the CANS statute itself, enacted for the purpose of more harshly penalizing the offering of oral and anal sex for compensation, was enacted as a proclamation against "sexual immorality." In light of *Romer*, *Lawrence*, and *Windsor*, it is questionable at best whether such state-sponsored moral proclamation against commercial, specifically sodomitical acts by consenting adults withstands constitutional scrutiny, particularly since Prostitution already criminalizes sodomitical and vaginal sex for compensation.

More pointedly, the *Ryans* court admits that "the defendant's conduct arguably violated La. R.S. 14:82 [Prostitution] as well as La. R.S. 14:89 [CANS]" but opines that district attorneys are granted prosecutorial discretion.[23] This is true, but it seems impossible to square the court's admission of an equivalence between Prostitution and CANS with its earlier insistence that the difference between Prostitution and CANS legitimates the harsher penalties of the latter.

Baxley *(1995)*

In *Baxley*, the state supreme court rejected a trial judge's decision "that the sentencing provision of the crime against nature statute discriminates against gay men and lesbians in violation of their equal protection rights, and thereby imposes unconstitutionally excessive punishment."[24] For the trial judge, that the penalties for CANS—that is, for sexual conduct associated with gays and lesbians—were greater than the penalties for Prostitution made the statute itself unconstitutionally discriminatory. The *Baxley* court pointed out, rightfully, that CANS only refers to sexual conduct, not to the gender or sexual orientations of the participants: "the statute does not single out gay men or lesbians."[25]

Importantly, though, *Baxley* adds the following qualification:

> A statute, though facially neutral, may still be challenged as constitutionally infirm if the challenger can prove that the statute was enacted because of a discriminatory purpose. . . . In the present case, the record *is devoid of any evidence that the crime against nature statute was enacted for the purpose of discriminating against gay men and lesbians.*[26]

To the contrary, the record reveals discrimination to be the sole purpose of the law. It is true that *simple* Crime Against Nature was not enacted to discriminate against gays and lesbians, social identities that arrived far after 1805. But the 1982 Crime Against Nature by Solicitation statute, along with its harsher penalties than the penalties for Prostitution, were explicitly directed at gay men soliciting sex for compensation. The Louisiana House Criminal Justice Committee record (Section IV) includes comments and behaviors by state representatives that can only be described as animus-soaked.

The *Baxley* court further defends the harsher penalties of CANS, explaining:

> [T]he legislature may, in its discretion, deem *one form of conduct more offensive to the public's morals than another*, and punish that conduct more severely. In the present case, the legislature has determined that solicitation for "unnatural carnal copulation" is more offensive than solicitation for "indiscriminate sexual intercourse."[27]

This analysis too is inaccurate. Although the statutory language is indeed different between the laws (CANS proscribes soliciting "unnatural carnal copulation"; Prostitution proscribes soliciting "indiscriminate sexual intercourse"), Prostitution has been statutorily specified to criminalize anal and oral sex for compensation (La R.S. 14:82.B), and CANS has been judicially interpreted to criminalize offering anal and oral sex for compensation.[28] Moreover, oral sex and anal sex for compensation was criminalized by the state before the 1982 CANS law.[29] Neither CANS nor Prostitution are gender-specific. The only significant difference between the laws as applied (but not as enforced) is that Prostitution also criminalizes vaginal sex for compensation.

Baxley missteps twice. First, the court claims there is no historical evidence that CANS reflects antigay animus, but the law was enacted to target teenage gay male prostitutes whose conduct was already criminalized by the state's revised Prostitution law. Second, the court interprets CANS and Prostitution as proscribing different forms of sexual conduct. The statutes criminalize identical sexual conduct; Prostitution additionally criminalizes vaginal sex for compensation.

Smith *(2000)*

Smith upheld the constitutionality of Louisiana's simple sodomy statute (La. R.S. 14:89.A[1]), predominantly leaning on *Bowers v. Hardwick*[30] to do so (substantively and stylistically; compare "the defendant would have us announce . . . a constitutional right to engage in oral sex. This we are unwilling to do" [*Smith*][31] with "respondent would have us announce . . . a fundamental right to engage in homosexual sodomy. This we are quite unwilling to do" [*Bowers*][32]). As the *Thomas* court would note five years later, Louisiana's simple sodomy statute would not survive a post-*Lawrence* challenge, for both the *Bowers* Court and then the *Smith* court misconfigured the liberty interests of the respective defendants.[33]

The *Smith* court consolidated into its decision, though, a reversal of several lower court appeals that had successfully challenged CANS on multiple grounds, among them cruel and unusual punishment and equal protection.

In response to the equal protection challenges, *Smith* reiterates the faulty distinction from *Ryans* and *Baxley*: "the different punishments of two types of different conduct does not constitute an equal protection violation."[34] But to reiterate: the conduct criminalized across statutes is identical. Should a woman solicit oral or anal sex for compensation, she could be prosecuted under either Prostitution or CANS. Should a man solicit oral or anal sex for compensation, he could be prosecuted under Prostitution or CANS.

Symbolically, CANS singles out sex practices connoting homosexuality, which is why, in responding to the cruel and unusual punishment challenge, the *Smith* court relies not upon its different conduct/different penalties line of reasoning but rather upon the legitimacy of morals legislation: "the legislature may declare one form of conduct more offensive to the public's morals than another, and punish that conduct more severely."[35] But since the conduct is in fact the same or could be, the distinction is less between sexual practices than between its terms, "indiscriminate sexual intercourse" and "unnatural carnal copulation."[36] While the *Smith* court is surely right—even after *Lawrence*—that "the same arguments made for privacy rights of non-commercial, consensual sex are simply not as persuasive for commercial sex acts,"[37] it seems especially dubious—after *Lawrence*—that "offense to the public's morals" constitutionally legitimates either severer penalties for, or the statutory isolation of, commercial sodomy.

The *Smith* court maintains that should it hold different penalties for CANS and Prostitution unconstitutional, it would be forced to hold stricter penalties for higher degrees of rape unconstitutional, or stricter penalties for the "distribution of heroin" over the "distribution of cocaine" unconstitutional.[38]

These analogies weaken rather than strengthen *Smith*'s holding, for the state legislature may reasonably contend that gradations of punishment correspond to the maintenance of public health, the deterrence of violence and gangs, or some other legitimate public reason. The only reason for separating CANS and its penalties from Prostitution and its penalties is the preservation and state endorsement of sexual morality held by private citizens. Moreover, forced sexual intercourse against a sixty-five-year-old person (La. R.S. 14:42.A, first degree rape) is quite different from sex procured under false pretense of identity (La. R.S. 14:43.A[3], third degree rape). Consensual, commercial oral sex (Prostitution) *is* consensual, commercial oral sex (CANS).

Shortly after *Lawrence*, the Kansas Supreme Court held unconstitutional the state's "Romeo and Juliet" law, which penalized sex between younger and older teenagers of the same sex more severely than sex between younger and older teenagers of different sexes.[39] As in the present case, the underlying conduct remains criminal (commercial sex in Louisiana; sex between minors in Kansas), but the state supreme court found that any further distinctions between "voluntary sexual conduct" affronts *Lawrence*'s holding that "moral disapproval of a group cannot be a legitimate government interest."[40] Strictly speaking, in neither Kansas nor Louisiana is the "group" at issue "homosexuals." The Kansas law more severely punished teenagers who engage in same-sex sex; the Louisiana law more severely punished people who solicit oral and anal sex for money, some of whom presumably identify as homosexual. Less important than the status classification or "group" is the rationale for isolating and punishing the group: moral disapproval alone. The constitutional question is not about suspect classification and tiers of scrutiny but whether sexual immorality provides a rational basis for discriminatory legislation. It does not.

Thomas *(2005)*

The *Thomas* court hears and swiftly rejects a post-*Lawrence*, substantive liberty challenge to CANS. The court's rejection of Tina Thomas's liberty claim depends upon the distinction the *Lawrence* Court itself drew between private and public consensual sexual conduct ("the present case does not involve . . . public conduct or prostitution").[41]

Less persuasively, the court hastily rejects the equal protection "classification" challenge, repeating, as in earlier decisions, that "punishment of one type of conduct more severely than another similar type of conduct is not, of itself, and equal protection violation."[42] The problem with this analysis, still, is that the same conduct has been criminalized as either Prostitution or CANS. And while the differing penalty schemes might survive an equal protection challenge if 1) the conduct covered under each statute were in fact different and/or 2) CANS were drawn and enforced for public-regarding, legitimate government objectives, neither of those conditions holds true.

Chief Justice Calogero noted that while his earlier expressed view—that the then-harsher penalties for CANS over Prostitution are "unconstitution-ally excessive"[43]—was not at issue in *Thomas*, it is "only bolstered by the *Lawrence* decision."[44] *Lawrence* endorses, indeed constitutionalizes, the Chief Justice's long-held position that the greater penalties for CANS are constitutionally unsupportable. As he noted in *Baxley*, CANS is "a sex act for money involving no harm or injury, or the threat thereof, to any 'victim;' it is a 'victimless' crime."[45] This chapter contends that it is not only the formerly stricter penalties for CANS that cannot withstand constitutional scrutiny but also that CANS itself, because of its arbitrary enactment, its prejudicial enforcement, and its symbolic degradation of sex acts "traditionally associ-ated with homosexuality," cannot withstand constitutional scrutiny either.[46] CANS "effectively brand[s]" people as "deviant by nature."[47]

Jindal *(2012) and* Caldwell *(2013)*

In 2012, the United States District Court of the Eastern District of Louisiana held the state sex offender registration requirements triggered by CANS unconstitutional. Judge Feldman adhered to "the simple and clear injunc-tion of the Fourteenth Amendment," that a state scheme mandating sex offender registration for "identical conduct" convicted under one statute (CANS) but not another (Prostitution) violates equal protection of the laws.[48] The *Jindal* court is the only one of the aforementioned to acknowledge that Prostitution and CANS proscribe identical, not just similar, conduct, further admonishing that "any contention to the contrary—to the extent it relies on the 'distinctions' between 'unnatural carnal copulation' and 'indiscriminate sexual intercourse'—is an exercise that is without substance."[49]

Jindal ordered the nine plaintiffs convicted of CANS to be declassified as sex offenders and to be removed from the Louisiana Sex Offender and Child Predatory Registry. A year later, the *Caldwell* settlement declassified nearly all persons previously convicted of CANS as sex offenders too, mandating their removal from the Registry.

But since the "the very same public health and moral purposes apply to both statutes,"[50] to CANS and to Prostitution, *Jindal* beseeches us to ques-tion not only the constitutionality of CANS's now defunct sex offender reg-istration requirements but also the constitutionality of the CANS statute itself. If there is not "even one unique legitimating governmental interest that can rationally explain" why CANS triggered sex offender registration requirements but Prostitution does not, can there be any such public interest that explains CANS's redundancy on Prostitution?[51] No. This same district court, it should be noted, was a holdout from its sister courts in recognizing legitimate purposes for Louisiana's prior restriction on marriage licenses to one woman and one man (purposes like linking children to their biological parents and respect for democratic processes of social change).[52] One need not carry a brief for gay rights to recognize that the separate classification of CANS from Prostitution is both arbitrary and prejudicial.

Judge Feldman bookended his ruling with cautions against "class legislation" as anathema to the U.S. Constitution. He opened his inquiry with an historical observation from two legal scholars that the idea of equal protection "not only aimed to prevent class privilege but also invidious oppression."[53] And he concluded his analysis with reminders from landmark rulings such as *Cleburne*[54]—that the Fourteenth Amendment is "essentially a direction that all persons similarly [identically] situated should be treated alike"[55]—and *Skinner*[56]—that "the equal protection clause would . . . be a formula of empty words if such conspicuously artificial lines could be drawn."[57]

Despite their now equalized penalties, and despite their now identically prescribed conduct, CANS, but not Prostitution, singles out, and thereby humiliates and demeans, a class of individuals—queer people—associated with certain sex practices.

IV. Equal Protection Violation #1: CANS Bears No Rational Relationship to a Legitimate Government Objective

From the outset, Crime Against Nature by Solicitation was redundant and arbitrary. In 1982, the state legislators enacted the CANS statute, and with more severe punishments than Prostitution, to remedy what they understood to be a growing social problem of young male sex work in the French Quarter of New Orleans. According to committee records, legislators were informed that "in Louisiana, there is no law specifically directed at male prostitution,"[58] that La. R.S. 14:82 could only be charged against a "female" practicing "indiscriminate sexual intercourse with others for compensation." The gender-specificity of the Prostitution law supposedly impeded the NOPD from curbing commercial sex between men.

However, this legislative presumption about the Prostitution law is contravened by the fact that, in 1977, five years prior to the enactment of CANS, the Louisiana Legislature had already gender-neutralized the statute. The Legislature redefined Prostitution as "the practice by a *female* of indiscriminate sexual intercourse with others for compensation" to "the practice by a *person* of indiscriminate sexual intercourse with others for compensation."[59] The Legislature revised the Prostitution statute in 1977 for the same reasons they enacted CANS in 1982: as a response to male street prostitution in New Orleans.[60] At the time of CANS's codification, then, the NOPD already had at its disposal a law criminalizing commercial sex between men as well as solicitation for such sex. CANS was arbitrary from the outset; rather than overlapping in its coverage with Prostitution, CANS criminalized a subset of the conduct criminalized by Prostitution, but did so much more harshly, to reflect the Legislature's greater moral disapproval of commercial sex between men than between men and women.

There are two possible rebuttals to the proposition that CANS was always unnecessary and therefore unreasonable: first, legislators may not have known or fully understood that the Prostitution law already reached the conduct it sought to criminalize through CANS; second, legislators may have thought that men's offering *oral sex* was not criminalized by Prostitution, a presumption that would have been buttressed by the ambiguous language of "indiscriminate sexual intercourse."

As for the first rebuttal: if ignorance is rarely a defense for lawbreakers, it should not be a defense for lawmakers.

As for the second: since, typically, men do not have vaginal sex with other men, the 1977 gender-neutralization revision to the Prostitution statutes was intended to reach some other form of commercial sexual conduct. And since the Legislature had recently statutorily relocated forced anal sex from "aggravated crime against nature" to "rape,"[61] it is safe to assume that, minimally, the 1977 revision criminalized the solicitation of anal sex by one man to another for compensation.

But what about oral sex? Was oral sex "sex," statutorily speaking, in 1982? Legislative and case history document time and again that "oral sex" qualified as "unnatural carnal copulation" and so a "crime against nature" in Louisiana; but not until 2008 was "oral sex" statutorily "clarified" as "sexual intercourse" under another revision to the Prostitution law.[62] However, if in fact (commercial) oral sex did not count as (commercial) sex until 2008 for legislative and policing purposes, then no person, *male or female*, should have been charged or convicted under Prostitution for such conduct—attempted, solicited, or performed—until 2008. This proposition is belied by police and news reports from the late 1970s and early 1980s, which document both men and women being arrested for Prostitution for soliciting or performing oral sex.[63] The legislative clarification in 2008 that "sexual intercourse" "means anal, oral, or vaginal sex"[64] spelled out in statute what was already clear and common in police practice: oral sex for money is Prostitution. Moreover, the 2008 definitional revision only underscores CANS's offensiveness to the state and federal constitutions: unquestionably, CANS serves no rational purpose beyond the purposes served by the Prostitution statute.

Instructive to the rational relationship inquiry at issue is a holding from the Ninth Circuit Court of Appeals, *Erotic Serv. Provider Legal Educ. Research Project v. Gascon*,[65] in which plaintiffs contended that *Lawrence v. Texas* protects commercial sexual transactions between adults, or prostitution. Affirming the district court's ruling, the Ninth Circuit Court held that *Lawrence* does not extend its liberty protections to prostitution, and that California's stipulated reasons for the law were legitimate, namely: "discouraging human trafficking and violence against women, discouraging illegal drug use, and preventing contagious and infectious diseases."[66] Of course, the constitutional question is not whether prostitution laws are the most efficacious means of achieving these governmental objectives, but whether such objectives are rationally related to the law's purpose. At the same time, California did not propose upholding "public morality" as one of its objectives for criminalizing commercial sex. As the district court had earlier observed: "following the holding in *Lawrence*, moral disapproval is not an adequate or rational basis for criminalizing conduct."[67]

The Louisiana CANS law serves no legitimate government objective; any health, violence, or drug use concerns associated with the commercial exchange of anal and oral sex would be met by the Prostitution statute. Given that CANS was superfluously enacted to criminalize male prostitutes; given that CANS's stricter penalties were formerly justified as expressive disapproval of "sexual immorality"; and given that CANS has disparately impacted transgender women (see Section V), we must conclude "that the principal purpose and the necessary effect of this law are to demean those persons" whose sex practices are associated with homosexuality.[68] But unlike the federal Defense of Marriage Act, which arguably entailed at least some reasons for its enactment beyond moral disapproval,[69] the CANS legislative and enforcement record is, summarily, a record of moral opprobrium. By continuing to statutorily isolate sex practices associated with homosexuality, CANS sanctions the sentiment expressed by the Louisiana Supreme Court not so long ago: that "unnatural carnal copulation," or nonvaginal sex acts, are "loathsome and disgusting."[70] Moral disapproval of sexual conduct serves no rational purpose for state action.

V. Equal Protection Violation #2: CANS Is Motivated by Animus, in Both Codification and Enforcement

From the outset, and discoverable from the legislative record, CANS was enacted out of a "bare congressional desire to harm a politically unpopular group."[71] Later, CANS disproportionately impacted, and has been discriminatorily enforced against, transgender women. As such, CANS offends the equal protection guarantees of the Louisiana and federal constitutions, injecting an impermissibly high degree of bias into the law that ought to be proscribed under the "quadrilogy"[72] of United States Supreme Court animus opinions.

Animus and CANS Codification

While evidence of legislators' "subjective dislike" of a targeted group is neither sufficient nor necessary to prove animus-based legislation, in the present case the evidence is uncharacteristically persuasive.[73] The 1982 Louisiana House Criminal Justice Committee had invited a local news stations to its chambers to play a recording of its segment on "young hustlers" in the French Quarter.[74] The recording features teenage boys and younger men talking about the commercial sex trade; they sound incapacitated by drug use. The committee members laugh at the boys' and young men's interviews before turning to a discussion of the new law that would harshly criminalize male prostitution (which was already criminalized).

One committee member proposed that fairness would dictate equalizing the penalties for Prostitution and CANS.[75] His proposal was rejected by another committee member, who, adopting the newscast's sentiment that the hustlers are "streetwise," responded that the men would fast learn how to avoid arrest.[76] By making CANS a felony—whereas Prostitution was and remains a misdemeanor—the Legislature sought to punish a few male sex workers swiftly and severely before they were smart to the law. Contrary to *Ryans, Baxley, Smith,* and *Thomas,* the legislative motivation behind making CANS felonious was not to register, abstractly, the state's greater moral disapproval for "unnatural carnal copulation" over "indiscriminate sexual intercourse" but to punish, concretely, young men soliciting other men for sex; and to punish them more severely than their women counterparts.

Additionally, then-Representative James Donelon, as of this writing the Louisiana Commissioner of Insurance, told his fellow Justice Committee members that venereal disease and herpes are "rampant" with "these people," thus putting NOPD officers pursuing and arresting the young men at risk of contracting sexually transmitted infections.[77] While Representative Donelon's derision and prejudicial assumptions (regarding the rate of infections among male sex workers as well as, and more importantly for this animus inquiry, his apparent fear that the young men would sexually assault the officers) cannot be taken to represent the collective intent of the Louisiana Legislature,[78] his statement nevertheless evidences the congressional temperament that drove the enactment of CANS and its harsh penalties. In its totality, the recorded minutes from the June 17, 1982, Louisiana House Criminal Justice Committee show that CANS is steeped in illegitimate bias against young men perceived to be gay.

Animus and CANS Enforcement

There are neither citywide nor statewide data that demonstrate conclusively that CANS is discriminately and disproportionately enforced against transgender women. However, several occurrences constellate the claim of bias, especially bias against transgender women of color:

1. In March 2011, the Civil Rights Division of the United States Department of Justice published its "Investigation of the New Orleans Police Department," the report that resulted in the federal consent decree between DOJ and NOPD. Among many issues raised about policing policy and practice was bias against the LGBT community:

   > Members of the LGBT community complained that NOPD officers subject them to unjustified arrests for prostitution, targeting bars frequented by the community and sometimes fabricating evidence of solicitation for compensation. Moreover, *transgender residents reported that officers elect to charge them under Louisiana's statute criminalizing solicitation of "crimes against nature," rather than the state's generic solicitation law. The crimes against nature statute, a statute whose history reflects anti-LGBT sentiment*, in part criminalizes the solicitation of an individual "with the intent to engage in any unnatural carnal copulation for compensation." . . . Of the registrants convicted of solicitation of a crime against nature, 80 percent are African American, suggesting an element of racial bias as well. Indeed, *community members told us they believe some officers equate being African American and transgender with being a prostitute.*[79]

2. At the time of the DOJ Investigation, then-Assistant Attorney General for Civil Rights Thomas Perez stated, "we found regular harassment of LGBT individuals, and the use of the 'crimes against nature' statute almost solely against LGBT individuals."[80] (In the context of the DOJ Investigation, Perez is referring to "Crime Against Nature by Solicitation," not simple "Crime Against Nature.")

3. In 2018, a transgender woman plaintiff of *Doe v. Jindal* founded the campaign "CANScantSTAND," which, according to its Facebook page, "was instigated to liberated individuals by the CANS

(Crime Against Nature [by Solicitation]) law, RS 14:89, mostly transgender women of color."[81]

   a. In coordination with the organization Operation Restoration, CANScantSTAND inaugurated a focus group in 2018 for transgender women of color who are "disproportionately target[ed]" by CANS.[82]

   b. In April 2019, CANScantSTAND and Operation Restoration held a symposium at Tulane University, at which seven transgender women of color spoke about their experiences having been convicted of CANS.[83]

   c. In August 2019, during the Southern Decadence festival in New Orleans, CANScantSTAND organized a street march protesting CANS because the "anti-sodomy law has continued to be used to punish sex workers, particularly trans women of color."[84]

   d. The political campaign led by Black transgender women against CANS is chronicled in the documentary, *CANS Can't Stand: Liberation for Black Trans Women*, distributed by the *New Yorker* in 2023, which has drawn national media attention to antigay codification and antitransgender enforcement patterns of the law.[85]

4. Of the nine plaintiffs in *Doe v. Jindal* that challenged the constitutionality of CANS's sex offender registration requirements, three are transgender women (at least two of whom are African American) and one is a man. Slightly fewer than half the plaintiffs, then, are or would be perceived to be part of the LGBT community, in a city that, as of 2015, is 5.1 percent LGBT.[86]

5. In its amicus brief on behalf of plaintiffs in *Doe v. Jindal*, four LGBTQ rights organizations argued:

   > Without access to housing and employment, LGBT youth and transgender women are often forced into criminalized economic activities, including prostitution, in order to survive. An even greater number of LGBT young people and transgender women are profiled by police as being engaged in prostitution-related offenses when simply walking down the street, hailing a cab, or talking to friends. For these reasons, *LGBT people are one of the populations that have been particularly harmed by the CANS statute's disparate, discriminatory, and disproportionate punishment scheme.*[87]
   >
   > According to preliminary results from a study of African-American transgender young women in New

Orleans conducted by BreakOUT!, *70 percent of those surveyed indicated they felt targeted or profiled by the New Orleans Police Department* ("NOPD"). . . . Many of the Black transgender women surveyed by BreakOUT! said they were stopped by police on Tulane Avenue or in the French Quarter and accused of engaging in prostitution simply because they were transgender and in areas where prostitution occurs. . . .

LGBT youth and transgender women commonly face staggering rates of poverty, violence, unemployment, and discrimination. Some are forced into prostitution to survive while living on the streets, while many others are wrongly profiled and arrested by police. As a result, *LGBT people have been particularly harmed by the CANS statute's disparate and discriminatory mandatory sex offender registration requirement.*[88]

6. In their 2014 quantitative and qualitative analysis of Louisiana's sex offender registries, professors Susan Dewey and Tonia P. St. Germain found that "CANS' application disproportionately affected African American women and transgender individuals," and in particular that "Orleans Parish disproportionately issued CANS convictions to African Americans and transgender sex workers relative to the size of these populations."[89]

Animus Doctrine

Several legal scholars have pointed to an array of U.S. Supreme Court decisions that outline the beginnings of an animus doctrine: what constitutes animus, how courts may identify animus, and ways animus unconstitutionally infect state action.[90] While other Court decisions reference animus, bias, prejudice, or discriminatory intent, *Department of Agriculture v. Moreno*,[91] *City of Cleburne v. Cleburne Living Center*,[92] *Romer v. Evans*,[93] and *United States v. Windsor*[94] control the present animus inquiry. Taken separately and together, these decisions direct the conclusion that CANS is permanently and unconstitutionally tainted by animus.

Moreno (1973)

The *Moreno* Court held that Congress's amendment to the Food Stamp Act to deny food stamps to households with unrelated individuals violated the equal protection clause of the Fourteenth Amendment. The Court focused its inquiry upon legislators' derogatory comments about "hippies," famously stating that "[I]f the constitutional conception of 'equal protection of the laws' means anything, it must at the very least mean that a bare congressional desire to harm a politically unpopular group cannot constitute a legitimate governmental interest."[95]

As evidenced by the 1982 House Criminal Justice Committee record, the Louisiana Legislature sought to harm young men they perceived as gay. The legislators' laughter at the young men interviewed by the local news station, the reference to "these people" and their "rampant" sexually transmitted infections, and, most pertinently, the harsher penalties quickly and spitefully assigned to CANS over Prostitution reflect legislators' animus.

Cleburne (1985)

Cleburne is not as integral to the present inquiry, for in that case the Court held that council members of the City of Cleburne could not codify their constituents' bias into law by prohibiting a permit to a group home for people with cognitive disabilities. There is no relevant record of New Orleans residents lobbying for CANS (although one could argue that the legislators mobilized media bias).

On the other hand, the *Cleburne* Court, while refusing to grant suspect classification to the cognitively disabled, nevertheless held that the city's decision had no rational basis—or rather, that the city's purported legitimate reasons for denying the housing permit were outweighed by evidence of bias.[96] The city's "discrimination failed even a lower level of judicial scrutiny."[97]

While CANS facially applies to conduct and not to status, its purpose to target gay men might warrant a higher level of judicial scrutiny. As with *Cleburne*, though, such suspect classification is unnecessary. First, because the alleged governmental objective for CANS—public denouncement of sexual immorality—no longer survives rational basis review. Second, because any additional government objectives are met by the Prostitution statute, which does not carry—or at least not as baldly—the same animus baggage.[98] Simply, there is no "benign explanation for the statute."[99] Rational basis review is deferential—but not "ultradeferential"[100]—to state action; the selective denigration of sexual conduct by the CANS statute, like the selective denial of food stamps to "hippies," like the selective residential restrictions against people with cognitive disabilities, is void of any public purpose.

Romer (1996)

The *Romer* Court, sidestepping the issue of legislators' or citizens' bias, nevertheless found that Colorado's Amendment 2, which broadly denied gays, lesbians, and bisexuals from making antidiscrimination claims based on sexual orientation, was "inexplicable by anything but animus."[101] The Court discovered animus not in intent but in the "radical lack of fit" between the scope of the law and the justification for it.[102] In *Romer*, the state justifications—rights of citizens' association and distribution of resources to other discriminated groups—were contravened by the sweeping denial of protections to gays, lesbians, and bisexuals across an array of social and economic vectors.

The CANS statute presents the opposite relation of scope and justification, but to the same discriminatory effect. The scope of CANS, rather than being broad and sweeping, is in fact narrow if not null: it criminalizes no additional conduct. But the justification for CANS—to swiftly and harshly punish teenage male prostitutes, and later transgender women of color—reflects bias. In *Romer*, the state's tailored justification is belied by the wide scope of the law; with the CANS statute, scope (null) belies any nondiscriminatory justification for the law.

Windsor (2013)

Windsor struck down the federal Defense of Marriage Act (DOMA) as an unconstitutional violation of the Fifth Amendment (with equal protection read into the Amendment's Due Process Clause). Section 3 of DOMA, which defined marriage in federal law as between one man and one woman, denied recognition and thousands of benefits to same-sex couples married under state law. "The principal purpose and necessary effect of" DOMA, wrote Justice Kennedy, "are to demean those persons who are in a lawful same-sex marriage."[103] Indeed, throughout the opinion Justice Kennedy observes the dignitary harms gays and lesbians suffer as a result of DOMA.[104]

Windsor is critical to an animus-based analysis of CANS, for it registers the ongoing dignitary injuries of the statute against the LGBT community, even though the penalties for CANS and Prostitution have now been equalized.

DOMA did not deny federal marriage recognition to "gays" and "lesbians" but restricted the definition of marriage to a "man" and a "woman."[105] Ostensibly, a gay man could marry a lesbian woman. This may sound facetious since clearly DOMA was designed to prevent gays and lesbians from marrying the same-sex partners of their choice. Indeed, *Windsor* "stands for the proposition that a government's use of *identity-based classifications* to purposefully inflict dignitary injury is impermissible animus,"[106] even though "gays" and "lesbians" were not identified as such under DOMA. As with CANS: while the conduct proscribed is not sexual orientation- or gender-specific, its enactment and enforcement leave an enduring and stigmatizing imprint upon the gay and transgender community. This observation is supported by the *Lawrence* Court's assessment of an equal protection challenge to Texas's Homosexual Conduct Law: "If protected conduct is made criminal and the law which does so remains unexamined for its substantive validity, its stigma might remain even if it were not enforceable as drawn for equal protection reasons."[107] As one law scholar explains:

> [T]he [*Lawrence*] Court wanted to be sure that neither Texas nor any other state could reenact a sodomy law applying facially to hetero-sexuals and homosexuals under the guise of "equality," for such a law would continue to impose stigma on homosexuals.[108]

Indeed, while Prostitution and CANS now criminalize identical conduct with identical penalties, the latter "continue[s] to impose stigma on homosexuals" and transgender women.

As for "homosexuals and transgender women": let me address in closing the "floating" animus problem of CANS. CANS was designed to target gay men; it was later disparately and discriminately enforced against transgender women; in absolute terms, Black citizens and cis women make up the largest portion of persons convicted for CANS and persons who were required to register as sex offenders.

Is CANS codification and enforcement, then, homophobic, transphobic, racist, or sexist? Yes. More germanely, should the law's multiply targeted, multiply purposed prejudice immunize it from an animus-based equal protection challenge? No. Just as, in criminal law, "intent to murder does not disappear merely because, in the course of his murderous errand, the murderer kills someone other than the intended victim," so too, as law professor Juan Perea argues in an analogous context of "floating" state discrimination, "the same principle of transferred intent should apply here."[109] A law designed to persecute gays ought not to survive constitutional attack because it was later used to persecute transgender women.

A lawyer for plaintiffs in *Jindal*, which held CANS's severer penalties over Prostitution unconstitutional, wrote the following about an equal protection challenge to the statute itself:

> Equal protection cases are notoriously difficult to win, requiring a showing that a particular group—African Americans, say, or women—was animated by illicit intent (i.e., a base desire to harm that group). This is already difficult enough to prove as a general matter; it would have been nearly impossible in this context, where the CANS statute was adopted and then enforced in ways that involve sometimes overlapping and sometimes distinct discriminatory purposes.[110]

I am in no position to doubt this assessment as a practical one about litigation strategy. It nevertheless seems to me that a law with a documented and indisputable history of prejudicial codification and enforcement against multiple vulnerable populations should be on just as shaky constitutional grounds as a law disadvantaging one vulnerable population. Similarly, the policies, amendments, and statutes at issue in *Moreno, Cleburne, Romer,* and *Windsor* disadvantaged not only "hippies," the cognitively disabled, and gays and lesbians, just as CANS not only disadvantages gay men and trans women; but this empirical observation does not undercut impermissible bias, discriminatory intent, and disparate treatment.

Whether or not the populations targeted by CANS shift across time and space, they share a common denominator: they are demeaned and humiliated under a law that associates them with "unnatural," nonvaginal sex acts. What the preceding sections of this chapter have demonstrated is that legislators enacted CANS with a "desire to politically harm an unpopular group"; that there is, never has been, and there cannot be a "benign explanation for" CANS; and that CANS segregates out demographic groups for "invidious oppression," regardless of the groups' changing membership.

VI. Conclusion

CANS bears no rational relationship to a legitimate government purpose; there are no public-regarding reasons for Louisiana to criminalize identical conduct under two separate statutes. CANS is poisoned by animus; the law demeans gay and transgender citizens of Louisiana. CANS violates the equal protection guarantees of the Louisiana and federal constitutions.

5

Sex Work, Sex, Work

The last chapter was something of a slog: doctrinal, technical, and dry, my occasional efforts at pith notwithstanding. Of course, I stand by its claims: the Louisiana Crime Against Nature by Solicitation statute (CANS), discriminatorily codified and enforced, has wreaked havoc upon thousands of the state's citizens, disproportionately Black trans women, cis women, and gay men, and for absolutely no legitimate state purpose. CANS is bad law, and not just as policy. It offends the Louisiana state and federal constitutions.

But if you were paying attention in the previous chapter you would notice that the doctrinal argument appears to paint itself into a sex-regressive corner. By positing that the legitimate, public-facing reasons the state might proffer for the CANS statute are already met by its Prostitution statute, have I thereby justified laws criminalizing commercial sex?

This chapter answers that question by making the not-as-doctrinal case that laws criminalizing commercial sex are unconstitutional as well, and that they too violate the Fourteenth Amendment to the U.S. Constitution. If CANS offends the guarantee of "equal protection" under the Fourteenth Amendment, antiprostitution laws offend the Amendment's "liberty" guarantee.[1] In my estimation, the constitutional case against CANS is a slam

A previous version of this chapter appeared as Joseph J. Fischel, "Is There a Constitutional Right to Sex Work?" *Boston Review*, February 1, 2022, https://www.bostonreview.net/articles/is-there-a-constitutional-right-to-sex-work/.

dunk; the constitutional case against antiprostitution laws less so, as this chapter's everything-and-the-kitchen-sink strategy betrays. This chapter is also not as doctrinal as the previous one because while CANS is anomalous to Louisiana and yet to be confronted with a facial equal protection challenge, prostitution is criminalized everywhere in the United States but for several counties in Nevada, and antiprostitution laws have been unsuccessfully challenged in many jurisdictions. Rather than deep dive into the legislative and case histories of Louisiana's Prostitution statute, I opt instead to advance broadly encompassing and not statutory text-specific arguments against laws prohibiting commercial sex. I do so in part by moving across several state and federal courts' rejections of a right to sex work, explaining why those rejections are unsupportable, erotophobic, contradictory, or all three.

There are several paths to the recognition of a constitutional right to sex work; the most promising one is—or was[2]—through *Lawrence v. Texas*, the 2003 Supreme Court decision holding that antisodomy laws (laws criminalizing anal and oral sex) violate the liberty protections of the Fourteenth Amendment.[3] As we will see, several sex workers and sex worker collectives have challenged antiprostitution laws in lower courts, claiming that if, according to *Lawrence*, the Constitution protects gay sex from criminalization, then it should protect commercial sex too. No court has yet agreed. Hovering over this chapter is the meta-observation that the judicial wedge between gay sex and commercial sex is as doctrinally dubious as it is culturally explainable. Through decades of remarkable social transformation and political advocacy, gays became the beneficiaries of constitutional rights; sex workers still are not.

The *Lawrence* Court, in countenancing the gay plaintiffs before it, characterized them as "two adults who, with full and mutual consent from each other, engaged in sexual practices common to a homosexual lifestyle."[4] But how *uncommon* is commercial sex to the heterosexual lifestyle? And is commonality really the issue, or is "full and mutual consent"? And if, for the moment, we will admit that at least some commercial sex, some of the time, is consensual, then what privileges noncommercial sodomy over and against sex for money? How have lower courts wedged a constitutional distinction? And why, to slightly readjust the admonition of the late Justice Antonin Scalia, should we "not believe it"?[5]

To adumbrate: do laws criminalizing prostitution violate the Constitution? Probably. Until recently, such a proposition would have been as absurd as suggesting, as in 1971, that the Constitution guaranteed a right to same-sex marriage.[6] How ridiculous?[7] How ridiculous![8] But cultural winds shift, social and sexual norms evolve, and political movements shape law (as should queer legal theory, or so is this author's naïve, wholly unwarranted ambition).

Section I of this chapter catalogs and counters U.S. lower courts' oft-repeated insistence that the Supreme Court already—and fatally—rejected a constitutional right to prostitution in its *Lawrence v. Texas* holding. Whether courts' misreading of *Lawrence* is deliberately deceptive or simply sloppy, the misreading must be overcome before a constitutional right to sex work can be either seriously entertained or substantively elaborated.

Ground so cleared, Section II builds out a constitutional right to sex work drawn principally from a *Lawrence*-based liberty interest in sexual freedom.[9]

Building out the *Lawrence*-based liberty interest for commercial sex entails a) refuting state and federal courts' classification of prostitution as ineluctably "public" and thereby constitutionally unprotected; b) refuting the holding of the Ninth Circuit Court of Appeals—the highest court as of this writing to adjudicate a *Lawrence*-based challenge to antiprostitution statutes—that prostitution is necessarily void of "intimacy" and thereby constitutionally unprotected; but then c) showing that "intimacy" is not a constitutional prerequisite to sexual freedom in the first place, since *Lawrence* established not a right to love—the opinion's Hallmark rhetorical flourishes notwithstanding—but a right to fuck.[10] The constitutional right to fuck has justifiable—as in compelling-or-just-legitimate-state-interest—limits. The right need not and should not authorize sexual assault, child sexual abuse, (some) incestuous relations, sex involving capability-diminishing injuries, or (some) sex between persons in positions of authority and their subordinates, like teachers and students.[11] Commerciality, though, or so I will argue d), is not a justifiable limit on the right to fuck, despite protestations about prostitution's alleged social ills: increases in crime, violence against women, HIV and other sexually transmitted infections, and so on.

Until the summer of 2022, the best, as in judicially cognizable, constitutional argument for a right to sex work would likely have derived from the right to *sex*, a right founded upon the Fourteenth Amendment's protection against liberty deprivations "without due process of law" (what is known as the Due Process Clause). Now, though, it is quite possible that the best, as in judicially cognizable, constitutional argument for a right to sex derives from a right to *work*, also as a Fourteenth Amendment–protected liberty, and not despite but because of that right's contractarian, libertarian, antiregulatory origins. Yet as I will elaborate, there is a constitutional as well as ethical distinction between regulating an occupation and proscribing it, between statutorily limiting the hours a baker may bake and criminalizing commercial baking *in toto*.[12] Section III of this chapter explains why *Dobbs v. Jackson Women's Health Organization* (2022), the Supreme Court decision abrogating a right to an abortion, jeopardizes an already-tenuous *Lawrence*-based liberty to commercial sex.[13] This part then revisits two Fourteenth Amendment due process cases from the *Lochner* era, *Meyer v. Nebraska* (1923) and *Pierce v. Society of Sisters* (1925).[14] Although these cases have been jurisprudentially repurposed as protoprivacy, proto-personal-autonomy, proto-procreative-and-family-rights holdings (i.e., as prologues for later-breaking substantive rights to contraception, interracial marriage, abortion, sodomy, and same-sex marriage), these cases more immediately assert and affirm rights to earn a living, pursue an occupation, and run a business.[15] Reestablishing *Meyer* and *Pierce* as primarily economic liberty cases, and only secondarily as personal autonomy cases, may make liberals squirm, but carrying a right to work brief for prostitution has the double advantage of syncopating with sex workers' own preferred political idiom (e.g., "sex work is work"[16]) and sounding in the conservative judiciary's albeit-attenuated deference to "unenumerated rights that are 'deeply rooted in this Nation's history and tradition.'"[17] A *Meyer*- and *Pierce*-anchored right to earn a living, I evidence, has been substantiated, or we might say constitutionalized, by legal advocacy and case law.

I. Misreading *Lawrence*

In response to sex workers', sex worker clients', and sex worker collectives' assertions that the U.S. Constitution protects commercial sex, judges often repeat the same mistaken claim that *Lawrence v. Texas* already answered what we might call the prostitution–Constitution question, and that the answer is a definitive "no." In 2004, an Illinois state appellate court found that the "*Lawrence* Court specifically excluded prostitution from its analysis."[18] The court clunkily reiterates the point: "Included in the conduct the *Lawrence* Court specifically excluded from its opinion were acts of prostitution."[19] Drawing on similar language, the Supreme Court of Hawaii wrongly posited that prostitution is "expressly rejected as a protected liberty interest under *Lawrence*."[20] The Louisiana Supreme Court followed suit: "*Lawrence* specifically states the court's decision does not disturb state statutes prohibiting public sexual conduct or prostitution."[21] And in 2019, a Texas appellate court put it plainly: *Lawrence* "has no bearing on our analysis here because the Supreme Court specifically noted that that 'case . . . does not involve prostitution.'"

But *Lawrence* did not "exclude," and absolutely did not "reject," prostitution from its holding. The *Lawrence* Court punted on prostitution, and rightly so, because neither sex work nor sex workers were before the Court. *The opinion's* statement about its *own limits* is one of its most cited passages, but has been erroneously deployed to limit its future applications:

The present case does not involve minors. It does not involve persons who might be injured or coerced or who are situated in relationships where consent might not easily be refused. It does not involve public conduct or prostitution.[22]

In legalese, this kind of passage in a court decision is known as dicta, words and opinions that neither directly bear on the present case nor bind future ones. The lower courts, however, have treated these dicta as prescriptive rather than descriptive, transforming "the present case does not involve . . . prostitution" into *the Supreme Court rejected a right to commercial sex*. This is bad reading and bad judging.

In so many words, the *Lawrence* Court said: *The precise scope of this sexual liberty we are announcing is TBD, but it* minimally *extends to gay sex in the bedroom. Sex workers, exhibitionists, and polyamorists will have to have their own days in court.* For lower courts to then claim the *Lawrence* decision precludes sex workers' constitutional claims shirks their own interpretive responsibilities. After all, in the *Lawrence* decision, Justice Anthony Kennedy chastises his yesteryear colleagues for too narrowly defining the question before them as one of "'whether the Federal Constitution confers a fundamental right upon homosexual to engage in sodomy.' . . . That statement . . . discloses the Court's own failure to appreciate the extent of the liberty at stake."[23] Our constitutionally protected sexual liberty does not cash out as a mere right to have anal sex in one's own house without getting arrested. *Lawrence* must "bear" in some way on a right to commercial sex, then, even if, ultimately, courts hold that such a right is outweighed or cabined by countervailing state interests. So what, then, are the right, good, and constitutional parameters of our sexual liberty? What decisions about sex—our sexual practices, sexual partners, and the conditions of our sexual exchange—ought to be protected from state and police interference? The Supreme Court of Virginia held that *Lawrence*'s liberty extends to a right to fornicate (to have nonmarital sex).[24] What makes sex for money so patently different? Why does the presence of money mean the absence of rights?

The preceding point is not really one about textual misinterpretation, but rather about how social misperception lubricates bad reading. Judges' stereotypes about prostitution on the one hand (nonintimate, emotionless, dangerous) and noncommercial sex on the other (intimate, enduring, consensual, nonabusive, marital) enable courts to hastily write off prostitution as outside the ambit of constitutionally protected sexual liberty.

Even when courts do not flatly reject the prostitution–Constitution question from the outset, their dismissals are tellingly contemptuous. Here is a federal district court from Indiana: "[I]t would be an *untenable stretch*

to find that *Lawrence* necessarily renders (or even implies) laws prohibiting prostitution . . . unconstitutional."[25] Here is the federal district court
of D.C.: "Defendant *stretches* the holding in *Lawrence* beyond any recognition."[26] In Illinois, defendant Sherry Conroy smartly asserted that, just
as the *Obergefell* Court drew on *Lawrence* to establish a right to marriage
for same-sex couples even though *Lawrence* itself concerned sodomitical,
not spousal, relations, so might the state's appellate court consider applying *Lawrence*'s sexual liberty to commercial sex. The court's rebuttal: "If
the *Obergefell* Court was seeking to strengthen the institution of marriage,
one can hardly imagine how extending constitutional protection to prostitution would promote that goal."[27] But it is the court that has shifted the
goal post, and circularly, as if Sherry Conroy were proposing that sex work
improves marriage. (Not incidentally, such a proposition, far from being
"hardy imagin[able]," is likely the oldest and most misogynistic defense for
prostitution: "sewers are necessary to guarantee the sanitation of palaces,
said the Church Fathers."[28])

Do these courts have in mind a "stretched"-out woman? A woman
whose sexual choices—to have sex outside marriage, to not give up sex
for free—render her unfit for constitutional protection, "hardly" a rights-
claiming citizen-subject? In 1993, a few years after the Supreme Court first
heard a constitutional challenge to antisodomy laws in *Bowers v. Hardwick*
(1986), law professor Kendall Thomas observed that the Court rhetorically
couched its refusal to countenance that right as if the Court itself were under
sexual assault by the gay appellant, Michael Hardwick. "Situating itself in
the place and position of a woman, the *Hardwick* Court seeks to persuade
readers of its institutional chastity. . . . [It] demands 'great resistance' to
Hardwick's attempted seduction."[29] If, in the 1980s, gay men were perceived
"to be a threatened attack on patriarchal power," might sex workers continue
to occupy a similar role today? By "stretching" sexual rights across the com-
mercial/noncommercial divide, sex workers are seen to endanger family,
marriage, procreation, and gendered divisions of labor, just as homosexuals were seen to before the advent of dignified, respectable homonormativity, when gays can now *just happen* to be gay.[30] Sex workers cannot yet, in
assimilative fashion, *just happen* to be sex workers.

As we have seen, many courts have refused to seriously entertain questions of if and how *Lawrence v. Texas* pertains to sex workers' rights. But
when courts have taken up the question of whether *Lawrence*'s liberty interest extends to commercial sex, or at least some forms of it, they have unilat-
erally concluded it does not. That conclusion is based on three interrelated
arguments: that *Lawrence*'s sexual liberty is subsumed under a right to *privacy*, and prostitution is not private; that *Lawrence* protects *intimate* liberty, not sexual liberty, and commercial sexual exchange definitionally lacks

intimacy; and finally, that states have more legitimate reasons to criminalize sex work than to criminalize gay sex. All three arguments are spurious.

II. The Right to Sex (Work)

a) Is Sex Work Public or Private? It's a Trick Question

Lower courts have declared commercial sex to be intrinsically public and so beyond *Lawrence*'s boundary. Donna Williams, appealing her four-year prison sentence under Illinois's antiprostitution statute, "characterize[d] her conduct as private sexual activity between two consenting adults." Prosecutors argued instead that "Williams' activity is more aptly described as the commercial sale of sex."[31] By accepting and defending the state's account, the Illinois court leans on an absolute opposition between commerciality and privacy, as if that opposition is metaphysical rather than manufactured by the state.[32] The D.C. federal district court trumpets the same note:

> In contrast to the private, non-commercial activity at issue in *Lawrence*, the conduct . . . in this case concerns the sale of sexual acts in the commercial marketplace. . . . This activity is unquestionably both public and commercial. It does not fall within the reasoning of *Lawrence*.[33]

Even if sexual acts are sold in public, they are almost always performed in private, at least in the spatial sense of indoors and hidden from others' view (for a queer theoretic, Black feminist-inflected, liberal-legalism-supported argument against criminalizing nearly all incidences of nudity, sexual expression, and sexual activity performed *not-as-hidden* from others' view, see Chapter 2). As a constitutional matter, the court is probably right: *Lawrence*'s liberty does not extend to *commercial solicitations* for sex (*Lawrence*'s liberty may not even protect *noncommercial solicitations* for anal or oral sex).[34] But if I negotiate, in the mythical marketplace, caretaking services for my father who suffered dementia, and those very bodily, very intimate services were then performed in my father's bedroom and bathroom at his assisted living facility, are those exchanges "public"? And what about, more to the point, the commercial facilitation of masturbation and sex for cognitively and physically disabled persons, whether in their own residences or group homes?[35] Surely this is "sex work" of some kind, but I would hesitate to classify such sexual services as irrevocably "public."

In her survey of sex work in Johannesburg, law professor I. India Thusi writes, "sex work frustrates [the] public-private dichotomy by making the presumably private act of sex into a public transaction." Thusi complicates her own dichotomy further still:

> [A]lthough the sale of sex occurs in private areas, the procurement of strangers for sexual activity is necessarily a *somewhat* public act. For there to be an efficient market for sex, there must be public or *quasi-public* spaces where strangers can purchase sex.[36]

Thusi's "somewhat" and "quasi-public" qualifiers betray the ideological-turned-constitutional fiction of privacy. Is purchasing sex in a side alley in fact "public"? What about in a brothel? Online? What if you take someone home, and then, upon arrival, he asks for $20 for oral sex? What if someone takes you home and gets off on paying to service you? Is that a public, sexual exchange? Under more conventional, spatialized understandings of privacy, nearly all commercial sex is "private" if we just mean in some sort of residence or dwelling (although publicly funded or subsidized group homes for the elderly and disabled question even this thin account of "privacy").

Over the past several decades, both the *transaction* and the *sex* of transactional sex have shifted indoors and online by the effects of urban gentrification, vice policing, and the internet. Drawing upon the work of sociologist Elizabeth Bernstein, journalist Alison Bass notes that "by 2001, only about 2 percent of American sex workers were streetwalkers."[37] Ironically, as both Bass and Thusi illustrate, the policing of "public" sex helped "privatize its geography," confounding the moralized binary between commerciality and privacy that justified aggressive policing in the first place.[38] Meanwhile and from another direction, social media, webcamming, and platforms like OnlyFans have forever confounded the already-fuzzy distinctions between pornography and prostitution, sex work and erotic labor. A critical difference between conventional pornography and conventional prostitution is the presence and absence of a camera, respectively.[39] Even if we accept as right and good that the presence of a camera triggers First Amendment obstacles to criminalization, how ought we to classify the labor (or is it "expression"?) of performers who sell erotic, explicit content online to individual clients? Private or public? More to the point, once sexual and erotic labor are reperceived to capture a much wider array of conduct than the "woman of the night," it is no longer clear, or all too clear, why the state criminalizes the one slice of labor disproportionately populated by lower-income, racial minority women.[40]

In *Lawrence*, the Supreme Court held that choices regarding sex, family, and procreation should be shielded from undue state interference:

[T]here are other spheres of our lives and existence, outside the home, where the State should not be a dominant presence. Freedom extends beyond spatial bounds. Liberty presumes an autonomy of the self that includes freedom of thought, belief, expression, and *certain* intimate conduct.[41]

What, though, are the contours of Justice Kennedy's "certain" if, as I have insisted, those contours cannot merely inscribe the "intimate conduct" at issue in *Lawrence*: indoor, noncommercial, consensual sex?[42] May the state imprison fornicators, adulterers, and sex workers, or not?

Some legal commentators have argued that *Lawrence* delivers a far "less expansive, rather geographized, and in the end, domesticated . . . concept of freedom" than it otherwise appears to promise.[43] But if a sex worker has[44]—excuse me, had[45]—the private-decisional right to terminate her pregnancy, why would she not have the private-decisional right to engage in the very sex that got her pregnant? Under the modern idealization *cum* judicialization of privacy, a woman and anyone else has a right to purchase contraception, and had the right to purchase abortion services, in the nominally public sphere of a clinic, hospital, or pharmacy.[46] So commercialization does not, judicially speaking, convert private, sex-*adjacent* acts into public ones, even if "privacy is an odd way of protecting the right to contraception" and even if "abortion, similarly, is not a private act" in any commonsense understanding of the term "private."[47] Why then does commercialization automatically make sex public, especially since, from the outset, the contraception and abortion cases are more plainly about the right to fuck (without procreative consequence) than a right to privacy?[48] The current constitutional regime, confusing and probably crumbling, extends the notion of privacy to protect buying and selling condoms at the local CVS, but not to buying or selling sex in one's bedroom. "Go figure," as Judge Richard Posner might say.[49]

b) Intimacy for Me but Not for Thee

In 2017, the Ninth Circuit Court of Appeals heard a post-*Lawrence* constitutional challenge to California's antiprostitution laws.[50] The court rejected plaintiffs' arguments not, chiefly, because sex work is not private, but rather because sex work is purportedly not intimate. In *Erotic Service Providers Legal Education and Research Project v. Gascon* (*ESP*), the court reasoned that the Fourteenth Amendment's sexual liberty protections, articulated by *Lawrence*, applies only to conduct characterizable as intimate. Prostitution is not, avers the court, and for two reasons: first, "a prostitute's relationship with a client 'lasts for a short period and only as long as the client is willing to pay the fee'"; and, second, "the commercial nature of the relationship between prostitute and client suggests a far less selective relationship than that which previously has been held to constitute an intimate association."[51] Let's call these two assertions the durational thesis and the fungibility thesis. Crudely, commercial sex is 1) quick and dirty and 2) sex workers are interchangeable.

It should not take an ethnography of sex work (and there are some great ones)[52] to see that both the durational and fungibility theses are false, at least as universally proclaimed by the Ninth Circuit. Commercial sex is not necessarily any longer or any shorter than noncommercial sex—and, at any rate, *Lawrence* protected gays and lesbians from criminalization for having sex, not for holding hands. Sex does not take up that much time in people's relationships, and that holds true for relationships between clients and sex workers too. Yet the relationship between a client and sex worker may go on for days, months, or years, just like noncommercial relationships. As for fungibility, clearly both clients and sex workers discriminate. Different clients have different preferences, and different sex workers have different areas of expertise.

Probably the most popular preference of contemporary clients of sex work is the "Girlfriend Experience," or GFE. Details of the GFE vary, but the basic idea is that clients want a partner—a paid one—with whom to talk, travel, share dates and meals, and cuddle. On the podcast *The Science of Sex*, then–doctoral student Christina Pareirra described the GFE as "the most pricey service" among Nevada's brothels. Pareirra, who wrote her dissertation on the brothels, found that the GFE was the service clients sought most, and the one sex workers most sought to perform (the GFE's inverse, the "Porn Star Experience," is quicker, cheaper, and generally perceived by brothel sex workers as unbecoming). The GFE might involve multiple days and nights spent with a sex worker, including dates to shows and dinners.[53]

Elizabeth Bernstein cautions us against thinking of these encounters as ersatz intimacy.[54] Rather, and as a function of several broad political, economic, and cultural transformations, the defining features of modern street prostitution (the prostitute as a public and therefore disreputable woman; the exchange of cash for expedient sexual release as ideological antithesis to private-sphere sex and love) have become muted. In their place has emerged a world of commercially available intimate encounters normalized for sex workers and clients alike, although the commingling of cash and intimacy is not altogether new, either. As Simone de Beauvoir observed in the 1940s, "some prostitutes . . . specialize in 'fantasy' because it brings in more money."[55] (Under most state antiprostitution laws, the exchange of cash for "fantasy" is perfectly permissible provided the fantasy does not involve genital contact.) In any case, just as commercialization is not the antithesis to privacy, Bernstein wishes to "complicate the view that the commodification of sexuality is transparently equatable with diminished intimacy and erotic experience."[56] Care, cooking, babysitting, and sex may all be purchased intimacies.[57] The real difference is that paid sex generally pays better than babysitting.[58] But sex is often only a small fraction of the GFE. This testimonial from sex worker Michelle Christy, as reported to journalist Alison Bass, captures some defining features of commercial intimacy:

> Sex is the least of what they want. I've got the CEO of a major NASDAQ company who comes to see me twice a month. . . . His second wife hates his first wife, and he needs a place where he can go and unwind. He's thrilled to give me $1,000 to sit and talk.[59]

Like *privacy*, *intimacy* is abstract and subjective, its meaning contingent on norms, history, and power. Nevertheless, and however underdefined, it takes judicial hubris to declare that commercial sexual relationships are altogether void of intimacy, at least for many clients. But what about for the sex workers? Is the intimacy of the GFE one-sided, and if so, should that augur against the constitutional protection of commercial sex?

There are three responses to this question; the third is the best.

The first, simplest, least persuasive answer is that even if the happy hooker is a patriarchal lie[60] peddled by "Cinde-fuckin'-rella,"[61] it would be equally tendentious to suppose that all commercial sexual relationships are not and could never be intimate for the seller. Feelings may commingle with cash. One may come to care for a client, even if not sexually, or at any rate sympathize with his frustrations about work, family, or whatever.

Still, sex workers and sex workers' rights activists, like Molly Smith and Juno Mac, are rightfully wary of defenses of prostitution anchored in rights to intimacy, pleasure, sexual freedom, sexual expression, and so forth. They worry that a politics of sex positivity can sanitize the material challenges of sex work. "Labour rights and safety are not the same as pleasure."[62] Likewise, Lorelei Lee, in her searing essay "Cash/Consent," explains how dominant political discourses admit "only two options" for sex workers: either they are victimized by traffickers or empowered by their own sexual choices. Lost between narratives of victimization and empowerment are the experiences of real-life sex workers, experiences most often contoured by poverty, limited opportunities, and sometimes violence.[63] "You don't have to like your job to want to keep it," remind Smith and Mac.[64] Yet as a constitutional question rather than a policy one, courts since the New Deal have been more likely to recognize rights to intimacy than unfettered rights to work—but see Section III.[65] Perhaps, though, we can avoid the whitewashing danger of *fucking-is-freedom* by delimiting what we mean by *intimacy*.

So the second answer to the question, *Is sex work "intimate" for the sex worker?*, would entail recasting intimacy not as deep feelings and cuddly attachments, but as a referent for choices, behaviors, and beliefs culturally coded as personal—that is, closely connected with one's sense of self and with one's meaningful relationships. In the contemporary United States, sex is freighted with significance. Even for the most promiscuous person or busiest sex worker, choices about sex (and about marriage, family, and children) are likely more intimate, so reconstructed, than choices about, say, what to have for breakfast, whether to walk or bike to work, or when and where to brush your teeth.[66]

This second answer is nearly tautological. It comes close to redefining as "intimate" whatever is "sexual." But the tautology is *Lawrence*'s, not mine: "The question before the Court is the validity of a Texas statute making it a crime for two persons of the same sex to engage in certain intimate conduct."[67] But what the Texas statute actually criminalized was "deviate sexual intercourse," which Kennedy has alchemized into "intimate conduct."[68] So alchemized, does cash so fully reverse the spell? Yes, but should it?

c) The Constitutional Right to Fuck

The third answer, though, is that the Ninth Circuit erred from the outset, because *Lawrence* was never really about intimacy; it was about sex. No legal commentator seriously thinks *Lawrence* does not guarantee the right to a "zipless fuck."[69] So whether the oral or anal sex occurs between a lifelong monogamous couple or people who met fifteen minutes before on a dating app, the police cannot break into their home and arrest them. "The *Lawrence* Court did not make intimacy a precondition for constitutional protection," as legal scholar Cass Sunstein succinctly summarizes.[70] Nevertheless, a cruel irony is that for gays to achieve rights to sex they had to appear sexless before the court.[71] Sex cannot be so easily cleansed from the sex worker, culturally and constitutionally speaking, which accounts, at least in part, for why homosexuals have fared better than sex workers in winning rights.

Under *ESP*'s lights, a commercial sexual relationship, no matter how private, how intimate, how GFE, and how long-lasting, may be criminalized. Yet the one-night (or one-minute) stand, so long as no money is exchanged between partners, may not be. Perverting incentives, it is only when "a woman might refuse to be paid by a client she liked," that she escapes criminality.[72] Conversely, hate-fucks are covered by *Lawrence*. Sometimes we want sex because it is a break from intimacy rather than its fulfillment; sometimes sex is hot (and meaningful) because it is nonintimate. Hot or not, intimate or casual, dyadic or orgiastic, *Lawrence* constitutionalizes a right to fuck between or among consenting adults; in doing so, it made manifest what earlier cases enshrining rights to contraception and abortion so clearly intimated. Law professor Nan Hunter observes:

> Although the Court in *Lawrence* treats its discussion of the early [contraception and abortion] cases as merely descriptive, it subtly regrounds those cases with a greater acknowledgment that what had been before the Court was sexual activity, not simply decisions about whether to become a parent.[73]

Citing Hunter, law professor Mary Anne Case drives home the point: "what emerges [from *Griswold* and its progeny] is the right to fuck, as generations of distinguished scholars using much politer language, have been arguing from the start."[74]

As of now, cash vitiates the right to fuck. It should not.

d) The Enduring Myth of Nonphobic Prostitution Laws

Sex work may or may not be *private*, and it may or may not be *intimate*. Constitutionally, it might not make a difference one way or the other, if states have better reasons for criminalizing prostitution than criminalizing oral and anal sex. A driving point of *Lawrence*, developed from several earlier landmark equal protection cases, is that animus toward gay people and gay sex is not a legitimate reason for states to criminalize sodomy.[75] Surely there are better reasons to criminalize prostitution than moral disapproval of prostitutes, right? Or could it be that animus—animus against sex workers, specifically, and animus, generally, against women who refuse the gendered labors of making babies and giving sex to men for free—underwrites antiprostitution laws?

Cass Sunstein suggests that "restrictions on prostitution are easily defensible," and he is correct, given our running cultural presumptions about sex work. States might, for example, claim that the legalization of sex work would "contribute to the sexual subordination of women."[76] Consider for a moment all the gendered labor, in the service sector, entertainment industry, and beyond, that the state would be authorized to ban under such a rationale ("the prostitute who only gives her body is perhaps less of a slave that the woman whose occupation it is to entertain").[77] A few weeks after the *Lawrence* decision was delivered, another legal commentator offered, "antiprostitution laws can still be justified based on concerns about coercion, exploitation of women, and the public health."[78] Indeed, this is exactly the line toed by the *ESP* court: "discouraging human trafficking and violence against women, discouraging illegal drug use, and preventing contagious and infectious diseases" are "legitimate reasons" for California to criminalize prostitution.[79]

Yet anal sex may cause anal fissures, once claimed the state of New York in defense of its sodomy law. More ludicrously, New York put forward that "injury from" fellatio "has also been reported."[80] But less ludicrously, "anal sex is the riskiest type of sex for getting or transmitting HIV."[81] Historically, as we saw in the Introduction, sodomy laws were enforced against men who committed sexual assault (but not vaginal rape).[82] Are these not good, nonphobic reasons for criminalizing sodomy? What about criminalizing activities that directly, and not speculatively, endanger citizens: smoking tobacco, drinking alcohol, eating fatty foods, playing full contact sports like hockey and football, mining, logging, or serving as president of the United States?[83]

Ass pain notwithstanding, courts came around to the position that legislators' proclaimed reasons for criminalizing same-sex sex (or discriminating against gays and lesbians,[84] or withholding federal recognition of same-sex marriage[85]) were not legitimate but rather pretexts for prejudice.

It is past time to interrogate the allegedly good, righteous-sounding reasons for outlawing prostitution. If no criminalizing regime—whether that regime prohibits the sale of sex, the buying of sex, or both—demonstrably advances state interests like public health and sex equality, and if in fact all such regimes demonstrably regress those state interests by endangering and impoverishing women and other sex workers, then maybe the good reasons for outlawing sex work are not so good after all.

Aggregating studies on sex work policies and collecting testimonies from sex workers, philosopher Amia Srinivasan summarizes "that legal restrictions on sex work make [sex workers'] lives harder, more dangerous, more violent, and more precarious. When prostitution is criminalized, as in most of the US, sex workers are raped by johns, and by the police, with impunity."[86] Srinivasan catalogs other countries' regulatory models, less draconian than the United States', but nevertheless finds that "under none of these criminalizing regimes are sex workers, as a class, better off."[87] Study after study after study after study show that criminalizing sex work—including criminalizing just the buyers, as in Sweden—puts sex workers at far greater risk of physical and sexual violence, from both clients and police; and criminalization regimes disproportionately endanger sex workers who are queer, transgender, racial minorities, and immigrants.[88]

Astonishingly, several of the studies *ESP* cites to legitimate California's antiprostitution law advocate—wait for it—repealing antiprostitution laws. One cited study reports that decriminalization would "make it easier to protect sex workers from violence and rape, because women could complain without fearing prosecution"[89]; and that "with the closing of the brothels [in France in the 1960s], venereal diseases, public solicitation, and police corruption all increased and women were more dependent upon pimps."[90] Another cited study suggests that increased drug use among African American women sex workers must be "contextualize[d] within a broader framework that acknowledges the social, economic, and political factors that indirectly shape the lives of prostitutes."[91] In other words, it might not be sex work per se that causes drug use, but poverty, violence, and criminality. *ESP* cites a Centers for Disease Control and Prevention (CDC) study to claim that "prostitution is linked to the transmission of AIDS and other sexually transmitted diseases," but that same CDC study warns that "the illegal—and often criminalized—nature of exchange sex makes it difficult to gather population-level data on HIV risk among this population." The CDC study points out that "many persons who exchange sex face stigma, poverty, and lack of access to health care and other social services—all of which pose challenges to HIV prevention efforts."[92]

When we uncover a string of sex workers murdered by serial killers in Long Island or Vancouver, which is more likely: that criminalization and aggressive policing literally and figuratively marginalize sex workers, that criminalization amplifies their vulnerability to violence, and that criminalization degrades their moral worth in the eyes of others, or that criminalization promotes gender equality?[93] So often we are told that prostitutes are symbols and victims of patriarchy. But what is more patriarchal: a woman selling sex, or public authorities disallowing her to do so? "People committed to gender hierarchy," argues philosopher Martha Nussbaum, "frequently have viewed the prostitute, a sexually active woman, as a threat to male control of women."[94] Less forgivingly, anarchist Emma Goldman wryly commented during the white slavery scare of the Progressive Era, "It is merely a question of degree" whether a woman "sells herself to one man, in or out of marriage, or to many men."[95] Or as Venus Xtravaganza observes in the queer-classic documentary *Paris Is Burning*, if a married suburban woman wants her husband to purchase a new washing machine, "I'm sure she'd have to go to bed with him anyway to give him what he wants, for her to get what she wants, so in the long run it all ends up the same way."[96]

After the sexual revolution and second-wave feminism, the line between marriage and sex work may no longer be as vanishing as Goldman supposes or Xtravaganza implies; but when states criminalize sex work and courts uphold that criminalization, women's (and folks of all genders') sexual choices—and their livelihoods—are commandeered and confined.

III. The Right to (Sex) Work?

In 2022, the United States Supreme Court overturned the constitutional right to an abortion. An extremely conservative judiciary, the majority could have voted to support Mississippi's restrictive anti-abortion law without abrogating the right to terminate one's pregnancy completely,[97] a right first announced in *Roe v. Wade* (1973) and then affirmed, if fatally qualified, in *Casey v. Planned Parenthood* (1992).[98] But the path the Court chose instead—to reverse *Roe* and *Casey* as bad law—has the not-so-unintended effect of throwing its "substantive due process" holdings into question.[99] *Roe* and *Casey* are part of a constellation of cases related to family, marriage, sex, and procreation in which the Court has held that the Constitution protects certain individual liberties against (most forms of) state interference, even if those liberties are not explicitly enumerated in the Constitution. The right to contraception, the right to marry someone of a different race or someone of the same sex, (formerly) the right to an abortion, and, as we saw previously, the right to fuck, are all such liberties that have no textual location in the Constitution but have been read out of the amendments in the Bill of Rights, chiefly but not exclusively the Fourteenth Amendment and its Due Process Clause: "nor shall any State deprive any person of life, liberty, or property, without due process of law."[100] The *Dobbs* Court expounds that a substantive due process right to an abortion is both "farcical"[101] and political. Calling forth another line of cases reining in the Due Process Clause's substantive reach, the Court maintains that only rights "implicit in the concept of ordered liberty" and "deeply rooted in this Nation's history and tradition" warrant constitutional protection from state interference.[102]

This is all a wind up for me to concur with Justice Thomas's concurrence, as do *Dobbs*'s dissenting Justices. If the Court now finds there is no constitutional liberty guarantee for abortion, what prevents states from reenacting laws to racially and sex-segregate marriage, to prohibit contraception, or criminalize oral and anal sex?[103] The weak sauce reply from Justice Alito's majority opinion is that these other practices are not counterbalanced by state interests in "potential life" and "the life of an 'unborn human being.'"[104] Yet once the Court commands, as snidely paraphrased by the dissenting Justices, that "[i]f the ratifiers [of the Fourteenth Amendment] did not understand something as central to freedom, then neither can we," a state's rationale for proscribing this or that intimate or sexual practice may be quite thin.[105] The more precise problem for this chapter's foregoing argument is not that, as some fear and others hope, the Court will revisit and then repeal other heretofore protected sexual and intimate freedoms, but that, in a post-*Dobbs* juridical landscape, courts are even less likely than they were before 2022 to announce a *Lawrence*-based liberty interest in sex for money. Consider *Dobbs*'s own ridiculing reference to prostitution:

> These attempts to justify abortion through appeals to a broader right to autonomy and to define one's "concept of existence" proves too much. Those criteria, at a high level of generality, could license fundamental rights to illicit drug use, prostitution, and the like.... None of these rights has any claim to being deeply rooted in history.[106]

The Court's rationale for not extending a right to sex work is identical to what would be the rationale for rescinding the right to sex sans work, that is for overturning *Lawrence*, since the right to fuck has no United Statesean transhistorical roots either.

If a right to *sex* may not encompass sex work, and if a right to sex (work) is not "deeply rooted in history," might a right to *work*?[107]

Many readers will be immediately skeptical of such a notion, for the Court long ago renounced[108] its infamous *Lochner v. New York* decision and several of its *Lochner*-era opinions, which held various state economic regulations (for example, maximum hour and minimum wage laws) to be unconstitutional violations of a right to contract, a right discovered as a protected liberty interest of the Fourteenth Amendment. Until recently, the *Lochner* era has been generally understood, historiographically and jurisprudentially, as a disgraced period when the Court baldly pressed a free(r)-market politics from the bench;[109] its later, regulatory-deferential decisions from the New Deal onward were critical in upholding, inter alia, workplace health and safety policies, minimum wage and maximum hour laws, and nondiscrimination protections for racial minorities, women, and other disadvantaged groups.

The pertinent question is whether or not anchoring a constitutional right to sex work in a right to work, not sex, slippery-slides us toward a nightmarish, deregulatory frenzy of judicial activism; or if, conversely, the "*Lochner* bogeyman"[110] preempts us from a more discriminating defense, whereby one may pursue their livelihoods (baking or sex, for example) and sell their wares (bread loaves or blowjobs, for example) but under legitimate regulatory oversight. I am suggesting the latter, and by way of two other *Lochner*-era Supreme Court decisions.

Meyer v. Nebraska and *Pierce v. Society of Sisters* not only survived the New Deal regulatory-friendly Court decisions but also have had a thriving career since, redrafted as prologues for an array of rights to sexual, marital, and reproductive freedoms.

In *Meyer*, a schoolteacher had been convicted under a 1919 Nebraska law that prohibited instructing schoolchildren in any language other than

English. The teacher, Robert Meyer, successfully challenged the constitutionality of the (post–World War I, avowedly xenophobic) law. The Court held that the law "conflict[ed] with rights assured to plaintiff" by the Fourteenth Amendment, specifically (but more on this anon) "the right of the individual to contract [and] to engage in any of the common occupations of life."[111]

At issue in *Pierce* was an Oregon law compelling nearly all children in the state to attend public school. "[T]wo Oregon corporations owning and conducting schools," a Catholic orphanage and a private military academy, brought suit, and like Robert Meyer the corporations alleged that the statute deprived them of their Fourteenth Amendment–protected liberty.[112] Liberty to what? The Court specified (but more on this anon, too): the "corporations owning and conducting schools are threatened with destruction of their business and property through the improper and unconstitutional compulsion exercised by this statute upon parents and guardians."[113]

These cases manifestly involve children and child-rearing, parents and parenting, family and education. It is for this reason that the Court has so often marshaled *Pierce* and *Meyer* in its landmark decisions announcing constitutional rights to privacy, contraception, abortion, interracial marriage, same-sex marriage, and (noncommercial) sex.[114] Nor are such references disingenuous. The language in both *Meyer* and *Pierce* easily lends itself to such appropriation. For example, *Meyer* lists off the rights to "to marry [and] establish a home and bring up children" as also subsumed under the Fourteenth Amendment.[115] Less abstractly, the *Meyer* Court opines that Meyer's "right thus to teach and the right of the parents to engage him so to instruct their children . . . are within the liberty of the Amendment."[116] *Pierce* echoes *Meyer*: "we think it is entirely plain that the [law] unreasonably interferes with the liberty of parents and guardians to direct the upbringing and education of their children."[117]

Yet it is critical to remember, as does law professor Jed Rubenfeld, that the parties in these cases were neither parents nor children, but a teacher and two corporations, deprived of their business and property.[118] Even as the *Pierce* Court waxes poetic that "those who nurture [the child] and direct his destiny have the right, coupled with the high duty, to recognize and prepare him for additional obligations," that is not the immediate issue the Court is adjudicating nor the liberty it is sculpting out of the Fourteenth Amendment.[119] Surely it is of nontrivial consequence that the business these businesses are in are instructing children and cultivating young citizen-soldiers for the nation. Both *Meyer* and *Pierce* make plain that not every business, party to a contract, or worker has a right to an occupation, let alone an absolute one. *Meyer*, *Pierce*, and even *Lochner* attest that states may regulate commerce and regulate working conditions, provided those regulations are "reasonable," a point on which this chapter will close.[120] But for now I want to convey the simple observation that *Pierce* and *Meyer*, although later conscripted as laying the foundation for rights to privacy, sexual and intimate freedoms, and reproductive autonomy, are straightforwardly about the right to an occupation. Or even more granularly, these cases reject state laws that would *categorically* proscribe an occupation (*Meyer*) and shut down a business (*Pierce*).

Jed Rubenfeld revisits *Meyer* and *Pierce* to make a complementary argument to the one I am introducing here. Writing after *Bowers* but before *Lawrence*, Rubenfeld provocatively and rather persuasively proposes that laws against contraception, abortion, interracial marriage, and gay sex are better comprehended, both normatively and constitutionally, not as violations of a right to privacy (and the "personhood" that privacy purports to protect),[121] but as antidemocratic, totalitarian overreaches that coerce citizens into social conformity and standardize them under traditional norms. Under Rubenfeld's lights, the common and unconstitutional denominator across anticontraception, anti-abortion, and antisodomy laws is that they "forcibly direc[t] individuals into the pathways of reproductive sexuality."[122] "Anti-abortion laws," additionally, "produce motherhood: they take diverse women with every variety of career, life-plan, and so on, and make mothers of them all."[123] Rubenfeld's enemy of democracy, and of the Constitution, is social standardization. "The danger of standardization," he summarizes, "can in part be understood as the danger of treating individuals as mere instrumentalities of the state, rather than as citizens with independent minds."[124]

Despite the later judicial rebranding of *Meyer* and *Pierce* as protoprivacy and protopersonhood cases, Rubenfeld posits that these cases are better read as establishing constitutional checks against laws that coercively conform their citizens. The *Meyer* Court, notes Rubenfeld, cautioned that Nebraska was "attempting to 'foster a homogenous people' with American ideals."[125] Banning the teaching of foreign languages is tantamount to the state "inculcat[ing] one acceptable way of thinking."[126] The Oregon law adjudicated in *Pierce* "presented this threat [of coerced uniformity] even more starkly," and Rubenfeld quotes powerful passages from the opinion to that effect: "the fundamental theory of liberty upon which all governments in this Union repose excludes any general power of the State to standardize its children"[127]; and "[t]he child is not the mere creature of the state."[128]

I have taken this detour through Rubenfeld's read of *Meyer*, *Pierce*, and the antitotalitarian principles for which he extols them as I think his analysis applies with equal force to sex work, the people—most often women—who perform it, and the laws that criminalize it. If a "child is not the mere creature of the state," nor is a woman. And if the state cannot "standardize its children," it should not standardize its women, either. As laws against abortion force women (and others) into motherhood, laws against prostitution compel women (and others) into a norm of amative sex, itself a rarely realized fiction. But whereas Rubenfeld supposes that *Pierce*'s true objection is to totalitarian overreach and not "*merely* to a deprivation of the 'liberty of contract [i.e., *Lochner*],'" I am Goldilocksing the critique, proposing that the state's outright prohibition on an occupation—whether baker, German teacher, or prostitute—is in itself presumptively unconstitutional and impermissibly standardizing.[129] For even if, as Rubenfeld contends, "minimum wage or maximum rent laws . . . do not positively take over and redirect lives" like government bans on abortion, government bans on professions get pretty close.[130]

In *Pierce*, in other words, the deprivation of liberty to contract was no "mere" regulatory interference but exactly what would have effectuated the socially standardizing, coercively conformist world Rubenfeld fears. Liberals and leftists (this book's audience, let's be honest) may find it more appealing to criticize antiprostitution laws as socially and sexually normative rather than as economically restrictive, but I am arguing that, in this instance, economic restriction installs social and sexual normativity.

A constitutionally guaranteed right to earn a living, what I will shorthand as an "occupational right," has been championed by not only free marketers and libertarians but also civil rights leaders and litigators. During World War II, explains law professor Risa Goluboff, lawyers for the National Association for the Advancement of Colored People (NAACP) shifted its litigation focus to African American workers and union discrimination cases.[131] As the constitutional location of "civil rights claims . . . remained uncertain"[132] in the 1940s (would relief come from the "equal protection," "due process," or "privileges and immunities" clauses of the Fourteenth Amendment?[133]), NAACP lawyers advanced a Fourteenth Amendment-based, due process, occupational right argument on behalf of African American workers in segregated and/or otherwise discriminating unions. Surveying NAACP briefs in employment discrimination cases at the time, Goluboff writes, perhaps surprisingly, that

> the NAACP lawyers did not see a necessary disjunction between *Lochner* reasoning and the New Deal. Rather they saw continuity: New Deal labor regulation represented a deepening of government protection for the right to a livelihood precisely by safeguarding unions.[134]

Regulatory oversight was a condition of possibility for "collective rights of laborers" and for equal employment opportunities.[135] In their briefs, NAACP lawyers cited several lower courts' espousal of a right to work even after—and importantly for my argument, not in conflict with—the Supreme Court's about-face on *Lochner.* For example: "[e]veryone must be free to pursue his lawful calling; that is fundamental"; "the constitutional right to earn a livelihood"; and "the right to earn a livelihood is a property right guaranteed by the Fifth and Fourteenth Amendments to the United States Constitution."[136] The strategy proved victorious:

> The NAACP thus argued, and the state courts embraced, *Lochner*-like right to work arguments as justifying limits on union freedom to discriminate. This fact focused the cases at least as much, if not more, on the substantive right to work (as it happened, without racial discrimination) as on the substantive right to be free from racial discrimination (as it happened, in the context of work).[137]
>
> The most successful legal arguments the NAACP marshaled in the union discrimination cases were based on a substantive reading of the Due Process Clause and closely related common law doctrine, not on the Equal Protection Clause. . . . [These arguments] saw considerable success even in the post-*Lochner* era.[138]

The right at issue is "*Lochner*-like," but not strictly Lochnerian. These cases were not about the right to work for however little wage or for however many hours, but about, "at base, the right to work," full stop.[139] As the NAACP legal team saw it, unions specifically and government regulations generally buttressed or potentially buttressed a *nondiscriminatory right to an occupation.* This right is not to be confused, and is in fact oppositional to, a right to unfettered contract.

Reconsider *Meyer, Pierce,* and, circuitously, earning a livelihood via sex. State governments may intervene on all kinds of matters in their educational institutions, from health and safety measures to curricular content to staff and faculty salaries.[140] One might make the case, as NAACP litigators did in the context of racially discriminating unions, that these sorts of interventions protect or enrich schools, students, faculty, and staff. But laws that outright ban a profession, like teaching a foreign language, sound the constitutional alarm.

Undoubtedly, the market in commercial sex ought to be regulated to secure the safety and well-being of sex workers and their clients (even if the history of such regulation heretofore tends toward the discriminatory, stigmatizing, and misogynistic).[141] But a market cannot be officially regulated, and people's occupational rights thereby realized through such regulation, if that market is a black one. While specifically *antidiscrimination* regulatory measures for sex work are rather downstream from the contemporary condition of near total criminalization in the United States,[142] we should recognize, if not as a constitutional matter, that antiprostitution laws and enforcement disparately disadvantage racial minority women, queer and trans communities, and poor people.[143] A regulatory regime of legalized sex work thus extends a right to occupation to social groups for whom it has been historically and contemporarily denied. In this sense, a *Meyer*- and *Pierce*-based right to earn a livelihood for sex workers finds affinity in the NAACP's "brief but significant foray into labor-related litigation in the 1940s."[144]

Beyond the union discrimination cases, throughout the twentieth and twenty-first centuries, and before and after the "sexual freedom" cases of which the *Dobbs* Court is so dangerously skeptical,[145] courts have repeatedly insisted upon a constitutionally protected right to earn a living—or "a right to choose and follow one's calling"[146]—as a protected liberty interest of the Due Process Clause of the Fourteenth Amendment.

Herewith, several examples to buttress the claim that an occupational right has deep, historical, doctrinal roots:

In 1915 (so maybe not that "deep," but deeper in the nation's history than 1973), shortly after *Lochner*, the Supreme Court gave its originalist, most full-throated defense of an occupational right in *Truax v. Raich*:

> It requires no argument to show that the right to work for a living in the common occupations [and what is more common than prostitution?] of the community is of the very essence of the personal freedom and opportunity that it was the purpose of the [Fourteenth] Amendment to secure.[147]

In *Greene v. McElroy*, a McCarthy-era case involving a government subcontractor terminated for his alleged affiliations with Communism, Chief Justice Earl Warren, writing for the majority, pronounced that "the right to hold specific private employment and to follow a chosen profession free from unreasonable governmental interference comes within the 'liberty' and 'property' concepts of the Fifth Amendment," a right presumably incorporated against states through the Fourteenth Amendment.[148] Although the Court ultimately ruled for Greene on other grounds, the Court cites *Greene* in another Communist-affiliation/employment-termination case several years later to suggest a right to private employment, against which statutory interference has "serious constitutional implications."[149]

In 1987, the Ninth Circuit Court of Appeals, citing *Greene* but sounding like *Raich*, noted that "it is indisputable that an individual may have a protected property interest in private employment."[150]

Most pertinent for the purpose of this chapter—anchoring a right to sex work in the right to work—the Supreme Court held in 1999 that the "liberty component of the Fourteenth Amendment's Due Process Clause includes some generalized due process right to choose one's field of private employment, but a right which is nevertheless subject to reasonable government regulation."[151] Chief Justice Rehnquist clarifies that this unenumerated-but-protected right has materialized against "cases [that] all deal with *a complete prohibition of the right to engage in a calling*, and not the sort of brief interruption which occurred here."[152] If one has a protected "liberty interest in practicing law,"[153] or in baking, or in commercial sex, that in no way prevents states, nay may require them (see the NAACP union discrimination cases), to regulate said lawyering, baking, and fucking. Chief Justice Rehnquist's distinction presciently anticipates law professor David Bernstein's ruminations, written a generation later, on a constitutionally carved out occupational right:

> One imagines the Court could also find a way to define the right carefully and narrowly [it did!], protecting the specific right not to be excluded from a profession by arbitrary and oppressive licensing rules [or complete criminalization?], and not a broader and much less historically grounded right to be free from occupational regulations that impinge on freedom of contract, such as minimum wage laws.[154]

Like me, Bernstein wishes to advance a constitutional right to lawful occupation. He spotlights, inter alia, a 2015 Texas Supreme Court opinion that "invalidated a law that required individuals who make their living by threading eyebrows to obtain a cosmetology license, which requires costly, time-consuming training that is almost entirely irrelevant to eyebrow threading."[155] Despite courts longstanding, post-*Lochner* deference to states' economic interventions, some forms of licensure, avers Bernstein, have the impermissible, *Pierce*-like effect of quashing rather than regulating business.

The sampling of "occupation" cases assembled here begins to substantiate that "[t]he right to purse an occupation free from arbitrary government action is certainly deeply rooted in American history."[156] In Section II of this chapter I referred to the 2018 Ninth Circuit *ESP* case as entailing a *Lawrence*-based, right-to-fuck liberty challenge to anticommercial sex laws, and I explained that the appellate court's blinkered definition of *intimacy* carried the day against sex work. But three of the plaintiffs in the case, "former erotic service providers,"[157] asserted *occupational rights* against the California antiprostitution law as well, claiming that the law "severely infringes on [their] ability to earn a living through one's chosen livelihood or profession" and "unconstitutionally burdens the right to follow any of the ordinary callings in life; to live and work where one will; and for that purpose to enter into all contracts which may be necessary and essential to carrying out these pursuits."[158] In their brief to the court, the erotic service providers cite *Meyer v. Nebraska*, the German teacher case from the 1920s, to this effect.[159]

The Ninth Circuit ignores the sex workers' assertion of an occupational right and fails to address *Meyer* at all. Barely entertaining the challenge, the court recircuits the occupational right claim as if it is a *Lawrence*-based sexual right claim, and then tautologically concludes that "there is no constitutional right to engage in illegal employment, namely prostitution."[160] But that's a bit like replying to Robert Meyer that he has no right to teach German because there is a law against teaching German. The illegality of the occupation is the very constitutional question before the court. Either 1) the *ESP* court is prejudicially unable to conceive of sexual labor as labor, 2) the occupational right claim smells too much like *Lochner* for the court to countenance it, 3) taking *Meyer* and its occupational rights, not just privacy rights, progeny seriously would launch a formidable attack against sex work criminalization, or 4) some combination of all three. Whatever permutation, *ESP*'s insufficient gloss on a sex worker's right to a livelihood ought to be rectified in future constitutional challenges.

If and when *ESP*'s oversight is redressed, the final concern or counterbalance, as always, will be reasonability. Just as a sex right, even if constitutional, might be and very often is curtailed for legitimate state purposes (one's right to sex cannot be exercised on a child, for example), so too may an occupational right (one's right to work as a coalminer may be limited by a host of municipal and state protocols, for example). The judicial question then becomes what constitutes "reasonable government regulation," and what is unreasonable. The criminalization of sex work is unreasonable for all the reasons outlined in the enduring myth of nonphobic prostitution laws section earlier in this chapter. Antiprostitution laws and "repressive policing practices" isolate and endanger (indexically) women, subject them to violence and sexual violence from police and clients, increase their likelihood of contracting HIV and other STIs, and decrease the likelihood of condom use.[161] The market in sex work cannot be regulated to protect women, nor to reduce violence and sexually transmitted infections, while antiprostitution laws remain on the books. In his dissent in *Lochner*, quoting an earlier case over licensure for cigarette sellers, Justice Harlan wrote that

> unless the regulations are so *utterly unreasonable and extravagant* in their nature and purpose that the property and personal rights of the citizen are unnecessarily, and in a manner wholly arbitrary, interfered with or destroyed without due process of law, they do not extend beyond the power of the State to pass.[162]

If the standard for the unconstitutionality of a statute were "utterly unreasonable and extravagant," that would be a high bar, but one nonetheless antiprostitution laws fail to meet. Banning boxing[163] or banning American football,[164] given the direct, serious, and capability-corroding harms they inflict upon their practitioners, would seem to me a far more reasonable use of state power than banning sex work, yet I would argue that the boxer's and the football player's right to earn a living should not be so easily dismissed, either. Boxing and football are regulated, of course, concussions and chronic traumatic encephalopathy notwithstanding. Would a state be permitted to criminalize either sport?

If a right to be concussed for cash is questionable—after all, we call boxing without compensation *assault*—a right to sex for cash should not be.

Throughout this last section of the chapter I have insisted that a right to earn a livelihood cannot be realized without regulatory oversight: for example, one cannot pursue an occupation if she is sexually harassed at her workplace. I hope therefore that my qualified defense of a right to sex work survives the criticism that queer legal thought is necessarily antistatist, a handmaiden to deregulatory neoliberalism.[165]

IV. Paraidentitarian Sexual Freedom, Redux

In 1957, the influential Report of the Departmental Committee on Homosexual Offences and Prostitution, also known as the Wolfenden Report, called for the decriminalization of homosexual acts in the United Kingdom.[166] At the same time, the report advocated punishing street prostitution more harshly and criminalizing male sex workers. Across the pond and around the same time, the MPC, promulgated by the American Law Institute, recommended that states decriminalize consensual sodomy yet criminalize prostitution, brothel-keeping, and similar offenses.[167]

The Wolfenden Report and the MPC do not, of course, exhaustively explain why gays and sex workers have received such disparate political, cultural, and legal treatment over the past several generations. But these documents, which have so powerfully shaped criminal law and police practices, forecast an identitarian hierarchy of moral worth, a stratification of respectability that frames how we understand sexual rights and who we think are entitled to them.

"The raid on the Stonewall Inn one June night in 1969 would not have become a police riot were it not for the street-hustling transvestites (as they then referred to themselves) who resisted when threatened with arrest, who tossed coins and bottles back at the police," writes former sex worker and journalist Melissa Grant.[168] Molly Smith and Juno Mac concur:

[T]he bravery and resilience of sex workers has played a part in many liberation struggles. . . . [T]hey were part of the riots at Compton's Cafeteria in San Francisco and the Stonewall Inn in New York that kickstarted the LGBTQ liberation movement in the United States.[169]

U.S. courts have affirmed the criminality of prostitution by distancing sex work from gay sex conceptually and morally, with commerciality as their pretext. The courts' maneuver "judicializes" the Wolfenden Report's and MPC's recommendations yet belies queers' and sex workers' historical affinity and common struggle.

Queers and sex workers—evidently, not discrete populations—share or ought to share a political project: to build a world in which sex practices, gender identities, and gender expressions are policed a whole lot less. The fight for sexual freedom should not be artificially cabined by sexual identity, whether on the streets, in statehouses, or in the courts.

Coda

Sodomy's Solicitations

Children's Edition

This coda is occasioned by the 2020s, U.S.-led, renewed war on queer, trans, and nonbinary children—which is to say all children[1]—waged by conservative lawmakers. We are living through an extended moment of "naked political violence against trans life."[2] Some of us are not living through it.[3] In the contemporary moment, violence against trans life is most aggressively violence against trans children, wherein "trans" signifies not just young people who definitively desire to inhabit life in a gender other than the gender that conventionally correlates with their assigned sex at birth, but also signifies any and every deviation from the strictest, most unforgiving, most toxic, most unfun gender norms.[4] From this description or prescription of "trans," "Don't Say Gay" ordinances, statewide bans on affirming healthcare, near-bans on drag performances, and restrictions on students' movement—to and from bathrooms and locker rooms, in and out of swimming pools, on and off the athletic field—are all cut from the same cloth: political manipulations of adults' desire to extinguish the strangeness, queerness, and curiosity of children.[5]

"It's always open season on gay kids."[6] The war on kids—gay and trans, queer and gender-exploratory—and their flourishing now taking place in the United States, the United Kingdom, and elsewhere urges a retrospective on the three sodomitical episodes and the two constitutional cases for commercial sex discussed in the preceding chapters. For the symbolic Child who sits at the vacant center of the antitrans movement—white and woundable, innocent and incompetent, always corruptible to perverts and perversion[7]—is the very same Child who contains or regresses what would be a more expansive, paraidentitarian politics of sexual justice, in Louisiana and far beyond.

In the first chapter, it was the alleged monstrosity of sexual violence against imagined white children, or the "pedophilic function," that legitimates the illegitimate: sex offender registration and notification systems and the antifeminist, carceral machine those systems fuel and amplify.[8] The New Orleans–based political campaign to declassify sex workers as sex offenders hinged on distancing women from pedophiles, from child rapists. The political opportunity lost in that maneuver is challenging the state's deployment of sex for unjust governance; unjust both because sex offender regulatory regimes are worse than ineffective remedies against sexual violence and because the regime perpetuates its own form of state-sponsored sexual violence. That latter claim, if somewhat speculatively made in Chapter 1, has been horrifically literalized in the war on queer and trans children, as newly enacted laws authorize state actors to inspect the genitals of children under the auspices of protecting them—while in the summer of 2024, the Louisiana Legislature passed a bill permitting the state to surgically castrate child sex offenders.[9] The state threatens to sexually abuse children in order to shield them from gender diversity, or queerness; that such sexual abuse is normalized, if it is, is in part due to the sex exceptionalism manifested in sex offender regulatory regimes.

Recall, too, as parsed in my constitutional case against CANS, that the law was enacted to target and imprison Brown and Black boys selling sex in the French Quarter. The whole historico-political episode was driven by Southern white male conservative legislators' desire to send poor Brown and Black kids to prison longer, begging the question, to paraphrase law professor Dorothy Roberts, whether and under what conditions "children of color" is a political oxymoron.[10]

In the second sodomitical episode, the child did the most regressive political labor despite but really because there were no actual children on the scene.[11] The specter of the witnessing child, witnessing sex in public, neutralized what should have been a noncontroversial reform to repeal the state's already unlawful antisodomy law. And as I mentioned in that chapter as well, another reform bill—this one to decriminalize commercial sex—panicked one state representative to agonize aloud at a public hearing that children might come to watch their parents having sex with prostitutes. I thus meditated on the incest palimpsest that underscores aversion-attraction to sex in public.

And as we saw in the third sodomitical episode, the animal sexual abuse law, with its proscriptions on animal pornography and its sex offender treatment mandates, is modeled on child pornography and child molestation statutes. The state senator's alarmist appeal for his bill—"Strong punishment for this heinous act is important because the sexual abuse of animals is an indicator of other violent, predatory sex crimes, especially against children";[12] and, "the people who do these things abuse children, and they later graduate to murder and other horrific things"[13]—throws into relief the nearly irrefutable political power of the sexually abused child. The heady blend of expertise talk ("an indicator of"), gateway talk ("they later graduate"), careful vagueness ("these things"), and child sexual abuse talk makes it particularly challenging to recognize that each of the senator's propositions is senseless and dangerous. In this last episode, the injured or injurable child, and the injuring image of the child, directs our theories and our policies away from mass-scale animal suffering and back onto strange, predatory, and despicably indiscriminate male desire.

While the Child and children are not manifest in my claims for a constitutional right to commercial sex, I noted earlier that opposition to a decriminalization bill invoked the specter of the violated child; more generally, sexually injurable children have long served as ideological bludgeons for neutralizing sex workers' movements and for censoring pornography.[14] It is also worth pointing out that the occupational right I deduced from two 1920s Supreme Court cases to plea for a sex worker's right to work first arose with regard to rearing and educating children. That fact cuts dialectically: the moral force of an occupational right is drawn from teachers and schools acting in loco parentis. But so proximate to the child, that occupational right was conscripted into modern privacy jurisprudence, obfuscating a right to work as a proto-right to child-rearing, marriage, contraception, abortion, and, indeed, sodomy.

In the sodomitical episodes I parse, the Child cabins a paraidentitarian, more progressive politics of sexual justice. In the contemporary backlash against queer and trans lives, the nonconforming Child figures as corrupted, deluded, and soon to be mutilated by woke ideology.

A first question, then: how might we countenance the moralization and weaponization of the figurative Child over and against the flourishing of actually existing children, adults, and nonhuman animals?

In the Introduction, I proposed that the affinities and attachments enacted through sodomy locate nonprocreative desires as immanent sources of, rather than external constitutive threats to, the polity and so to politics. Both sodomy and antisodomy law invite us to avow and then politicize what we might think of as a universal queerness, rather than to offload that queerness onto racial, gendered, and sexualized others. And yet, while I suggested that left political theory and adjacent scholarship diagnose how women and people of color are historically burdened as figures of excess, unruliness, and incompetence in opposition to the deliberative, temperate capacities of ruling white men, the truth of the matter is that, under liberalism and late liberalism, no category of persons figures as so wholly dependent, heteronomous, and incapable of reason as the child.[15] As legal scholar Annette Appell argues, liberalism needs childhood to prop up adults as deliberative, reasoning, independent agents capable of self-governance. Under U.S. law, whereas formal racial and (nearly all) sex discriminations are, after long struggles, now understood to be noxious to the Constitution, age-based restrictions are ubiquitous across state and federal laws.[16] Childhood philosopher John Wall predicts, if optimistically, that

> in a century, we will likely look back on today's attitudes about children's rights that same way we look back on attitudes about women's and minorities' rights a century ago. We will see how profoundly young people are treated as second-class citizens in our time.[17]

And so a second question: how might children figure otherwise in a paraidentitarian politics?

Lee Edelman's infamous answer was to "fuck the social order and Child in whose name we're collectively terrorized," by which he meant that those of us who are socially ascribed as queer ought to reject a political structure that incessantly, insidiously, and heteronormatively valorizes the Child as the summary source of our collective meaning and purpose.[18] I am more sympathetic to this structural, symbolic provocation than some other critics, but I agree with Paul Amar that such a refusal is not and should not be synonymous with disengaging from projects of investing children with political power and recognizing their political agency.[19] To the contrary, empowering young people, and cataloging their political activism, participation, and protest, confounds the Child as the inert prop of adult projections, or what Amar names "political infantilization."[20]

Queer scholar Steven Angelides's counterproposal to the erotophobic conservatism of the Child is to protect and promote children's sexual agency, supposing that the recognition of children's desires and pleasures would serve as a ballast against recurring child sex panics, of which today's anti-trans movement might be considered a latest iteration.[21] Sociologist Jane Ward, meanwhile, offers a gorgeous, biographic plea for suspending gender as much as possible in child-rearing practices. She describes how she and her partner have deliberately raised their child without markers of traditional gender, encouraging their child to pick for themselves clothes, toys, styles, activities, and so forth. "To parent queerly is to offer children an array of gendered objects, colors, and narratives—including queer and cross-gender narrative—and then invite children to interact with this expanded field of possibilities."[22] The backlash Ward, her partner, and other queerly creative parents encounter in their labors to suspend the social imposition of gender on their children is testament to the violent, collective investment in its binary form.[23]

I adore Ward's parenting practices, although I am unsure if they are scalable; and I admire Angelides's courage in defending the sexuality of children, although I worry that, absent other institutional reforms, permitting young people more sexual license (for example, by repealing laws that criminalize sex between teachers and students) might end up further exploiting them.[24]

In any case, I want to take the last few paragraphs of this coda to propose an alternative, more structural path forward for facilitating young people's gender and sexual flourishing, a path that synchronizes with the paraidentitarian politics of the book.

It is beyond time to politically enfranchise young people.[25] "It is difficult to justify to children why they are disenfranchised for nearly two decades of their lives, during which time they have little authority and fewer claims to power."[26] Indeed, young people should have the right to vote, to hold political office, to sit on juries, to participate in the political and institutional decisions, to sit on school boards, and so on. Young people ought to serve on advising boards for matters pertaining to their healthcare, including but not limited to contraception access, birth control availability, abortion services, and gender affirming care. "At the very least, children should participate in or be consulted in their governance, regulations that affect them, public works, and the design of the institutions that affect them most directly, such as school, streets, homes, and neighborhoods."[27] I am following the lead of, among other political and legal theorists,[28] Appell, who advocates not only negative rights for children (so delimiting or abolishing age-based restrictions on political participation, employment, and sexual activity, for example) but also positive accommodations for young people—like robust civics, vocational and sexual education, not to mention lower tables in the home and more compact automobiles—so that they may enjoy equal citizenship.[29] We might add to her list education in human anatomy and physiology so that young people are better informed about the decisions they make regarding their health and welfare.[30]

Whether current age-based restrictions on political, economic, and civic participation should be lowered or outright abolished is not my concern here. Rather, the point is twofold: first, to recognize that, despite age-correlated developmental processes, it is in fact modern and late modern social and political constructions of childhood, rather than any categorical and ontological deficiency of minors aged one day to eighteen years, that renders children so utterly helpless. "Children lack voting rights not, as generally thought, because of something deficient in children; they lack voting rights . . .

because of something deficient in democracy."[31] And second, to point out how glaringly absent, or at least exceedingly rare,[32] are young people's voices and opinions from the legislative reforms now curtailing or extinguishing their freedoms.

Accommodationist policies for children, policies tailored to the physical, emotional, and educational needs of young people but calibrated to equal citizenship and participation, would recognize children as a separate social class (identitarian) while expecting and affirming their involvement and leadership in intergenerational community (para). Consider too the kinds of paraidentitarian coalitions that might materialize among subjects sexualized by the state: the hundreds of thousands of people placed on sex offender registries for crimes they committed as children;[33] parents who may be investigated for child abuse because they provided their children with healthcare;[34] minors whose genitals may be subject to inspection by state actors.[35]

Negative and positive liberties are recursive. Enfranchised, children overall would likely vote for better public housing, a living wage for their parents (and maybe themselves), stricter gun control, easier access to books and educational resources, and easier access to necessary healthcare.[36] Better educated, better nourished, and better sheltered children make for better actors in the polity.

My suggestion for beefing up young people's political agency, and not just their gendered or sexual agency, is to point toward a more political, less personal, more procedural, less subjective, more radical, and less reactive agenda for defending the queerness of kids. The suggestion is also an avowedly political-as-in-partisan one: young people are more progressive than their elders, more concerned about climate change, more likely to identify as vegan, vegetarian, or "flexitarian" (talk about paraidentitarian!), and more likely to identify as trans or nonbinary.[37] Their increased political involvement, I would wager, would be a boon for gender diversity, for interspecies welfare, and for planet Earth.

Despite Taylor Swift's analgesic that "shade never made anybody less gay,"[38] historical materialists tell us otherwise.[39] The contours of political economy, political ideology, and scientific development shape sexual subjectivity, gender identity, and possibilities for intimacy. And so, a final reason for engendering young people's political participation is that *there would likely be more trans people in the world.*[40] Then, the rationale for providing gender affirming care for queer, trans, and nonbinary children would not only be that such kids will otherwise suffer or commit suicide,[41] but also that the world would be more joyful, filled with more queerness.

Chronology

1805   Louisiana first criminalizes "crime against nature" (CAN).[1]

1900   *State v. Vicknair.* Louisiana Supreme Court rejects argument that oral sex is "natural," thereby upholding crime against nature conviction.[2]

1912   *State v. Aenspacker.* Louisiana Supreme Court rejects argument that crime against nature refers only to sex "per anum."[3]

1942   Legislature revises CAN statute to criminalize "unnatural carnal copulation by a human being with another of the same or opposite sex or with an animal." Solicitation for "unnatural" sexual practices does not constitute CAN but is instead a misdemeanor under the obscenity statute.[4]

1962   Legislature adds "Aggravated" to "Crime Against Nature" (CAN) statute, which includes forcible anal and oral sex.[5]

1975   Legislature reclassifies forcible anal sex as "rape," thereby excluding such conduct from "aggravated" CAN.[6]

1977   Legislature gender-neutralizes "prostitution" statute; men can be convicted for prostitution.[7]

1978   *State v. Phillips.* Louisiana Supreme Court holds that both anal penetration and oral-genital contact (penetration not required) qualify as a "crime against nature."[8]

1982   Legislature enacts "Crime Against Nature by Solicitation" (CANS) statute, prohibiting oral and anal sex for compensation.[9] CANS carries significantly harsher penalties than "prostitution" despite criminalizing identical conduct.

1987   *State v. Ryans.* Louisiana Court of Appeals rejects argument that penalties for a CANS conviction are disproportionate and excessive as compared to "prostitution."[10]

1992   Legislature enacts first sex offender registration law. CAN is classified as a registerable sex offense.[11]

1995   *State v. Baxley.* Louisiana Supreme Court rejects that the harsher penalties attached to a CANS conviction compared to the penalties attached to a "prostitution" conviction unconstitutionally discriminates against homosexuals.[12]

1995   *State v. Spitz.* Louisiana state appellate court rejects argument that fellatio is "natural," thereby upholding crime against nature conviction.[13]

2000   *State v. Smith.* Louisiana Supreme Court upholds both CAN and CANS as constitutionally permissible.[14]

2001   *State v. Moore.* Louisiana state appellate court rejects argument that homosexuality is "natural," thereby upholding crime against nature conviction.[15]

2001   Legislature adds "oral sexual intercourse" to the definition of "rape."[16] Defendants convicted of forcible oral sex continue to be prosecuted under aggravated CAN.

2005   *State v. Thomas.* Louisiana Supreme Court rejects argument that punishing CANS more harshly than prostitution violates due process. However, the court implies that the simple CAN statute (which criminalizes consensual, noncommercial sex) is unconstitutional.[17]

2008   Legislature clarifies that "oral sex" is "sexual intercourse" under the "prostitution statute."[18]

2010   Legislature equalizes penalties for first conviction of CANS and prostitution. People do not have to register as sex offenders for a first conviction of CANS. However, subsequent CANS convictions are still registerable sex offenses.[19]

2011   Legislature declassifies CANS as a registerable sex offense.[20] However, previous offenders are not removed from the sex offender registry.

2012   *Doe v. Jindal.* Federal district court holds that sex offender registration and notification requirements are unconstitutional as applied to nine plaintiffs convicted of CANS.[21]

2013   *Doe v. Caldwell.* Federal class action lawsuit removes all people convicted of CANS from the state sex offender registry.[22]

2013   News report reveals that men were arrested for attempted CAN by officers of the East Baton Rouge Sheriff's Office,[23] even though antisodomy laws were held unconstitutional by the U.S. Supreme Court in 2003.[24]

2014   Legislature repeals "incest" laws, reclassifying incestuous conduct under CAN.[25]

2014   State representative Patricia Smith's bill to repeal CAN law fails in Louisiana House.[26]

2018   Legislature enacts freestanding animal sexual abuse law, replacing and expanding upon provision in CAN that had proscribed bestial sex ("or with an animal").[27]

2021   State representative Mandie Landry's bill to decriminalize commercial sex—which would have repealed the CANS and "prostitution" statutes—is voluntarily deferred in Louisiana House Criminal Justice Committee. The bill would not have survived a committee vote.[28]

2024   State senator Royce Duplessis's bill to repeal CANS law fails in Louisiana Senate.[29]

Notes

INTRODUCTION

1. For an excellent text that avowedly limits "sexual justice" mainly to gender equality and the dangers sexual harassment poses for gender equality, see Alexandra Brodsky, *Sexual Justice: Supporting Victims, Ensuring Due Process, and Resisting the Conservative Backlash* (New York: Metropolitan Books, 2021).

2. See Janet Halley, *Split Decisions: How and Why to Take a Break from Feminism* (Princeton: Princeton University Press, 2006); see also Aziza Ahmed, "Janet Halley in Conversation with Aziza Ahmed: Interview," in *Beyond Virtue and Vice: Rethinking Human Rights and Criminal Law*, edited by Alice M. Miller and Mindy Jane Roseman (Philadelphia: University of Pennsylvania Press, 2019), 17, 23 ("I've started to try to remind people that 'taking a break' has a very important connotation, like a cigarette break. A person can be a feminist all day long and then take a break. . . . If you're only wearing your feminist glasses all the time, you'll only see the things that those feminist glasses let you see, and they may blind you to things that the feminist idea set doesn't already include").

3. See Janet E. Halley, "Reasoning about Sodomy: Act and Identity in and after *Bowers v. Hardwick*," *Virginia Law Review* 79 (1993): 1770–1772.

4. On the varying referents for "sodomite" and "sodomy" across time and space see, for example, H. G. Cocks, *Visions of Sodom: Religion, Homoerotic Desire, and the End of the World in England, C. 1550–1850* (Chicago: University of Chicago Press, 2017), 12–22.

5. Madhavi Menon, "Universalism and Partition: A Queer Theory," *differences: A Journal of Feminist Cultural Studies* 26 (2015): 122, 130. Menon's (and my) queer universalism syncopates with the universal but nonessentialist commitments of the reproductive justice movement. See Loretta J. Ross and Rickie Solinger, *Reproductive Justice: An Introduction* (Oakland, CA: University of California Press, 2017), 72.

6. Cathy J. Cohen, "Punks, Bulldaggers, and Welfare Queens: The Radical Potential of Queer Politics?" *GLQ* 3 (1997): 437–465.

7. Hortense J. Spillers, "Mama's Baby, Papa's Maybe: An American Grammar Book," *Diacritics* 17 (1987): 67; see also Alexander G. Weheliye, "Pornotropes," *Journal of Visual Culture* 7 (2008): 67 ("How does the historical question of violent political domination activate a surplus and excess of sexuality that simultaneously sustains and disfigures such brutality?").

8. See essays by Cohen and Cohen's interlocutors collected in "GLQ at 25" issue of *GLQ: A Journal of Lesbian and Gay Studies* 25 (2019): 140–193.

9. Cohen, "Punks," 438.

10. Cathy Cohen, "The Radical Potential of Queer? Twenty Years Later," *GLQ: A Journal of Lesbian and Gay Studies* 25 (2019): 143.

11. In the contemporary taxonomic lexicon of sexuality, *zoophile* more properly refers to humans with professed emotional and intimate, not just erotic, attachments to non-human animals whereas *bestialist* refers to humans whose interests in nonhuman animals are exclusively sexual and (so) arguably objectifying. On the political implications of the distinction, see Joanna Bourke, *Loving Animals: On Bestiality, Zoophilia and Post-Human Love* (London: Reaktion, 2020). I interchange the terms in the introduction and in Chapter 3 because, from the lawmaker's perspective, it is a distinction without a difference (even as the zoophile more likely implicates our puppy love; see Midas Dekkers, *Dearest Pet: On Bestiality* [London: Verso, 1994]).

12. Lauren Berlant and Michael Warner, "Sex in Public," *Critical Inquiry* 24 (1998): 548, note 2.

13. Cohen, "Punks," 437.

14. Ibid., 442–443.

15. Ibid., 452. To their credit, Berlant and Warner were careful from the get-go to explain that "contexts that have little visible relation to sex practice, such as life narrative and generational identity, can be heteronormative . . . while in other contexts *forms of sex between men and women might* not *be heteronormative.*" Berlant and Warner, "Sex in Public," 548 note 2, emphasis added.

16. See also Ummni Khan, "Chester Brown and the Queerness of Johns," *Critical Analysis of Law* 6 (2019): 39–62.

17. Cohen, "Punks," 457.

18. Ibid.

19. On the state's (but not just the state's) biopoweristic deployment of sex to stratify, control, and constitute populations, see, most famously, Michel Foucault, *The History of Sexuality, Volume 1: An Introduction,* translated by Robert Hurley (New York: Vintage, 1990), 145–159.

20. Cohen, "Punks," 444.

21. Cohen, "Radical Potential," 142.

22. Cohen, "Punks," 438 ("I envision a politics where one's relation to power, and not some homogenized identity, is privileged in determining one's political comrades").

23. Ibid., 447.

24. Cohen, "Radical Potential," 143.

25. Laura A. Belmonte et al., "Colloquy: Queering America and the World," *Diplomatic History* 40 (2016): 68. On similar non- or paraidentitarian appropriations for *trans*, see C. Riley Snorton, *Black on Both Sides: A Racial History of Trans Identity* (Minneapolis: University of Minnesota Press, 2017); Susan Stryker, "Transgender History, Homonormativity, and Disciplinarity," *Radical History Review* 100 (2008): 145–157. For a review of scholarship pressing *queer* and *trans* as analytics for relations of power, see Regina Kunzel, "The Power of Queer History," *American Historical Review* 123 (2018): 1560–1582.

26. Cohen, "Punks," 447.

27. David M. Halperin, "The War on Sex," in *The War on Sex*, edited by David M. Halperin and Trevor Hoppe (Durham: Duke University Press, 2017), 12.

28. See, for example (and the very tip of the non- or quasi-taxonomic identities iceberg), Gayatri Reddy, *With Respect to Sex: Negotiating Hijra Identity in South India* (Chicago: University of Chicago Press, 2005); Travis S. K. Kong, *Chinese Male Homosexualities: Memba, Tongzhi, and Golden Boy* (Milton Park: Routledge, 2011); Don Kulick, *Travesti: Sex, Gender, and Culture among Brazilian Transgendered Prostitutes* (Chicago: University of Chicago Press, 1998). Despite the book's subtitle ("transgendered . . ."), Kulick records travestis' "desire to embody homosexuality." Ibid., 224.

29. See, for example (and the very tip of the intersectional LGBT identities iceberg), Snorton, *Black on Both Sides*; Julian Gill-Peterson, *Histories of the Transgender Child* (Minneapolis: University of Minnesota Press, 2018); Eli Clare, *Brilliant Imperfection: Grappling with Cure* (Durham: Duke University Press, 2017); Eli Clare, *Exile and Pride: Disability, Queerness, and Liberation* (Durham: Duke University Press, 1999). The classic here remains Cohen, "Punks."

30. For a historical account of the ways sexuality articulated across imprisonment and criminalization, see Regina Kunzel, *Criminal Intimacy: Prison and the Uneven History of Modern American Sexuality* (Chicago: University of Chicago Press, 2008); for accounts of the ways mass incarceration and carceral politics disparately impact already marginalized queers, see, for example, Joey L. Mogul, Andrea J. Ritchie, and Kay Whitlock, *Queer (In)justice: The Criminalization of LGBT People in the United States* (Boston: Beacon Press, 2011); Eric A. Stanley and Nat Smith, eds., *Captive Genders: Trans Embodiment and the Prison Industrial Complex* (Oakland: AK Press, 2011).

31. See, for example (and the very tip of the queer-studies-without-[much]-sex iceberg), Mel Y. Chen, *Animacies: Biopolitics, Racial Mattering and Queer Affect* (Durham: Duke University Press, 2012). Chen's theorization of sex rotates primarily on the cultural and literal desexing and degendering of nonhuman animals. Ibid., 127–155; David L. Eng, *The Feeling of Kinship: Queer Liberalism and the Racialization of Intimacy* (Durham: Duke University Press, 2010); Anne M. Harris and Stacy Holman Jones, *The Queer Life of Things: Performance, Affect, and the More-Than-Human* (Lanham: Lexington Books, 2019); Tom Roach, *Friendship as a Way of Life: Foucault, AIDS, and the Politics of Shared Estrangement* (Albany: SUNY Press, 2012). To be fair, Roach devotes a chapter to canvassing "the material role of [promiscuous, anonymous, gay] sexuality in a political model of love." Ibid., 121. See generally, David L. Eng, Judith Halberstam, and José Esteban Muñoz, eds., "What's Queer about Queer Studies Now," *Social Text* 23 (2005); Janet Halley and Andrew Parker, eds., *After Sex? On Writing Since Queer Theory* (Durham: Duke University Press, 2011).

32. David L. Eng with Judith Halberstam and José Esteban Muñoz, "Introduction: What's Queer about Queer Studies Now?" *Social Text* 23 (2005): 2, quoted in Oliver Davis and Tim Dean, *Hatred of Sex* (Lincoln: University of Nebraska Press, 2022), 45.

33. Davis and Dean, *Hatred of Sex*, 46.

34. Jennifer V. Evans, *The Queer Art of History: Queer Kinship after Fascism* (Durham: Duke University Press, 2023), 3, 14.

35. Charles Upchurch, *"Beyond the Law": The Politics of Ending the Death Penalty for Sodomy in Britain* (Philadelphia: Temple University Press, 2021), 201.

36. Stefan Vogler, *Sorting Sexualities: Expertise and the Politics of Legal Classification* (Chicago: University of Chicago Press, 2021), 23.

37. Avgi Saketopoulou and Ann Pellegrini, *Gender Without Identity* (New York: The Unconscious in Translation, 2023), xxiv.

38. Davis and Dean, *Hatred of Sex*, 45.

39. Ibid., 47.

40. Ibid., 57.

41. Ibid.

42. Ibid., 56.

43. Ibid., 64.

44. Jennifer C. Nash, "Black Anality," *GLQ: A Journal of Lesbian and Gay Studies* 20 (2014): 439–460; Jennifer C. Nash, *The Black Body in Ecstasy: Reading Race, Reading Pornography* (Durham: Duke University Press, 2014); Amber Jamilla Musser, *Sensual Excess: Queer Femininity and Brown Jouissance* (New York: New York University Press, 2019); Ariane Cruz, *The Color of Kink: Black Women, BDSM, and Pornography* (New York: New York University Press, 2016); Mireille Miller-Young, *A Taste for Brown Sugar: Black Women in Pornography* (Durham: Duke University Press, 2014); Angela Jones, *Camming: Money, Power, and Pleasure in the Sex Work Industry* (New York: New York University Press, 2020); Deborah R. Vargas, "Ruminations on *Lo Sucio* as a Latino Queer Analytic," *American Quarterly* 66 (2014): 715–726.

45. Davis and Dean, *Hatred of* Sex, 46.

46. Not all queer work on sex, obviously, cohabitates in ethnic and Black studies. Jasbir Puar and Robert McRuer, for example, observe and affix disability and sexuality in nonidentitarian idioms of assemblage and emergence, although Puar is less interested in sex per se than in processes of gendering and sexualizing. Jasbir K. Puar, *The Right to Maim: Debility, Capacity, Disability* (Durham: Duke University Press, 2017); Robert McRuer, *Crip Times: Disability, Globalization, and Resistance* (New York: New York University Press, 2018). Tim Dean powerfully describes how some gay men, racially diverse and intergenerational, create cultural belonging through sex, semen, and fantasies of virality rather than through appeals to social recognition. Still, his study limits itself to gay men. Tim Dean, *Unlimited Intimacy: Reflections on the Subculture of Barebacking* (Chicago: University of Chicago Press, 2009).

47. For a methodologically and topically eclectic grab bag of work in and around queer studies that is, if not antistatist, profoundly skeptical about political engagement with the state, see Lee Edelman, *No Future: Queer Theory and the Death Drive* (Durham: Duke University Press, 2004); Eng, *The Feeling of Kinship*; Katherine Franke, *Wedlocked: The Perils of Marriage Equality* (New York: New York University Press, 2015); Halley, *Split Decisions*; José Esteban Muñoz, *Cruising Utopia, Tenth Anniversary Edition: The Then and There of Queer Futurity* (New York: New York University Press, 2019); Jasbir K. Puar, *Terrorist Assemblages: Homonationalism in Queer Times* (Durham: Duke University Press, 2007); Puar, *Right to Maim*; Eric A. Stanley, *Atmospheres of Violence: Structuring Antagonism and the Trans/Queer Ungovernable* (Durham: Duke University Press, 2021); Sarah Schulman, *Israel/Palestine and the Queer International* (Durham: Duke University, 2012). As counterpoints, see Samuel Clowes Huneke, *A Queer Theory of the State* (New York: Columbia University Press, 2023); Evren Savci, *Queer in Translation: Sexual Politics under Neoliberalism* (Durham: Duke University Press, 2021), 109–141.

48. The exemplar here is Frank B. Wilderson, III, *Afropessimism* (New York: Liveright, 2020).

49. See Jennifer C. Nash, "On the Beginning of the World: Dominance Feminism, Afropessimism, and the Meanings of Gender," *Feminist Theory* 23 (2021): 556–574.

50. Edelman, *Bad Education*, xv, xvi.

51. Ibid., xvii.

52. Ibid., xviii–xix, emphasis added.

53. See, for example, William N. Eskridge Jr., and Christopher R. Riano, "*Bostock*: A Statutory Super-Precedent for Sex and Gender Minorities," *American Constitution Society*, July 1, 2020, www.acslaw.org/expertforum/bostock-a-statutory-super-precedent-for-sex-and-gender-minorities/.

54. In *Price Waterhouse v. Hopkins*, 490 U.S. 228 (1989), the Supreme Court held that employment discrimination based on sex stereotyping violates Title VII of the Civil Rights Act of 1964; see also Eskridge and Riano, "*Bostock*." ("Because Justice Gorsuch's *Bostock* opinion cited *Price Waterhouse v. Hopkins*, and because neither dissenting opinion questioned its authority, we believe that *Hopkins*'s gender-stereotyping rule is entrenched in Title VII law.")

55. Esteban Muñoz, *Cruising Utopia, Tenth Anniversary Edition*, 87; Edelman, *Bad Education*, xvii.

56. Ibid., xix.

57. Ibid., 213.

58. Cohen, "Punks," 453.

59. Carole Pateman, *The Sexual Contract* (Cambridge: Polity, 1988); Charles W. Mills, *The Racial Contract* (Ithaca: Cornell University Press, 1997).

60. Carole Pateman and Charles W. Mills, *Contract and Domination* (Cambridge: Polity, 2007).

61. Robyn Wiegman, *Object Lessons* (Durham: Duke University Press, 2014), 1, note 1.

62. For powerful iterations of the offloading thesis see, inter alia, Elizabeth R. Anker, *Ugly Freedoms* (Durham: Duke University Press, 2022); Claire E. Rasmussen, *The Autonomous Animal: Self-Governance and the Modern Subject* (Minneapolis: University of Minnesota Press, 2011); Chandan Reddy, *Freedom with Violence: Race, Sexuality and the US State* (Durham: Duke University Press, 2011); Sylvia Wynter, "Unsettling the Coloniality of Being/Truth/Power/Freedom: Towards the Human, after Man, Its Overrepresentation—An Argument," *CR: The New Centennial Review* 3 (2003): 257–337.

63. Carole Pateman, "Race, Sex, and Indifference," in Pateman and Mills, *Contract and Domination*, 135–147; Charles W. Mills, "Intersecting Contracts," in Pateman and Mills, *Contract and Domination*, 185, 194.

64. Sina Kramer, *Excluded Within: The (Un)Intelligibility of Radical Political Actors* (New York: New York University Press, 2017).

65. Pateman, *Sexual Contract*, 225–227; Pateman, "Race, Sex, and Indifference," 338, 136; Mills, "Intersecting Contracts," 185, 194. For a contrasting account of the "bestialization of Blackness," see Zakkiyah Iman Jackson, *Becoming Human: Matter and Meaning in an Antiblack World* (New York: New York University Press, 2020), 18, 23 ("I replace the notion of 'denied humanity' and 'exclusion' with bestialized humanization, because *the African's humanity is not denied but appropriated, inverted, and ultimately plasticized in the methodology of abjecting animality*") (emphasis in original). Kramer's concept of "constitutive exclusion" is more temporal and multiplicative than the rendition presented here. Kramer, *Excluded Within*, 144–152.

66. Or precarious. See Judith Butler, *Frames of War: When Is Life Grievable?* (London: Verso, 2009); Kramer, *Excluded Within*, 15–16.

67. See Bonnie Honig, *Political Theory and the Displacement of Politics* (Ithaca: Cornell University Press, 1993).

68. Kramer, *Excluded Within*, 23.

69. See Foucault, *History of Sexuality*, 101; Jonathan Goldberg, "Sodomy in the New World: Anthropologies Old and New," *Social Text* 29 (1991): 46–56.

70. Charles W. Mills, "The Racial Contract Revisited: Still Unbroken after All These Years," *Politics, Groups and Identities* 3 (2015), 541.

71. Halley, "Reasoning about Sodomy," 1738–1739.

72. See Cocks, *Visions of Sodom*, 6–20; Karma Lochrie, "Presumptive Sodomy and Its Exclusions," *Textual Practice* 13 (1999): 295–310.

73. See Eoghan Ahern, "The Sin of Sodomy in Late Antiquity," *Journal of the History of Sexuality* 27 (2018): 210–213; Sir William Blackstone, *Commentaries on the Laws of England Book 4: On Public Wrongs* (New York: Wallachia Publishers, 2015), 215; Immanuel Kant, *Lectures on Ethics*, translated by Louis Infield (London: Methuen & Co., 1930), 163.

74. According to Mark Jordan, Aquinas misconstrues Augustine's condemnation of Sodomite lust and perversity as a pronouncement against the "misuse of reproductive powers." Mark D. Jordan, *The Invention of Sodomy in Christian Theology* (Chicago: University of Chicago Press, 1998), 148–149.

75. See George Painter, "The Sensibilities of Our Forefathers: The History of Sodomy Laws in the United States," *Gay & Lesbian Archives of the Pacific Northwest*, www.glapn .org/sodomylaws/sensibilities/introduction.htm ("Even though English courts were generous in defining who could be prosecuted under the law, they were restrictive in defining the indictable act. A 1781 case decided that emission of semen had to occur for an act of sodomy to exist. Thus, it became an absolute defense to a charge of sodomy if the inserter withdrew prior to ejaculation, even if ejaculation occurred. This decision was controversial, effectively permitting 'sodomy interruptus' to go unpunished. This was the only aspect of English case law on sodomy rejected in the United States, beginning with the Virginia Supreme Court in 1812. Most other state courts, when presented with the issue, deferred to Virginia, rather than England").

76. See Immanuel Kant, *Metaphysics of Morals*, edited by Mary Gregor (Cambridge: Cambridge University Press, 1996), 61–62.

77. Lee Edelman, *Bad Education: Why Queer Theory Teaches Us Nothing* (Durham: Duke University Press, 2022), 20; see also Brenda Cossman, *Sexual Citizens: The Legal and Cultural Regulation of Sex and Belonging* (Stanford: Stanford University Press, 2007), 29–30; Joseph J. Fischel, "Transcendent Homosexuals and Dangerous Sex Offenders: Sexual Harm and Freedom in the Judicial Imaginary," *Duke Journal of Gender Law & Policy* 17 (2010): 277–312.

78. Mills, "Intersecting Contracts," 172.

79. Michael Warner, "New English Sodom," *American Literature* 64 (1992): 19–47.

80. Ibid., 20.

81. Ibid., 21.

82. Ibid.

83. Ibid., 38.

84. Ibid., 24.

85. Ibid., 25.

86. Pateman, "Race, Sex, and Indifference," 140; Mills, "Intersecting Contracts," 172.

87. Warner, "New English Sodom," 26–27.

88. Ibid., 34–35.

89. Ibid., 29.

90. Ibid., 33.

91. Ibid., 35, quoting Perry Miller, *The New England Mind: The Seventeenth Century (Volume I)* (Cambridge, MA: Harvard University Press, 1982 [1939]), 418.

92. See David John Frank, Steven A. Boucher, and Bayliss Camp, "The Reform of Sodomy Laws from a World Society Perspective," in *Queer Mobilizations: LGBT Activists Confront the Law*, edited by Scott Barclay, Mary Bernstein, and Anna-Maria Marshall (New York: New York University Press, 2009), 123–141; William N. Eskridge Jr., *Dishonorable Passions: Sodomy Laws in America, 1861–2003* (New York: Viking, 2008).

93. Warner, "New English Sodom," 36.

94. See Kramer, *Excluded Within*, 148.

95. Warner, "New English Sodom," 38.

96. See Mills, "Racial Contract Revisited," 545–546.

97. Warner, "New English Sodom," 35, citing Alan Bray, "Homosexuality and the Signs of Male Friendship in Elizabethan England," *History Workshop* 29 (1990): 1–19.

98. Zachary Herz, "The Epistemology of the Courthouse: Classical Antiquity in American LGBT-Rights Litigation," in *Enticements: Queer Legal Studies*, edited by Joseph J. Fischel and Brenda Cossman (New York: New York University Press, 2024), 50; see also Randall B. Clark, "Platonic Love in a Colorado Courtroom: Martha Nussbaum, John Finnis, and Plato's *Laws* in *Evans v. Romer*," *Yale Journal of Law & the Humanities* 12 (2000): 1–38.

99. Ibid., 50.

100. Christopher Chitty, *Sexual Hegemony: Statecraft, Sodomy, and Capital in the Rise of the World System* (Durham: Duke University Press, 2020), 59.

101. Michael Rocke, *Forbidden Friendships: Homosexuality and Male Culture in Renaissance Florence* (New York: Oxford University Press, 1996), 35.

102. Ibid., 39.

103. Ibid., 42.

104. Chitty, *Sexual Hegemony*, 57.

105. Ibid., 57, 58, emphasis added. Chitty's account of how sodomy and sodomy regulations were politicized in Florence—not to mention his more global, historical materialist, and brilliant theses on the dialectics of same-sex sex, sexual regulations, ascension of class hegemonies, and state power—is far more dimensional than the sliver of argument presented here.

106. Kant, *Metaphysics*, 109.

107. For yet another account of sodomy as a political counterforce, see Jordan, *Invention of Sodomy*, 50 ("[eleventh-century monk] Peter Damian fears a church of Sodom within the church of God. He suspects or infers the operation of a shadow hierarchy with its own means of governance and of recruitment").

108. See generally Wendy Brown, *States of Injury: Power and Freedom in Late Modernity* (Princeton: Princeton University Press 1995); see also Kramer, *Excluded Within*, 188–191.

109. See, for example, Pateman, *Sexual Contract*, 224–225; Catharine A. MacKinnon, "Feminism, Marxism, Method and the State: Toward Feminist Jurisprudence," *Signs* 8 (1983): 635–658; Charles W. Mills, "Alternative Epistemologies," *Social Theory and Practice* 14 (1988): 237–263; Angela Y. Davis, *Women, Race and Class* (New York: Random House, 1983), 172–201.

110. See Kimberlé Crenshaw, "Mapping the Margins: Intersectionality, Identity Politics, and Violence against Women of Color," *Stanford Law Journal* 43 (1991): 1265–1282; Davis, *Women, Race and Class*.

111. Emily A. Owens, *Consent in the Presence of Force: Sexual Violence and Black Women's Survival in Antebellum New Orleans* (Chapel Hill: University of North Carolina Press, 2023).

112. See Stephen Robertson, "Shifting the Scene of the Crime: Sodomy and the American History of Sexual Violence," *Journal of the History of Sexuality* 19 (2010): 223–242.

113. See Human Rights Watch, "This Alien Legacy: The Origins of 'Sodomy' Laws in British Colonialism," *Human Rights Watch*, December 17, 2008, www.hrw.org/report /2008/12/17/alien-legacy/origins-sodomy-laws-british-colonialism; Estelle B. Freedman, *Redefining Rape: Sexual Violence in the Era of Suffrage and Segregation* (Cambridge, MA: Harvard University Press, 2015), 168–190; Nayan Shah, *Stranger Intimacy: Contesting Race, Sexuality, and the Law in the North American West* (Berkeley: University of California Press, 2011).

114. Gayle S. Rubin, "Thinking Sex: Notes for a Radical Theory of the Politics of Sexuality," in *Deviations: A Gayle Rubin Reader*, edited by Gayle S. Rubin (Durham: Duke University Press, 2011 [1984]), 159.

115. The offline and online archives of Louisiana sodomy cases are hodgepodge, but in summary I reviewed: all sodomy (or "buggery") cases heard by the Criminal District Court for the Parish of Orleans from the 1880s to the 1920s housed in the City Archives, New Orleans Public Library; all sixty-four sodomy cases heard by the Louisiana Supreme Court between 1957 and 2005 available on LEXIS; all 222 sodomy cases heard by Louisiana appellate courts between 1980 and 2015 available on LEXIS, of which 180 involved incidents of noncommercial sodomy.

116. My research assistant Luke Maher reviewed eighty-seven sodomy cases heard in Georgia appellate courts between 1970 and 2003, available on LEXIS. For nationwide data I looked primarily to William N. Eskridge Jr., *Gaylaw: Challenging the Apartheid of the Closet* (Cambridge, MA: Harvard University Press, 1999), appendix c, 373–384.

117. Joseph J. Fischel, "Sodomy's Penumbra" *Journal of Homosexuality* 64 (2017): 203–256.

118. See, for example, Rubin, "Thinking Sex"; for a more recent, public-facing, Louisiana-focused framing of U.S. antisodomy laws as homophobic through and through, see Mark Joseph Stern, "You Can Still Be Arrested for Being Gay in Red-State America," *Slate*, August 5, 2013, https://slate.com/human-interest/2013/08/gay-people -are-still-being-arrested-for-having-consensual-sex-in-some-red-states-like-louisiana .html. While Rubin's constructivism might not allow for the anachronistic usage of "homophobia," her account of the sodomite exemplar, the Earl of Castlehaven, gauges sodomy law, like other sex laws, as "the most adamantine instrument of sexual stratification and erotic persecution." Rubin, "Thinking Sex," 156, 159.

119. See, for example, Eskridge, *Gaylaw*; Eskridge, *Dishonorable Passions*; Freedman, *Redefining Rape*; Robertson, "Shifting the Scene."

120. See Eskridge, *Gaylaw*; Lynne Huffer, *Are the Lips a Grave? A Queer Feminist on the Ethics of Sex* (New York: Columbia University Press, 2013), 91–117.

121. See George Chauncey, "'What Gay Studies Taught the Court': The Historians Amicus Brief in *Lawrence v. Texas*," *GLQ: A Journal of Lesbian and Gay Studies* 10 (2004): 509–538.

122. La. Rev. Stat. 14:89.1. The state's Crime Against Nature law was amended to include aggravating circumstances in 1962. Louisiana House Bill 789, Act 60 (1962).

123. Eskridge, *Gaylaw*; Eskridge, *Dishonorable Passions*.

124. Huffer, *Lips*, 91–117.

125. Huffer's thesis rotates on the fact that *Lawrence v. Texas*, the 2003 Supreme Court decision holding state sodomy laws unconstitutional, was propelled in part by the strategic eclipse of sexual violence from a case out of Georgia. *Lawrence*, in striking down Texas's sodomy law as unconstitutional, cited as precedent *Powell v. State*, a Georgia Supreme Court decision holding that state's sodomy law in violation of its own constitution. In *Powell*, Anthony Powell was initially charged with forcing oral sex and vaginal sex on his wife's seventeen-year-old niece, Quashana. The trial jury found Powell not guilty of "rape" or "forcible sodomy," but guilty of "simple sodomy," even though the complainant testified that she "was crying" as Powell performed oral sex on her. Yet Quashana "never said the word 'no.'" Ibid., 109, 111. Powell appealed his conviction for simple sodomy to the Georgia Supreme Court, which held the law unconstitutional. However horrific, *Powell* is an outlier, not a dramatization of a pattern whereby defendants are convicted of simple sodomy as a strict liability offense but held not guilty on other sexual assault charges.

126. *State v. Gamble*, 504 So.2d 1100 (La. Ct. App. 1987).

127. *Bowers v. Hardwick*, 478 U.S. 186 (1986); *Lawrence v. Texas*, 539 U.S. 558 (2003).

128. Eskridge, *Gaylaw*, 375.

129. Eskridge, *Dishonorable Passions*, 50.

130. Ibid., 55.

131. Ellen Anderson periodizes twentieth-century, U.S. antisodomy law reforms into four stages, across which she finds a pattern of "plateau, flux, plateau, flux." The first stage, running until 1970, is the "*status quo ante*" of antisodomy laws codified in all fifty states. In the second stage, 1971–1983, many states repealed their antisodomy laws while others specified them to criminalize only same-sex sexual activity. Running from 1984 to 1991, the third stage "encompasses a period of backsliding," when states ceased repealing antisodomy statutes, but others continued to enact laws targeting same-sex sex. Stage four, from 1992 onward, marks the increasing invalidation of same-sex, antisodomy state laws. Ellen Ann Andersen, "The Stages of Sodomy Law Reform," *Thurgood Marshall Law Review* 23 (1998): 284–286.

132. Louisiana Senate Bill 400, Act 612 (1975; emphasis added). The Act retained a marital exemption that would not be lifted until 1990 and not without significant resistance from male legislators. Louisiana House Bill 236, Act 722 (1990); Senate Committee on Judiciary A, minutes of meeting of July 3, 1990.

133. Surveying an earlier historical moment, the colonial period, Robertson notes the predominance of sodomy cases "directed against servants or minors," leading him to conclude that "sexual violence created not just a gender hierarchy but also other relations of dominance and subordination." Like Robertson, I am suggesting that more careful attention to antisodomy law brooks a less identitarian, less gender-dominance theory of sexual violence. Robertson, "Shifting the Scene," 235.

134. *State v. Phillips*, 365 So.2d 1304 (La. 1978).

135. At the turn of the twentieth century, a defendant before the Louisiana Supreme Court asserted the naturalness of cunnilingus to overturn his crime against nature conviction. *State v. Aenspacker*, 19276 (1912), Box 2640, Louisiana and Special Collections, Earl K. Long Library, University of New Orleans. Another argued that crime against nature could refer only to sex "per anum," without further statutory definition. *State v. Vicknair*, 13506 (1900), Box 1559, Louisiana and Special Collections, Earl K. Long Library, University of New Orleans. At the end of that century, a defendant before a state appellate court asserted the naturalness of homosexual oral sex to overturn his crime against nature conviction. *State v. Moore*, 797 So.2d 756 (La. Ct. App. 2001). Another

contested the presumptive unnaturalness of fellatio. *State v. Spitz*, 650 So.2d 271 (La. Ct. App. 1995). None of these defendants convinced the court.

In 2001, Louisiana amended its rape statute to include oral sex, although persons were still convicted of aggravated crime against nature after that year. Louisiana House Bill 604, Act 301 (2001). Interestingly, the bill's sponsor, then State Representative Emma Devillier, proposed the reclassification of forcible oral sex as rape based on concerns of HIV transmission. Although HIV transmission rates from oral sex are minimal, it is the specter of contagion and vulnerable women, not an expanding definition of "sex," that facilitated the punitive reclassification.

136. *State v. Lambert*, 550 So.2d 847 (La. Ct. App. 1989; emphasis added).

137. *State v. Ketton*, 468 So.2d 707 (La. Ct. App. 1985; emphasis added).

138. *State v. White*, 495 So.2d 340 (La. Ct. App. 1986; emphasis added).

139. *State v. Mills*, 505 So.2d 933 (La. Ct. App. 1987; emphasis added).

140. See Sharon Marcus, "Fighting Bodies, Fighting Words: A Theory and Politics of Rape Prevention," in *Feminists Theorize the Political*, edited by Judith Butler and Joan Scott (New York: Routledge, 1992): 385–403.

141. *State v. Yancy*, 465 So.2d 48 (La. Ct. App. 1985; emphasis added).

142. Catharine A. MacKinnon, "Feminism, Marxism, Method, and the State: An Agenda for Theory," *Signs* 7 (1982): 541.

143. Leo Bersani, "Is the Rectum a Grave?" *AIDS: Cultural Analysis/Cultural Activism* 43 (1987): 197–222; see also Lee Edelman, *Homographesis: Essays in Gay Literary and Cultural Theory* (New York: Routledge, 1994).

144. Edelman, *Homographesis*.

145. Judith Butler, *Frames of War*, 149.

146. See Susan Dewey and Tonia P. St. Germain, "Sex Workers/Sex Offenders: Exclusionary Criminal Justice Practices in New Orleans," *Feminist Criminology* 10 (2015): 211–234; Fischel, "Sodomy's Penumbra."

147. For various stakeholders' accounts of WWAV's successful campaign and its broader implications for social and sexual justice, see Alexis Agathocleous, "Building a Movement for Justice: *Doe v. Jindal* and the Campaign against Louisiana's Crime Against Nature Statute," in *The War on Sex*, edited by David M. Halperin and Trevor Hoppe (Durham: Duke University Press, 2017), 429–453; Laura McTighe and Deon Haywood, "'There Is NO Justice in Louisiana': Crimes against Nature and the Spirit of Black Feminist Resistance," *Souls: A Critical Journal of Black Politics, Culture, and Society* 19 (2017): 261–285; Andrea J. Ritchie, "Crimes against Nature: Challenging Criminalization of Queerness and Black Women's Sexuality," *Loyola Journal of Public Interest Law* 14 (2013): 355–374.

148. Matt Nadel and Megan Plotka, *CANS Can't Stand* (Lynwood Films, 2022).

149. At Liberty Podcast, "This Law Criminalizes Black Trans Women," *ACLU*, March 30, 2023, www.aclu.org/podcast/fighting-for-the-liberation-of-black-trans-women-in-louisiana

150. Joseph J. Fischel, "Social Justice for Gender and Sexual Minorities: A Discussion with Paisley Currah and Aeyal Gross," *Critical Analysis of Law* 6 (2019): 89.

151. This argument develops my earlier treatment of sex offender registration and notification systems. Joseph J. Fischel, "Transcendent Homosexuals"; Joseph J. Fischel, *Sex and Harm in the Age of Consent* (Minneapolis: University of Minnesota Press, 2016).

152. Associated Press, "Louisiana: Anti-sodomy Law Stands," *New York Times*, April 15, 2014.

153. Walter Einenkel, "40% of Louisiana State Senators Voted against Making Bestiality a Crime—Because They're Homophobic," *Daily Kos*, April 12, 2018, www .dailykos.com/stories/2018/4/12/1756467/-40-of-Louisiana-state-senators-voted -against-making-bestiality-a-crime-because-they-re-homophobic; Anthony Izaguirre, "Christian Conservatives Fight Bid to Toughen Louisiana Anti-bestiality Law," *Talking Points Memo*, April 25, 2018, https://talkingpointsmemo.com/news/christian -conservatives-fight-toughening-louisiana-anti-bestiality-law; WPMI Web Staff, "Ten Louisiana Lawmakers Vote against 'Sex with Animals' Ban," *NBC*, April 11, 2018, https:// mynbc15.com/news/local/ten-louisiana-lawmakers-vote-against-sex-with-animals-ban.

154. Greta LaFleur, *The Natural History of Sexuality in Early America* (Baltimore: Johns Hopkins University Press, 2018), 189.

155. Joseph J. Fischel, *Screw Consent: A Better Politics of Sexual Justice* (Oakland: University of California Press, 2019), 117–134.

156. As this book goes to press, documentarian Matt Nadel and I are working with Operation Restoration in Louisiana to lobby the state legislature to repeal the CANS law. In summer 2024, the state legislature voted against a repeal bill.

157. Dale Carpenter, "Windsor Products: Equal Protection from Animus," *The Supreme Court Review* 2013 (2013): 183–285.

158. *Dobbs v. Jackson Women's Health Org.*, 142 S.Ct. 2228 (2022).

159. *Erotic Serv. Provider Legal Educ. and Research Project v. Gascon*, 880 F.3d 450, 459 (9th Cir. 2018).

160. On the many publics at issue in the problem of "public sex," see Chapter 2.

161. Lee Edelman, *No Future*.

162. See, for example, Jennifer M. Spear, *Race, Sex, and Social Order in Early New Orleans* (Baltimore: Johns Hopkins University Press, 2008).

163. See, for example, Owens, *Consent in the Presence of Force*.

164. See, for example, Sarah Haley, *No Mercy Here: Gender, Punishment, and the Making of Jim Crow Modernity* (Chapel Hill: University of North Carolina Press, 2016). My contemporary, normative account of a paraidentitarian politics of sexual justice in no way conflicts with Haley's historical, descriptive account that "southern punishment [under Jim Crow] was a technology of gender construction, reconstituting and reinforcing ideologies of absolute racial difference through black female abjection." Ibid., 251. The postbellum solidification of racial difference and racial subordination through sexual difference and sexualization is the hard side constraint for any United Statesean, paraidentitarian, queer political project.

165. For texts that thematize the exceptional/representational tension, see for example, Vincanne Adams, *Markets of Sorrow, Labors of Faith: New Orleans in the Wake of Katrina* (Durham: Duke University Press, 2013); Tom Piazza, *Why New Orleans Matters* (New York: HarperCollins Publishers, 2005); see generally Cedric Johnson, ed., *The Neoliberal Deluge: Hurricane Katrina, Late Capitalism, and the Remaking of New Orleans* (Minneapolis: University of Minnesota Press, 2011).

166. Elizabeth Fussell, "Constructing New Orleans, Constructing Race: A Population History of New Orleans," *Journal of American History* 94 (2007): 846–855; see also Jenn Bentley, "Pushed Out: The Changing Demographics of New Orleans," *Big Easy*, February 11, 2019, www.bigeasymagazine.com/2019/2/11pushed-out-the-changing-demographics -of-new-orleans/.

167. See Lynnell L. Thomas, *Desire and Disaster in New Orleans: Tourism, Race, and Historical Memory* (Durham: Duke University Press, 2014), 47.

168. See Richard Fausset, "A Black Group Says Mardi Gras Blackface Honors Tradition. Others Call It 'Disgusting,'" *New York Times*, February 14, 2019, www.nyti mes.com/2019/02/14/us/zulu-parade-new-orleans.html; see also Cynthia Becker, "New Orleans Mardi Gras Indians: Mediating Racial Politics from the Backstreets to Main Street," *African Arts* 46 (2013): 36–49; George Lipsitz, "Mardi-Gras Indians: Carnival and Counter-Narrative in Black New Orleans," *Culture Critique* 10 (1988): 99–121. The definitive study on Mardi Gras and its competing and collaborating social groups is Reid Mitchell, *All on a Mardi Gras Day: Episodes in the History of New Orleans Carnival* (Cambridge, MA: Harvard University Press, 1999).

169. See Gary Richards, "Queering Katrina: Gay Discourses of the Disaster in New Orleans," *Journal of American Studies* 44 (2010): 521–522.

170. See Susan Stryker and Jim Van Buskirk, *Gay by the Bay: A History of Queer Culture in the San Francisco Bay Area* (San Francisco: Chronicle Books, 1996), 18.

171. Warner, "New English Sodom," 21.

172. Rev. Philo Tower, *Slavery Unmasked: Being a Truthful Narrative* (Rochester: E. Darrow & Brother, 1856), 390.

173. Reprinted in Anthony J. Stanonis, *Creating the Big Easy: New Orleans and the Emergence of Modern Tourism, 1918–1945* (Athens: University of Georgia Press, 2006), 6.

174. Ibid.

175. Reprinted in George Painter, "The Sensibilities of Our Forefathers: The History of Sodomy Laws in the United States," *Gay & Lesbian Archives of the Pacific Northwest*, August 10, 2004, www.glapn.org/sodomylaws/sensibilities/louisiana.htm.

176. Richards, "Queering Katrina," 521.

177. On the various and contradictory sins scripturally ascribed to Sodom, see Mark Jordan, *The Invention of Sodomy in Christian Theology* (Chicago: University of Chicago Press, 1997).

178. Cocks, *Visions of Sodom*.

CHAPTER 1

1. Eric, interview by author, January 16, 2012. Interviews with registered sex offenders were conducted in confidentiality; as mutually agreed upon, names of interviewed sex offenders are pseudonyms.

2. Complaint at 5, *Doe v. Jindal* (E.D. La. 2011).

3. Louisiana Revised Statutes 14:82.

4. Louisiana Revised Statutes 14:89.2; *State v. Phillips*, 365 So.2d 1304 (La. 1978), specified that the "unnatural carnal copulation" proscribed under the Louisiana's sodomy law refers to anal penetration and oral-genital contact.

5. Zeb Tortorici, "Against Nature: Sodomy and Homosexuality in Colonial Latin America," *History Compass* 10 (2012): 169.

6. This quotation is from an attorney interviewed in Susan Dewey and Tonia P. St. Germain, "Sex Workers/Sex Offenders: Exclusionary Criminal Justice Practices in New Orleans," *Feminist Criminology* 10 (2015): 218. The offering of oral sex to a police officer for money is the most common fact pattern across Louisiana appellate cases. See Joseph J. Fischel, "Sodomy's Penumbra," *Journal of Homosexuality* 64 (2017): 2053 note 37.

7. Greg Mottola, *Superbad* (Columbia Pictures, 2007).

8. In the summer of 2010, the Louisiana Legislature passed a bill that made a first conviction of CANS misdemeanant. Between summer 2010 and summer 2011, only a second CANS conviction mandated sex offender registration. In 2011, the legislature

fully equalized penalties for CANS and Prostitution. *Doe v. Jindal*, 851 F. Supp. 2d 995, 998 note 4 (E.D. La. 2012).

9. Complaint at 5, *Doe v. Jindal*.

10. See Alexis Agathocleous, "Building a Movement for Justice: *Doe v. Jindal* and the Campaign against Louisiana's Crime Against Nature Statute," in *The War on Sex*, edited by David M. Halperin and Trevor Hoppe (Durham: Duke University Press, 2017), 437–438; Laura McTighe and Deon Haywood, "'There Is NO Justice in Louisiana': Crimes against Nature and the Spirit of Black Feminist Resistance," *Souls: A Critical Journal of Black Politics, Culture, and Society* 19 (2017): 270–271.

11. See Andrea J. Ritchie, "Crimes against Nature: Challenging Criminalization of Queerness and Black Women's Sexuality," *Loyola Journal of Public Interest Law* 14 (2013): 358; McTighe and Haywood, "NO Justice," 267.

12. McTighe and Haywood, "NO Justice," 268–274.

13. Ibid., 274; see also Complaint at 16, *Doe v. Jindal*.

14. Plaintiffs' Motion for Summary Judgment, *Doe v. Jindal* (E.D. La. 2011), 1–18.

15. *Doe v. Jindal*, 851. F. Supp. 2d 995,1006 (E.D. La. 2012).

16. Class Action Complaint, *Doe v. Caldwell*, 913 F. Supp. 2d 262 (E.D. La. 2012) (No. 12CV01670), 2012 WL 2417737; see also "Louisiana to Remove Hundreds of Individuals Unconstitutionally Placed on Sex Offender Registry," *Center for Constitutional Rights*, June 12, 2013, https://ccrjustice.org/home/press-center/press-releases/louisiana-remove -hundreds-individuals-unconstitutionally-placed-sex.

17. See note 6; see also Brendan M. Connor, Andrea J. Ritchie, and Women With A Vision, "'Just a Talking Crime': A Policy Brief in Support of the Repeal of Louisiana's Solicitation of a Crime Against Nature (SCAN) Statute," February 2011, https://ccrjustice .org/home/what-we-do/our-cases/crimes-against-nature-solicitation-cans-litigation.

18. In the summer of 2020, and at the excellent suggestion of Bill Araiza, I connected with Susan Hazeldean, who directs the Brooklyn Law School LGBT Advocacy Clinic. I sent Professor Hazeldean and her clinic students an early draft of what is now Chapter 4 of this book, which lays out an animus-based, equal protection attack on the CANS statute. Since then, Professor Hazeldean and her students have extensively researched possible litigation strategies against CANS, and they are, as of this writing, working with attorneys at the American Civil Liberties Union to challenge the law.

I served as the historical consultant for, helped fund, and briefly appear as a talking head in the documentary *CANS Can't Stand* (2022), considered (and fully cited) later, which draws attention to the discriminatory codification history and enforcement patterns of CANS. The film's critical acclaim and popularity accelerated my collaboration with the film's codirector, Matt Nadel, and the film's lead subject, Wendi Cooper, to lobby state legislators to repeal CANS. The New Orleans-based Operation Restoration, and its executive director Syrita Steib, have taken the lead in this legislative effort, encouraging Louisiana state senator Roy Duplessis to introduce a repeal bill.

Nadel, a former student and research assistant of mine, and I curated a virtual exhibit on CANS that functioned as something of a prologue to the documentary and helped publicize CANS's injustices against racial, gender, and sexual minorities. Matt Nadel and Joseph Fischel, "Crimes Against Nature by Solicitation," *ArcGIS*, October 5, 2021, https://storymaps.arcgis.com/stories/cf4facb7fb5d4cbd9e8e76a9c3f40c56.

I provide this partial account of my political activism against CANS neither to virtue signal nor to toot my own horn but because the critique of this chapter is borne out of sustained solidarity. For my broader analysis of the policing of racial minority and transgender communities in New Orleans, see Joseph J. Fischel, "In the Fight for

Policing Reform, LGBT Is a Threadbare Alliance," *Boston Review*, June 17, 2020. This article developed from my volunteering with the ACLU of Louisiana in the spring of 2019.

19. At Liberty Podcast, "This Law Criminalizes Black Trans Women," *ACLU*, March 30, 2023, www.aclu.org/podcast/fighting-for-the-liberation-of-black-trans-women-in-louisiana.

20. Joseph J. Fischel, "Against Nature, against Consent: A Sexual Politics of Debility," *differences: A Journal of Feminist Cultural Studies* 24 (2013): 55–103.

21. Terrance Wooten, "'The Streets Are My Home': Black Male Sex Offenders, Hypersurveillance, and the Liminality of Home," *Feminist Formations* 33 (2021): 36, emphasis in original.

22. Matt Nadel and Megan Plotka, *CANS Can't Stand* (Lynwood Films, 2022).

23. Ibid.

24. Crispin Long, "Fighting the Louisiana Law that Makes Sex Work a 'Crime against Nature,'" *New Yorker*, February 8, 2023, www.newyorker.com/culture/the-new-yorker-documentary/fighting-the-louisiana-law-that-makes-sex-work-a-crime-against-nature. For example, the documentary's "focus is a group of Black trans women who are fighting today to liberate their community from the policy's grasp." Ibid. The synopsis, not wrong, underplays Cooper's and Sherry's solidarity with and movement for all those impacted by CANS. See "The Movement," *CANS Can't Stand*, www.canscantstandfilm.com/#the-movement.

25. "CANS Can't Stand: Liberation for Black Trans Women," *New Yorker*, February 8, 2023, www.newyorker.com/video/watch/the-new-yorker-documentary-cans-cant-stand-liberation-for-black-trans-women.

26. See Brief of *Amici Curiae* Breakout!, *Doe v. Jindal* (E.D. La. 2011), 10; Dewey and St. Germain, "Sex Workers/Sex Offenders," 220–221.

27. At Liberty Podcast, "Black Trans Women."

28. Nadel and Plotka, *CANS Can't Stand*.

29. See Fischel, "Sodomy's Penumbra," 2036–2037.

30. Minutes of the Louisiana House Criminal Justice Committee, House Bill 853, June 17, 1982, audiocassette recording.

31. Act 49, 1977; Criminal Court News, "AC/DC Prostitution," *The Times-Picayune*, March 2, 1978; see also Jeanie Blake, "Who'll Take a Hooker's Word over the Word of a Lawman?" *The Times-Picayune*, April 12, 1981; "Police Reports [461 W. Napoleon Ave.]," *The Times-Picayune*, December 6, 1980.

32. Complaint, *Doe v. Jindal*, 30; see also Dewey and St. Germain, "Sex Workers/Sex Offenders," 225.

33. See Kate Sosin, "Against Backdrop of Anti-Trans Bills, Transgender Homicides Double," *The 19th*, April 16, 2021, https://19thnews.org/2021/04/against-backdrop-anti-trans-bills-transgender-homicides-double/.

34. At Liberty, "Black Trans Women."

35. See generally McTighe and Haywood, "NO Justice"; Ritchie, "Crimes against Nature."

36. McTighe and Haywood, "NO Justice," 268.

37. Ibid., 270.

38. Ibid., 276.

39. Ritchie, "Crime against Nature," 361.

40. Ibid., 371.

41. Dewey and St. Germain, "Sex Workers/Sex Offenders," 214. On the other hand, based on their analyses of sex offender registries across Louisiana parishes, the researchers point out that a nontrivial number of "men" on the registry for CANS are likely transgender. "[T]ransgender persons constitute 6.66% of those who must register as sex offenders solely due to a CANS conviction, but it is possible that there were many more transgender persons in the sex offender registry who did not self-present [as women]." Ibid., 277.

42. Michel Foucault, *The History of Sexuality, Volume 1: An Introduction*, translated by Robert Hurley (New York: Vintage, 1990), 43; Jonathan Goldberg, *Sodometries: Renaissance Texts, Modern Sexualities* (New York: Fordham University Press, 2010), 18.

43. See also Christopher Chitty, *Sexual Hegemony: Statecraft, Sodomy, and Capital in the Rise of the World System* (Durham: Duke University Press, 2020), 67 ("In fourteenth- and fifteenth-century Florence, however, sodomy was far from a confused legal category. Juridically speaking, it included only men who had sexual relations with other men").

44. Ritchie, "Crime against Nature," 371.

45. My thinking here is influenced by Jasbir Puar's argument that the "reracialization of sodomy elsewhere," onto Arabs and Muslims after September 11th, normalized and normativized privacy rights for indexically white gay subjects. Jasbir K. Puar, *Terrorist Assemblages: Homonationalism in Queer Times* (Durham: Duke University Press, 2007), 120.

46. Michael Merricks (Detective, Sex Crimes Unit, New Orleans Police Department), interview by author, January 14, 2012.

47. See James R. Kincaid, "Producing Erotic Children," in *Curiouser: On the Queerness of Children*, edited by Steven Bruhm and Natasha Hurley (Minneapolis: University of Minnesota Press, 2004), 3–14.

48. At Liberty, "Black Trans Women."

49. Nadel and Plotka, *CANS Can't Stand*.

50. Louisiana Revised Statutes 14:91.5.

51. Louisiana Revised Statutes 14:91.2.

52. Complaint, *Doe v. Jindal*, 24–26.

53. Louisiana Revised Statutes 14:313, 14:313.1.

54. Joseph J. Fischel, "Transcendent Homosexuals and Dangerous Sex Offenders: Sexual Harm and Freedom in the Judicial Imaginary," *Duke Journal of Gender Law & Policy* 17 (2010): 277–312; see generally Human Rights Watch, "No Easy Answers: Sex Offender Laws in the US," *Human Rights Watch* 19 (2007): 1–141, www.hrw .org/report/2007/09/11/no-easy-answers/sex-offender-laws-us; *Sex Offender Laws: Failed Policies, New Directions, 2nd Edition*, edited by Richard G. Wright (New York: Springer, 2015); Judith Levine and Erica R. Meiners, *The Feminist and the Sex Offender: Confronting Sexual Harm, Ending State Violence* (London: Verso, 2020).

55. See, for example, Richard G. Wright, "An Interview with Patty Wetterling," in Wright, *Sex Offender Laws*, 69–79; Hayley Forrestal, "The Sex Offender Registry Doesn't Work," *Chicago Alliance Against Sexual Exploitation*, October 9, 2019, www.caase .org/the-sex-offender-registry-doesnt-work/; Reina Gattuso, "Why Should Feminists Be against the Sex Offender Registry?" *Feministing*, December 21, 2018, https://feministing .com/2018/12/21/why-should-feminists-be-against-the-sex-offender-registry/; see also note 200 and accompanying text.

56. See, for example, Amanda Y. Agan and J. J. Prescott, "Sex Offender Law and the Geography of Victimization," *Journal of Empirical Legal Studies* 11 (2014): 786–828; Jeffrey C. Sandler, Naomi J. Freeman, and Kelly Michael Socia, "Does a Watched Pot Boil?

A Time-Series Analysis of New York State's Sex Offender Registration and Notification Law," *Psychology Public Policy and Law* 14 (2008): 284–302; Bob Edward Vásquez, Sean Maddan, and Jeffery T. Walker, "The Influence of Sex Offender Registration and Notification Laws in the United States: A Time-Series Analysis," *Crime & Delinquency* 54 (2008): 175–192. "The empirical findings of this research is that the sex offender legislation seems to have had no uniform and observable influence on the number of rapes reported in the states analyzed. . . . Taken collectively, the findings reported here indicate that sex offender registration and notification laws may have had little general deterrent effects on the incidence of rape offenses analyze." Ibid., 188.

57. "Program Purpose," *State Sex Offender and Child Predator Registry, Louisiana State Police Public Safety Services*, www.lsp.org/community-outreach/sex-offender -registry/program-purpose/.

58. See, for example, Mariel Alper and Matthew R. Durose, "Recidivism of Sex Offenders Released from State Prison: A 9-Year Follow-Up (2005–14)," *Bureau of Justice Statistics, Office of Justice Programs, U.S. Department of Justice*; Jeffrey S. Jones et al., "Comparisons of Sexual Assaults by Strangers Versus Known Assailants in a Community-Based Population," *American Journal of Emergency Medicine* 22 (2004): 454–459; Rape, Abuse and Incest National Network, "Perpetrators of Sexual Violence: Statistics," *RAINN*, www.rainn.org/statistics/perpetrators-sexual-violence.

59. Linda Gordon, "The Politics of Child Sexual Abuse: Notes from American History," *Feminist Review* 28 (1988): 61.

60. Rose Corrigan, *Up Against a Wall: Rape Reform and the Failure of Success* (New York: New York University Press, 2013), 206.

61. "It is not only men convicted of rape who believe that the only thing they did different from what men do all the time is get caught." Feminists believe so too, is MacKinnon's provocation. Catharine A. MacKinnon, "Feminism, Marxism, Method, and the State: Toward Feminist Jurisprudence," *Signs* 8 (1983): 650.

62. Gordon, "Child Sexual Abuse," 62.

63. Judith Levine and Erica R. Meiners, *The Feminist and the Sex Offender* (London: Verso, 2020), 159–185; for a set of noncarceral proposals and policies to remedy intimate partner violence, see Leigh Goodmark, *Decriminalizing Domestic Violence: A Balanced Policy Approach to Intimate Partner Violence* (Oakland: University of California Press, 2018).

64. Michel Foucault, *Discipline and Punish: The Birth of the Prison*, translated by Alan Sheridan (New York: Vintage, 1995), 297.

65. Sabrina Axster et al., "Colonial Lives of the Carceral Archipelago: Rethinking the Neoliberal Security State," *International Political Sociology* 15 (2021): 471, note 2.

66. Paul M. Renfro, "Sex Offender Registries Are Fueling Mass Incarceration—And They Aren't Helping Survivors," *Jacobin*, June 22, 2020, https://jacobin.com/2020/06/sex -offender-registries-mass-incarceration.

67. Levine and Meiners, *Feminist and the Sex Offender*, 11.

68. Ibid., 11–12; see also Eric S. Janus, *Failure to Protect: America's Sexual Predator Laws and the Rise of the Preventative State* (Ithaca: Cornell University Press, 2006); Roger N. Lancaster, *Sex Panic and the Punitive State* (Berkeley: University of California Press, 2011).

69. Sarah Haley, *No Mercy Here: Gender, Punishment, and the Making of Jim Crow Modernity* (Chapel Hill: University of North Carolina Press, 2015), 16, 156–194.

70. Gillian Harkins, *Virtual Pedophilia: Sex Offender Profiling and U.S. Security Culture* (Durham: Duke University Press, 2020), 4–5.

71. Ibid., 20–23.

72. Foucault, *History of Sexuality*, 43; see also Stefan Vogler, *Sorting Sexualities: Expertise and the Politics of Legal Classification* (Chicago: University of Chicago Press, 2021), 46 ("the law works to constitute the very sexual subjects it aims to govern"). In the summer of 2024, the Louisiana Legislature passed a bill that indisputably authorizes state sexual violence against sex offenders. David W. Chen, "Louisiana Passes Surgical Castration Bill for Child Sex Offenders," *New York Times*, June 4, 2024, www.nyt.com /2024/06/04.

73. "By now, most people who pay any attention to criminal justice reform know better than to label people convicted of drug offenses 'drug offenders,' a dehumanizing label that presumes these individuals will be criminals for life. But we continue to label people 'sex offenders'—implying that people convicted of sex offenses are somehow difference." Wendy Sawyer, "BJS Fuels Myths about Sex Offense Recidivism, Contradicting Its Own New Data," *Policy Prison Initiative*, June 6, 2019, www.prisonpolicy.org/blog /2019/06/06/sexoffenses/.

74. Michelle Alexander, *The New Jim Crow: Mass Incarceration in the Age of Colorblindness, Tenth Anniversary Edition* (New York: The New Press, 2020), xix.

75. Susan Faupel, "Etiology of Adult Sexual Offending," *Sex Offender Management Assessment and Planning Initiative, Office of Justice Programs, U.S. Department of Justice*, July 2015.

76. See Nadel and Plotka, *CANS Can't Stand*; see also Ritchie, "Crime against Nature," 370; McTighe and Haywood, "NO Justice," 270–271.

77. On the "sex offender" as a cultural, racialized category, nonidentical with but inseparable from the "sex offender" as a legal category, see Terrance Wooten, "Keyword 4: Sex Offender," *differences: A Journal of Feminist Cultural Studies* 30 (2019): 82–90.

78. Wooten, "Black Male Sex Offenders," 46.

79. See Brief of *Amici Curiae* Breakout!, *Doe v. Jindal*, 19–20; "Investigation of the New Orleans Police Department," *U.S. Department of Justice Civil Rights Division*, March 16, 2011, www.justice.gov/crt/about/spl/nopd_report.pdf: 36.

80. Wooten, "Black Male Sex Offenders," 40, citing Trevor Hoppe, "Punishing Sex: Sex Offenders and the Missing Punitive Turn in Sexuality Studies," *Law and Social Inquiry* 41 (2016): 573–594; see also Vogler, *Sorting Sexualities*, 49 ("Black men are disproportionately represented on public sex offender registries and in state civil commitment programs for sex offenders, and are more likely than White men to be diagnosed with a coercive rape paraphilia as the rationale for civil commitment").

81. Minutes of the Louisiana Senate Judiciary C Committee, House Bill 141, June 14, 2011, video recording.

82. Barbara Lacen-Keller (Director of Constituent Services for Councilmember-at-Large Stacy Head, New Orleans City Council), interview by author, January 31, 2012.

83. Lucy, interview by author, January 18, 2012; Kathy, interview by author, January 16, 2012.

84. Kathy, interview.

85. Andy, interview by author, January 12, 2012.

86. Cathy J. Cohen, *The Boundaries of Blackness: AIDS and the Breakdown of Black Politics* (Chicago: University of Chicago Press, 1999), 70.

87. For an excellent criticism of this scholarship and activism, see Harkins, *Virtual Pedophilia*, 194–207; for my earlier, similar gloss, see Joseph J. Fischel, *Sex and Harm in the Age of Consent* (Minneapolis: University of Minnesota Press, 2019), 1–6.

88. Evan, interview by author, January 24, 2012.

89. Ken, interview by author, January 19, 2012.

90. Phillip, interview by author, January 26, 2012.

91. Harkins, *Virtual Pedophilia*, 31.

92. NO Justice Project, "Constitutional Challenge Launched," *Women With a Vision*, https://wwav-no.org/no-justice-project/, emphasis added.

93. Connor, Ritchie, and Women With A Vision, "Talking Crime" (emphasis in original).

94. Ibid.

95. Editorial, "These Two Sex Crimes Should be Treated the Same," *The Times-Picayune*, May 30, 2011, www.nola.com/opinions/article_c3634d66-ab39-5f2f-a542 -e63989f18f64.html.

96. Complaint, *Doe v. Jindal*, 3, 5, 18, 19, 20, 20, 30, 31, 32, 40, 41. Ingeniously, the Complaint reverses the force of "force" discourse, positioning the plaintiffs as (sexually) victimized by the state, as in the phrases "[Audrey Doe] has been forced to explain to neighbors why she is registered as a sex offender," and "Diane Doe feels forced to explain that she did not molest anyone when she presents her identification at banks, the doctor's office, and other businesses," and "Eve Doe was first forced to circulate community notification disclosing her registration as a sex offender from her grandmother's home." Ibid., 32, 35.

97. Ibid., 5, emphasis added.

98. Of course, "whether a law and society deems a given behavior 'violent' in the first place is the outcome of complex political, racial, and ideological forces." Aya Gruber, "The Critique of Carceral Feminism," *Yale Journal of Law and Feminism* 34 (2023): 61.

99. Agathocleous, "Building a Movement," 444; Fischel, "Against Nature."

100. Complaint, *Doe v. Jindal*, 40.

101. *Doe v. Jindal*, 1009 note 28, emphasis in original.

102. Agathocleous, "Building a Movement," 444–445.

103. "Offenses," *State Sex Offender and Child Predator Registry, Louisiana State Police Public Safety Services*, www.lsp.org/community-outreach/sex-offender-registry /offenses/; "Program History," *State Sex Offender and Child Predator Registry, Louisiana State Police Public Safety Services*, www.lsp.org/community-outreach/sex-offender -registry/program-history/.

104. Bobby Jindal, "Governor Signs Chemical Castration Bill, Authorizing the Castration of Sex Offenders in Louisiana," *Office of the Governor Bobby Jindal*, June 25, 2008, https://votesmart.org/public-statement/353973/governor-signs-chemical-castration -bill-authorizing-the-castration-of-sex-offenders-in-louisiana.

105. "New Law Requires Sex Offenders to List Their Status on Facebook," *Fox Business*, July 5, 2012, http://video.foxbusiness.com/v/1721708504001/new-law-requires -sexoffenders-to-list-their-status-on-facebook/.

106. The majority of sex offenses do not involve Internet recruitment. A 2004 national study found that those offenders who do use the Internet target young teenagers, not children. They rarely deceive their victims about their age or intentions, and they rarely use violence. Janis Wolak, David Finkelhor, and Kimberly Mitchell, "Internet-Initiated Sex Crimes against Minors: Implications for Prevention Based on Findings from a National Study," *Journal of Adolescent Health* 35 (2004): 424e11–e20; see also David Finkelhor et al., "Youth Internet Safety Education: Aligning Programs with the Evidence Base," *Trauma, Violence, & Abuse* 22 (2020): 1233–1247.

107. Louisiana Revised Statutes 14:91.2; see also "Sex Offender Policy," *New Orleans Public Library*, www.nolalibrary.org/page/134/library-policies/203/sex-offender-policy.

108. Louisiana Revised Statutes 14.89.3.

109. As quoted in "Louisiana Strengthens Law against the Sexual Abuse of Animals," *The Humane Society of the United States*, May 31, 2018, www.humanesociety.org/news /louisiana-strengthens-law-against-sexual-abuse-animals.

110. See also Levine and Meiners, *Feminist and the Sex Offender*, 137 ("Unfortunately, the New Orleans campaign did not demand an end to the sex offender registry. Nor did it directly and clearly state that public registries make no one safer").

111. John Rawls, *A Theory of Justice* (Cambridge, MA: Harvard University Press, 1999 [1971]); John Rawls, *Political Liberalism* (New York: Columbia University Press, 2005 [1993]); John Rawls, *Justice as Fairness: A Restatement* (Cambridge, MA: Harvard University Press, 2001).

112. Rawls, *Justice as Fairness*, 42–43.

113. Nicole, interview by author, January 12, 2012; Kathy, interview; Ken, interview.

114. See Hoppe, "Punishing Sex." However, in the years since this chapter was first drafted, there have been several queer-inflected contributions to questions of carceral governance and punishment. See David M. Halperin and Trevor Hoppe, eds., *The War on Sex* (Durham: Duke University Press, 2017); Joey L. Mogul, Andrea Ritchie, and Kay Whitlock, *Queer (In)Justice: The Criminalization of LGBT People in the United States* (Boston: Beacon Press, 2011); Regina Kunzel, *Criminal Intimacy: Prison and the Uneven History of Modern American Sexuality* (Chicago: University of Chicago Press, 2008); Eric A. Stanley and Nat Smith, eds., *Captive Genders: Trans Embodiment and the Prison Industrial Complex* (Oakland: AK Press, 2011); Wooten, "Keyword 4"; Wooten, "Black Male Sex Offenders."

115. Bonnie Honig, "Rawls on Politics and Punishment," *Political Research Quarterly* 46 (1993): 102.

116. The original position is Rawls's thought-location to delineate and contract into agreed upon principles of justice for the basic structure of society. Rawls, *Theory*, 102–168. Parties in the original position function as representative citizens. Potentially biasing information such as the social status, wealth, religious belief, race, and sex of each member is made unknown through the "veil of ignorance." Ibid., 14–18. The device is designed, in part, to purify the contracted principles of justice from partiality and arbitrariness so that they rest squarely on rationality and reason.

117. Honig, "Rawls on Politics," 115.

118. Ibid., 104.

119. Rawls, *Theory*, 87–88.

120. Honig, "Rawls on Politics," 104.

121. If, for Honig, the problem of punishment reveals an immanent contradiction in Rawls, for political theorist Andrew Dilts, the indeterminacy of punishment is a foundational contradiction to the Lockean political commonwealth. In an excellent exposition, Dilts demonstrates that, since the thief in John Locke's state of nature is a threat in perpetuity (as there is no third party adjudicator), proportionality, ironically, knows no limit. To ground the right to punish, to bound proportionality, and to protect property, political society is contracted into existence. The transfer of punishment rights stabilizes the contractors as rational, innocent, proportionate, and unthreatening, while epistemologically figuring thieves as "animalistic and dangerous." Andrew Dilts, "To Kill a Thief: Punishment, Proportionality, and Criminal Subjectivity in Locke's Second Treatise," *Political Theory* 40 (2012): 72. "[I]n the moment of identification as a criminal, an individual simultaneously becomes responsible for a specific transgression and becomes a kind of person who embodies transgression itself . . . marked as the bad

actor that must be handled and managed, not simply for criminal actions but for a way of being." Ibid., 76. The instability of proportionate punishment constitutes the boundaries of political membership. Ibid., 73. For a more historical account of market order and criminal disorderliness as twin rationales for modern practices of punishment, see Bernard E. Harcourt, *The Illusion of Free Markets: Punishment and the Myth of Natural Order* (Cambridge, MA: Harvard University Press, 2011).

122. Honig, "Rawls on Politics," 122.

123. Ibid.

124. Ibid., 123.

125. Corey Brettschneider, *Democratic Rights: The Substance of Self-Government* (Princeton: Princeton University Press, 2007), 97.

126. Ibid., 96.

127. Ibid., 100.

128. To meet the requirements of Rawls's overlapping consensus, citizens are to offer "fair terms of social cooperation" that they themselves believe to be reasonable and believe others will find reasonable, given divergent comprehensive doctrines of the good. Rawls, *Political Liberalism*, xlii.

129. Brettschneider, *Democratic Rights*, 97.

130. Ibid., 99.

131. Ibid., 100.

132. Ibid., 110–111.

133. Ibid., 96, emphasis added.

134. Ibid., 99.

135. Ibid., 102.

136. Ibid., 103.

137. Evidently, Foucault influences the theoretical orientation of this chapter: first, in the chapter's documentation of moral/juridical subject types resultant from intersecting languages of expertise and disciplinary practices; and second, in its assumption that sexuality, under Western modernity and late modernity, expectedly harbors "limitless etiological power." Foucault, *Discipline and Punish*; Michel Foucault, "The Abnormals," in *Ethics: Subjectivity and Truth (The Essential Works of Michel Foucault, 1954–1984), Vol. 1*, edited by Paul Rabinow (New York: New Press, 1994), 54. As Foucault later observed of *Discipline and Punish*, his research there never asked about "justification" or the "right to punish" but instead surveyed relationships between forms of punishment—their expressed rationalities, their productions of subjectivities—and regimes of power. Michel Foucault, "What Is Called 'Punishing?'" in *Power (The Essential Works of Michel Foucault, 1954–1984, Vol. 3)*, edited by James D. Faubion (New York: New Press, 2001), 388.

138. Political theorist Benjamin McKean offers a "counterintuitive reading" of Rawls's ideal theory, noting that in the philosopher's later work, Rawls reconceives ideal theory as cultivating an "orientation" for citizens to "interpret society as a cooperative project with others as equal partners." Still, that Rawls "fails to develop a language to talk about power that would make it possible to orient one's action to it," seems to me to gut from the outset any project that would ideal-theorize just punishments for "criminals" who violate others' equal citizenship. Benjamin L. McKean, "What Makes a Utopia Inconvenient? On the Advantages and Disadvantages of a Realist Orientation to Politics," *American Political Science Review* 110 (2016): 877, 887.

139. See Angela Y. Davis, *Are Prisons Obsolete?* (New York: Seven Stories, 2003), 85.

140. Keally McBride, *Punishment and Political Order* (Ann Arbor: University of Michigan Press, 2007), 112.

141. Ibid., 148.

142. See Deborah W. Denno, "Life Before the Modern Sex Offender Statutes," *Northwestern University Law Review* 92 (1998): 1317–1414.

143. See Vogler, *Sorting Sexualities*, 176–186.

144. Honig, "Rawls on Politics," 123.

145. Patrick, interview by author, January 25, 2012.

146. Janus, *Failure to Protect*, 20.

147. Alexander, *New Jim Crow*. Although Alexander is tracking a national phenomenon, it is noteworthy that Louisiana was dubbed "the world's prison capital" by the *Times-Picayune*. Louisiana incarcerates a greater percentage of its residents than any other state in the nation or any other country in the world. Too, Louisiana's sentencing schemes are far stricter than those of most other states. The conditions of local prisons are uniquely atrocious on account of a roughly two-decades-old profit system between sheriffs and the state whereby sheriffs are incentivized to build prisons and retain prisoners at low cost. Cindy Chang, "Louisiana Incarcerated: How We Built the World's Prison Capital," *The Times-Picayune*, May 13, 2012.

148. Alexander, *New Jim Crow*, 51.

149. Ibid., 94.

150. Ibid., xxix; see also James Forman Jr., "Racial Critiques of Mass Incarceration: Beyond the New Jim Crow," *New York University Law Review* 87 (2012): 21–69; Rachel Kushner, "Is Prison Necessary? Ruth Wilson Gilmore Might Change Your Mind," *New York Times Magazine*, April 17, 2019, www.nytimes.com/2019/04/17/magazine/prison-abolition-ruth-wilson-gilmore.html ("I think the failure of some academics like myself [Michelle Alexander] to squarely respond to the question of violence in our work has created a situation in which it almost seems like we're approving of mass incarceration for violent people. Those of us who are committed to ending the system of mass criminalization have to begin talking more about violence. Not only the harm it causes, but the fact that building more cages will never solve it").

151. Ibid.

152. See, for example, Jill S. Levenson and Leo P. Cotter, "The Effect of Megan's Law on Sex Offender Reintegration," *Journal of Contemporary Criminal Justice* 21 (2005): 49–66; Richard Tewksbury, "Collateral Consequences of Sex Offender Registration," *Journal of Contemporary Criminal Justice* 21 (2005): 67–81; Richard G. Zevits and Mary Ann Farkas, "Sex Offender Community Notification: Managing High Risk Criminals or Exacting Further Vengeance?" *Behavioral Sciences and the Law* 18 (2000): 375–391.

153. Alexander, *New Jim Crow*, xxiii.

154. Ian Doe, an anonymized plaintiff in *Doe v. Jindal*, quoted in Agathocleous, "Building a Movement," 435.

155. Patrick, interview.

156. See also Martha T. McCluskey, "How Queer Theory Makes Neoliberalism Sexy," in *Feminist and Queer Legal Theory: Intimate Encounters, Uncomfortable Conversations*, edited by Martha Albertson Fineman, Jack E. Jackson, and Adam P. Romero (Surrey: Ashgate, 2009).

157. I found the following essay collections additionally helpful for theorizing debility: Mairian Corker and Tom Shakespeare, eds., *Disability/Postmodernity: Embodying Disability Theory* (London: Continuum, 2002); Robert McRuer and Anna Mollow, eds., *Sex and Disability* (Durham: Duke University Press, 2012); Tom Shakespeare,

ed., *The Disability Studies Reader: Social Science Perspectives* (London: Cassell, 1998); Tom Shakespeare, Kath Gillespie-Sells, and Dominic Davies, eds., *The Sexual Politics of Disability: Untold Stories* (London: Cassell, 1996); Sharon L. Snyder, Brenda Jo Brueggemann, and Rosemarie Garland-Thomson, eds., *Disability Studies: Enabling the Humanities* (New York: Modern Language Association of America, 2002).

158. See, for example, Lennard J. Davis, *Enforcing Normality: Disability, Deafness, and the Body* (London: Verso, 1995); Andrew Dilts, "Incurable Blackness: Criminal Disenfranchisement, Mental Disability, and the White Citizen," *Disability Studies Quarterly* 32 (2012): http://dsq-sds.org/article/view/3268/3101.

159. Jasbir K. Puar, "Prognosis Time: Towards a Geopolitics of Affect, Debility, and Capacity," *Women and Performance: A Journal of Feminist Theory* 19 (2009): 165; see also Jasbir K. Puar, *The Right to Maim: Debility, Capacity, Disability* (Durham: Duke University Press, 2017), xiii–xiv.

160. Puar, "Prognosis Time," 166; *Right to Maim*, xvi. Puar cites Julie Livingston's usage of the term debility, which encompasses "impairment, chronic illness, and senescence." Puar, "Prognosis Time," 167; Julie Livingston, *Debility and the Moral Imagination in Botswana* (Bloomington: Indiana University Press, 2005), 6. Contrasted against "disability," "debility" allows Livingston to more powerfully catalog how transformations in political economy, migration patterns, and medicine have—at the level of the human body and its caretakers—affected the southeastern populations of Botswana over the past hundred years. For me, provisionally, debility refers not only to incapacitations of the body but also to incapacitations against the person (of course, for Livingston, misfortunes and injuries to the body implicate horizons of personhood, too. Ibid., 2–4). While my specification of the state as the debilitating agent may stretch grammatical sensibility, my bid is not primarily to redefine a term but to retheorize an injustice.

161. Ibid., 163; see also Puar, *Right to Maim*, xvii.

162. Puar, *Right to Maim*, 157–158.

163. See Shakespeare, Gillespie-Sells, and Davies, *Sexual Politics*, 2–3; Michael Oliver, *The Politics of Disablement* (London: Macmillan, 1990); A. J. Withers, *Disability Politics and Theory* (Halifax: Fernwood, 2012), 86.

164. Puar, *Right to Maim*, 15–16.

165. Ibid., 160.

166. Ibid., xiii.

167. Puar, "Prognosis Time," 162, 167. "One wonders, at times, whether the Deleuzian mechanisms used in [*The Right to Maim*] are themselves too broad, encompassing, and cumbersome to describe, let alone remedy, the problems raised." Lennard Davis, "The Right to Maim: Debility, Capacity, Disability" [Book Review], *Critical Inquiry* 45 (2018): 237–238.

168. Ibid., 169.

169. Martha Albertson Fineman, "The Vulnerable Subject: Anchoring Equality in the Human Condition," *Yale Journal of Law and Feminism* 20 (2008): 8–9.

170. Martha C. Nussbaum, *Frontiers of Justice: Disability, Nationality, Species Membership* (Cambridge, MA: Harvard University Press, 2007): 87–88.

171. Ibid., 135.

172. Ibid., 167.

173. Ibid., 104–105.

174. Although *dignity* only became foundational in later iterations of Nussbaum's capabilities approach. See Rutger Claassen, "Human Dignity in the Capability Approach," in *The Cambridge Handbook of Human Dignity: Interdisciplinary Perspectives*, edited by

Marcus Düwell et al. (Cambridge: Cambridge University Press, 2014): 240–249. It is not clear to me that dignity must ground Nussbaum's capabilities approach as it now does, especially since dignity jurisprudence has generated significant obstacles for sexual and reproductive freedom. Joseph J. Fischel and Claire McKinney, "Capability without Dignity?" *Contemporary Political Theory* 19 (2020): 404–429.

175. Fineman, "Vulnerable Subject," 14 note 39.

176. Ibid., 1.

177. Ibid., 9.

178. Ibid., 4–6.

179. Ibid., 21.

180. Judith Butler, *Precarious Life: The Powers of Mourning and Violence* (London: Verso, 2004), 29.

181. Bryan S. Turner, *Vulnerability and Human Rights* (University Park: Penn State University Press, 2006), 32.

182. Neither Fineman nor Nussbaum neglect the statutory production of vulnerability, but the political consequences of this acknowledgment are not fleshed out. Fineman, "Vulnerable Subject," 21; Nussbaum, *Frontiers*, 165. Fineman criticizes Judith Butler's vulnerability thesis in *Precarious Life* for its overemphasis on grieving and loss and its inattention to state structures. Fineman, "Vulnerable Subject," 12 note 31.

183. See Cathy J. Cohen, "Punks, Bulldaggers, and Welfare Queens: The Radical Potential of Queer Politics?" *GLQ* 3 (1997): 437–465; see also Erica R. Meiners, "Awful Acts and the Trouble with Normal," in *Captive Genders: Trans Embodiment and the Prison Industrial Complex*, edited by Eric A. Stanley and Nat Smith (Oakland: AK Press, 2011), 118.

184. Thanks to Stephen Bush for helping clarify this potential ambiguity.

185. See Puar, *Right to Maim*, 80–81.

186. Fineman, "Vulnerable Subject," 9–10.

187. Ani B. Satz, "Disability, Vulnerability, and the Limits of Antidiscrimination," *Washington Law Review* 83 (2008): 527, 552.

188. Kathy, interview.

189. See, for example, Shelley Tremain, "On the Subject of Impairment," in *Disability/Postmodernity: Embodying Disability Theory*, edited by Mairian Corker and Tom Shakespeare (London: Continuum, 2002), 32–47.

190. See Michael Eric Dyson, *Come Hell or High Water: Hurricane Katrina and the Color of Disaster* (Cambridge, MA: Basic Civitas, 2006), 97–110.

191. Fischel, "Against Nature"; Fischel, *Sex and Harm*.

192. Minutes of the Louisiana Senate Judiciary C Committee, House Bill 141, June 14, 2011, video recording.

193. For a similar form of feminist-calibrated, anticarceral consequentalism, see I. India Thusi, "Radical Feminist Harms on Sex Workers," *Lewis and Clark Law Review* 22 (2018): 185–229.

194. For my more extended nonanswer to the question of sex's specialness, see Joseph J. Fischel, *Screw Consent: A Better Politics of Sexual Justice* (Berkeley: University of California Press, 2019), 27–30.

195. See Corrigan, *Up against a Wall*, 217–227; 247–248.

196. Barbara Lacen-Keller, the New Orleans city hall official who was, as discussed earlier, explicitly committed to the exonerative logic of the consenting adult, was also keenly attuned to compulsory heterosexuality. She asked me how oral or anal sex for compensation could be a sex offense when married couples routinely perform such

activities. I thought perhaps she misunderstood the law and explained that oral and anal sex had to be solicited in exchange for compensation in order for the acts to be criminal. To which she replied: "What do you think marriage is? . . . If a man don't bring no money home, no sugar tonight. And I don't mean out the sugar jar. Think about it! What do you think marriage is? Marriage is an installment. A long-term plan." Lacen-Keller is, of course, in good, radical company with Emma Goldman and Simone de Beauvoir on the point.

197. See Fineman, "Vulnerable Subject"; Satz, "Disability."

198. See, for example, Megan Comfort, *Doing Time Together: Love and Family in the Shadow of Prison* (Chicago: University of Chicago Press, 2008). Comfort, though, also describes how women sometimes benefit from the incarceration or threat of incarceration of their male partners.

199. See, for example, Joe Rollins, *AIDS and the Sexuality of Law: Ironic Jurisprudence* (New York: Palgrave Macmillan, 2004), 105–138; on the sexualized violence disproportionately experienced by transgender and gender nonconforming people in prison, see Paisley Currah, *Sex Is as Sex Does: Governing Transgender Identity* (New York: New York University Press, 2022), 121.

200. On "destructive masculinity" as a motor of extreme sexual and gendered violence across the criminal justice system, see Angela P. Harris, "Heteropatriarchy Kills: Challenging Gender Violence in a Prison Nation," *Washington University Journal of Law & Policy* 37 (2011): 13–65.

201. See, for example, Adaora A. Adimora and Victor J. Schoenbach, "Social Context, Sexual Networks, and Racial Disparities in Rates of Sexually Transmitted Infections," *Journal of Infectious Diseases* 191, Supp. 1 (2005): S119–120; Kathryn M. Nowotny et al., "Incarceration Rates and Incidence of Sexually Transmitted Infections in US Counties, 2011–2016," *American Journal of Public Health* 110, Suppl 1 (2020): S130–136.

202. Morgan Bassichis, Alexander Lee, and Dean Spade, "Building an Abolitionist and Queer Movement with Everything We've Got," in *Captive Genders: Trans Embodiment and the Prison Industrial Complex*, edited by Eric A. Stanley and Nat Smith (Oakland: AK Press, 2011), 34.

203. Ibid.

204. Currah, *Sex Is as Sex Does*, 127–128.

205. Goodmark, *Decriminalizing Domestic Violence*. For more information on the aforementioned organizations, visit "About Us," *Stop It Now!*, www.stopitnow.org /about-us/who-we-are; "About the Sexual Violence Prevention Program," *Minnesota Department of Health*, www.health.state.mn.us/communities/svp/index.html; "Analysis," *INCITE!*, https://incite-national.org/analysis/; "Learn," *ATSA*, www.atsa .com/learn; on restorative justice models for sexual violence, the models' feminist advocates and critics, and "transformative justice" as a potential successor, see Harris, "Heteropatriarchy Kills," 38–65.

206. Michel Foucault, Guy Hocquenghem, and Jean Danet, "Sexual Morality and the Law," in *Politics, Philosophy, Culture: Interviews and Other Writings, 1977–1984*, edited by Lawrence D. Kritzman (New York: Routledge, 1988), 276–277.

CHAPTER 2

1. Julia O'Donoghue, "Louisiana House Votes 27–67 to Keep Unconstitutional Antisodomy Law on the Books," *The Times-Picayune*, April 15, 2014.

2. Different criminal codes define sodomy differently, of course, but in Louisiana, by case law, "unnatural carnal copulation" includes oral sexual contact and penetrative anal sex between people of same or different genders. *State v. Phillips*, 365 So. 2d 1304 (La. 1978).

3. *Lawrence v. Texas*, 539 U.S. 558 (2003).

4. Jim Mustian, "Gay Men Arrested in Louisiana under Invalid Sodomy Law," *Advocate*, July 29, 2013, http://sdgln.com/news/2013/07/29/gay-men-arrested-louisiana -via-invalid-sodomy-law.

5. Raffy Ermac, "Baton Rouge Police Chief Apologizes for Unconstitutional 'Sodomy' Arrests," *Advocate*, February 19, 2015.

6. But see *State v. Thomas*, 891 So.2d 1233 (La. 2005) (implying that the state's non-commercial sodomy statute is unconstitutional). Then again, see *Dobbs v. Jackson Women's Health Org.*, 142 S.Ct. 2228 (2022).

7. Lauren McGaughy, "Committee Votes to Remove Anti-sodomy Statute from Louisiana Law," *The Times-Picayune*, April 9, 2014.

8. Julie Compton, "American Men Are Still Being Arrested for Sodomy," *Advocate*, May 23, 2016, quoting Matt Patterson, then the managing director of Equality Louisiana, www.advocate.com/crime/2016/5/23/american-men-are-still-being-arrested-sodomy.

9. Katie McDonough, "Louisiana Police Use Invalid Anti-sodomy Law to Arrest Gay Men for Agreeing to Consensual Sex," *Salon*, July 28, 2013.

10. As William Leap glosses the contributions to his edited volume: "Sexual-site-as-public-site, sexual-privacy-as-fiction—these are the cornerstone claims for the essays in this collection. While the sites under discussion here range rather widely—highway rest stops, beaches, health club saunas, bookstore backrooms, bathhouses, street corners, bus terminals, parks, and gay resorts, these case studies describe *efforts to create opportunities for sexual privacy in the face of public access, object, and regulation*." William L. Leap, *Public Sex /Gay Space* (New York: Columbia University Press, 1999), 12.

11. See Introduction, notes 111–127 and accompanying text.

12. Louisiana State Legislature Act No. 177 (2014).

13. For my cursory gloss on regulating incestuous relations, see Joseph J. Fischel, *Screw Consent: A Better Politics of Sexual Justice* (Berkeley: University of California Press, 2019), 78–86.

14. Lee Edelman, *Bad Education: Why Queer Theory Teaches Us Nothing* (Durham: Duke University Press, 2022), 218.

15. Ibid., 224.

16. But to scratch the surface, on the queer studies side, see, for example and seminally (haha), Eve Kosofksy Sedgwick, *Epistemology of the Closet* (Berkeley: University of California Press, 1990), 22–35; on the disability studies side, see, for example Anna Mollow, "Is Sex Disability? Queer Theory and the Disability Drive," in *Sex and Disability*, edited by Robert McRuer and Anna Mollow (Durham: Duke University Press, 2012), 285–312; Tony Siebers, "A Sexual Culture for Disabled People," in McRuer and Anna Mollow, *Sex and Disability*, 37–53.

17. For an instructive taxonomy of the many meanings of "private" and "public" under liberal jurisprudence, see Martha C. Nussbaum, "Protecting Intimacy: Sex Clubs, Public Sex, Risky Choices," in *From Disgust to Humanity: Sexual Orientation and Constitutional Law* (Oxford: Oxford University Press, 2010), especially 193–195.

18. Joel Feinberg, *Offense to Others: The Moral Limits of the Criminal Law, Vol. 2* (New York: Oxford University Press, 1988), 4–5.

19. Richard A. Posner, *Sex and Reason* (Cambridge, MA: Harvard University Press, 1992), 381.

20. Stuart P. Green, *Criminalizing Sex: A Unified Liberal Theory* (New York: Oxford University Press, 2020), 227.

21. Ibid., 248. On the other hand, Green surmises that legal enforcement against indecent exposure is likely justifiable when the conduct "offend[s] all but the most insensitive members of society" and takes as an instructive example when "everyone, or almost everyone, would be offended by being forced to witness people having sexual intercourse on a public bus." Ibid., 247; see also Feinberg, *Offense to Others*, 12. But I think this conclusion is not as dispositive as it first seems and for two reasons, the first empirical, the second conceptual. First: if we surveyed the passengers on the bus, would all of them or nearly all of them be offended by the copulating couple, or might several people be intrigued or indifferent? Offense might commingle with fascination. Feinberg, *Offense to Others*, 17–18. Second: a whole lot normatively, maybe everything, depends on the "force" of "forced to witness." In only the most peculiar iterations of this scenario would passengers be forced, other than by their own impulses, to watch their fellow passengers have sex. Moreover, in such scenarios—or its more common cousin, in which a man purposefully and directly flashes his penis to another passenger caught unaware—it seems what is socially objected to is not exposed genitals per se but that the genitals are exposed *at* others.

22. *State v. Thomas* (La. 2005).

23. *Lawrence v. Texas*, 539 U.S. 558 (2003).

24. *Lawrence*, 590, Scalia, J., dissenting.

25. Joseph J. Fischel, *Sex and Harm in the Age of Consent* (Minneapolis: University of Minnesota Press, 2016), 79.

26. *Lawrence*, 578, emphasis added.

27. For my criticism of these court decisions, see Chapter 5.

28. See *Erotic Serv. Provider Legal Educ. Research Project v. Gascon*, 880 F.3d 450 (9th Cir. 2018); MacKinnon has argued that prostitution as well as prostitution laws that criminalize the prostitute violate the Thirteenth Amendment of the United States Constitution. Catharine A. MacKinnon, "Prostitution and Civil Rights," *Michigan Journal of Gender & Law* 1 (1993): 13–31. Posner proposes that antiprostitution laws differ from laws against obscenity and public indecency in that a "principal purpose of punishing prostitution . . . is to protect marriage by discouraging men from seeking sexual satisfaction outside of it and from dissipating in that quest resources needed by their family." Posner, *Sex and Reason*, 378–339. This argument is antiquated, unsubstantiated, presumptuous, sexist, heteronormative, and so on.

In Chapter 5, I argue that prostitution laws violate the Due Process Clause of the Fourteenth Amendment. Prosecutors' and judges' insistence that prostitution is necessarily public are either immanently contradictory with their operative definitions of "publicity" or tautological (money = public).

29. Catharine A. MacKinnon, "Feminism, Marxism, Method, and the State: An Agenda for Feminist Jurisprudence," *Signs* 8 (1983): 635–658.

30. University of Chicago, "Trafficking, Prostitution and Inequality: A Public Lecture by Catharine MacKinnon," *YouTube*, December 14, 2011; see also Catharine A. MacKinnon, "The Road Not Taken: Sex Equality in *Lawrence v. Texas*," *Ohio State Law Journal* 65 (2004): 1081–1095; Marc Spindelman, "Surviving *Lawrence v. Texas*," *Michigan Law Review* 102 (2004): 1615–1667.

31. But see Green, *Criminalizing Sex*, 229 (reporting universities that have banned "streaking and mooning as forms of sexual harassment").

32. Green queries whether unsolicited dick pics (my phrasing) are "public" enough to be publicly indecent. Green, *Criminalizing Sex*, 245.

33. Livia Albeck-Ripka, "Tennessee Bans Drag Shows on Public Property," *New York Times*, March 2, 2023, www.nytimes.com/2023/03/02/us/tennessee-bans-drag-shows .html.

34. Ibid.

35. "Chaos, Law, and Order," *The Problem with John Stewart*, Apple+, March 3, 2023.

36. My reconstruction of sexual autonomy is developed in Fischel, *Screw Consent*, 140–149.

37. Nussbaum, "Protecting Intimacy," 174.

38. Ibid., 200.

39. Stephen J. Schulhofer, *Unwanted Sex: The Culture of Intimidation and the Failure of Law* (Cambridge, MA: Harvard University Press, 2000), 111; but see Gowri Ramachandran, "Against the Right to Bodily Integrity: Of Cyborgs and Human Right," *Denver University Law Review* 87 (2009): 1–57.

40. For an early and now foundational essay on virtuality, sex, sexual violence, and ethics, see Julian Dibbell, "A Rape in Cyberspace (or TINYSOCIETY, and How to Make One)," in *My Tiny Life: Crime and Passion in a Virtual World* (New York: Henry Holt, 1999), 11–30; see also Anastasia Powell and Nicola Henry, *Sexual Violence in a Digital Age* (London: Palgrave MacMillan, 2017); Tom Roach, *Screen Love: Queer Intimacies in the Grindr Era* (Albany: SUNY Press, 2021).

41. Katherine M. Franke, "The Domesticated Liberty of *Lawrence v. Texas*," *Columbia Law Review* 104 (2004): 1399–1426.

42. Ibid., 1404.

43. Ibid., 1406, quoting *National Coalition for Gay & Lesbian Equality v. Minister of Justice* 1999 (1) SALR 6 (CC) at para 29 (S. Afr.).

44. Ibid., 1406.

45. Allan Bérubé refers to bathhouses as "the first urban zone of privacy, as well as safety, for gay men." Allan Bérubé, "The History of Gay Bathhouses," *Journal of Homosexuality* 44 (2003): 37; see also Nussbaum's distinction between public accommodations and private facilities. "Protecting Intimacy," 195–196.

46. Lauren Berlant and Michael Warner, "Sex in Public," *Critical Inquiry* 24 (1998): 564–566.

47. Judith Butler, *Bodies that Matter: On the Discursive Limits of Sex* (Routledge: New York, 1993), 85.

48. Berlant and Warner, "Sex in Public," 564.

49. Ibid., 547, note 1, citing Herbert Marcuse, *Eros and Civilization: A Philosophical Inquiry into Freud* (Boston: Beacon Press, 1966).

50. Joseph J. Fischel, "Keep Pride Nude," *Boston Review*, June 23, 2021, https://bost onreview.net/articles/keep-pride-nude/.

51. Saidiya Hartman, *Wayward Lives, Beautiful Experiments: Intimate Histories of Social Upheaval* (New York: W.W. Norton & Company, 2019), 181.

52. Ibid., 180.

53. Ibid., 61.

54. See, for example, Marie Solis, "Sex Workers Will Finally Be Able to Carry Condoms without Fear of Arrest in California," *Vice*, July 29, 2019, www.vice.com/en /article/j5wymd/sex-workers-condoms-abuse-california-law; Jaclyn Diaz, "New York

Repeals 'Walking While Trans' Law," *NPR*, February 3, 2021, www.npr.org/2021/02/03/963513022/new-york-repeals-walking-while-trans-law.

55. Hartman, *Wayward Lives*, 182.

56. On Black counterpublics, see Michael C. Dawson, "A Black Counterpublic?: Economic Earthquakes, Racial Agenda(s), and Black Politics," *Public Culture* 7 (1994): 195–223; Marc Lamont Hill, "'Thank You, Black Twitter': State Violence, Digital Counterpublics and Pedagogies of Resistance," *Urban Education* 53 (2018): 286–302; Shatema Threadcraft, "North American Necropolitics and Gender: On #BlackLivesMatter and Black Femicide," *South Atlantic Quarterly* 116 (2017): 553–579.

57. Jennifer C. Nash, *The Black Body in Ecstasy: Reading Race, Reading Pornography* (Durham: Duke University Press, 2014); Amber Jamilla Musser, *Sensual Excess: Queer Femininity and Brown Jouissance* (New York: New York University Press, 2018); Ariane Cruz, *The Color of Kink: Black Women, BDSM, and Pornography* (New York: New York University Press, 2016); Darieck Scott, *Extravagant Abjection: Blackness, Power, and Sexuality in the African American Literary Imagination* (New York: New York University Press, 2010); Roderick A. Ferguson, *Aberrations in Black: Toward a Queer of Color Critique* (Minneapolis: University of Minnesota Press, 2004); Mireille Miller-Young, *A Taste for Brown Sugar: Black Women in Pornography* (Durham: Duke University Press, 2014); L. H. Stallings, *A Dirty South Manifesto: Sexual Resistance and Imagination in the New South* (Oakland: University of California Press, 2020); Deb Vargas, "Ruminations on *Lo Sucio* as a Latino Queer Analytic," *American Quarterly* 66 (2014): 715–726.

58. Shoniqua Roach and Erica Edwards offer excellent, cautionary essays on the political risks of resignifying Black women's sexuality. Shoniqua Roach, "Black Sex in the Quiet," *differences: A Journal of Feminist Cultural Studies* 30 (2019): 126–147; Erica R. Edwards, "Sex after the Black Normal," *differences: A Journal of Feminist Cultural Studies* 26 (2015): 141–167.

59. Stallings, *Dirty Southern Manifesto*.

60. Ibid., 58–59.

61. Ibid., 53–54, citing Audre Lorde, "Jessehelms," *Callalloo* 14 (1991): 60–61.

62. Lorde, "Jesse Helms," 60.

63. Stallings, *Dirty Southern Manifesto*, 62.

64. Ibid., 63.

65. Ibid., 69–70.

66. Ibid.., 70.

67. Compton, "American Men."

68. Nussbaum gives the example of city of Amsterdam permitting sexual activity in its public parks so long as such activity takes places within specific times zones, in secluded areas, and away from children. "Protecting Intimacy," 199.

69. Stallings, *Dirty Southern Manifesto*, 87.

70. Ibid., 88.

71. Samuel R. Delaney, *Time Square Red, Time Square Blue: 20th Anniversary Edition* (New York: New York University Press, 2019).

72. Vargas, "Ruminations on *Lo Sucio*," 724–725.

73. Ibid., 721.

74. Ibid., 722.

75. Ibid., 717.

76. Cathy Cohen, *The Boundaries of Blackness: AIDS and the Breakdown of Black Politics* (Chicago: University of Chicago Press, 1999).

77. Vargas, "*Lo Sucio*," 717–718.

78. Ibid., 718.

79. Ibid., 715, citing José Esteban Muñoz, *Cruising Utopia, Tenth Anniversary Edition: The Then and There of Queer Futurity* (New York: New York University Press, 2019).

80. Joseph Osmundson, *Virology: Essays for the Living, the Dead, and the Small Things in Between* (New York: W.W. Norton & Company, 2022), 108

81. See Elizabeth Brake, *Minimizing Marriage: Marriage, Morality, and the Law* (New York: Oxford University Press, 2012).

82. GerShun Avilez, *Black Queer Freedom: Spaces of Injury and Paths of Desire* (Urbana: University of Illinois Press, 2020).

83. Ibid., 4–5, emphasis added.

84. Ibid., 8.

85. Ibid., 8.

86. Ibid., 11, emphasis added.

87. Ibid., 48.

88. Ibid., 89, 99.

89. Ibid., 154.

90. Ibid., 16, emphasis added.

91. Ibid., 14.

92. Ibid., 29.

93. Ibid., 152.

94. Ibid., 152.

95. Joseph J. Fischel, "Keep Pride Nude," *Boston Review*, June 23, 2021, https://bostonreview.net/articles/keep-pride-nude/; Diaz, "New York Repeals 'Walking While Trans' Law"; Salman Masood and Mike Ives, "Rapes of Woman and 5-Year-Old Fuel Outrage in Pakistan," *New York Times*, September 11, 2020, www.nytimes.com/2020/09/11/world/asia/pakistan-rape-5-year-old-lahore-karachi.html.

96. See Kathryn Bond Stockton, *The Queer Child, or Growing Sideways in the Twentieth Century* (Durham: Duke University Press, 2009).

97. Ferguson, *Aberrations in Black*, 3; M. Jacqui Alexander, *Pedagogies of Crossing: Meditations on Feminism, Sexual Politics, Memory, and the Sacred* (Durham: Duke University Press, 2005); Musser, *Sensual Excess*.

98. Emily A. Owens, *Consent in the Presence of Force: Sexual Violence and Black Women's Survival in Antebellum New Orleans* (Chapel Hill: University of North Carolina Press, 2023), 22–23.

99. Ibid., 24.

100. But see, of course, Muñoz's reconstruction of Ernst Bloch's "critical notion of utopia" on behalf of "queer futurity." Muñoz, *Cruising Utopia*, 22. For radically democratic, insistently present-oriented transvaluations of utopian thinking, see also Benjamin L. McKean, "What Makes a Utopia Inconvenient? On the Advantages and Disadvantages of a Realist Orientation to Politics," *American Political Science Review* 110 (2016): 876–888; Tehama Lopez Bunyasi and Candis Watts Smith, "Get in Formation: Black Women's Participation in the Women's March on Washington as an Act of Pragmatic Utopianism," *The Black Scholar: Journal of Black Studies and Research* 48 (2018): 4–16; see generally Angela Jones, ed., *A Critical Inquiry into Queer Utopias* (New York: Palgrave MacMillan, 2013).

101. Jeremy Atherton Lin, *Gay Bar: Why We Went Out* (New York: Little, Brown and Company, 2021), 21, citing Johan Andersson, "Vauxhall's Post-industrial Pleasure Gardens: 'Death Wish' and Hedonism in 21st Century London," *Urban Studies* 48 (2011): 85–100.

102. Lin, *Gay Bar*, 31–32.

103. Franke, "Domesticated Liberty."

104. Osmundson, *Virology*, 139.

105. Bérubé, *History of Gay Bathhouses*, 34.

106. George Chauncey, "Privacy Could Only Be Had in Public: Gay Uses of the Street," in *The People, Place, and Space Reader*, edited by Jen Jack Gieseking and William Mangold (New York: Routledge, 2014).

107. Nussbaum, "Protecting Intimacy," 176–182.

108. Near the end of her writing on the matter, Nussbaum considers sexual activity at road stops and at public parks, advocating that such sexual activity ought likely to be legally permitted when conducted away from children and "unwilling" witnesses. Nussbaum makes public sex private to afford it ethical and constitutional protection. Ibid., 199–201.

109. *Bowers v. Hardwick*, 478 U.S. 186, 212–213 (1986), Blackmun, J., dissenting, emphasis added.

110. Gayle S. Rubin, "Thinking Sex: Notes for a Radical Theory of the Politics of Sexuality," in *Deviations: A Gayle Rubin Reader*, edited by Gayle S. Rubin (Durham: Duke University Press, 2011 [1984]), 149.

111. See Jed Rubenfeld, "The Right of Privacy," *Harvard Law Review* 102 (1989): 781–782. Hovering over the sex-as-ordinary component of my argument, as many readers will already know, are Foucault's admonitions against a politics of freedom anchored in the alleged specialness of sex. See Michel Foucault, *The History of Sexuality, Volume 1: An Introduction*, translated by Robert Hurley (New York: Vintage Books, 1980): 150–158.

112. Rubenfeld, "The Right of Privacy," 778–779; see also Janet E. Halley, "Reasoning about Sodomy: Act and Identity in and after *Bowers v. Hardwick*," *Virginia Law Review* 79 (1993): 1737–1739, 1770–1772.

113. Posner, *Sex and Reason*, 380.

114. Feinberg, *Offense to Others*, 8.

115. Ibid., 24.

116. Green, *Criminalizing Sex*, 234.

117. Ibid., 232.

118. Ibid., 229–230.

119. In the late 1980s, a group of women sunbathed topless in Central Park to protest New York's gender-asymmetric law criminalizing exposure of female breasts. After several years of litigation, the state's highest court punted on the equal protection challenge, holding instead that the law did not apply to nonlewd, noncommercial exposure of breasts. *People v. Santorelli*, 600 N.E.2d 232 (N.Y. 1992).

120. See Kate Mann, *Down Girl: The Logic of Misogyny* (Oxford: Oxford University Press, 2018), 177–219.

121. See Andrew Gilden, "Punishing Sexual Fantasy," *William & Mary Law Review* 58 (2016–2017): 419–491.

122. See *Commonwealth v. Bell*, 67 Mass. App. Ct. 266, 266 (2006) (holding "that a criminal defendant could be guilty of attempting to rape a child or of soliciting sexual conduct for a fee where, unbeknownst to him, he was negotiating with an undercover police officer to arrange for sexual intercourse with a child, and there was no actual child at risk in the negotiations, because the nonexistence of the child was a factual, not a legal, impossibility, and therefore was not a defense to the crime").

123. Model Penal Code: § 213.5 Indecent Exposure.

124. Model Penal Code: § 213.5 Indecent Exposure, Note 2: Definition of the Offense ("Display of buttocks or breast is not covered").

125. Model Penal Code: §2.02(b)(i). Alternatively, read as a result element ("likely to *cause*"), a defendant would be provided an even stronger shield from liability; he would need to be "practically certain" that his exposed genitals would cause affront or alarm. Model Penal Code: §2.02(b)(ii).

126. See Associated Press, "Berlin to Let Everyone Go Topless at Public Swimming Pools," *AP News*, March 9, 2023, https://apnews.com/article/germany-berlin-topless-swimming-pools-women-discrimination-292399fcd4290414d33ee8e8f46e1922.

127. Richard A. Posner and Katharine B. Silbaugh, *A Guide to America's Sex Laws* (Chicago: University of Chicago Press, 1996), 83–97.

128. Louisiana Revised Statutes 14:106G(4), emphases added.

129. Louisiana Revised Statutes 14:106A(1).

130. Louisiana Revised Statutes 14:106G(1).

131. See Fischel, *Screw Consent*, 126–131.

132. Louisiana Revised Statutes 14:80A(1).

133. Nussbaum, "Protecting Intimacy," 178.

134. Ibid., 199.

135. Green, *Criminalizing Sex*, 237.

136. Feinberg, *Offense to Others*, 11. Even regarding these Stories, which I find the most noxious of Feinberg's hypotheticals, I am disinclined to propose criminalization as a solution. However, should the picknickers absolutely refuse to pack up their boar penises and refuse to cease consuming their poop, it seems reasonable that the police might be called upon to escort the picknickers off the bus and too that the picknickers might be issued a summons.

137. Fischel, *Sex and Harm*, 127–128.

138. Fischel, *Screw Consent*, 64–93.

139. Ibid., 15.

140. Feinberg, *Offense to Others*, 17.

141. See Clifford J. Rosky, "Fear of the Queer Child," *Buffalo Law Review* 61 (2013): 607–697.

142. "The acceptance of children as dependents, as belonging to parents, is so deeply ingrained that we can scarcely imagine what it would mean to treat them as autonomous human beings, particularly in the realm of sexual expression and choice. . . . We do need, however, structures and programs that will help dissolve the boundaries that isolate the family, particularly those that privatize childrearing. We need community- or worker-controlled daycare, housing where *privacy and community co-exist*, neighborhood institutions—from medical clinics to performance centers—that enlarge the social unity where each of us has a secure place. As we create structures beyond the nuclear family that provide a sense of belonging, the family will wane in significance." John D'Emilio, "Capitalism and Gay Identity," in *The Lesbian and Gay Studies Reader*, edited by Henry Abelove, Michèle Aina Barale, and David M. Halperin (New York: Routledge, 1993), 474–475.

143. See Rubenfeld, "The Right of Privacy," 800.

144. After the scorched earth holding in *Dobbs v. Jackson Women's Health Org.*, 142 S. Ct. 2228 (2022), the state may very well relitigate—off the lives and livelihoods of gay men, trans women, and/or sex workers—its crime against nature statute; that is to say, antisodomy law might be reconstitutionalized, although *fetal personhood* seems to me a

more persuasive rational basis for conservative justices than, say, state representatives' discomfort with or disgust toward the butt stuff. See Chapter 5.

145. Judith Butler, *Antigone's Claim: Kinship Between Life and Death* (New York: Columbia University Press, 2000), 71, emphasis added; see also Franke, "Domesticated Liberty," 1408, note 49.

146. Butler, *Antigone's Claim*, 80, emphasis added.

147. Ibid., 58.

148. Ibid., 62.

149. Ibid., 82.

150. Ibid., 72 ("Although not quite a queer heroine, Antigone does emblematize a certain heterosexual fatality that remains to be read").

151. Ibid., 75.

152. Damon R. Young, *Making Sex Public and Other Cinematic Fantasies* (Durham: Duke University Press, 2018), 7.

153. *Paris Adult Theater I v. Slaton*, 413 U.S. 49, 67 (1973).

154. Young, *Making Sex Public*, 7, internal citations omitted.

155. Christina Sharpe, *Monstrous Intimacies: Making Post-Slavery Subjects* (Durham: Duke University Press, 2010), 27–36.

156. Oliver Davis and Tim Dean, *Hatred of Sex* (Lincoln: University of Nebraska Press, 2022), 88.

157. Ibid., 42.

158. Ibid., 33, 35 ("No other can ever be regarded as truly equal from an identitarian perspective. . . . We are all unmastered equally, though this aspect of equality is one that many progressives appear less than enthusiastic to acknowledge or accept").

159. Bloodhound Gang, "The Bad Touch," *Hooray for Boobies* (1999).

160. Lauren Berlant, "Live Sex Acts: (Parental Advisory: Explicit Material)," *Feminist Studies* 21 (1995): 390.

161. Meeting of the House Committee on Administration of Criminal Justice, Louisiana House of Representatives, Tuesday, May 4, 2021, https://house.louisiana.gov/H_Video/VideoArchivePlayer?v=house/2021/may/0504_21_CJ.

162. Ibid.

163. Ibid.

164. Ibid.

165. Ibid.

166. See Judith Butler, *The Psychic Life of Power: Theories in Subjection* (Stanford: Stanford University Press, 1997), 135–136.

167. Nussbaum, "Protecting Intimacy," 181.

168. Butler, *Antigone's Claim*, 71.

169. *Bowers*, 209, note 4, Blackmun, J., dissenting.

170. Rubenfeld, "The Right of Privacy," 757–758, note 110.

171. Butler, *Antigone's Claim*, 66–67.

172. Butler, *Psychic Life*, 135.

173. Ibid., 148–150; Butler, *Antigone's Claim*, 69.

174. I deliberately avoid use of the word "homosexual" since I know nothing about how the arrested men self-identify. "Sodomite," then, in a Louisianian juridical lexicon, would refer to anyone (of any gender and sexuality) soliciting or performing oral or anal sex. "The [commercial sodomy statute] applies equally to all individuals—male, female, heterosexual and homosexual. The statute punishes conduct—solicitation with the intent to engage in oral and anal sex." *State v. Baxley*, 656 So.2d 973, 978 (La. 1995).

While the *Baxley* Court insidiously and incorrectly points to the gender-neutrality of the state's commercial sodomy statute as prima facie proof of its nondiscriminatory purpose (the law was explicitly codified for discriminatory purposes and has never not been enforced discriminatorily; see Chapter 4), here I deliberately misread the Court's misreading to imagine populations similarly and sodomitically situated, populations including and *exceeding* "male, female, heterosexual and homosexual." Ibid.

175. For an account of prison gender-regulatory policies and practices as legitimating mechanisms of gendered, sexual violence, see Eric A. Stanley, *Atmospheres of Violence: Structuring Antagonism and the Trans/Queer Ungovernable* (Durham: Duke University Press, 2021), 101–108.

176. See Oliver and Davis, *Hatred of Sex*, 54–73; Halley, "Reasoning about Sodomy," 1771–1772.

177. Andrew Israel Ross, *Public City/Public Sex: Homosexuality, Prostitution, and Urban Culture in Nineteenth-Century Paris* (Philadelphia: Temple University Press, 2019), 15, emphasis added.

178. Ibid., 99; see also Chauncey, "Privacy Could Only Be Had in Public," 203–204.

179. Ibid., 96.

CHAPTER 3

1. Kate Gagliano, "Bill to Toughen Louisiana Anti-bestiality Law Advances over Some Objections," *New Orleans Advocate*, April 25, 2018, www.theadvocate.com/baton _rouge/news/politics/legislature/article_e3b67b0c-48e2-11e8-85fb-6b108a0373ca.html.

2. Rosenberg tracks the reenactment of antibestiality laws from the 1990s onwards, the great majority of which exempt livestock breeding and other animal husbandry practices from their ambit. Gabriel N. Rosenberg. "How Meat Changed Sex: The Law of Interspecies Intimacy after Industrial Reproduction," *GLQ: A Journal of Lesbian and Gay Studies* 23 (2017): 473–507.

3. Gagliano, "Louisiana Anti-bestiality Law."

4. Anthony Izaguirre, "Why Bid to Toughen Louisiana Anti-bestiality Law Is Drawing Unexpected Pushback," *The Times-Picayune*, April 24, 2018, www.nola.com /article_273f2287-6382-5d80-b576-d0b709618ea1.html.

5. Louisiana Revised Statutes 14:89A(1). However, as discussed in the preceding chapter, Louisiana repealed its criminal incest law, relocating consanguineous sex and marriage under CAN. Louisiana Revised Statutes 14:89A(2).

6. Izaguirre, "Louisiana Anti-bestiality Law."

7. Marie Simoneaux, "Stricter Bestiality Law Passes in House Committee," *The Times-Picayune*, April 25, 2018, www.nola.com/news/crime_police/article_08fd563a -65c9-5878-929a-c8a64077d636.html.

8. This political contestation might be the limit case for historian Joanna Bourke's observation that an alliance between conservative Christian moralists and liberal animal rights activists has hardened the taboo around bestiality in Europe and the United States in the last century, although such alliances have occurred in other state-level efforts to criminalize bestiality in the United States. Bourke convincingly argues that modern antibestiality laws tell us more about normative sexual relations among humans than they do about how to treat animals. See Joanna Bourke, *Loving Animals: On Bestiality, Zoophilia and Post-Human Love* (London: Reaktion, 2020).

9. Izaguirre, "Louisiana Anti-bestiality Law."

10. See, for example, Walter Einenkel, "40% of Louisiana State Senators Voted against Making Bestiality a Crime—Because They're Homophobic," *Daily Kos*, April 12, 2018, www.dailykos.com/stories/2018/4/12/1756467/-40-of-Louisiana-state-senat ors-voted-against-making-bestiality-a-crime-because-they-re-homophobic; Anthony Izaguirre, "Christian Conservatives Fight Bid to Toughen Louisiana Anti-bestiality Law," *Talking Points Memo*, April 25, 2018, https://talkingpointsmemo.com/news/christian -conservatives-fight-toughening-louisiana-anti-bestiality-law; WPMI Web Staff, "Ten Louisiana Lawmakers Vote against 'Sex with Animals' Ban," *NBC*, April 11, 2018, https:// mynbc15.com/news/local/ten-louisiana-lawmakers-vote-against-sex-with-animals-ban.

11. Marie Simoneaux, "John Bel Edwards Signs Tougher Bestiality Bill into Law," *The Times-Picayune*, May 31, 2018, www.nola.com/news/crime_police/john-bel-edwards -signs-tougher-bestiality-bill-into-law/article_1a432925-1107-56b6-8a71-e34b9b1a350b .html.

12. Louisiana Revised Statutes 14:89.3.

13. Factory farming is but one of many human practices that oppress, impede, and injure animals, as Martha Nussbaum powerfully illuminates. Martha C. Nussbaum, *Justice for Animals: Our Collective Responsibility* (New York: Simon & Schuster, 2022), 232–233.

14. Louisiana Revised Statutes 14:89.3.B(2)(a)(b).

15. Louisiana Revised Statutes 14:89.3.A(7).

16. *United States v. Stevens*, 559 U.S. 460 (2010) (holding a federal statute criminal- izing depictions of animal cruelty unconstitutional).

17. Louisiana Revised Statutes 14:89.3.D(2)(c)(d).

18. See Midas Dekkers, *Dearest Pet: On Bestiality* (London: Verso, 1994); Kathy Rudy, "LGBTQ . . . Z?" *Hypatia* 27 (2012): 601–615.

19. Louisiana Revised Statutes 14:89.3.B(1).

20. See Jonathan Haidt, *The Righteous Mind: Why Good People Are Divided by Politics and Religion* (New York: Vintage Books, 2012), 4, 111–112.

21. Louisiana Revised Statutes 14:102.1.A(b) (defining cruelty to animals as "any person who intentionally or with criminal negligence . . . torments, cruelly beats, or unjustifiably injures any living animal").

22. See Joseph J. Fischel, *Screw Consent: A Better Politics of Sexual Justice* (Berkeley: University of California Press, 2019), 115, 126.

23. Louisiana Revised Statutes 14:89.3.C(2)(3).

24. See Rosenberg, "How Meat Changed Sex"; Gabriel N. Rosenberg, "Animals," in *The Routledge History of American Sexuality*, edited by Kevin P. Murphy, Jason Ruiz, and David Serlin (New York: Routledge, 2020), 32–41.

25. Wayne Pacelle, "Deliver Us from the Evils of Bestiality," *A Humane World*, May 15, 2017, https://blog.humanesociety.org/2017/05/deliver-us-evils-bestiality.html.

26. "Animal sexual abuse" and "animal sexual assault" are the typical statutory terms, but some laws retain the archaic "bestiality." See, for example, Arizona Revised Statutes 13–141 ("Bestiality"). Louisiana, like other states, uses the updated "animal sex- ual abuse." Louisiana Revised Statutes 14:89.3. See also Oregon Revised Statutes 167.333 ("Sexual Assault of an Animal"); California Penal Code 286.5 ("Sexual Assaulting an Animal").

27. Rosenberg, "How Meat Changed Sex"; see also Jan Dutkiewicz and Gabriel N. Rosenberg, "The Meat Industry's Bestiality Problem," *The New Republic*, December 11, 2020, https://newrepublic.com/article/160448/meat-bestiality-artificial-insemination. The two holdouts are New Mexico and West Virginia.

28. Piers Beirne, "Rethinking Bestiality: Towards a Concept of Interspecies Sexual Assault," *Theoretical Criminology* 1 (1997): 317–340.

29. Ibid., 319–327.

30. Ibid., 332.

31. Ibid., 325–327; Carol J. Adams, *The Sexual Politics of Meat: A Feminist-Vegetarian Critical Theory* (New York: Bloomsbury Academic, 2015 [1990]).

32. Piers Beirne, "Peter Singer's 'Heavy Petting' and the Politics of Animal Sexual Assault," *Critical Criminology* 10 (2001): 44, 52–53.

33. Beirne, "Rethinking Bestiality," 319.

34. Beirne, "Animal Sexual Assault," 48.

35. Ibid., 43.

36. Beirne, "Rethinking Bestiality," 318.

37. Ibid., 327.

38. Ibid., 327.

39. Ibid., 330.

40. Ibid., 326.

41. Ibid., 328–331.

42. Ibid., 320–324.

43. Ibid., 328–331.

44. Michel Foucault, *The History of Sexuality, Volume 1: An Introduction*, translated by Robert Hy (New York: Vintage Books, 1990), 43.

45. Beirne, "Animal Sexual Assault," 51.

46. Compare Beirne, "Animal Sexual Assault," 49 ("[bestiality] should presumably encompass any form of oral-genital contact between humans and animals in a wide variety of social contexts"), with Beirne, "Rethinking Bestiality," 327 ("This innocent and affectionate suckling [by a girl on her dog's nipples] was probably not sexual in nature, it certainly was not assaultive and it doubtless caused the dog no harm").

47. Beirne, "Animal Sexual Assault," 44.

48. Sunaura Taylor, *Beasts of Burden: Animal and Disability Liberation* (New York: New Press, 2017), 62–63; see also Rudy, "LGBTQ . . . Z?," 607.

49. Beirne, "Rethinking Bestiality," 318.

50. Beirne, "Animal Sexual Assault," 51.

51. Catharine A. MacKinnon, "Feminism, Marxism, Method, and the State: Toward Feminist Jurisprudence," *Signs* 8 (1983): 647.

52. Beirne, "Rethinking Bestiality," 326–327.

53. Ibid., 325–326.

54. Ibid., 326–327.

55. Ibid., 325.

56. Ibid., 327.

57. For a thorough defense of the abolitionist position, see Gary L. Francione, *Why Veganism Matters: The Moral Value of Animals* (New York: Columbia University Press, 2020); but see Nussbaum, *Justice for Animals*, 197–202, 220–222.

58. "Stallions can be formidable, especially when in the presence of an ovulating mare; their aggressive behavior is a risk factor in itself. And while a mare in season is generally in a receptive mood, that doesn't mean she is not capable of aiming a good kick in her suitor's direction—or her handlers." Karen Briggs, "Restraint Techniques for Breeding," *The Horse*, October 8, 2001, https://thehorse.com/14702/restraint-techniques-for-breeding/.

59. Maine Revised Statutes 1031.1.I.

60. Maine Revised Statutes 1031.1.I.5.

61. Beirne, "Animal Sexual Assault," 44.

62. Maine Revised Statutes 1031.1.I.1; Louisiana Revised Statutes 14.89.3.B(2)(a).

63. See Alice Crary and Lori Gruen, *Animal Crisis: A New Critical Theory* (Cambridge: Polity Press, 2022).

64. Rudy, "LGBTQ . . . Z?," 601.

65. Beirne, "Animal Sexual Assault," 44.

66. Marie Simoneaux, "Bestiality Bill Is Not an Attempt to Strike Unconstitutional Sodomy Laws, Senator Says," *The Times-Picayune*, April 10, 2018, www.nola.com/news /crime_police/article_67fa6c79-5d0d-5202-bc60-33a96cacfa3c.html.

67. Jason Nark, "Animal-Cruelty Charges Dropped against Burlington County Cop," *Philadelphia Inquirer*, September 24, 2009, www.inquirer.com/philly/news/year -in-review/20090924_Animal-cruelty_charges_dropped_against_Burlington_County _cop.html.

68. Associated Press, "Former Moorestown Police Officer Sentenced to 30 Years for Sexually Assaulting Girls," *NJ.com*, October 11, 2012, www.nj.com/burlington/2012/10 /former_moorestown_police_officer_sentenced_to_30_years_for_sexually_assuaslting _girls.html.

69. Matt Friedman, "Bestiality Now Illegal in N.J.," *Politico*, November 9, 2015, www.politico.com/states/new-jersey/story/2015/11/bestiality-now-illegal-in-nj-094941; New Jersey Statutes 4:22–17.c.(4).

70. Peggy Ackerman, "Former N.J. Judge Not Reappointed by Gov., Christie Says He Was Kicked Off Bench Unfairly," *NJ.com*, June 17, 2010, www.nj.com/news/2010/06 /former_superior_court_judge_no.html.

71. Louisiana Revised Statutes 14:102.1.A.

72. Louisiana Revised Statutes 14:102.1.C.

73. "But sex with animals does not have to be cruel. Who has not been at a party disrupted by the household dog gripping the legs of a visitor and vigorously rubbing its penis against them?" It seems we are attending the wrong parties. Peter Singer, "Heavy Petting," *Prospect*, April 20, 2001, www.prospectmagazine.co.uk/magazine/heavypetting. Singer backtracked in his correspondence with Beirne: "[I] did not say that there is nothing wrong with sex with animals except when it involves cruelty. . . . I wanted to raise that question, but I did not answer it." Beirne, "Animal Sexual Assault," 54 note 4. This chapter answers the question: noninjurious sexual activity with animals may be wrong but should not be a crime. Nearly all "accepted animal husbandry practices" in the context of industrial agriculture are morally impermissible and should be legally impermissible, too.

74. Fischel, *Screw Consent*, 118–119.

75. Rudy, "LGBTQ . . . Z?," 607.

76. Martha C. Nussbaum and Jeremy Bendik-Keymer, "On Justice for Animals," *Boston Review*, February 8, 2023, www.bostonreview.net/articles/on-justice-for-anim als/.

77. The foundational tome on nonprocreative, but not simply homosexual, animal sex is Bruce Bagemihl, *Biological Exuberance: Animal Homosexuality and Natural Diversity* (New York: St. Martin's Press, 1999); see also Joan Roughgarden, *Evolution's Rainbow: Diversity, Gender, and Sexuality in Nature and People* (Berkeley: University of California Press, 2013); Jonathan Balcombe, *Pleasurable Kingdom: Animals and the Nature of Feeling Good* (London: Macmillan, 2006).

78. Barbara J. King, *How Animals Grieve* (Chicago: University of Chicago Press, 2013).

79. Marc Bekoff and Jessica Pierce, *Wild Justice: The Moral Lives of Animals* (Chicago: University of Chicago Press, 2009), 19, 55–84.

80. Ibid., 85–135.

81. Ibid., 85–86.

82. Sarah F. Brosnan and Frans B. M. de Waal, "Monkeys Reject Unequal Pay," *Nature* 425 (2003): 297–299.

83. See Friederike Range et al., "The Absence of Reward Induces Inequity Aversion in Dogs," *PNAS* 106 (2009): 340–345; see also Maria Konnikova, "How We Learn Fairness," *New Yorker*, January 7, 2016, www.newyorker.com/science/maria-konnikova/how-we-learn-fairness.

84. In a fascinating study of chimpanzees and inequity, researchers found that chimpanzees grew more frustrated when a human distributed uneven rewards than when a machine did so. The researchers conclude that "the inequity aversion task reveals special expectations of social agents and not fairness considerations" drives chimpanzees' response. Jan M. Engelman et al., "Social Disappointment Explains Chimpanzees' Behaviour in the Inequity Aversion Task," *Proceedings of the Royal Society B* 284 (2017): 2.

85. Friedrich Nietzsche, *On the Genealogy of Morals*, translated by Walter Kauffmann (New York: Vintage Books, 1969), 57. On Nietzschean promise as the idiom for a technologized future free of suffering and full of meat, see Benjamin Aldes Wurgraft, *Meat Planet: Artificial Flesh and the Future of Food* (Berkeley: University of California Press, 2019), 44–51.

86. Lori Gruen, *Entangled Empathy: An Alternative Ethic for Our Relationships with Animals* (New York: Lantern Books, 2015), 22–23.

87. Friedrich Nietzsche, *Thus Spoke Zarathustra*, edited by Adrian Del Caro and Robert Pippin (Cambridge: Cambridge University Press, 2006), 126; see also Colin Dayan, *The Law Is a White Dog: How Legal Rituals Make and Unmake Persons* (Princeton: Princeton University Press, 2011), 16, 1–38.

88. Rupert Sheldrake and Pamela Smart, "A Dog that Seems to Know When His Owner Is Coming Home: Videotaped Experiments and Observations," *Journal of Scientific Exploration* 14 (2000): 233–255; see also King, *Animals*, 28.

89. See Sylvia Wynter, "Unsettling the Coloniality of Being/Power/Truth/Freedom: Towards the Human, after Man, Its Overrepresentation—An Argument," *CR: The New Centennial Review* 3 (2003): 257–337; Sylvia Wynter, "On How We Mistook the Map for the Territory and Re-imprisoned Ourselves in Our Unbearable Wrongness of Being, of Desêtre: Black Studies toward the Human Project," in *Not Only the Master's Tools: African-American Studies in Theory and Practice*, edited by Lewis R. Gordon and Jane Anna Gordon (New York: Routledge, 2006), 107–169; see also Katherine McKittrick, ed., *Sylvia Wynter: On Being Human as Praxis* (Durham: Duke University Press, 2015). On connections between racial capitalism and intimacy with animals see Gabriel N. Rosenberg, "On the Scene of Zoonotic Intimacies: Jungle, Market, Pork Plant," *Transgender Studies Quarterly* 7 (2020): 646–656. The literature on race, animality, and multispecies justice is vast, but influential entries include Bénédicte Boisseron, *Afro-Dog: Blackness and the Animal Question* (New York: Columbia University Press, 2018); Harlan Weaver, *Bad Dog: Pit Bull Politics and Multispecies Justice* (Seattle: University of Washington Press, 2021); Zakiyyah Iman Jackson, *Becoming Human: Matter and Meaning in an Antiblack World* (New York: New York University Press, 2020). On murderous removal, see Clapperton Chakanetsa Mavhunga, "Vermin Beings: On Pestiferous Animals and Human Game," *Social Text* 29 (2011): 151–176.

90. Jackson, *Becoming Human*. Jackson is responding to a tendency in animal studies literature to interpret the human/animal binary as foundational to racial categorizations, a tendency arguably attributable to the influence of Italian posthumanist theorist Giorgio Agamben. For a parallel critique of animal studies, see Alexander G. Weheliye, *Habeas Viscus: Racializing Assemblages, Biopolitics, and Black Feminist Theories of the Human* (Durham: Duke University Press, 2014). For Agamben on animality as the master term of racial biopolitics, see Giorgio Agamben, *The Open: Man and Animal*, translated by Kevin Attell (Stanford: Stanford University Press, 2003). One of us (Rosenberg) has cautioned against flat analogies between race and species, noting that the categories are historically co-constitutive but particular, contextual, fragile, and reversible in their relations. See Gabriel N. Rosenberg, "A Race Suicide among the Hogs: The Biopolitics of Pork in the United States, 1865–1930," *American Quarterly* 68 (March 2016); Gabriel N. Rosenberg, "No Scrubs: Livestock Breeding, Eugenics, and the State in the Early Twentieth-Century United States," *Journal of American History* 107 (2020): 362–387; see also Mackenzie Cooley, *The Perfection of Nature: Animals, Breeding, and Race in the Renaissance* (Chicago: University of Chicago Press, 2022).

91. See Sue Donaldson and Will Kymlicka, *Zoopolis: A Political Theory of Animal Rights* (Oxford: Oxford University Press, 2011).

92. Ibid., 62–65; see also Kathy Rudy, *Loving Animals: Toward a New Animal Advocacy* (Minneapolis: University of Minnesota Press, 2013), x–xiii. On the nonexistence of the "wild" free from human dominion and domination, see Nussbaum, *Justice for Animals*, 227–231.

93. Ibid., 122 ("So we must keep an open mind about the potential scope of animal agency, recognizing that it will always be highly variable, and dependent on individual, contextual, and structural factors").

94. David M. Halperin, "Is There a History of Sexuality?" *History and Theory* 28 (1989): 259.

95. Bagemihl, *Biological*, 305.

96. But see Jeannette Vaught, "Is It Sex if the Veterinarian Does the Work? The Problem of Pleasure in Multispecies Sexual Labor," in *The Relational Horse*, edited by Gala Argent and Jeannette Vaught (Leiden: Brill, 2022): 135–146; Jeannette Vaught, "How to Make a Horse Have an Orgasm," in *Living with Animals: Bonds across Species*, edited by Natalie Porter and Ilana Gershon (Ithaca: Cornell University Press, 2018): 157–167.

97. See Samantha Cooney, "PETA Actually Compared Rape Victims to Meat Products," *Time*, November 8, 2016, https://time.com/4557329/peta-ad-sexual-assault -veganism/.

98. Rudy, "LGBTQ . . . Z?," 604.

99. Ethnographies of conventional meat production show that many workers form substantial attachments to livestock animals and that some of their work can be understood through the lens of "care." But *governance* and *rule-making* in those spaces is determined by extractive market logics. See Alexander Blanchette, *Porkopolis: American Animality, Standardized Life, and the Factory Farm* (Durham: Duke University Press, 2020).

100. Gabriel N. Rosenberg, *The 4-H Harvest: Sexuality and the State in Rural America* (Philadelphia: University of Pennsylvania Press, 2016); Gabriel Rosenberg, "Fetishizing Family Farms," *Boston Globe*, April 16, 2016, www.bostonglobe.com/ideas/2016/04/09 /fetishizing-family-farms/NJszoKdCSQWaq2XBw7kvIL/story.html.

101. Rudy, "LGBTQ . . . Z?," 609.

102. See Nussbaum, *Justice for Animals*, 261.

103. Caleb, interview by authors, February 1, 2019.

104. Andy and Sue, interview by authors, February 2, 2019.

105. Ibid.

106. Frank and Kim, interview by authors, February 2, 2019; see Michael Pollan, *The Omnivore's Dilemma: A Natural History of Four Meals* (New York: Penguin, 2007).

107. Ibid.

108. Peter Singer introduced *speciesism* to name "a prejudice or attitude of bias in favor of the interests of members' of one's own species and against those of members of other species"; it is therefore unlikely he would approve our appropriation of the term as a mode of humbled superintendence. Peter Singer, *Animal Liberation* (New York: Harper Perennial, 2009 [1975]), 6. Our qualification—*empathetic*—draws from Lori Gruen's brief for "entangled empathy," which she characterizes as "a way for oneself to perceive and to connect with a specific other in their particular circumstances, and to recognize and assess one's place in reference to the other." Gruen, *Entangled*, 67.

109. Nussbaum, *Justice for Animals*, 231.

110. Caleb, interview.

111. King, *Animals*, 8.

112. Andy and Sue, interview. On the playfulness, precocity, independence, intelligence, and good humor of goats, see also Jeffrey Masson, *The Secret World of Farm Animals* (London: Vintage, 2005), 119–128.

113. See Rudy, "LGBTQ . . . Z?," 608–609.

114. Andy and Sue, interview; see also Nussbaum, *Justice for Animals*, 260.

115. Nussbaum and Bendik-Keymer, "On Justice for Animals"; see also Nussbaum, *Justice for Animals*, 202–205.

116. Caleb, interview. Grandin is prolific; see, for example, Temple Grandin, *Temple Grandin's Guide to Working with Farm Animals: Safe, Humane Livestock Handling Practices for the Small Farm* (North Adams, MA: Storey, 2017).

117. Caleb, interview.

118. Ibid.

119. Frank and Kim, interview.

120. Andy and Sue, interview.

121. Frank and Kim, interview. Circumventing the debate among ethologists and anthropologists about whether or not nonhuman animals can "rape" or "be raped," Juno Parreñas instead draws our attention to the ways human constructs of captivity foment forced, violent copulation, feared by female orangutans. Juno Salazar Parreñas, *Decolonizing Extinction: The Work of Care in Orangutan Rehabilitation* (Durham: Duke University Press, 2018), 83–104.

122. Frank and Kim, interview.

123. See Rosenberg, "Race Suicide."

124. See Nussbaum, *Justice for Animals*, 251–252.

125. Martha C. Nussbaum, *Frontiers of Justice: Disability, Nationality, Species Membership* (Cambridge, MA: Harvard University Press, 2007), 325–407. Nussbaum's capabilities approach, though calibrated to a species norm, must flexibly heed "a conception of flourishing that is more sensitive to both interspecies community membership and intraspecies individual variation." Donaldson and Kymlicka, *Zoopolis*, 99. Some humans may have more fun and find more meaning in the company of dogs than with fellow humans. Some dogs may require opportunities and resources to flourish that are quite unlike those opportunities and resources needed by other dogs. Ibid., 98–99.

Nussbaum has since built out her earlier capabilities approach to justice for nonhuman animals in *Justice for Animals*.

126. Like Nussbaum, we recognize that sociopolitical arrangements keyed to the species-specific capabilities of animals differs from utilitarian arrangements keyed to animal pleasure or preference, and that the former is both more realizable (for what is the orangutan's preference?) and more just (what if the male orangutans' preference is to "gang rape" the female?). See Parreñas, *Decolonizing*, 91.

127. Frank and Kim, interview.

128. Ibid.; see also Nussbaum, *Frontiers*, 395 ("the castrating of certain male animals [horses, dogs, cats] seems [on the basis of long experience] to be compatible with flourishing lives for those animals . . . and often lives of less violence toward other animals, some of which typically results in pain and injury to the male animal himself"); Nussbaum, *Justice for Animals*, 216.

129. Andy and Sue, interview.

130. See Balcombe, *Pleasurable*; Bagemihl, *Biological*; Roughgarden, *Rainbow*.

131. Gayle S. Rubin, "Thinking Sex: Notes for a Radical Theory of the Politics of Sexuality," in *Deviations: A Gayle Rubin Reader*, edited by Gayle S. Rubin (Durham: Duke University Press, 2011 [1984]), 149; but see also Chapter 2.

132. Andy and Sue, interview.

133. In a similar vein, Nussbaum proposes that we must reconcile "species-sensitive paternalism" with "species autonomy" to best realize the capabilities of nonhuman animals. Nussbaum, *Frontiers*, 372–380.

134. Francione, *Veganism*. Francione's ethical schema—deontological and categorically abolitionist—contrasts sharply with Peter Singer's utilitarian argument, keyed to sentience, nonsuffering, and cognitive capacities. Singer, *Animal Liberation*.

135. Immanuel Kant, *Lectures on Ethics*, translated by Louis Infield (London: Methuen, 1930), 164.

136. Consider the fabulous and what should be infamous prescription from John D'Emilio to collectivize child-rearing so we make more children queer. John D'Emilio, "Capitalism and Gay Identity," in *The Lesbian and Gay Studies Reader*, edited by Henry Abelove, Michèle Aina Barale, and David M. Halperin (New York: Routledge, 1993), 475.

137. Jane Ward, *Not Gay: Sex between Straight White Men* (New York: New York University Press, 2015), 203.

138. See, for example, David L. Rosenfeld and Anthony L. Burrow, "The Unified Model of Vegetarian Identity: A Conceptual Framework for Understanding Plant-Based Food Choices," *Appetite* 112 (2017): 78–95; Hank Rothgerber, "A Comparison of Attitudes toward Meat and Animals among Strict and Semi-vegetarians," *Appetite* 72 (2014): 98–105.

139. On the ethics of and various policies regarding spaying and neutering, see Clare Palmer, Sandra Corr, and Peter Sandøe, "Inconvenient Desires: Should We Routinely Neuter Companion Animals?" *Anthrozoös* 25 (2012): s153–s172.

140. Our point is not that "painless death" for nonhuman animals is necessarily ethically sound; but surely a happy, hedonic life before slaughter is better than a tormented one. See Nussbaum, *Frontiers*, 384–388.

141. Adams, *Sexual Politics*, 195.

142. Lauren Berlant, "Risky Bigness: On Obesity, Eating, and the Ambiguity of 'Health,'" in *Against Health: How Health Became the New Morality*, edited by Jonathan M. Metzel and Anna Kirkland (New York: New York University Press, 2010), 26.

143. Ibid., 27.

144. Jonathan Safran Foer, "The End of Meat Is Here," *New York Times*, May 21, 2020, www.nytimes.com/2020/05/21/opinion/coronavirus-meat-vegetarianism.html; see also Mary Douglas, "Deciphering a Meal," *Daedalus* 101 (1972): 61–81.

145. Adams, *Sexual Politics*, 180.

146. Aazan Ahmad and Gary L. Francioni, "If Animals Matter Morally, Then We Cannot Treat Them as Commodities," *Animal Rights: The Abolitionist Approach*, August 1, 2016, www.abolitionistapproach.com/wp-content/uploads/2016/08/If-Animals-Matter-Morally-Interview-with-GLF-20160801.pdf.

147. Nussbaum, *Justice for Animals*, 184.

148. See Wurgraft, *Planet*; Chase Purdy, *Billion Dollar Burger: Inside Big Tech's Race for the Future of Food* (New York: Portfolio, 2020); Jan Dutkiewicz and Gabriel N. Rosenberg, "Man v Food: Is Lab-Grown Meat Really Going to Solve Our Nasty Agriculture Problem?" *The Guardian*, July 29, 2021, www.theguardian.com/news/2021/jul/29/lab-grown-meat-factory-farms-industrial-agriculture-animals.

149. See Jack Kloppenburg, *First the Seed: The Political Economy of Plant Biotechnology, 1492–2000* (Madison: University of Wisconsin Press, 1988); Nick Cullather, *The Hungry World: America's Cold War Battle Against Poverty in Asia* (Cambridge: Harvard University Press, 2010); Jason Moore, *Capitalism in the Web of Life: Ecology and the Accumulation of Capital* (New York: Verso, 2015); Christine Frison, *Redesigning the Global Seed Commons: Law and Policy for Agrobiodiversity and Food Security* (London: Routledge, 2018).

150. *New Harvest*, www.new-harvest.org/; *Good Food Institute*, www.gfi.org/; see also Jan Dutkiewicz, "Socialize Lab Meat," *Jacobin*, August 2019, https://jacobinmag.com/2019/08/lab-meat-socialism-green-new-deal.

151. On democratic hedonism as applied to humans, across sex inequality rather than speciative subordination, see Fischel, *Screw Consent*, 165–182.

152. To Beirne's credit, the United States's bad habits of overcriminalization and mass incarceration gave him pause before endorsing Maine's law against animal sexual assault. Beirne, "Animal Sexual Assault," 53.

153. We add the corrective that simply because a sexual preference or practice is non-injurious does not mean it is not worth further interrogating, even occasionally criticizing (not criminalizing). Sexual desire is or is often a powerful force. Sexual practices, however benign, are more commanding, stirring and absorbing, than benign nonsexual practices, which we suppose is to say they are not as benign. Two people fucking in the middle of a public park is more eye-grabbing than two people playing catch, even to the most radical of sex radicals (see Chapter 2). When our white gay friends tell us they are "just not into Asians" we do not pretend as they do that their desires are purified of history; nor are those desires immunized from a follow-up by virtue of being "personal." If you don't get out much because your dog is licking your testicles all the time, that might be a problem (there, we said it). It is quite possible sex with one's pet or one's livestock could corrode one's intimacies with other humans, or could hasten an especially exploitative, one-sided relationship to the animal. A human repeatedly having sex with animals *might* tell us something unfortunate, etiologically or environmentally, about the human, Foucauldian hackles notwithstanding. That does not mean we should put the person in prison, or a ward.

154. "If animals feel, then we have a responsibility towards them. And if they feel more than just pain—if they are capable of pleasure—then that responsibility is greater than if they did not." Balcombe, *Pleasurable*, 209. See also Balcombe's brief for "hedonic ethology." Ibid., 220–221.

155. See notes 64–65 and accompanying text.

156. See Fischel, *Screw Consent*, 117–122.

157. As far as we can tell, the only sound reason to proscribe a stallion from penetrating the anus or vagina of a human is to prevent injury to the *human*, not the horse. And we are not talking about the allegedly degraded dignity of the human for pruriently crossing the species divide, but about his ruptured stomach. See Fischel, *Screw Consent*, 117.

158. See Nussbaum, *Frontiers*, 396; see also Mary Anne Case, "Pets or Meat," *Chicago Kent Law Review* 80 (2005): 1144 ("It may therefore be worth asking whether training one's pets, for example, to perform oral sex on one, is anything different or worse than what David Letterman calls 'stupid pet tricks.' If we think there should be more strict or rigorous legal controls on having one's pets trained to do what would violate the bestiality laws than on other stupid pet tricks, we should acknowledge straightforwardly that it is our attitude toward sex, more than our concern for animal freedom of choice or animal welfare, that motivates us").

159. See Nussbaum, *Frontiers*, 393–401; Nussbaum, *Justice for Animals*, 102; Balcombe, *Pleasurable*, 207–227.

CHAPTER 4

1. *State v. Bonnano*, 163 So.2d 72 (La. 1964).

2. But see Chapter 5.

3. See Matt Nadel and Megan Plotka, "CANS Can't Stand," *New Yorker* (2023).

4. *United States Dept. of Agriculture v. Moreno*, 413 U.S. 528, 534 (1973).

5. See Joseph J. Fischel, "Sodomy's Penumbra," *Journal of Homosexuality* 64 (2017): 2030–2056.

6. Minutes of the Louisiana House Criminal Justice Committee, House Bill 853, June 17, 1982, audiocassette recording.

7. Criminal Court News, "AC/DC Prostitution," *The Times-Picayune*, March 2, 1978.

8. Louisiana Revised Statutes 14:82.C(1).

9. Complaint, *Doe v. Jindal* (E.D. La. 2011), 16.

10. Ibid., 3.

11. Louisiana Senate Bill 381, Act 882 (2010).

12. Louisiana House Bill 141, Act 223 (2011).

13. See Andrea J. Ritchie, "Crimes against Nature: Challenging Criminalization of Queerness and Black Women's Sexuality," *Loyola Journal of Public Interest Law* 14 (2013), 356.

14. *State v. Ryans*, 513 So.2d 386 (La. Ct. App. 1987).

15. *State v. Baxley*, 656 So.2d 973 (La. 1995).

16. *State v. Smith*, 766 So.2d 501 (La. 2000).

17. *State v. Thomas*, 891 So.2d 1233 (La. 2005).

18. *Lawrence v. Texas*, 539 U.S. 558 (2003).

19. *Doe v. Jindal*, 851 F.Supp.2d 995 (E.D. La. 2012).

20. *Doe v. Caldwell*, 913 F. Supp. 2d 262 (E.D. La. 2013).

21. *Ryans*, 387.

22. Ibid., 387–388.

23. Ibid., 387–388.

24. *Baxley*, 977.

25. Ibid., 978.

26. Ibid., 978, emphasis added.

27. Ibid., 980, emphasis added.

28. More specifically, anal penetration and oral-genital contact both qualify as a crime against nature. *State v. Phillips*, 365 So.2d 1304 (La. 1978).

29. See Jeanie Blake, "Who'll Take a Hooker's Word over the Word of a Lawman?" *The Times-Picayune*, April 12, 1981; "Police Reports [4631 W. Napoleon Ave.]," *The Times-Picayune*, December 6, 1980.

30. *Bowers v. Hardwick*, 478 U.S. 186 (1986).

31. *Smith*, 506.

32. *Bowers*, 191.

33. *Thomas*, 1239, Calogero, C. J., concurring; *Lawrence*, 567.

34. *Smith*, 514.

35. Ibid., 517.

36. Ibid., 517.

37. Ibid., 513; but see Chapter 5.

38. Ibid., 516.

39. *State v. Limon*, 280 Kan. 275, 276 (Kan. 2005).

40. *Limon*, 295.

41. *Lawrence*, 578, qtd. in *Thomas*, 1235; on the judicial use and abuse of this passage from *Lawrence*, see Chapter 5.

42. *Thomas*, 1238.

43. *Baxley*, 981, Calogero, C. J., concurring.

44. *Thomas*, 1238, Calogero, C. J., concurring.

45. *Baxley*, 982, Calogero, C. J., concurring.

46. Ritchie, "Crimes against Nature," 356.

47. Ibid., 355.

48. *Jindal*, 1000, 1009.

49. Ibid., 1008, note 27.

50. Ibid., 1007.

51. Ibid., 1009.

52. *Robicheaux v. Caldwell*, 2 F. Supp. 3d 910 (E.D. La. 2014).

53. V. F. Nourse and Sarah A. Maguire, "The Lost History of Governance and Equal Protection," *Duke Law Journal* 58 (2009): 968, qtd. in *Jindal*, 997.

54. *City of Cleburne, Tex. v. Cleburne Living Center*, 473 U.S. 432 (1985).

55. *Cleburne*, 440, qtd. in *Jindal*, 1005.

56. *Skinner v. Okla. ex rel. Williamson*, 316 U.S. 535 (1942).

57. *Skinner*, 542, qtd. in *Jindal*, 1009 note 30.

58. Minutes of the Louisiana House Criminal Justice Committee, House Bill 853, June 17, 1982, audiocassette recording.

59. Louisiana Revised Statutes 14:82.A(1), emphasis added; see also Linton W. Carney et al., "The Work of the Louisiana Legislature for the 1977 Regular Session: A Student Symposium," *Louisiana Law Review* 38 (1977): 127.

60. Carney et al., "Louisiana Legislature," 127; Ed Anderson, "Prostitution by Males DA's Target," *The Times-Picayune*, April 6, 1977.

61. Louisiana Senate Bill 400, Act 612 (1975).

62. Louisiana House Bill 40, Act 138 (2008).

63. See Blake, "Who'll Take a Hooker's Word?"; "Police Reports [4631 W. Napoleon Ave.]."

64. Ibid.

65. *Erotic Serv. Provider Legal Educ. Research Project v. Gascon*, 880 F.3d 450 (9th Cir. 2018).

66. Ibid. Chapter 5 refutes the Ninth Circuit's assertion that commercial sex is definitionally nonintimate and doubts the legitimacy of California's "legitimate purposes" for criminalizing prostitution.

67. *Erotic Serv. Provider Legal Educ. Research Project v. Gascon*, No. C 15-01007 (N.D. Cal. 2016); see also *Reliable Consultants, Inc. v. Earle*, 517 F.3d 738 (5th Cir. 2008).

68. *United States v. Windsor*, 133. S. Ct. 2675, 2695 (2013).

69. *Windsor*, 2707-09, Scalia, J., dissenting.

70. *State v. Bonnano*, 163 So.2d 72 (La. 1964).

71. *Moreno*, 534.

72. Dale Carpenter, "Windsor Products: Equal Protection from Animus," *The Supreme Court Review* 2013 (2013): 183.

73. On the challenges of sourcing legislation to "subjective dislike," see William D. Araiza, *Animus: A Short Introduction to Bias in the Law* (New York: New York University Press, 2017), 79–88. On the challenges of perceiving "animus" as anything other than subjective dislike, see Katie R. Eyer, "Animus Trouble," *Stetson Law Review* 48 (2019): 229.

74. Minutes of the Louisiana House Criminal Justice Committee, House Bill 853, June 17, 1982, audiocassette recording.

75. For a normative reclamation of *fairness* that eschews comparators for treating like cases alike (i.e., equally penalizing persons convicted of Prostitution and CANS), and instead substitutes a measure of state penalty against social outcome, see Chapter 1.

76. Minutes of the Louisiana House Criminal Justice Committee.

77. Ibid.

78. Araiza, *Animus*, 83; see also *Trump v. Hawaii*, 138 S.Ct. 2392, 2421 (2018) ("because there is persuasive evidence that the entry suspension [President Trump's 'travel ban'] has a legitimate grounding in national security concerns, quite apart from any religious hostility, we must accept that independent justification"). In the present case, there is no "justification" for the CANS statute "independent" of animus.

79. United States Department of Justice, Civil Rights Division, "Investigation of the New Orleans Police Department" (2017): 36–37, emphasis added.

80. Chris Geidner, "DOJ's New Scrutiny," *Metro Weekly*, March 23, 2011, www.metroweekly.com/2011/03/dojs-new-scrutiny/.

81. "CANScantSTAND," *Facebook*, October 17, 2018, www.facebook.com/1009945452523242/photos/a.1012811605569960/1012823818902072/.

82. "CANScantSTAND," *Facebook*, November 30, 2018, www.facebook.com/100994545452523242/photos/a.1039009952950125/1039043659613421/.

83. CANScantSTAND Symposium, Tulane University, April 30, 2019, https://events.tulane.edu/content/canscantstand-symposium ("This campaign focuses on eradicating the provisions of the Crime Against Nature Law which unfairly targets LGBTQ people, especially Trans-women of color").

84. Nico Lang, "Louisiana Is Using Its Anti-gay Sodomy Laws to Harass Sex Workers," *Out Magazine*, September 5, 2019, www.out.com/news/2019/9/05/louisiana-using-its-anti-gay-sodomy-laws-harass-sex-workers.

85. Matt Nadel and Megan Plotka, *CANS Can't Stand* (Lynwood Films, 2022).

86. David Leonhardt and Claire Cain Miller, "The Metro Areas with the Largest, and Smallest, Gay Populations," *New York Times*, March 20, 2015, www.nytimes.com/2015/03/21/upshot/the-metro-areas-with-the-largest-and-smallest-gay-population.html.

87. Brief of *Amici Curiae, Doe v. Jindal* (E.D. La. 2011), 6, emphasis added.

88. Ibid., 11–12, emphasis added, internal citations omitted.

89. Susan Dewey and Tonia P. St. Germain, "Sex Workers/Sex Offenders: Exclusionary Criminal Justice Practices in New Orleans," *Feminist Criminology* 10 (2015): 212, 225.

90. See, for example, Araiza, *Animus*; Carpenter, "Windsor Products"; Susannah W. Pollvogt, "Unconstitutional Animus," *Fordham Law Review* 81 (2012): 887–937.

91. *United States Dept. of Agriculture v. Moreno*, 413 U.S. 528 (1973).

92. *City of Cleburne, Tex. v. Cleburne Living Center*, 473 U.S. 432 (1985).

93. *Romer v Evans*, 517 U.S. 620 (1996).

94. *United States v. Windsor*, 570 U.S. 744 (2013).

95. *Moreno*, 534.

96. *Cleburne*, 449.

97. Araiza, *Animus*, 40.

98. But see Catharine A. MacKinnon, "Prostitution and Civil Rights," *Michigan Journal of Gender and Law* 1 (1993): 20 ("Criminal laws against prostitution make women into criminals for being victimized as women, yet there are no cases challenging these laws as sex discrimination on this ground. Criminal prosecution laws collaborate elaborately in women's social inequality; through them, the state enforces the exploitation of prostituted women directly. *When legal victimization is piled on top of social victimization*, women are dug deeper and deeper into civil inferiority, their subordination and isolation legally ratified and legitimated. *Disparate enforcement combines with this discriminatory design to violate women's Fourteenth Amendment right to equal protection of the laws*"). Emphasis added, internal citations omitted.

99. Araiza, *Animus*, 73.

100. Katie R. Eyer, "The Canon of Rational Basis Review," *Notre Dame Law Review* 93 (2018): 1321.

101. *Romer*, 632.

102. Pollvogt, "Unconstitutional Animus," 911.

103. *Windsor*, 774.

104. *Windsor*, 746, 768, 772, 775; see also Eric Merriam, "Fire, Aim, Ready! Militarizing Animus: 'Unit Cohesion' and the Transgender Ban," *Dickinson Law Review* 123 (2018): 76–78.

105. Defense of Marriage Act, Public Law 104–199, 110 Stat. 2419 (1996).

106. Merriam, "Fire Aim Ready," 77.

107. *Lawrence*, 575; see also *Lawrence*, 579–586, O'Connor, J., concurring.

108. Carpenter, "Windsor Products," 214.

109. Juan F. Perea, "The Echoes of Slavery: Recognizing the Racist Origins of the Agricultural and Domestic Worker Exclusion from the National Labor Relations Act," *Ohio State Law Journal* 72 (2011), 134. Perea argues that the exclusion of domestic and agricultural workers from the National Labor Relations Act violates constitutional equal protection, not despite but in part because an exemption designed to "exclude black employees from the New Deal" today "reproduces the same debilitating effects upon Latinos as upon blacks in an earlier era." Ibid., 98, 135.

110. Alexis Agathocleous, "Building a Movement for Justice: *Doe v. Jindal* and the Campaign against Louisiana's Crime Against Nature Statute," in *The War on Sex*, edited by David M. Halperin and Trevor Hoppe (Durham: Duke University Press, 2017), 443, internal citation omitted.

CHAPTER 5

1. U.S. Const. amend. XIV ("nor shall any state deprive any person of life, liberty, or property, without due process of law; nor deny to any person within its jurisdiction the equal protection of the laws").

2. See Section III of this chapter.

3. *Lawrence v. Texas*, 538 U.S. 558 (2003).

4. Ibid., 578.

5. Ibid., 604, Scalia, J., dissenting; see also Michael McGough, "Gay Marriage: Scalia Knew This Day Would Come," *Los Angeles Times*, December 12, 2012, www.latimes.com /opinion/la-xpm-2012-dec-07-la-ol-court-gaymarriage-scalia--20121207-story.html. Will the day come for sex workers?

6. *Baker v. Nelson*, 191 N.W.2d 185 (Minn. 1971); see also Erik Eckholm, "The Same-Sex Couple who Got a Marriage License in 1971," *New York Times*, May 16, 2015, www .nytimes.com/2015/05/17/us/the-same-sex-couple-who-got-a-marriage-license-in-1971 .html.

7. *Obergefell v. Hodges*, 576 U.S. 644 (2015).

8. *Dobbs v. Jackson Women's Health Org.*, 142 S.Ct. 2228 (2022), Thomas, J., concurring, at 2301–2302.

9. For several reasons, this chapter does not entertain First Amendment challenges to laws criminalizing commercial sex and solicitation for commercial sex. In addition to all such challenges being swatted down in courts because speech regarding criminal conduct has been held to be outside the remit of First Amendment protection, prostitution itself has not been recognized as protected expressive conduct. *Giboney v. Empire Storage & Ice Co.*, 336 U.S. 490, 498 (1949); *Arcara v. Cloud Books, Inc.*, 478 U.S. 697, 705 (1986). Other First Amendment lines of attack (for example, challenges to ordinances regulating sexual businesses) are indirect and so ultimately unhelpful. See *City of Renton v. Playtime Theatres, Inc.*, 475 U.S. 41 (1986) (upholding the constitutionality of a zoning ordinance for adult movie theaters). Challenges lodged in the language of "intimate association" read out of the First Amendment are doubly ill-fated. First, they have been met with incredulity by courts; and second, such challenges offer nothing for commercial sex that is avowedly nonintimate, casual, zipless, and so forth. See *Mills v. City of Harrisburg*, 589 F. Supp. 2d 544 (M.D. Penn. 2008) (rejecting First Amendment right of intimate association claim for commercial sex relationship because actions did not implicate "relationships that 'by their nature involve deep attachments and commitments'" [quoting *Roberts v. U.S. Jaycees*, 468 U.S. 609, 619–620 (1984)]). On the other hand, it is at least worth pausing to note that otherwise criminal commercial sex is made legal when it is pornography. See *Miller v. California*, 413 U.S. 15 (1973).

10. On the "right to fuck" and its genealogy in U.S. constitutional case law, see Mary Anne Case, "Donorsexuality," in *Enticements: Queer Legal Studies*, edited by Joseph J. Fischel and Brenda Cossman (New York: New York University Press, 2024).

11. For my gloss on regulating capability-extinguishing consensual sex, and on regulating consensual sex across vertical relations of dependence, see Joseph J. Fischel, *Screw Consent: A Better Politics of Sexual Justice* (Oakland: University of California Press, 2019).

12. *Lochner v. New York*, 198 U.S. 45 (1905) infamously held that a New York law stipulating maximum work hours for commercial bakers violated a constitutional right to contract. This chapter defends a distinction that the *Lochner* Court denies: "If this statute be valid . . . there would seem to be no length to which legislation of this nature might not go." Ibid. at 58. The counterargument: "unless the regulations are so utterly

unreasonable and extravagant in their nature and purpose that the property and personal rights of the citizen are unnecessarily, and in a manner wholly arbitrary, interfered with or destroyed without due process of law, they do not extend beyond the power of the State to pass, and they form no subject for Federal interference." Ibid. at 67, Harlan, J., dissenting, quoting *Gundling v. Chi.*, 177 U.S. 183, 188 (1900). In Section III, I will suggest categorical prohibitions on prostitution are "utterly unreasonable and extravagant."

13. *Dobbs v. Jackson Women's Health Org.*, 142 S.Ct. 2228 (2022).

14. *Meyer v. Nebraska*, 262 U.S. 390 (1923); *Pierce v. Society of Sisters*, 268 U.S. 510 (1925).

15. See David E. Bernstein, "The Due Process Right to Pursue a Lawful Occupation: A Brighter Future Ahead?" *Yale Law Journal Forum* 126 (2016–2017), 301; Jed Rubenfeld, "The Right of Privacy," *Harvard Law Review* 102 (1989), 743, note 34.

16. See, for example, LaLa B Holston-Zannell, "Sex Work Is Real Work, and It's Time to Treat It That Way," *ACLU*, June 10, 2020, www.aclu.org/news/lgbtq-rights/sex-work-is-real-work-and-its-time-to-treat-it-that-way.

17. *Dobbs*, Kavanaugh J., concurring, at 2304.

18. *People v. Williams*, 811 N.E.2d 1197, 1199 (Ill. App. Ct. 2004).

19. Ibid.

20. *State v. Romano*, 155 P.3d 1102 (Haw. 2007).

21. *State v. Thomas*, 891 So. 2d 1233, 1236 (La. 2005).

22. *Lawrence*, 578.

23. Ibid., 566–567, quoting *Bowers v. Hardwick*, 478 U.S. 186, 190 (1986).

24. *Martin v. Ziherl*, 607 S. E. 2d 367 (Va. 2005).

25. *U.S. v. Thompson*, 458 F. Supp. 2d 730, 732 (N.D. Ind. 2006), emphasis added.

26. *U.S. v. Palfrey*, 499 F. Supp. 2d 34, 41 (D.D.C. 2007), emphasis added.

27. *People v. Conroy*, 145 N.E.3d 537, 543 (Ill. App. Ct. 2019).

28. Simone de Beauvoir, *The Second Sex*, translated by Constance Borde and Sheila Malovany-Chevallier (New York: Vintage Books, 2011 [1949]), 599. Beauvoir's synopsis is a sendup, of course.

29. Kendall Thomas, "Corpus Juris (Hetero)sexualis: Doctrine, Discourse, and Desire in *Bowers v. Hardwick*," *GLQ: A Journal of Lesbian & Gay Studies* 1 (1993), 41.

30. See Lisa Duggan, *The Twilight of Equality: Neoliberalism, Cultural Politics, and the Attack on Democracy* (Boston: Beacon Press, 2003).

31. *Williams*, 275.

32. Ibid., 276.

33. *Palfrey*, 41.

34. See Mary Anne Case, "Of 'This' and 'That' in *Lawrence v. Texas*," *Supreme Court Review* 2003 (2003), 133–137; see also note 9.

35. See Don Kulick and Jens Rydström, *Loneliness and Its Opposite: Sex, Disability, and the Ethics of Engagement* (Durham: Duke University Press, 2015).

36. I. India Thusi, *Policies Bodies: Law, Sex Work, and Desire in Johannesburg* (Stanford: Stanford University Press, 2022), 72–73, emphases added.

37. Alison Bass, *Getting Screwed: Sex Workers and the Law* (Lebanon, NH: ForeEdge, 2015), 45.

38. Thusi, *Policing Bodies*, 72, quoting Philip Howell, "A Private Contagious Disease Act: Prostitution and Public Space in Victorian Cambridge," *Journal of Historical Geography* 26 (2000), 377.

39. See generally Jessica Spector, ed., *Prostitution and Pornography: Philosophical Debate about the Sex Industry* (Stanford: Stanford University Press, 2006); see also

Joseph J. Fischel, "Pornography's Contradictions," *Boston Review*, September 21, 2021, www.bostonreview.net/articles/pornographys-contradictions; *U.S. v. Thompson*, 458 F. Supp. 2d 730, 732 (N.D. Ind. 2006) (quoting defendant's recognition of "the current extremely absurd nature of applied prostitution law enforcement that protects the dominant European pornography . . . industry under the 1st Amendment but leaves the dominant Asian Massage Parlor . . . prostitution industry subject to Mann Act prosecutions").

40. See Jasmine Sankofa, "From Margin to Center: Sex Work Decriminalization Is a Racial Justice Issue," *Amnesty International*, December 12, 2016, www.bostonreview .net/articles/pornographys-contradictions/ ("In 2015, nearly 40% of adults arrested for prostitution were Black. This disparity is larger for minors, where approximately 60% of youth under the age of 18 arrested for prostitution were Black—despite being categorized as victims of sex trafficking under federal law").

41. *Lawrence*, 562, emphasis added.

42. Another irony here is that plaintiffs in *Lawrence* were likely not having oral, anal, or any other kind of sex with each other, let alone intimate sex, however defined. See Dale Carpenter, *Flagrant Conduct: The Story of* Lawrence v. Texas (New York: W.W. Norton, 2012).

43. Katherine M. Franke, "The Domesticated Liberty of *Lawrence v. Texas*," *Columbia Law Review* 104 (2004): 1401.

44. *Roe v. Wade*, 410 U.S. 113 (1973); *Planned Parenthood v. Casey*, 505 U.S. 833 (1992).

45. *Dobbs v. Jackson Women's Health Org.*, 142 S.Ct. 2228 (2022).

46. *Griswold v. Conn.*, 381 U.S. 479 (1965) (protecting married couples' use and access to contraception under a right to privacy read out of several constitutional amendments, notably not the Fourteenth, but see White, J., concurring, at 502); *Eisenstadt v. Baird*, 405 U.S. 438 (1971) (extending the right to use and access contraception to unmarried persons, but under the equal protection guarantee of the Fourteenth Amendment); *Roe* (1973).

47. Martha C. Nussbaum, "Is Privacy Bad for Women?" *Boston Review*, April 1, 2000, www.bostonreview.net/articles/martha-c-nussbaum-privacy-bad-women/.

48. Case, "Donorsexuality"; Nan D. Hunter, "Living with *Lawrence*," *Minnesota Law Review* 88 (2003–2004): 1103–1139.

49. *Baskin v. Bogan*, 766 F.3d 648, 662 (7th Cir. 2014).

50. *Erotic Serv. Provider Legal Educ. and Research Project (ESP) v. Gascon*, 880 F.3d 450 (9th Cir. 2018).

51. Ibid., 459, internal citation omitted.

52. See, for example, Elizabeth Bernstein, *Temporarily Yours: Intimacy, Authenticity, and the Commerce of Sex* (Chicago: University of Chicago Press, 2007); Gregory Mitchell, *Tourist Attractions: Performing Race and Masculinity in Brazil's Sexual Economy* (Chicago: University of Chicago Press, 2015); Svati P. Shah, *Street Corner Secrets: Sex, Work, and Migration in the City of Mumbai* (Durham: Duke University Press, 2014); I. India Thusi, *Policing Bodies*.

53. The Science of Sex podcast, "Sex Work in America," March 12, 2019.

54. Bernstein, *Temporarily Yours*.

55. Beauvoir, *The Second Sex*, 609.

56. Bernstein, *Temporarily Yours*, 21.

57. Viviana A. Zelizer, *The Purchase of Intimacy* (Princeton: Princeton University Press, 2007).

58. Bass, *Getting Screwed*, 49.

59. Ibid., 55.

60. Clelia Smyth and Yolanda Estes, "The Myth of the Happy Hooker: Kantian Moral Reflections on a Phenomenology of Prostitution," in *Analyzing Violence against Women*, edited by Wanda Teays (Switzerland: Springer, 2019), 257–264.

61. Garry Marshall, *Pretty Woman* (Touchstone Pictures, 1990).

62. Molly Smith and Juno Mac, *Revolting Prostitutes: The Fight for Sex Workers' Rights* (Verso: London, 2020), 13.

63. Lorelei Lee, "Cash/Consent," *n + 1* (2019), www.nplusonemag.com/issue-35 /essays/cashconsent/.

64. Smith and Mac, *Revolting Prostitutes*, 55.

65. But see Joseph F. Morrisey, "*Lochner, Lawrence*, and Liberty," *Georgia State University Law Review* 27 (2011): 609–672. Morrisey argues that gay rights pertaining to marriage, adoption, and surrogacy would have a sounder constitutional basis in a modified *Lochnerian* contract right than in a right either to privacy or equality.

66. But see Nussbaum, "Is Privacy Bad for Women?" ("[W]omen take their [birth control] pills anywhere they happen to be, whereas they won't brush their teeth just anywhere").

67. *Lawrence*, 562.

68. Ibid., 563; see also Noa Ben-Asher, "Conferring Dignity: The Metamorphosis of the Legal Homosexual," *Harvard Journal of Law & Gender* 37 (2014), 255–257.

69. Erica Jong, *Fear of Flying* (New York: New American Library, 1973).

70. Cass R. Sunstein, "Liberty After *Lawrence*," *Ohio State Law Journal* 65 (2004), 1066.

71. See Mary Anne Case, "Missing Sex Talk in the Supreme Court's Same-Sex Marriage Cases," *University of Missouri-Kansas City Law Review* 84 (2015–2016): 675–692; see also Ben-Asher, "Conferring Dignity," 273 ("The moral ascent of the legal homosexual over the last three decades has depended on the declining visibility of erotic acts").

72. Beauvoir, *The Second Sex*, 608.

73. Hunter, "Living with *Lawrence*," 1110.

74. Case, "Donorsexuality," 192.

75. See William D. Araiza, *Animus: A Short Introduction to Bias in the Law* (New York: New York University Press, 2017).

76. Sunstein, "Liberty after *Lawrence*," 1067.

77. Beauvoir, *The Second Sex*, 614. See also Martha C. Nussbaum, "'Whether from Reason or Prejudice': Taking Money for Bodily Services," *Journal of Legal Studies* 27 (1998), 723 ("Worries about subordination more recently raised by feminists are much more serious concerns, but they apply to many types of work poor women do").

78. Joanna Grossman, "The Consequence of *Lawrence v. Texas*: Justice Scalia is Right that Same Sex Marriage Bans Are at Risk, but Wrong that a Host of Other Laws Are Vulnerable," *FindLaw*, July 8, 2003, https://supreme.findlaw.com/legal-commentary/the -consequences-of.html.

79. *ESP*, 457.

80. Appellant's Brief, *People v. Onofre*, 424 N.Y.S.2d 566 (N. Y. App. Div. 1980), 10, quoted in Ellen Ann Anderson, "The Stages of Sodomy Reform," *Thurgood Marshall Law Review* 23 (1998), 300, note 89.

81. "Ways HIV Can Be Transmitted," *Centers for Disease Control and Prevention*, www.cdc.gov/hiv/basics/hiv-transmission/ways-people-get-hiv.html.

82. See Stephen Robertson, "Shifting the Scene of the Crime: Sodomy and the American History of Sexual Violence," *Journal of the History of Sexuality* 19 (2010): 223–242.

83. John Elledge, "Does the US President Have the Most Dangerous Job in America?" *New Statesman*, October 25, 2016, www.newstatesman.com/world/2016/10/most-danger ous-job-america-us-presidents-have-fatality-rate-roughly-27.

84. *Romer v. Evans*, 517 U.S. 620 (1996).

85. *United States v. Windsor*, 570 U.S. 744 (2013).

86. Amia Srinivasan, *The Right to Sex: Feminism in the Twenty-First Century* (New York: Farrar, Straus, and Giroux, 2021), 151–152.

87. Ibid., 152.

88. See generally Sarah, Sakha, Emily Greytak, and Mya Haynes, "Is Sex Work Decriminalization the Answer?" ACLU Research Brief (2020), www.aclu.org/report/sex -work-decriminalization-answer-what-research-tells-us; Nina Luo, "Decriminalizing Survival: Policy Platform and Polling on the Decriminalization of Sex Work," *Data for Progress* (2020), www.dataforprogress.org/memos/decriminalizing-sex-work; Candace N. Hill, "Selling Sex: The Costs of Criminalization," *Quinnipiac Health Law* 21 (2018): 131–157; I. India Thusi, "Radical Feminist Harms on Sex Workers," *Lewis & Clark Law Review* 22 (2018): 185–229. In her ethnographic reflections on the Swedish model— which ostensibly criminalizes just the purchase of sexual services—Professor Thusi narrates how the model nonetheless authorizes police harassment, abuse, and hyper-surveillance of sex workers. I. India Thusi, "Ne Nya Sexpuritanerna," *Yale Journal of Law and Feminism* 34 (2023): 66–73.

89. Sylvia A. Law, "Commercial Sex: Beyond Decriminalization," *Southern California Law Review* 73 (2000): 583. "Commercial Sex" is cited in *ESP*, 457–458.

90. Ibid., 555.

91. Amy M. Young, Carol Boyd, and Amy Hubbell, "Prostitution, Drug Use, and Coping with Psychological Distress," *Journal of Drug Issues* 30 (2000): 797. "Prostitution, Drug Use, and Coping" is cited in *ESP*, 458.

92. "HIV Risk Among Persons Who Exchange Sex for Money or Nonmonetary Items," *Centers for Disease Control and Prevention*, www.cdc.gov/hiv/group/sexworkers .html. "HIV Risk among Persons" is cited in *ESP*, 458.

93. See Bass, *Getting Screwed*, 117–121, 201–202.

94. Nussbaum, "'Whether from Reason or Prejudice,'" 708.

95. Emma Goldman, "The Traffic in Women," in Emma Goldman, *Anarchism and Other Essays* (New York: Mother Earth Publishing Association, 1911), 185; see also Beauvoir, *The Second Sex*, 599–600.

96. Jennie Livingston, *Paris Is Burning* (Academy Entertainment, 1990).

97. See *Dobbs*, Roberts, C. J., concurring.

98. See Alison Gash, "The Erosion of *Roe v. Wade* and Abortion Access Didn't Begin in Texas or Mississippi—It Started in Pennsylvania in 1992," *The Conversation*, October 28, 2021, http://theconversation.com/amp/the-erosion-of-roe-v-wade-and-abortion -access-didnt-begin-in-texas-or-mississippi-it-started-in-pennsylvania-in-1992-169925.

99. "[The majority opinion] can (so it says) neatly extract the right to choose from the constitutional edifice without affecting any associated rights. (Think of someone telling you that the Jenga tower simply will not collapse.)" *Dobbs*, Breyer, Sotomayor, and Kagan, JJ., dissenting, at 2330.

100. U.S. Const. amend. XIV.

101. *Dobbs*, Thomas, J., concurring, at 2300, citing *June Medical Services L.L.C. v. Russo*, 140 S.Ct. 2103 (2020), Thomas, J., dissenting, at 2142.

102. *Dobbs*, 2242, citing *Washington v. Glucksberg*, 521 U.S. 702, 721 (1997).

103. *Dobbs*, Thomas, J., concurring, at 2301; *Dobbs*, Breyer, Sotomayor, and Kagan, J.J., dissenting, at 2332. Notably, however, while Justice Thomas calls out the Court's constitutional protections for contraception, sodomy, and same-sex marriage as "erroneous," he makes no explicit reference to interracial marriage. Ibid.

104. *Dobbs*, 2258.

105. *Dobbs*, Breyer, Sotomayor, and Kagan, J.J., dissenting, at 2324.

106. *Dobbs*, 2258.

107. James Bernstein introduces an argument, resonant with the one made in this chapter, that antiprostitution laws may unconstitutionally tread upon a property right to one's own body. James J. Bernstein, "Property Prohibitions: Why Criminalizing Prostitution Violates Constitutional Guarantees," *University of San Francisco Law Review* 56 (2021): 109–122.

108. *West Coast Hotel Co. v. Parrish*, 300 U.S. 379 (1937).

109. See Thomas B. Colby and Peter J. Smith, "The Return of *Lochner*," *Cornell Law Review* 100 (2015): 527–602.

110. *Patel v. Texas Department of Licensing and Regulation*, 469 S.W.3d 69, 94 note 11 (Tex. 2015), Willett, J., concurring.

111. *Meyer*, 399, 402.

112. *Pierce*, 528.

113. *Pierce*, 510.

114. *Griswold*, 481; *Loving v. Virginia*, 388 U.S. 1, 7 (1967); *Eisenstadt*, 457; *Roe*, 143; *Casey*, 848–849; *Lawrence*, 563; *Obergefell*, 675–676; see also Rubenfeld, "Right of Privacy," 743.

Leadingly, the *Griswold* Court opines that Planned Parenthood personnel "have standing to raise the constitutional rights of the married people with whom they had a professional relationship," just as, in *Pierce*, "the owners of private schools were entitled to assert the rights of potential pupils and their parents." Ibid. But the *Pierce* Court did not address the question of its appellees' standing and held the Oregon law to constitutionally violate the business and property rights of the corporations.

115. *Meyer*, 399.

116. Ibid., 400.

117. *Pierce*, 53.

118. "In both *Meyer* and *Pierce*, the party bringing suit was not a parent or child but an economic actor with whose occupation or business the challenged law was allegedly interfering. . . . Other language in the cases, however, indicates that the Court's essential concern was not so much for the liberty of contract as for freedom in upbringing or child-raising, issues much closer to those involved in modern privacy cases." Rubenfeld, "Right of Privacy," 743, note 34. Rubenfeld is right, but even if these loftier issues underlay the "Court's essential concern," they were not the essential concerns at law; occupation, property, and contract were.

119. *Pierce*, 535.

120. *Meyer*, 402 ("The power of the State to . . . make reasonable regulations for all schools . . . is not questioned"); *Pierce*, 534 ("No question is raised concerning the power of the State reasonably to regulate all schools"); *Lochner*, 58 ("We think the limit of the police power has been reached and passed in this case. There is, in our judgment, no reasonable foundation for holding this to be necessary or appropriate as a health law to safeguard the public health or the health of the individuals who are following the trade of a baker").

121. Rubenfeld, "Right of Privacy," 752.

122. Ibid., 800.

123. Ibid., 788.

124. Ibid., 790.

125. Ibid., 786, quoting *Meyer*, 402.

126. Ibid., 787.

127. Ibid., 787, quoting *Pierce*, 535.

128. Ibid., 790, note 205, quoting *Pierce*, 535.

129. Ibid., 787, emphasis added.

130. Ibid., 806.

131. Risa Lauren Goluboff, "'Let Economic Equality Take Care of Itself': The NAACP, Labor Litigation, and the Making of Civil Rights in the 1940s," *UCLA Law Review* 52 (2005): 1392–1486.

132. Ibid., 1399.

133. Ibid., 1399, 1430, 1435–1436.

134. Ibid., 1439.

135. Ibid., 1398.

136. Ibid., 1438–1439, 1441, citing NAACP briefs and lower court opinions.

137. Ibid., 1441.

138. Ibid., 1442.

139. Ibid., 1442.

140. See note 120.

141. See Adrienne D. Davis, "Regulating Sex Work: Erotic Assimilationism, Erotic Exceptionalism, and the Challenge of Intimate Labor," *California Law Review* 103 (2015): 1195–1275; see also Hila Shamir, "Feminist Approaches to the Regulation of Sex Work: Patterns in Transnational Governance Feminist Law Making," *Cornell International Law Journal* 52 (2019): 177–233.

142. See Davis, "Regulating Sex Work," 1231–1242.

143. See Sankofa, "From Margin to Center"; I. India Thusi, "Harm, Sex, and Consequences," *Utah Law Review* 2019 (2019): 193–194, 206–211.

144. Goluboff, "'Let Economic Equality Take Care of Itself,'" 1396.

145. Richard A. Posner, "The Uncertain Protection of Privacy by the Supreme Court," *Supreme Court Review* 1979 (1979): 214–215.

146. *Connecticut v. Gabbert*, 526 U.S. 286, 292 (1999).

147. *Truax v. Raich*, 239 U.S. 33, 41 (1915).

148. *Greene v. McElroy*, 360 U.S. 474, 492 (1959).

149. *U.S. v. Robel*, 389 U.S. 258, 263 (1967).

150. *Merritt v. Mackey*, 827 F.2d 1368, 1370 (9th Cir. 1987).

151. *Gabbert*, 291–292 (1999).

152. Ibid., 292, emphasis added.

153. Ibid., 291.

154. Bernstein, "Due Process Right," 295.

155. Ibid., 287–288.

156. Ibid., 295.

157. *ESP*, 455.

158. Ibid., 459, internal citation omitted.

159. Brief of Plaintiffs-Appellants at 44–45, *Erotic Serv. Provider Legal Educ. and Research Project v. Gascon*, 880 F.3d 450 (9th Cir. 2018) (No. 16-15927), 2016 WL 5787393.

160. *ESP*, 459.

161. Lucy Platt et al., "Associations Between Sex Work Laws and Sex Workers' Health: A Systematic Review and Meta-analysis of Quantitative and Qualitative Studies," *PLOS Medicine* 15 (2018): 1–54; see also sources in notes 85–91.

162. *Lochner*, 67, emphasis added; see also note 12.

163. See Nussbaum, "'Whether from Reason or Prejudice,'" 711 ("There is a stronger case for paternalistic regulation of boxing than of prostitution, and externalities [the glorification of violence as example to the young] make boxing at least as morally problematic, probably more so. And yet I would not defend the criminalization of boxing, and I doubt that very many Americans would either. Sensible regulation of both prostitution and boxing, by contrast, seems reasonable and compatible with personal liberty").

164. See Fischel, *Screw Consent*, 31–63.

165. See Martha T. McCluskey, "How Queer Theory Makes Neoliberalism Sexy," in *Feminist and Queer Legal Theory: Intimate Encounters, Uncomfortable Conversations*, edited by Marth Albertson Fineman, Jack E. Jackson, and Adam P. Romero (Aldershot, UK: Ashgate, 2009).

166. "Wolfenden Report, 1957," *British Library*, www.bl.uk/collection-items/wolfen den-report-conclusion.

167. See Derek Demeri, "The Model Penal Code & Sex Work Criminalization," *Vermont Law Review* 47 (2022): 156–219.

168. Melissa Gira Grant, *Playing the Whore* (London: Verso Books, 2014), 16.

169. Smith and Mac, *Revolting Prostitutes*, 7.

CODA

1. "If you scratch a child, you will find a queer, in the sense of someone 'gay' or just plain strange." Kathryn Bond Stockton, *The Queer Child, or Growing Sideways in the Twentieth Century* (Durham: Duke University Press, 2009), 1.

2. Jules Gill-Peterson, *Histories of the Transgender Child* (Minneapolis: University of Minnesota Press, 2018), 196.

3. See Amy Novotney, "'The Young People Feel It': A Look at the Mental Health Impact of Antitrans Legislation," *American Psychological Association*, June 29, 2023, www.apa.org/topics/lgbtq/mental-health-anti-transgender-legislation.

4. See Robin Dembroff, "'I Know What I Am': Reimagining the Meaning of Transgender," *Australian Broadcasting Company*, July 24, 2023, www.abc.net.au/religion /robin-dembroff-reimagining-the-meaning-of-transgender/102640594; Susan Stryker, Paisley Currah, and Lisa Jean Moore, "Introduction: Trans-, Trans, or Transgender?" *Women's Studies Quarterly* 36 (2008): 11–22.

5. See Sam Levin, "How Trans Children Became a 'Political Football' for the Republican Party," *The Guardian*, March 23, 2021.

6. Eve Kosofsky Sedgwick, "How to Bring Your Kids Up Gay," *Social Text* 29 (1991): 18; see also Jules Gill-Peterson, *Histories of the Transgender Child*, 195–207.

7. For some key queer studies' glosses on the politicizing and depoliticizing functions of children and childhood innocence, see Lauren Berlant, "Live Sex Acts (Parental Advisory: Explicit Material)," *Feminist Studies* 21 (1995): 379–404; Steven Bruhm and Natasha Hurley, eds., *Curiouser: On the Queerness of Children* (Minneapolis: University of Minnesota Press, 2004); Lee Edelman, *No Future: Queer Theory and the Death Drive* (Durham: Duke University Press, 2004); James Kincaid, *Erotic Innocence: The Culture of Child Molesting* (Durham: Duke University Press, 1998); Kathryn Bond Stockton, *The Queer Child*.

8. Gillian Harkins, *Virtual Pedophilia: Sex Offender Profiling and U.S. Security Culture* (Durham: Duke University Press, 2020).

9. See, for example, Anagha Srikanth, "Florida's New Ban on Transgender Sports Would Allow Schools to Subject Minors to Genital Inspections," *The Hill*, April 15, 2021, https://thehill.com/changing-america/respect/equality/548534-floridas-new-ban-on-transgender-students-in-sports-would/; see also Tey Meadow and Kristina R. Olson, "Laws Vilifying Transgender Children and Their Families Are Abusive," *Scientific American*, March 29, 2022, www.scientificamerican.com/article/laws-vilifying-transgender-children-and-their-families-are-abusive/; David W. Chen, "Louisiana Passes Surgical Castration Bill for Child Sex Offenders," *New York Times*, June 4, 2024, www.nyt.com/2024/06/04.

10. Dorothy E. Roberts, *Killing the Black Body: Race, Reproduction, and the Meaning of Liberty* (New York: Pantheon Books, 1997), 21 ("The powerful Western image of childhood innocence does not seem to benefit Black children. Black Children are born guilty"); but for accounts of political movements on behalf of children of color that leverage innocence, see, for example, Elizabeth Bernstein, *Brokered Subjects: Sex, Trafficking, and the Politics oof Freedom* (Chicago: University of Chicago Press, 2018); Robin Bernstein, *Racial Innocence: Performing American Childhood from Slavery to Civil Rights* (New York: New York University Press, 2011); Jessica Fields, *Risky Lessons: Sex Education and Social Inequality* (New Brunswick: Rutgers University Press, 2008).

11. See Berlant, "Live Sex Acts."

12. Jean-Paul Morrell, quoted in "Louisiana Strengthens Law against the Sexual Abuse of Animals," *The Humane Society of the United States*, May 31, 2018, www.humanesociety.org/news/louisiana-strengthens-law-against-sexual-abuse-animals.

13. Jean-Paul Morrell, quoted in Elizabeth Crisp, "Louisiana Looks to Clearly Outlaw Sexual Abuse of Animals, amid Concerns over Loopholes in Existing Law," *The Advocate*, April 9, 2018, www.theadvocate.com/baton_rouge/news/politics/legislature/louisiana-looks-to-clearly-outlaw-sexual-abuse-of-animals-amid-concerns-over-loopholes-in-existing/article_ccc31858-3c47-11e8-a09c-1f3d9daab565.html.

14. See, for example, Berlant, "Live Sex Acts"; Paul M. Renfro, *Stranger Danger: Family Values, Childhood, and the American Carceral State* (Oxford: Oxford University Press, 2020), 167–170; Sara Morrison, "The Danger of Making the Internet Safe for Kids," *Vox*, March 14, 2022, www.vox.com/recode/2022/3/14/22971618/earn-it-sesta-fosta-children-safety-internet-laws.

15. See Annette Ruth Appell, "Accommodating Childhood," *Cardozo Journal of Law & Gender* 19 (2013): 724–735; Holly Brewer, *By Birth or Consent: Children, Law, and the Anglo-American Revolution in Authority* (Chapel Hill: University of North Carolina Press, 2005).

16. Appell, "Accommodating Childhood," 734–745.

17. John Wall, *Children's Rights: Today's Global Challenge* (Lanham: Rowman & Littlefield, 2017), 3.

18. Edelman, *No Future*, 29.

19. Paul Amar, "The Street, the Sponge, and the Ultra: Queer Logics of Children's Rebellion," *GLQ: A Journal of Lesbian and Gay Studies* 22 (2016): 572–573.

20. Ibid., 569.

21. Steven Angelides, *The Fear of Child Sexuality: Young People, Sex, and Agency* (Chicago: University of Chicago Press, 2019).

22. Jane Ward, "Radical Experiments Involving Innocent Children: Locating Parenthood in Queer Utopia," in *A Critical Inquiry into Queer Utopias*, edited by Angela Jones (New York: Palgrave Macmillan, 2013), 242.

23. Ibid., 240–243.

24. For my review of Angelides' *Fear of Child Sexuality*, see Joseph J. Fischel, "Sexing the Child," *GLQ: A Journal of Lesbian and Gay Studies* 27 (2021): 658–661.

25. On political efforts to enforce young people's voting rights under the Twenty-Sixth Amendment of the U.S. Constitution, see Yael Bromberg, "The Youth Voting Rights Act Would Transform Access for Young Voters," *Teen Vogue*, July 27, 2022, www .teenvogue.com/story/youth-voting-rights-act-what-is.

26. Appell, "Accommodating Childhood," 749.

27. Ibid., 774.

28. See, for example, Allison James, "To Be (Come) or Not to Be (Come): Understanding Children's Citizenship," *The Annals of the American Academy of Political and Social Science* 633 (2011): 167–179; Lachlan Montgomery Umbers, "Enfranchising the Youth," *Critical Review of International Social and Political Philosophy* 23 (2020): 732–755; John Wall, *Children's Rights*; John Wall, *Give Children the Vote: On Democratizing Democracy* (London: Bloomsbury Academic, 2022).

29. Appell, "Accommodating Childhood," 755–778.

30. For well over a hundred years, trans children have petitioned medical and political authorities to recognize and respect their gender expressions and identifications. See Gilles-Peterson, *Histories of the Transgender Child*.

31. Wall, *Give Children the Vote*, 5.

32. See Madeleine Carlisle, "Kid of the Year Finalist Kai Shappley, 11, Takes on Lawmakers in Her Fight for Trans Rights," *Time*, January 12, 2022, https://time.com /6128490/kid-of-the-year-kai-shappley-trans-activist/.

33. See Malik Picket et al., "Labeled for Life: A Review of Youth Sex Offender Registration Laws," *Juvenile Law Center*, 2020, https://jlc.org.

34. J. David Goodman, "How Medical Care for Transgender Youth Became 'Child Abuse' in Texas," *New York Times*, March 11, 2022, www.nytimes.com/2022/03/11/us /texas-transgender-youth-medical-care-abuse.html.

35. See note 9.

36. See Appell, "Accommodating Childhood," 776.

37. See Dan Levin, "Young Voters Keep Moving to the Left of Social Issues, Republicans Included," *New York Times*, January 23, 2019; Jody L. Herman, Andrew R. Flores, and Kathryn K. O'Neill, "How Many Adults and Youth Identify as Transgender in the United States?" *Williams Institute*, June 2020, https://williamsinstitute.law.ucla .edu/publications/trans-adults-united-states/; Daniel de Visé, "Vegetarianism Is on the Rise—Especially the Part-Time Kind," *The Hill*, November 3, 2022, https://thehill.com /changing-america/sustainability/3747206-vegetarianism-is-on-the-rise-especially-the -part-time-kind/.

38. Taylor Swift, "You Need to Calm Down," *Lover* (Republic Records, 2019).

39. See, for example, John D'Emilio, "Capitalism and Gay Identity," in *The Lesbian and Gay Studies Reader*, edited by Henry Abelove, Michèle Aina Barale, and David M. Halperin (New York: Routledge, 1993), 467–476; Christopher Chitty, *Sexual Hegemony: Statecraft, Sodomy, and Capital in the Rise of the World System* (Durham: Duke University Press, 2020); Joanne Meyerowitz, *How Sex Changed: A History of Transsexuality in the United States* (Cambridge, MA: Harvard University Press, 2002).

40. D'Emilio, "Capitalism and Gay Identity," 474–475; Gilles-Peterson, *Histories of the Transgender Child*, 206–207.

41. For rather different shaves on the discursive limits of *suffering* and *suicide* as the idioms for queer children's political condition, see Andrew Gilden, "Cyberbullying and the Innocence Narrative," *Harvard Civil Rights-Civil Liberties Law Review* 48 (2013): 357–407; Jasbir K. Puar, "The Cost of Getting Better: Suicide, Sensation, Switchpoints," *GLQ* 18 (2011): 149–158; Ritch C. Savin-Williams, *The New Gay Teenager* (Cambridge, MA: Harvard University Press, 2006).

CHRONOLOGY

1. 1805 Louisiana Acts chap. I, § 2.
2. *State v. Vicknair*, 28 So. 273 (La. 1900).
3. *State v. Aenspacker*, 58 So. 520 (La. 1912).
4. La. Crim. Stat. Ann. § 43:89 (1943); see also Laura McTighe and Deon Haywood, "'There Is NO Justice in Louisiana:' Crimes against Nature and the Spirit of Black Feminist Resistance," *Souls: A Critical Journal of Black Politics, Culture, and Society* 19 (2017), 265–266.
5. Louisiana House Bill 789, Act 60 (1962).
6. Louisiana Senate Bill 400, Act 612 (1975).
7. Act 49.
8. *State v. Phillips*, 365 So.2d, 1304 (La. 1978).
9. Act 703.
10. *State v. Ryans*, 513 So.2d 386 (La. Ct. App. 1987).
11. Acts 1992, No. 388., §1.
12. *State v. Baxley*, 656 So.2d 973 (La. 1995).
13. *State v. Spitz*, 650 So.2d 271 (La. Ct. App. 1995).
14. *State v. Smith*, 766 So.2d 501 (La. 2000).
15. *State v. Moore*, 797 So.2d 756 (La. Ct. App. 2001).
16. Act 301.
17. *State v. Thomas*, 891 So.2d 1233 (La. 2005).
18. Louisiana House Bill 40, Act 138 (2008).
19. Louisiana Senate Bill 381, Act 882 (2010).
20. Louisiana House Bill 141, Act 223 (2011).
21. *Doe v. Jindal*, 851 F. Supp. 2d 995 (E.D. La. 2012).
22. *Doe v. Caldwell*, Civil Action No. 12–1670 (E.D. La. 2013).
23. Jim Mustian, "Gay Men Arrested in Louisiana under Invalid Sodomy Law," *Advocate*, July 29, 2013, http://sdgln.com/news/2013/07/29/gay-men-arrested-louisiana-via-invalid-sodomy-law.
24. *Lawrence v. Texas*, 539 U.S. 558 (2003).
25. Louisiana State Legislature Act No. 177 (2014).
26. Julia O'Donoghue, "Louisiana House Votes 27–67 to Keep Unconstitutional Anti-sodomy Law on the Books," *The Times-Picayune*, April 15, 2014.
27. Louisiana Revised Statutes 14:89.3.
28. Kaylee Poche, "Bill to Decriminalize Sex Work in Louisiana Fails to Make It Out of Committee," *Gambit*, May 4, 2021, www.nola.com/gambit/news/the_latest/bill-to-decriminalize-sex-work-in-louisiana-fails-to-make-it-out-of-committee/article_533f3 5da-ad22-11eb-8018-9ff9cf06337b.html.
29. Louisiana Senate Bill 283 (2024).

Bibliography

CASES

Arcara v. Cloud Books, Inc., 478 U.S. 697 (1986)
Baker v. Nelson, 191 N.W.2d 185 (Minn. 1971)
Baskin v. Bogan, 766 F.3d 648 (7th Cir. 2014)
Bowers v. Hardwick, 478 U.S. 186 (1986)
City of Cleburne, Tex. v. Cleburne Living Center, 473 U.S. 432 (1985)
City of Renton v. Playtime Theatres, Inc., 475 U.S. 41 (1986)
Commonwealth v. Bell, 67 Mass. App. Ct. 266 (2006)
Connecticut v. Gabbert, 526 U.S. 286 (1999)
Dobbs v. Jackson Women's Health Org., 142 S.Ct. 2228 (2022)
Doe v. Caldwell, 913 F. Supp. 2d 262 (E.D. La. 2013)
Doe v. Jindal, 851 F. Supp. 2d 995 (E.D. La. 2012)
Eisenstadt v. Baird, 405 U.S. 438 (1971)
Erotic Serv. Provider Legal Educ. and Research Project v. Gascon, 880 F.3d 450 (9th Cir. 2018)
Erotic Serv. Provider Legal Educ. Research Project v. Gascon, No. C 15-01007 (N.D. Cal. 2016)
Giboney v. Empire Storage & Ice Co., 336 U.S. 490 (1949)
Greene v. McElroy, 360 U.S. 474 (1959)
Griswold v. Connecticut, 381 U.S. 479 (1965)
Gundling v. Chicago, 177 U.S. 183 (1900)
June Medical Services L.L.C. v. Russo, 140 S.Ct. 2103 (2020)
Lawrence v. Texas, 539 U.S. 558 (2003)
Lochner v. New York, 198 U.S. 45 (1905)
Loving v. Virginia, 388 U.S. 1 (1967)
Martin v. Ziherl, 607 S. E. 2d 367 (Va. 2005)
Merritt v. Mackey, 827 F.2d 1368 (9th Cir. 1987)

Meyer v. Nebraska, 262 U.S. 390 (1923)

Miller v. California, 413 U.S. 15 (1973)

Mills v. City of Harrisburg, 589 F. Supp. 2d 544 (M.D. Penn. 2008)

National Coalition for Gay & Lesbian Equality v. Minister of Justice 1999 (1) SALR 6 (CC) at para. 29 (S. Afr.)

Obergefell v. Hodges, 576 U.S. 644 (2015)

Paris Adult Theater I v. Slaton, 413 U.S. 49 (1973)

Patel v. Texas Dep't of Licensing and Regulation, 469 S. W. 3d 69 (Tex. 2015)

People v. Conroy, 145 N.E.3d 537 (Ill. App. Ct. 2019)

People v. Onofre, 424 N.Y.S.2d 566 (N.Y. App. Div. 1980)

People v. Santorelli, 600 N.E.2d 232 (N.Y. 1992)

People v. Williams, 811 N.E.2d 1197 (Ill. App. Ct. 2004)

Pierce v. Society Sisters, 268 U.S. 510 (1925)

Planned Parenthood v. Casey, 505 U.S. 833 (1992)

Price Waterhouse v. Hopkins, 490 U.S. 228 (1989)

Reliable Consultants, Inc. v. Earle, 517 F.3d 738 (5th Cir. 2008)

Roe v. Wade, 410 U.S. 113 (1973)

Roberts v. U.S. Jaycees, 468 U.S. 609 (1984)

Robicheaux v. Caldwell, 2 F. Supp. 3d 910 (E.D. La. 2014)

Romer v. Evans, 517 U.S. 620 (1996)

Skinner v. Okla. ex rel. Williamson, 316 U.S. 535 (1942)

State v. Aenspacker, 58 So. 520 (La. 1912)

State v. Baxley, 656 So.2d 973 (La. 1995)

State v. Bonnano, 163 So.2d 72 (La. 1964)

State v. Gamble, 504 So.2d 1100 (La. Ct. App. 1987)

State v. Ketton, 468 So.2d 707 (La. Ct. App. 1985)

State v. Lambert, 550 So.2d 847 (La. Ct. App. 1989)

State v. Limon, 280 Kan. 275 (Kan. 2005)

State v. Mills, 505 So.2d 933 (La. Ct. App. 1987)

State v. Moore, 797 So.2d 756 (La. Ct. App. 2001)

State v. Phillips, 365 So.2d 1304 (La. 1978)

State v. Romano, 155 P.3d 1102 (Haw. 2007)

State v. Ryans, 513 So.2d 386 (La. Ct. App. 1987)

State v. Smith, 766 So.2d 501 (La. 2000)

State v. Spitz, 650 So.2d 271 (La. Ct. App. 1995)

State v. Thomas, 891 So.2d 1233 (La. 2005)

State v. Vicknair, 28 So. 273 (La. 1900)

State v. White, 495 So.2d 340 (La. Ct. App. 1986)

State v. Yancy, 465 So.2d 48 (La. Ct. App. 1985)

Truax v. Raich, 239 U.S. 33 (1915)

Trump v. Hawaii, 138 S.Ct. 2392 (2018)

U.S. Dept. of Agriculture v. Moreno, 413 U.S. 528 (1973)

U.S. v. Palfrey, 499 F. Supp. 2d 34 (D.D.C. 2007)

U.S. v. Robel, 389 U.S. 258 (1967)

U.S. v. Stevens, 559 U.S. 460 (2010)

U.S. v. Thompson, 458 F. Supp. 2d 730 (N.D. Ind. 2006)

U.S. v. Windsor, 570 U.S. 744 (2013)

Washington v. Glucksberg, 521 U.S. 702 (1997)

West Coast Hotel Co. v. Parrish, 300 U.S. 379 (1937)

GENERAL SOURCES

Ackerman, Peggy. "Former N.J. Judge Not Reappointed by Gov. Christie Says He Was Kicked Off Bench Unfairly." *NJ.com*, June 17, 2010. www.nj.com/news/2010/06/for mer_superior_court_judge_no.html.

Adams, Carol J. *The Sexual Politics of Meat: A Feminist-Vegetarian Critical Theory.* New York: Bloomsbury Academic, [1990] 2015.

Adams, Vincanne. *Markets of Sorrow, Labors of Faith: New Orleans in the Wake of Katrina.* Durham: Duke University Press, 2013.

Adimora, Adaora A., and Victor J. Schoenbach. "Social Context, Sexual Networks, and Racial Disparities in Rates of Sexually Transmitted Infections." *Journal of Infectious Diseases* 191, Supp. 1 (2005): S115–22.

Agamben, Giorgio. *The Open: Man and Animal.* Translated by Kevin Attell. Stanford: Stanford University Press, 2003.

Agan, Amanda Y., and J.J. Prescott. "Sex Offender Law and the Geography of Victimization." *Journal of Empirical Legal Studies* 11, no. 4 (2014): 786–828.

Agathocleous, Alexis. "Building a Movement for Justice: *Doe v. Jindal* and the Campaign against Louisiana's Crime Against Nature Statute." In *The War on Sex*, edited by David M. Halperin and Trevor Hoppe, 429–453. Durham: Duke University Press, 2017.

Ahern, Eoghan. "The Sin of Sodomy in Late Antiquity." *Journal of the History of Sexuality* 27, no. 2 (2018): 209–233.

Ahmad, Aazan, and Gary L. Francioni. "If Animals Matter Morally, Then We Cannot Treat Them as Commodities." *Animal Rights: The Abolitionist Approach*, August 1, 2016. www.abolitionistapproach.com/wp-content/uploads/2016/08/If-Animals-Mat ter-Morally-Interview-with-GLF-20160801.pdf.

Ahmed, Aziza. "Janet Halley in Conversation with Aziza Ahmed: Interview." In *Beyond Virtue and Vice: Rethinking Human Rights and Criminal Law*, edited by Alice M. Miller and Mindy Jane Roseman, 17–38. Philadelphia: University of Pennsylvania Press, 2019.

Albeck-Ripka, Livia. "Tennessee Bans Drag Shows on Public Property." *New York Times*, March 2, 2023. www.nytimes.com/2023/03/02/us/tennessee-bans-drag-shows.html.

Alexander, Michelle. *The New Jim Crow: Mass Incarceration in the Age of Colorblindness, Tenth Anniversary Edition.* New York: The New Press, 2020.

Alexander, M. Jacqui. *Pedagogies of Crossing: Meditations on Feminism, Sexual Politics, Memory, and the Sacred.* Durham: Duke University Press, 2005.

Allen, Andre, dir. *The Problem with John Stewart.* Season 2, episode 7, "Chaos, Law, and Order." Aired March 3, 2023, on Apple+.

Alper, Mariel, and Matthew R. Durose. *Recidivism of Sex Offenders Released from State Prison: A 9-Year Follow-Up (2005–14).* Washington, D.C.: Bureau of Justice Statistics, Office of Justice Programs, U.S. Department of Justice, 2019.

Amar, Paul. "The Street, the Sponge, and the Ultra: Queer Logics of Children's Rebellion." *GLQ: A Journal of Lesbian and Gay Studies* 22, no. 4 (2016): 569–604.

Anderson, Ed. "Prostitution by Males DA's Target." *The Times-Picayune*, April 6, 1977.

Anderson, Ellen Ann. "The Stages of Sodomy Reform." *Thurgood Marshall Law Review* 23 (1998): 283–319.

Andersson, Johan. "Vauxhall's Post-industrial Pleasure Gardens: 'Death Wish' and Hedonism in 21st Century London." *Urban Studies* 48, no. 1 (2011): 85–100.

Angelides, Steven. *The Fear of Child Sexuality: Young People, Sex, and Agency.* Chicago: University of Chicago Press, 2019.

Anker, Elizabeth R. *Ugly Freedoms*. Durham: Duke University Press, 2022.

Appell, Annette Ruth. "Accommodating Childhood." *Cardozo Journal of Law and Gender* 19, no. 3 (2013): 715–779.

Araiza, William D. *Animus: A Short Introduction to Bias in the Law*. New York: New York University Press, 2017.

Associated Press. "Berlin to Let Everyone Go Topless at Public Swimming Pools." *AP News*, March 9, 2023. https://apnews.com/article/germany-berlin-topless-swimming-pools-women-discrimination-292399fcd4290414d33ee8e8f46e1922.

Associated Press. "Former Moorestown Police Officer Sentenced to 30 Years for Sexually Assaulting Girls." *NJ.com*, October 11, 2012. www.nj.com/burlington/2012/10/former_moorestown_police_officer_sentenced_to_30_years_for_sexually_assaulting_girls.html.

Associated Press. "Louisiana: Anti-sodomy Law Stands." *New York Times*, April 15, 2014. www.nytimes.com/2014/04/16/us/louisiana-anti-sodomy-law-stands.html.

Association for the Treatment and Prevention of Sexual Abuse. "Learn." www.atsa.com/learn.

Avilez, GerShun. *Black Queer Freedom: Spaces of Injury and Paths of Desire*. Urbana: University of Illinois Press, 2020.

Axster, Sabrina, Ida Danewid, Asher Goldstein, Matt Mahmoudi, Cemal Burak Tansel, and Lauren Wilcox. "Colonial Lives of the Carceral Archipelago: Rethinking the Neoliberal Security State." *International Political Sociology* 15, no. 3 (September 2021): 415–439. https://doi.org/10.1093/ips/olab013.

Bagemihl, Bruce. *Biological Exuberance: Animal Homosexuality and Natural Diversity*. New York: St. Martin's Press, 1999.

Balcombe, Jonathan. *Pleasurable Kingdom: Animals and the Nature of Feeling Good*. London: Macmillan, 2006.

Bass, Alison. *Getting Screwed: Sex Workers and the Law*. Lebanon, NH: ForeEdge, 2015.

Bassichis, Morgan, Alexander Lee, and Dean Spade. "Building an Abolitionist and Queer Movement with Everything We've Got." In *Captive Genders: Trans Embodiment and the Prison Industrial Complex*, edited by Eric A. Stanley and Nat Smith, 15–40. Oakland: AK Press, 2011.

Beauvoir, Simone de. *The Second Sex*. Translated by Constance Borde and Sheila Malovany-Chevallier. New York: Vintage Books, [1949] 2011.

Becker, Cynthia. "New Orleans Mardi Gras Indians: Mediating Racial Politics from the Backstreets to Main Street." *African Arts* 46, no. 2 (2013): 36–49.

Beirne, Piers. "Peter Singer's 'Heavy Petting' and the Politics of Animal Sexual Assault." *Critical Criminology* 10 (2001): 43–55.

Beirne, Piers. "Rethinking Bestiality: Towards a Concept of Interspecies Sexual Assault." *Theoretical Criminology* 1, no. 3 (1997): 317–340.

Bekoff, Marc, and Jessica Pierce. *Wild Justice: The Moral Lives of Animals*. Chicago: University of Chicago Press, 2009.

Belmonte, Laura A., et al. "Colloquy: Queering America and the World." *Diplomatic History* 40, no. 1 (2016): 19–80.

Ben-Asher, Noa. "Conferring Dignity: The Metamorphosis of the Legal Homosexual." *Harvard Journal of Law & Gender* 37 (2014): 243–284.

Bentley, Jenn. "Pushed Out: The Changing Demographics of New Orleans." *Big Easy*, February 11, 2019. www.bigeasymagazine.com/2019/2/11pushed-out-the-changing-demographics-of-new-orleans/.

Berlant, Lauren. "Live Sex Acts: (Parental Advisory: Explicit Material)." *Feminist Studies* 21, no. 2 (Summer 1995): 379–404.

Berlant, Lauren. "Risky Bigness: On Obesity, Eating, and the Ambiguity of 'Health.'" In *Against Health: How Health Became the New Morality*, edited by Jonathan M. Metzel and Anna Kirkland, 26–39. New York: New York University Press, 2010.

Berlant, Lauren, and Michael Warner. "Sex in Public." *Critical Inquiry* 24, no. 2 (1998): 547–566.

Bernstein, David E. "The Due Process Right to Pursue a Lawful Occupation: A Brighter Future Ahead?" *Yale Law Journal Forum* 126 (December 2016): 287–303.

Bernstein, Elizabeth. *Brokered Subjects: Sex, Trafficking, and the Politics oof Freedom*. Chicago: University of Chicago Press, 2018.

Bernstein, Elizabeth. *Temporarily Yours: Intimacy, Authenticity, and the Commerce of Sex*. Chicago: University of Chicago Press, 2007.

Bernstein, James J. "Property Prohibitions: Why Criminalizing Prostitution Violates Constitutional Guarantees." *University of San Francisco Law Review* 56 (2021): 109–122.

Bernstein, Robin. *Racial Innocence: Performing American Childhood from Slavery to Civil Rights*. New York: New York University Press, 2011.

Bersani, Leo. "Is the Rectum a Grave?" *AIDS: Cultural Analysis/Cultural Activism* 43 (1987): 197–222.

Bérubé, Allan. "The History of Gay Bathhouses." *Journal of Homosexuality* 44, no. 3–4 (2003): 33–53.

Blackstone, Sir William. *Commentaries on the Laws of England Book 4: On Public Wrongs*. New York: Wallachia Publishers, 2015.

Blake, Jeanie. "Who'll Take a Hooker's Word over the Word of a Lawman?" *The Times-Picayune*, April 12, 1981.

Blanchette, Alexander. *Porkopolis: American Animality, Standardized Life, and the Factory Farm*. Durham: Duke University Press, 2020.

Bloodhound Gang. "The Bad Touch." *Hooray for Boobies* (1999).

Boisseron, Bénédicte. *Afro-Dog: Blackness and the Animal Question*. New York: Columbia University Press, 2018.

Bourke, Joanna. *Loving Animals: On Bestiality, Zoophilia and Post-Human Love*. London: Reaktion, 2020.

Brake, Elizabeth. *Minimizing Marriage: Marriage, Morality, and the Law*. New York: Oxford University Press, 2012.

Bray, Alan. "Homosexuality and the Signs of Male Friendship in Elizabethan England." *History Workshop* 29, no. 1 (1990): 1–19.

Brettschneider, Corey. *Democratic Rights: The Substance of Self-Government*. Princeton: Princeton University Press, 2007.

Brewer, Holly. *By Birth or Consent: Children, Law, and the Anglo-American Revolution in Authority*. Chapel Hill: University of North Carolina Press, 2005.

Briggs, Karen. "Restraint Techniques for Breeding." *The Horse*, October 8, 2001. https://thehorse.com/14702/restraint-techniques-for-breeding/.

British Library. "Wolfenden Report, 1957." www.bl.uk/collection-items/wolfenden-report-conclusion.

Brodsky, Alexandra. *Sexual Justice: Supporting Victims, Ensuring Due Process, and Resisting the Conservative Backlash*. New York: Metropolitan Books, 2021.

Bromberg, Yael. "The Youth Voting Rights Act Would Transform Access for Young Voters." *Teen Vogue*, July 27, 2022. www.teenvogue.com/story/youth-voting-rights-act-what-is.

Brosnan, Sarah F., and Frans B. M. de Waal. "Monkeys Reject Unequal Pay." *Nature* 425 (2003): 297–299.

Brown, Wendy. *States of Injury: Power and Freedom in Late Modernity*. Princeton: Princeton University Press 1995.

Bruhm, Steven, and Natasha Hurley, eds. *Curiouser: On the Queerness of Children*. Minneapolis: University of Minnesota Press, 2004.

Bunyasi, Tehama Lopez, and Candis Watts Smith. "Get in Formation: Black Women's Participation in the Women's March on Washington as an Act of Pragmatic Utopianism." *The Black Scholar: Journal of Black Studies and Research* 48, no. 3 (2018): 4–16.

Butler, Judith. *Antigone's Claim: Kinship Between Life and Death*. New York: Columbia University Press, 2000.

Butler, Judith. *Bodies That Matter: On the Discursive Limits of Sex*. New York: Routledge, 1993.

Butler, Judith. *Frames of War: When Is Life Grievable?* London: Verso, 2009.

Butler, Judith. *Precarious Life: The Powers of Mourning and Violence*. London: Verso, 2004.

Butler, Judith. *The Psychic Life of Power: Theories in Subjection*. Stanford: Stanford University Press, 1997.

"CANScantSTAND." *Facebook*, October 17, 2018. www.facebook.com/1009945452523 242/photos/a.1012811605569960/1012823818902072/.

"CANScantSTAND." *Facebook*, November 30, 2018. www.facebook.com/1009945452523 242/photos/a.1039009952950125/1039043659613421/.

"CANS Can't Stand: Liberation for Black Trans Women." *New Yorker*, February 8, 2023. Video, 18:44. www.newyorker.com/video/watch/the-new-yorker-documentary-cans -cant-stand-liberation-for-black-trans-women.

CANScantSTAND Symposium, Tulane University. April 30, 2019. https://events.tulane .edu/content/canscantstand-symposium.

Carlisle, Madeleine. "Kid of the Year Finalist Kai Shappley, 11, Takes on Lawmakers in Her Fight for Trans Rights." *Time*, January 12, 2022. https://time.com/6128490/kid -of-the-year-kai-shappley-trans-activist/.

Carney, Linton W., Albert M. Hand Jr., William Hardy Patrick III, David S. Rubin, and John Miller Shuey Jr. "The Work of the Louisiana Legislature for the 1977 Regular Session: A Student Symposium." *Louisiana Law Review* 38, no. 1 (1977): 51–175.

Carpenter, Dale. *Flagrant Conduct: The Story of* Lawrence v. Texas. New York: W.W. Norton, 2012.

Carpenter, Dale. "Windsor Products: Equal Protection from Animus." *The Supreme Court Review* 2013 (2014): 183–285.

Case, Mary Anne. "Donorsexuality." In *Entanglements: Queer Legal Studies*, edited by Joseph J. Fischel and Brenda Cossman, 184–209. New York: New York University Press, 2024.

Case, Mary Anne. "Missing Sex Talk in the Supreme Court's Same-Sex Marriage Cases." *University of Missouri-Kansas City Law Review* 84 (2016): 675–692.

Case, Mary Anne. "Of 'This' and 'That' in *Lawrence v. Texas*." *Supreme Court Review* 2003 (2003): 75–142.

Case, Mary Anne. "Pets or Meat." *Chicago Kent Law Review* 80 (2005): 1129–1150.

Centers for Disease Control and Prevention. "HIV Risk Among Persons Who Exchange Sex for Money or Nonmonetary Items." Last reviewed March 16, 2022. www.cdc.gov /hiv/group/sexworkers.html.

Centers for Disease Control and Prevention. "Ways HIV Can Be Transmitted." Last reviewed March 4, 2022. www.cdc.gov/hiv/basics/hiv-transmission/ways-people -get-hiv.html.

Chang, Cindy. "Louisiana Incarcerated: How We Built the World's Prison Capital." *The Times-Picayune*, May 13, 2012.

Chauncey, George. "Privacy Could Only Be Had in Public: Gay Uses of the Street." In *The People, Place, and Space Reader*, edited by Jen Jack Gieseking and William Mangold. New York: Routledge, 2014.

Chauncey, George. "'What Gay Studies Taught the Court': The Historians Amicus Brief in *Lawrence v. Texas*." *GLQ: A Journal of Lesbian and Gay Studies* 10, no. 3 (2004): 509–538.

Chen, David W. "Louisiana Passes Surgical Castration Bill for Child Sex Offenders." *New York Times*, June 4, 2024. www.nytimes.com/2024/06/04/us/louisiana-castration-bill.html.

Chen, Mel Y. *Animacies: Biopolitics, Racial Mattering and Queer Affect*. Durham: Duke University Press, 2012.

Chitty, Christopher. *Sexual Hegemony: Statecraft, Sodomy, and Capital in the Rise of the World System*. Durham: Duke University Press, 2020.

Ciesemier, Kendall. "This Law Criminalizes Black Trans Women." Produced by ACLU. *At Liberty*, March 30, 2023. Podcast, 31:34. www.aclu.org/podcast/fighting-for-the-liberation-of-black-trans-women-in-louisiana.

Claassen, Rutger. "Human Dignity in the Capability Approach." In *The Cambridge Handbook of Human Dignity: Interdisciplinary Perspectives*, edited by Marcus Düwell, Jens Braarvig, Roger Brownsword, and Dietmar Mieth, 240–249. Cambridge: Cambridge University Press, 2014.

Clare, Eli. *Brilliant Imperfection: Grappling with Cure*. Durham: Duke University Press, 2017.

Clare, Eli. *Exile and Pride: Disability, Queerness, and Liberation*. Durham: Duke University Press, 1999.

Clark, Randall B. "Platonic Love in a Colorado Courtroom: Martha Nussbaum, John Finnis, and Plato's *Laws* in *Evans v. Romer*." *Yale Journal of Law & the Humanities* 12 (2000): 1–38.

Cocks, H. G. *Visions of Sodom: Religion, Homoerotic Desire, and the End of the World in England, C. 1550–1850*. Chicago: University of Chicago Press, 2017.

Cohen, Cathy J. *The Boundaries of Blackness: AIDS and the Breakdown of Black Politics*. Chicago: University of Chicago Press, 1999.

Cohen, Cathy J. "Punks, Bulldaggers, and Welfare Queens: The Radical Potential of Queer Politics?" *GLQ: A Journal of Lesbian and Gay Studies* 3, no. 4 (1997): 437–465.

Cohen, Cathy. "The Radical Potential of Queer? Twenty Years Later." *GLQ: A Journal of Lesbian and Gay Studies* 25, no. 1 (2019): 140–144.

Colby, Thomas B., and Peter J. Smith. "The Return of *Lochner*." *Cornell Law Review* 100 (March 2015): 527–602.

Comfort, Megan. *Doing Time Together: Love and Family in the Shadow of Prison*. Chicago: University of Chicago Press, 2008.

Compton, Julie. "American Men Are Still Being Arrested for Sodomy." *Advocate*, May 23, 2016. www.advocate.com/crime/2016/5/23/american-men-are-still-being-arrested-sodomy.

Connor, Brendan M., Andrea J. Ritchie, and Women With A Vision. "'Just a Talking Crime': A Policy Brief in Support of the Repeal of Louisiana's Solicitation of a Crime Against Nature (SCAN) Statute." *Center for Constitutional Rights*, February 2011. https://ccrjustice.org/home/what-we-do/our-cases/crimes-against-nature-solicitation-cans-litigation.

Cooley, Mackenzie. *The Perfection of Nature: Animals, Breeding, and Race in the Renaissance*. Chicago: University of Chicago Press, 2022.

Cooney, Samantha. "PETA Actually Compared Rape Victims to Meat Products." *Time*, November 8, 2016. https://time.com/4557329/peta-ad-sexual-assault-veganism/.

Corker, Mairian, and Tom Shakespeare, eds. *Disability/Postmodernity: Embodying Disability Theory*. London: Continuum, 2002.

Corrigan, Rose. *Up Against a Wall: Rape Reform and the Failure of Success*. New York: New York University Press, 2013.

Cossman, Brenda. *Sexual Citizens: The Legal and Cultural Regulation of Sex and Belonging*. Stanford: Stanford University Press, 2007.

Crary, Alice, and Lori Gruen. *Animal Crisis: A New Critical Theory*. Cambridge: Polity Press, 2022.

Crenshaw, Kimberlé. "Mapping the Margins: Intersectionality, Identity Politics, and Violence against Women of Color." *Stanford Law Journal* 43, no. 6 (1991): 1241–1299.

Criminal Court News. "AC/DC Prostitution." *The Times-Picayune*, March 2, 1978.

Crisp, Elizabeth. "Louisiana Looks to Clearly Outlaw Sexual Abuse of Animals, amid Concerns over Loopholes in Existing Law." *The Advocate*, April 9, 2018. www.thea dvocate.com/baton_rouge/news/politics/legislature/louisiana-looks-to-clearly-out law-sexual-abuse-of-animals-amid-concerns-over-loopholes-in-existing/article_c cc31858-3c47-11e8-a09c-1f3d9daab565.html.

Cruz, Ariane. *The Color of Kink: Black Women, BDSM, and Pornography*. New York: New York University Press, 2016.

Cullather, Nick. *The Hungry World: America's Cold War Battle Against Poverty in Asia*. Cambridge: Harvard University Press, 2010.

Currah, Paisley. *Sex Is as Sex Does: Governing Transgender Identity*. New York: New York University Press, 2022.

Davis, Adrienne D. "Regulating Sex Work: Erotic Assimilationism, Erotic Exceptionalism, and the Challenge of Intimate Labor." *California Law Review* 103, no. 5 (October 2015): 1195–1275.

Davis, Angela Y. *Are Prisons Obsolete?* New York: Seven Stories, 2003.

Davis, Angela Y. *Women, Race and Class*. New York: Random House, 1983.

Davis, Lennard J. *Enforcing Normality: Disability, Deafness, and the Body*. London: Verso, 1995.

Davis, Lennard J. "The Right to Maim: Debility, Capacity, Disability." Review of *The Right to Maim: Debility, Capacity, Disability*, by Jasbir K. Puar. *Critical Inquiry* 45, no. 1 (Autumn 2018): 237–238.

Davis, Oliver, and Tim Dean. *Hatred of Sex*. Lincoln: University of Nebraska Press, 2022.

Dawson, Michael C. "A Black Counterpublic?: Economic Earthquakes, Racial Agenda(s), and Black Politics." *Public Culture* 7, no. 1 (Fall 1994): 195–223.

Dayan, Colin. *The Law Is a White Dog: How Legal Rituals Make and Unmake Persons*. Princeton: Princeton University Press, 2011.

Dean, Tim. *Unlimited Intimacy: Reflections on the Subculture of Barebacking*. Chicago: University of Chicago Press, 2009.

Dekkers, Midas. *Dearest Pet: On Bestiality*. London: Verso, 1994.

Delaney, Samuel R. *Time Square Red, Time Square Blue: 20th Anniversary Edition*. New York: New York University Press, 2019.

Dembroff, Robin. "'I Know What I Am': Reimagining the Meaning of Transgender." *Australian Broadcasting Company*, July 24, 2023. www.abc.net.au/religion/robin -dembroff-reimagining-the-meaning-of-transgender/102640594

Demeri, Derek. "The Model Penal Code & Sex Work Criminalization." *Vermont Law Review* 47 (2022): 156–219.

D'Emilio, John. "Capitalism and Gay Identity." In *The Lesbian and Gay Studies Reader*, edited by Henry Abelove, Michèle Aina Barale, and David M. Halperin, 467–476. New York: Routledge, 1993.

Denno, Deborah W. "Life Before the Modern Sex Offender Statutes." *Northwestern University Law Review* 92 (1998): 1317–1414.

Dewey, Susan, and Tonia P. St. Germain. "Sex Workers/Sex Offenders: Exclusionary Criminal Justice Practices in New Orleans." *Feminist Criminology* 10, no. 3 (July 2015): 211–234.

Diaz, Jaclyn. "New York Repeals 'Walking While Trans' Law." *NPR*, February 3, 2021. www.npr.org/2021/02/03/963513022/new-york-repeals-walking-while-trans-law.

Dibbell, Julian. "A Rape in Cyberspace (or TINYSOCIETY, and How to Make One)." In *My Tiny Life: Crime and Passion in a Virtual World*. New York: Henry Holt, 1999.

Dilts, Andrew. "Incurable Blackness: Criminal Disenfranchisement, Mental Disability, and the White Citizen." *Disability Studies Quarterly* 32, no. 3 (2012): http://dsq-sds.org/article/view/3268/3101.

Dilts, Andrew. "To Kill a Thief: Punishment, Proportionality, and Criminal Subjectivity in Locke's *Second Treatise*." *Political Theory* 40, no. 1 (2012): 58–83.

Donaldson, Sue, and Will Kymlicka. *Zoopolis: A Political Theory of Animal Rights*. Oxford: Oxford University Press, 2011.

Douglas, Mary. "Deciphering a Meal." *Daedalus* 101, no. 1 (Winter 1972): 61–81.

Duggan, Lisa. *The Twilight of Equality: Neoliberalism, Cultural Politics, and the Attack on Democracy*. Boston: Beacon Press, 2003.

Dutkiewicz, Jan. "Socialize Lab Meat." *Jacobin*, August 11, 2019. https://jacobinmag.com/2019/08/lab-meat-socialism-green-new-deal.

Dutkiewicz, Jan, and Gabriel N. Rosenberg. "Man v Food: Is Lab-Grown Meat Really Going to Solve Our Nasty Agriculture Problem?" *The Guardian*, July 29, 2021. www.theguardian.com/news/2021/jul/29/lab-grown-meat-factory-farms-industrial-agriculture-animals.

Dutkiewicz, Jan, and Gabriel N. Rosenberg. "The Meat Industry's Bestiality Problem." *The New Republic*, December 11, 2020. https://newrepublic.com/article/160448/meat-bestiality-artificial-insemination.

Dyson, Michael Eric. *Come Hell or High Water: Hurricane Katrina and the Color of Disaster*. Cambridge, MA: Basic Civitas, 2006.

Eckholm, Erik. "The Same-Sex Couple Who Got a Marriage License in 1971." *New York Times*, May 16, 2015. www.nytimes.com/2015/05/17/us/the-same-sex-couple-who-got-a-marriage-license-in-1971.html.

Edelman, Lee. *Bad Education: Why Queer Theory Teaches Us Nothing*. Durham: Duke University Press, 2022.

Edelman, Lee. *Homographesis: Essays in Gay Literary and Cultural Theory*. New York: Routledge, 1994.

Edelman, Lee. *No Future: Queer Theory and the Death Drive*. Durham: Duke University Press, 2004.

Editorial. "These Two Sex Crimes Should Be Treated the Same." *The Times-Picayune*, May 30, 2011. www.nola.com/opinions/article_c3634d66-ab39-5f2f-a542-e63989f18f64.html.

Edwards, Erica R. "Sex after the Black Normal." *differences: A Journal of Feminist Cultural Studies* 26, no. 1 (2015): 141–167.

Einenkel, Walter. "40% of Louisiana State Senators Voted against Making Bestiality a Crime—Because They're Homophobic." *Daily Kos*, April 12, 2018. www.dailykos.com/stories/2018/4/12/1756467/-40-of-Louisiana-state-senators-voted-against-making-bestiality-a-crime-because-they-re-homophobic.

Elledge, John. "Does the US President Have the Most Dangerous Job in America?" *New Statesman*, October 25, 2016. www.newstatesman.com/world/2016/10/most-dangerous-job-america-us-presidents-have-fatality-rate-roughly-27.

Eng, David L. *The Feeling of Kinship: Queer Liberalism and the Racialization of Intimacy.* Durham: Duke University Press, 2010.

Eng, David L., with Judith Halberstam, and José Esteban Muñoz. "Introduction: What's Queer about Queer Studies Now." *Social Text* 23, no. 3/4 (2005): 1–17.

Engelman, Jan M., Jeremy B. Clift, Esther Herrmann, and Michael Tomasello. "Social Disappointment Explains Chimpanzees' Behaviour in the Inequity Aversion Task." *Proceedings of the Royal Society B* 284 (2017): 1–8.

Ermac, Raffy. "Baton Rouge Police Chief Apologizes for Unconstitutional 'Sodomy' Arrests." *Advocate*, February 19, 2015. www.advocate.com/politics/2015/02/19/baton-rouge-police-chief-apologizes-unconstitutional-sodomy-arrests.

Eskridge, William N., Jr. *Dishonorable Passions: Sodomy Laws in America, 1861–2003.* New York: Viking, 2008.

Eskridge, William N., Jr. *Gaylaw: Challenging the Apartheid of the Closet.* Cambridge, MA: Harvard University Press, 1999.

Eskridge, William N., Jr., and Christopher R. Riano. "*Bostock*: A Statutory Super-Precedent for Sex and Gender Minorities." *American Constitution Society*, July 1, 2020. www.acslaw.org/expertforum/bostock-a-statutory-super-precedent-for-sex-and-gender-minorities/.

Evans, Jennifer V. *The Queer Art of History: Queer Kinship after Fascism.* Durham: Duke University Press, 2023.

Eyer, Katie R. "Animus Trouble." *Stetson Law Review* 48, no. 2 (2019): 215–234.

Eyer, Katie R. "The Canon of Rational Basis Review." *Notre Dame Law Review* 93, no. 3 (2018): 1317–1370.

Faupel, Susan. "Etiology of Adult Sexual Offending." *Sex Offender Management Assessment and Planning Initiative, Office of Justice Programs, U.S. Department of Justice*, July 2015. https://smart.ojp.gov/SOMAPI-brief-etiology.

Fausset, Richard. "A Black Group Says Mardi Gras Blackface Honors Tradition. Others Call It 'Disgusting.'" *New York Times*, February 14, 2019. www.nytimes.com/2019/02/14/us/zulu-parade-new-orleans.html.

Feinberg, Joel. *Offense to Others: The Moral Limits of the Criminal Law, Vol. 2.* New York: Oxford University Press, 1988.

Ferguson, Roderick A. *Aberrations in Black: Toward a Queer of Color Critique.* Minneapolis: University of Minnesota Press, 2004.

Fields, Jessica. *Risky Lessons: Sex Education and Social Inequality.* New Brunswick: Rutgers University Press, 2008.

Fineman, Martha Albertson. "The Vulnerable Subject: Anchoring Equality in the Human Condition." *Yale Journal of Law and Feminism* 20, no. 1 (2008): 1–23.

Finkelhor, David, Kerryann Walsh, Lisa Jones, Kimberly Mitchell, and Anne Collier. "Youth Internet Safety Education: Aligning Programs with the Evidence Base." *Trauma, Violence, & Abuse* 22, no. 5 (2020): 1233–1247.

Fischel, Joseph J. "Against Nature, against Consent: A Sexual Politics of Debility." *differences: A Journal of Feminist Cultural Studies* 24, no. 1 (2013): 55–103.

Fischel, Joseph J. "In the Fight for Policing Reform, LGBT Is a Threadbare Alliance." *Boston Review*, June 17, 2020.

Fischel, Joseph J. "Keep Pride Nude." *Boston Review*, June 23, 2021. https://bostonreview .net/articles/keep-pride-nude/.

Fischel, Joseph J. "Pornography's Contradictions." *Boston Review*, September 21, 2021. www.bostonreview.net/articles/pornographys-contradictions.

Fischel, Joseph J. *Screw Consent: A Better Politics of Sexual Justice.* Berkeley: University of California Press, 2019.

Fischel, Joseph J. *Sex and Harm in the Age of Consent.* Minneapolis: University of Minnesota Press, 2016.

Fischel, Joseph J. "Sexing the Child." *GLQ: A Journal of Lesbian and Gay Studies* 27, no. 4 (2021): 658–661.

Fischel, Joseph J. "Social Justice for Gender and Sexual Minorities: A Discussion with Paisley Currah and Aeyal Gross." *Critical Analysis of Law* 6, no. 1 (2019): 82–101.

Fischel, Joseph J. "Sodomy's Penumbra." *Journal of Homosexuality* 64, no. 14 (2017): 2030–2056.

Fischel, Joseph J. "Transcendent Homosexuals and Dangerous Sex Offenders: Sexual Harm and Freedom in the Judicial Imaginary." *Duke Journal of Gender Law & Policy* 17, no. 2 (2010): 277–312.

Fischel, Joseph J., and Claire McKinney. "Capability without Dignity?" *Contemporary Political Theory* 19, no. 3 (2020): 404–429.

Foer, Jonathan Safran. "The End of Meat Is Here." *New York Times*, May 21, 2020. www .nytimes.com/2020/05/21/opinion/coronavirus-meat-vegetarianism.html.

Forman, James, Jr. "Racial Critiques of Mass Incarceration: Beyond the New Jim Crow." *New York University Law Review* 87, no. 1 (2012): 21–69

Forrestal, Hayley. "The Sex Offender Registry Doesn't Work." *Chicago Alliance Against Sexual Exploitation*, October 9, 2019. www.caase.org/the-sex-offender-registry -doesnt-work/.

Foucault, Michel. "The Abnormals." In *Ethics: Subjectivity and Truth (The Essential Works of Michel Foucault, 1954–1984), Vol. 1*, edited by Paul Rabinow, 51–58. New York: New Press, 1994.

Foucault, Michel. *Discipline and Punish: The Birth of the Prison.* Translated by Alan Sheridan. New York: Vintage, 1995.

Foucault, Michel. *The History of Sexuality, Volume 1: An Introduction.* Translated by Robert Hurley. New York: Vintage, [1978] 1990.

Foucault, Michel. "What Is Called 'Punishing?'" In *Power (The Essential Works of Michel Foucault, 1954–1984, Vol. 3)*, edited by James D. Faubion, 382–393. New York: New Press, 2001.

Foucault, Michel, Guy Hocquenghem, and Jean Danet. "Sexual Morality and the Law." In *Politics, Philosophy, Culture: Interviews and Other Writings, 1977–1984*, edited by Lawrence D. Kritzman, 271–285. New York: Routledge, 1988.

Francione, Gary L. *Why Veganism Matters: The Moral Value of Animals.* New York: Columbia University Press, 2020.

Frank, David John, Steven A. Boucher, and Bayliss Camp. "The Reform of Sodomy Laws from a World Society Perspective." In *Queer Mobilizations: LGBT Activists Confront the Law*, edited by Scott Barclay, Mary Bernstein, and Anna-Maria Marshall, 123–141. New York: New York University Press, 2009.

Franke, Katherine M. "The Domesticated Liberty of *Lawrence v. Texas.*" *Columbia Law Review* 104, no. 5 (2004): 1399–1426.

Franke, Katherine M. *Wedlocked: The Perils of Marriage Equality.* New York: New York University Press, 2015.

Freedman, Estelle B. *Redefining Rape: Sexual Violence in the Era of Suffrage and Segregation.* Cambridge, MA: Harvard University Press, 2015.

Friendman, Matt. "Bestiality Now Illegal in N.J." *Politico*, November 9, 2015. www.politico.com/states/new-jersey/story/2015/11/bestiality-now-illegal-in-nj-094941.

Frison, Christine. *Redesigning the Global Seed Commons: Law and Policy for Agrobiodiversity and Food Security.* London: Routledge, 2018.

Fussell, Elizabeth. "Constructing New Orleans, Constructing Race: A Population History of New Orleans." *Journal of American History* 94, no. 3 (2007): 846–855.

Gagliano, Kate. "Bill to Toughen Louisiana Anti-bestiality Law Advances over Some Objections." *New Orleans Advocate*, April 25, 2018. www.theadvocate.com/baton_rouge/news/politics/legislature/article_e3b67b0c-48e2-11e8-85fb-6b108a0373ca.html.

Gash, Alison. "The Erosion of *Roe v. Wade* and Abortion Access Didn't Begin in Texas or Mississippi—It Started in Pennsylvania in 1992." *The Conversation*, October 28, 2021. http://theconversation.com/amp/the-erosion-of-roe-v-wade-and-abortion-access-didnt-begin-in-texas-or-mississippi-it-started-in-pennsylvania-in-1992-169925.

Gattuso, Reina. "Why Should Feminists Be against the Sex Offender Registry?" *Feministing*, December 21, 2018. https://feministing.com/2018/12/21/why-should-feminists-be-against-the-sex-offender-registry/.

Geidner, Chris. "DOJ's New Scrutiny." *Metro Weekly*, March 23, 2011. www.metroweekly.com/2011/03/dojs-new-scrutiny/.

Gilden, Andrew. "Cyberbullying and the Innocence Narrative." *Harvard Civil Rights-Civil Liberties Law Review* 48 (2013): 357–407

Gilden, Andrew. "Punishing Sexual Fantasy." *William & Mary Law Review* 58, no. 2 (2016): 419–492.

Gill-Peterson, Julian. *Histories of the Transgender Child.* Minneapolis: University of Minnesota Press, 2018.

Goldberg, Jonathan. "Sodomy in the New World: Anthropologies Old and New." *Social Text* 29 (1991): 46–56.

Goldman, Emma. "The Traffic in Women." In *Anarchism and Other Essays*, 183–200. New York: Mother Earth Publishing Association, 1911.

Goluboff, Risa Lauren. "'Let Economic Equality Take Care of Itself': The NAACP, Labor Litigation, and the Making of Civil Rights in the 1940s." *UCLA Law Review* 52, no. 5 (2005): 1393–1486.

Good Food Institute. www.gfi.org/.

Goodman, J. David. "How Medical Care for Transgender Youth Became 'Child Abuse' in Texas." *New York Times*, March 11, 2022. www.nytimes.com/2022/03/11/us/texas-transgender-youth-medical-care-abuse.html.

Goodmark, Leigh. *Decriminalizing Domestic Violence: A Balanced Policy Approach to Intimate Partner Violence.* Oakland: University of California Press, 2018.

Gordon, Linda. "The Politics of Child Sexual Abuse: Notes from American History." *Feminist Review* 28 (1988): 56–64.

Grandin, Temple. *Temple Grandin's Guide to Working with Farm Animals: Safe, Humane Livestock Handling Practices for the Small Farm.* North Adams, MA: Storey, 2017.

Grant, Melissa Gira. *Playing the Whore.* London: Verso Books, 2014.

Green, Stuart P. *Criminalizing Sex: A Unified Liberal Theory*. New York: Oxford University Press, 2020.

Grossman, Joanna. "The Consequence of *Lawrence v. Texas*: Justice Scalia Is Right that Same Sex Marriage Bans Are at Risk, but Wrong that a Host of Other Laws Are Vulnerable." *FindLaw*, July 8, 2003. https://supreme.findlaw.com/legal-commentary /the-consequences-of.html.

Gruber, Aya. "The Critique of Carceral Feminism." *Yale Journal of Law and Feminism* 34, no. 2 (2023): 55–64.

Gruen, Lori. *Entangled Empathy: An Alternative Ethic for Our Relationships with Animals*. New York: Lantern Books, 2015.

Haidt, Jonathan. *The Righteous Mind: Why Good People Are Divided by Politics and Religion*. New York: Vintage Books, 2012.

Haley, Sarah. *No Mercy Here: Gender, Punishment, and the Making of Jim Crow Modernity*. Chapel Hill: University of North Carolina Press, 2016.

Halley, Janet. "Reasoning about Sodomy: Act and Identity in and after *Bowers v. Hardwick*." *Virginia Law Review* 79, no. 7 (1993): 1721–1780.

Halley, Janet. *Split Decisions: How and Why to Take a Break from Feminism*. Princeton: Princeton University Press, 2006.

Halley, Janet, and Andrew Parker, eds. *After Sex? On Writing Since Queer Theory*. Durham: Duke University Press, 2011.

Halperin, David M. "Is There a History of Sexuality?" *History and Theory* 28, no. 3 (1989): 257–274.

Halperin, David M. "The War on Sex." In *The War on Sex*, edited by David M. Halperin and Trevor Hoppe, 1–64. Durham: Duke University Press, 2017.

Halperin, David M., and Trevor Hoppe, eds. *The War on Sex*. Durham: Duke University Press, 2017.

Harcourt, Bernard E. *The Illusion of Free Markets: Punishment and the Myth of Natural Order*. Cambridge, MA: Harvard University Press, 2011.

Harkins, Gillian. *Virtual Pedophilia: Sex Offender Profiling and U.S. Security Culture*. Durham: Duke University Press, 2020.

Harris, Angela P. "Heteropatriarchy Kills: Challenging Gender Violence in a Prison Nation." *Washington University Journal of Law & Policy* 37, no. 1 (2011): 13–65.

Harris, Anne M., and Stacy Holman Jones. *The Queer Life of Things: Performance, Affect, and the More-Than-Human*. Lanham, MD: Lexington Books, 2019.

Hartman, Saidiya. *Wayward Lives, Beautiful Experiments: Intimate Histories of Social Upheaval*. New York: W.W. Norton & Company, 2019.

Herman, Jody L., Andrew R. Flores, and Kathryn K. O'Neill. "How Many Adults and Youth Identify as Transgender in the United States?" *Williams Institute*, June 2020. https://williamsinstitute.law.ucla.edu/publications/trans-adults-united-states/.

Herz, Zachary. "The Epistemology of the Courthouse: Classical Antiquity in American LGBT-Rights Litigation." In *Enticements: Queer Legal Studies*, edited by Joseph J. Fischel and Brenda Cossman, 29–58. New York: New York University Press, 2024.

Hill, Candace N. "Selling Sex: The Costs of Criminalization." *Quinnipiac Health Law* 21 (2018): 131–157.

Hill, Marc Lamont. "'Thank You, Black Twitter'; State Violence, Digital Counterpublics and Pedagogies of Resistance." *Urban Education* 53, no. 2 (2018): 286–302.

Holston-Zannell, LaLa B. "Sex Work Is Real Work, and It's Time to Treat It That Way." *ACLU*, June 10, 2020. www.aclu.org/news/lgbtq-rights/sex-work-is-real-work-and-its -time-to-treat-it-that-way.

Honig, Bonnie. *Political Theory and the Displacement of Politics*. Ithaca: Cornell University Press, 1993.

Honig, Bonnie. "Rawls on Politics and Punishment." *Political Research Quarterly* 46, no. 1 (March 1993): 99–125.

Hoppe, Trevor. "Punishing Sex: Sex Offenders and the Missing Punitive Turn in Sexuality Studies." *Law and Social Inquiry* 41, no. 3 (Summer 2016): 573–594.

Howell, Philip. "A Private Contagious Disease Act: Prostitution and Public Space in Victorian Cambridge." *Journal of Historical Geography* 26, no. 3 (July 2000): 376–402.

Huffer, Lynne. *Are the Lips a Grave? A Queer Feminist on the Ethics of Sex*. New York: Columbia University Press, 2013.

Human Rights Watch. "No Easy Answers: Sex Offender Laws in the US." *Human Rights Watch* 19, no. 4(G) (2007): 1–141. www.hrw.org/report/2007/09/11/no-easy-answers /sex-offender-laws-us.

Human Rights Watch. "This Alien Legacy: The Origins of 'Sodomy' Laws in British Colonialism," *Human Rights Watch*, December 17, 2008. www.hrw.org/report/2008 /12/17/alien-legacy/origins-sodomy-laws-british-colonialism.

Huneke, Samuel Clowes. *A Queer Theory of the State*. New York: Columbia University Press, 2023.

Hunter, Nan D. "Living with *Lawrence*." *Minnesota Law Review* 88 (2004): 1103–1139.

INCITE! "Analysis." https://incite-national.org/analysis/.

Izaguirre, Anthony. "Christian Conservatives Fight Bid to Toughen Louisiana Anti-bestiality Law." *Talking Points Memo*, April 25, 2018. https://talkingpointsmemo .com/news/christian-conservatives-fight-toughening-louisiana-anti-bestiality-law.

Izaguirre, Anthony. "Why Bid to Toughen Louisiana Anti-bestiality Law Is Drawing Unexpected Pushback." *The Times-Picayune*, April 24, 2018. www.nola.com/article _273f2287-6382-5d80-b576-d0b709618ea1.html.

Jackson, Zakiyyah Iman. *Becoming Human: Matter and Meaning in an Antiblack World*. New York: New York University Press, 2020.

James, Allison. "To Be (Come) or Not to Be (Come): Understanding Children's Citizenship." *The Annals of the American Academy of Political and Social Science* 633 (2011): 167–179.

Janus, Eric S. *Failure to Protect: America's Sexual Predator Laws and the Rise of the Preventative State*. Ithaca: Cornell University Press, 2006.

Jindal, Bobby. "Governor Signs Chemical Castration Bill, Authorizing the Castration of Sex Offenders in Louisiana." *Office of the Governor Bobby Jindal*, June 25, 2008. https://votesmart.org/public-statement/353973/governor-signs-chemical-castration -bill-authorizing-the-castration-of-sex-offenders-in-louisiana.

Johnson, Cedric, ed. *The Neoliberal Deluge: Hurricane Katrina, Late Capitalism, and the Remaking of New Orleans*. Minneapolis: University of Minnesota Press, 2011.

Jones, Angela. *Camming: Money, Power, and Pleasure in the Sex Work Industry*. New York: New York University Press, 2020.

Jones, Angela, ed. *A Critical Inquiry into Queer Utopias*. New York: Palgrave MacMillan, 2013.

Jones, Jeffrey S., Barbara N. Wynn, Boyd Kroeze, Chris Dunnuck, and Linda Rossman. "Comparisons of Sexual Assaults by Strangers Versus Known Assailants in a Community-Based Population." *American Journal of Emergency Medicine* 22, no. 6 (2004): 454–459.

Jong, Erica. *Fear of Flying*. New York: New American Library, 1973.

Jordan, Mark D. *The Invention of Sodomy in Christian Theology*. Chicago: University of Chicago Press, 1998.

Kant, Immanuel. *Lectures on Ethics*. Translated by Louis Infield. London: Methuen, 1930.

Kant, Immanuel. *Metaphysics of Morals*. Edited by Mary Gregor. Cambridge: Cambridge University Press, 1996.

Khan, Ummni. "Chester Brown and the Queerness of Johns." *Critical Analysis of Law* 6, no. 1 (2019): 39–62.

Kincaid, James R. *Erotic Innocence: The Culture of Child Molesting*. Durham: Duke University Press, 1998.

Kincaid, James R. "Producing Erotic Children." In *Curiouser: On the Queerness of Children*, edited by Steven Bruhm and Natasha Hurley, 3–16. Minneapolis: University of Minnesota Press, 2004.

King, Barbara J. *How Animals Grieve*. Chicago: University of Chicago Press, 2013.

Kloppenburg, Jack. *First the Seed: The Political Economy of Plant Biotechnology, 1492–2000*. Madison: University of Wisconsin Press, 1988.

Kong, Travis S. K. *Chinese Male Homosexualities: Memba, Tongzhi, and Golden Boy*. Milton Park: Routledge, 2011.

Konnikova, Maria. "How We Learn Fairness." *New Yorker*, January 7, 2016. www.newyorker.com/science/maria-konnikova/how-we-learn-fairness.

Kramer, Sina. *Excluded Within: The (Un)Intelligibility of Radical Political Actors*. New York: New York University Press, 2017.

Kulick, Don. *Travesti: Sex, Gender, and Culture among Brazilian Transgendered Prostitutes*. Chicago: University of Chicago Press, 1998.

Kulick, Don, and Jens Rydström. *Loneliness and Its Opposite: Sex, Disability, and the Ethics of Engagement*. Durham: Duke University Press, 2015.

Kunzel, Regina. *Criminal Intimacy: Prison and the Uneven History of Modern American Sexuality*. Chicago: University of Chicago Press, 2008.

Kunzel, Regina. "The Power of Queer History." *American Historical Review* 123, no. 5 (2018): 1560–1582.

Kushner, Rachel. "Is Prison Necessary? Ruth Wilson Gilmore Might Change Your Mind." *New York Times Magazine*, April 17, 2019. www.nytimes.com/2019/04/17/magazine/prison-abolition-ruth-wilson-gilmore.html.

LaFleur, Greta. *The Natural History of Sexuality in Early America*. Baltimore: Johns Hopkins University Press, 2018.

Lancaster, Roger N. *Sex Panic and the Punitive State*. Berkeley: University of California Press, 2011.

Lang, Nico. "Louisiana Is Using Its Anti-gay Sodomy Laws to Harass Sex Workers." *Out Magazine*, September 5, 2019. www.out.com/news/2019/9/05/louisiana-using-its-anti-gay-sodomy-laws-harass-sex-workers.

Law, Sylvia A. "Commercial Sex: Beyond Decriminalization." *Southern California Law Review* 73, no. 3 (2000): 523–610.

Leap, William L. *Public Sex /Gay Space*. New York: Columbia University Press, 1999.

Lee, Lorelei. "Cash/Consent." *n + 1* 35 (Fall 2019). www.nplusonemag.com/issue35/essays/cashconsent.

Leonhardt, David, and Claire Cain Miller. "The Metro Areas with the Largest, and Smallest, Gay Populations." *New York Times*, March 20, 2015. www.nytimes.com/2015/03/21/upshot/the-metro-areas-with-the-largest-and-smallest-gay-population.html.

Levenson, Jill S., and Leo P. Cotter. "The Effect of Megan's Law on Sex Offender Reintegration." *Journal of Contemporary Criminal Justice* 21, no. 1 (2005): 49–66.

Levin, Dan. "Young Voters Keep Moving to the Left of Social Issues, Republicans Included." *New York Times*, January 23, 2019. www.nytimes.com/2019/01/23/us/gop-liberal-america-millennials.html.

Levin, Sam. "How Trans Children Became a 'Political Football' for the Republican Party." *The Guardian*, March 23, 2021. www.theguardian.com/us-news/2021/mar/23/anti-trans-bills-us-transgender-youth-sports.

Levine, Judith, and Erica R. Meiners. *The Feminist and the Sex Offender: Confronting Sexual Harm, Ending State Violence*. London: Verso, 2020.

Lin, Jeremy Atherton. *Gay Bar: Why We Went Out*. New York: Little, Brown and Company, 2021.

Lipsitz, George. "Mardi-Gras Indians: Carnival and Counter-Narrative in Black New Orleans." *Culture Critique* 10 (1988): 99–121.

Livingston, Jennie, dir. *Paris Is Burning*. Academy Entertainment, 1990.

Livingston, Julie. *Debility and the Moral Imagination in Botswana*. Bloomington: Indiana University Press, 2005.

Lochrie, Karma. "Presumptive Sodomy and its Exclusions." *Textual Practice* 13, no. 2 (1999): 295–310.

Long, Crispin. "Fighting the Louisiana Law that Makes Sex Work a 'Crime against Nature.'" *New Yorker*, February 8, 2023. www.newyorker.com/culture/the-new-yorker-documentary/fighting-the-louisiana-law-that-makes-sex-work-a-crime-against-nature.

Lorde, Audre. "Jessehelms." *Callalloo* 14, no. 1 (Winter 1991): 60–61.

Louisiana State Police. "Offenses." *State Sex Offender and Child Predator Registry*. www.lsp.org/community-outreach/sex-offender-registry/offenses/.

Louisiana State Police. "Program History." *State Sex Offender and Child Predator Registry*. www.lsp.org/community-outreach/sex-offender-registry/program-history/.

Louisiana State Police. "Program Purpose." *State Sex Offender and Child Predator Registry*. www.lsp.org/community-outreach/sex-offender-registry/program-purpose/.

"Louisiana Strengthens Law against the Sexual Abuse of Animals." *The Humane Society of the United States*, May 31, 2018. www.humanesociety.org/news/louisiana-strengthens-law-against-sexual-abuse-animals.

"Louisiana to Remove Hundreds of Individuals Unconstitutionally Placed on Sex Offender Registry." *Center for Constitutional Rights*, June 12, 2013. https://ccrjustice.org/home/press-center/press-releases/louisiana-remove-hundreds-individuals-unconstitutionally-placed-sex.

Luo, Nina. "Decriminalizing Survival: Policy Platform and Polling on the Decriminalization of Sex Work." *Data for Progress*, January 30, 2020. www.dataforprogress.org/memos/decriminalizing-sex-work.

MacKinnon, Catharine A. "Feminism, Marxism, Method, and the State: Toward Feminist Jurisprudence." *Signs* 8, no. 4 (Summer 1983): 635–658.

MacKinnon, Catharine A. "Prostitution and Civil Rights." *Michigan Journal of Gender & Law* 1, no. 1 (1993): 13–31.

MacKinnon, Catharine A. "The Road Not Taken: Sex Equality in *Lawrence v. Texas*." *Ohio State Law Journal* 65, no. 5 (2004): 1081–1095.

Mann, Kate. *Down Girl: The Logic of Misogyny*. Oxford: Oxford University Press, 2018.

Marcus, Sharon. "Fighting Bodies, Fighting Words: A Theory and Politics of Rape Prevention." In *Feminists Theorize the Political*, edited by Judith Butler and Joan Scott, 385–403. New York: Routledge, 1992.

Marcuse, Herbert. *Eros and Civilization: A Philosophical Inquiry into Freud*. Boston: Beacon Press, 1966.

Marshall, Garry, dir. *Pretty Woman*. Touchstone Pictures, 1990.

Masood, Salman, and Mike Ives. "Rapes of Woman and 5-Year-Old Fuel Outrage in Pakistan." *New York Times*, September 11, 2020. www.nytimes.com/2020/09/11 /world/asia/pakistan-rape-5-year-old-lahore-karachi.html.

Masson, Jeffrey. *The Secret World of Farm Animals*. London: Vintage, 2005.

Mavhunga, Clapperton Chakanetsa. "Vermin Beings: On Pestiferous Animals and Human Game." *Social Text* 29, no. 1 (2011): 151–176.

McBride, Keally. *Punishment and Political Order*. Ann Arbor: University of Michigan Press, 2007.

McCluskey, Martha T. "How Queer Theory Makes Neoliberalism Sexy." In *Feminist and Queer Legal Theory: Intimate Encounters, Uncomfortable Conversations*, edited by Martha Albertson Fineman, Jack E. Jackson, and Adam P. Romero, 115–134. Surrey: Ashgate, 2009.

McDonough, Katie. "Louisiana Police Use Invalid Anti-sodomy Law to Arrest Gay Men for Agreeing to Consensual Sex." *Salon*, July 28, 2013.

McGaughy, Lauren. "Committee Votes to Remove Anti-sodomy Statute from Louisiana Law." *The Times-Picayune*, April 9, 2014.

McGough, Michael. "Gay Marriage: Scalia Knew This Day Would Come." *Los Angeles Times*, December 12, 2012. www.latimes.com/opinion/la-xpm-2012-dec-07-la-ol -court-gaymarriage-scalia--20121207-story.html.

McKean, Benjamin L. "What Makes a Utopia Inconvenient? On the Advantages and Disadvantages of a Realist Orientation to Politics." *American Political Science Review* 110, no. 4 (2016): 876–888.

McKittrick, Katherine, ed. *Sylvia Wynter: On Being Human as Praxis*. Durham: Duke University Press, 2015.

McRuer, Robert. *Crip Times: Disability, Globalization, and Resistance*. New York: New York University Press, 2018.

McRuer, Robert, and Anna Mollow, eds. *Sex and Disability*. Durham: Duke University Press, 2012.

McTighe, Laura, and Deon Haywood. "'There Is NO Justice in Louisiana': Crimes against Nature and the Spirit of Black Feminist Resistance." *Souls: A Critical Journal of Black Politics, Culture, and Society* 19, no. 3 (2017): 261–285.

Meadow, Tey, and Kristina R. Olson. "Laws Vilifying Transgender Children and Their Families Are Abusive." *Scientific American*, March 29, 2022. www.scientificamerican .com/article/laws-vilifying-transgender-children-and-their-families-are-abusive/.

Meiners, Erica R. "Awful Acts and the Trouble with Normal." In *Captive Genders: Trans Embodiment and the Prison Industrial Complex*, edited by Stanley, Eric A. Stanley, and Nat Smith, 113–122. Oakland, CA: AK Press, 2011.

Menon, Madhavi. "Universalism and Partition: A Queer Theory." *differences: A Journal of Feminist Cultural Studies* 26, no. 1 (2015): 117–140.

Merriam, Eric. "Fire, Aim, Ready! Militarizing Animus: 'Unit Cohesion' and the Transgender Ban." *Dickinson Law Review* 123, no. 1 (2018): 57–112.

Meyerowitz, Joanne. *How Sex Changed: A History of Transsexuality in the United States*. Cambridge, MA: Harvard University Press, 2002.

Miller, Perry. *The New England Mind: The Seventeenth Century (Volume I)*. Cambridge, MA: Harvard University Press, [1939] 1982.

Miller-Young, Mireille. *A Taste for Brown Sugar: Black Women in Pornography.* Durham: Duke University Press, 2014.

Mills, Charles W. "Alternative Epistemologies." *Social Theory and Practice* 14, no. 3 (1988): 237–263.

Mills, Charles W. *The Racial Contract.* Ithaca: Cornell University Press, 1997.

Mills, Charles W. "The Racial Contract Revisited: Still Unbroken after All These Years." *Politics, Groups and Identities* 3, no. 3 (2015): 541–557.

Minnesota Department of Health. "About the Sexual Violence Prevention Program." Accessed June 21, 2023. www.health.state.mn.us/communities/svp/index.html

Mitchell, Gregory. *Tourist Attractions: Performing Race and Masculinity in Brazil's Sexual Economy.* Chicago: University of Chicago Press, 2015.

Mitchell, Reid. *All on a Mardi Gras Day: Episodes in the History of New Orleans Carnival.* Cambridge, MA: Harvard University Press, 1999.

Mogul, Joey L., Andrea Ritchie, and Kay Whitlock. *Queer (In)Justice: The Criminalization of LGBT People in the United States.* Boston: Beacon Press, 2011.

Mollow, Anna. "Is Sex Disability? Queer Theory and the Disability Drive." In *Sex and Disability,* edited by Robert McRuer and Anna Mollow, 285–312. Durham: Duke University Press, 2012.

Moore, Jason. *Capitalism in the Web of Life: Ecology and the Accumulation of Capital.* New York: Verso, 2015.

Morrisey, Joseph F. "*Lochner, Lawrence,* and Liberty." *Georgia State University Law Review* 27, no. 3 (2011): 609–672.

Morrison, Sara. "The Danger of Making the Internet Safe for Kids." *Vox,* March 14, 2022. www.vox.com/recode/2022/3/14/22971618/earn-it-sesta-fosta-children-safety-internet-laws.

Mottola, Greg, dir. *Superbad.* Columbia Pictures, 2007.

"The Movement." *CANS Can't Stand.* www.canscantstandfilm.com/#the-movement.

Muñoz, José Esteban. *Cruising Utopia, Tenth Anniversary Edition: The Then and There of Queer Futurity.* New York: New York University Press, 2019.

Muñoz, José Esteban. *Disidentifications: Queers of Color and the Performance of Politics.* Minneapolis: University of Minnesota Press, 2009.

Musser, Amber Jamilla. *Sensual Excess: Queer Femininity and Brown Jouissance.* New York: New York University Press, 2018.

Mustian, Jim. "Gay Men Arrested in Louisiana under Invalid Sodomy Law." *Advocate,* July 29, 2013. http://sdgln.com/news/2013/07/29/gay-men-arrested-louisiana-via-invalid-sodomy-law.

Nadel, Matt, and Joseph Fischel. "Crimes against Nature by Solicitation." *ArcGIS,* October 5, 2021. https://storymaps.arcgis.com/stories/cf4facb7fb5d4cbd9e8e76a9c3f40c56.

Nadel, Matt, and Megan Plotka, dirs. *CANS Can't Stand.* Lynwood Films, 2022.

Nark, Jason. "Animal-Cruelty Charges Dropped against Burlington County Cop." *Philadelphia Inquirer,* September 24, 2009. www.inquirer.com/philly/news/year-in-review/20090924_Animal-cruelty_charges_dropped_against_Burlington_County_cop.html.

Nash, Jennifer C. "Black Anality." *GLQ: A Journal of Lesbian and Gay Studies* 20, no. 4 (2014): 439–460.

Nash, Jennifer C. *The Black Body in Ecstasy: Reading Race, Reading Pornography.* Durham: Duke University Press, 2014.

Nash, Jennifer C. "On the Beginning of the World: Dominance Feminism, Afropessimism, and the Meanings of Gender." *Feminist Theory* 23, no. 4 (2021): 556–574.

New Harvest. www.new-harvest.org/.

New Orleans Public Library. "Sex Offender Policy." Last modified April 2, 2019. www .nolalibrary.org/page/134/library-policies/203/sex-offender-policy.

Nietzsche, Friedrich. *On the Genealogy of Morals.* Translated by Walter Kauffmann. New York: Vintage Books 1969.

Nietzsche, Friedrich. *Thus Spoke Zarathustra.* Edited by Adrian Del Caro and Robert Pippin. Cambridge: Cambridge University Press, 2006.

Nourse, V. F., and Sarah A. Maguire. "The Lost History of Governance and Equal Protection." *Duke Law Journal* 58, no. 6 (2009): 955–1012.

Novotney, Amy. "'The Young People Feel It': A Look at the Mental Health Impact of Antitrans Legislation." *American Psychological Association*, June 29, 2023. www.apa .org/topics/lgbtq/mental-health-anti-transgender-legislation.

Nowotny, Kathryn M., Marisa Omori, Melanie McKenna, and Joshua Kleinman. "Incarceration Rates and Incidence of Sexually Transmitted Infections in US Counties, 2011–2016." *American Journal of Public Health* 110(Suppl 1) (2020): S130–S136.

Nussbaum, Martha C. *Frontiers of Justice: Disability, Nationality, Species Membership.* Cambridge, MA: Harvard University Press, 2007.

Nussbaum, Martha C. "Is Privacy Bad for Women?" *Boston Review*, April 1, 2000. www .bostonreview.net/articles/martha-c-nussbaum-privacy-bad-women/.

Nussbaum, Martha C. *Justice for Animals: Our Collective Responsibility.* New York: Simon & Schuster, 2022.

Nussbaum, Martha C. "Protecting Intimacy: Sex Clubs, Public Sex, Risky Choices." In *From Disgust to Humanity: Sexual Orientation and Constitutional Law*, 167–203. Oxford: Oxford University Press, 2010.

Nussbaum, Martha C. "'Whether from Reason or Prejudice': Taking Money for Bodily Services." *Journal of Legal Studies* 27, no. S2 (June 1998): 693–723.

Nussbaum, Martha C., and Jeremy Bendik-Keymer. "On Justice for Animals." *Boston Review*, February 8, 2023. www.bostonreview.net/articles/on-justice-for-animals/.

O'Donoghue, Julia. "Louisiana House Votes 27–67 to Keep Unconstitutional Anti-sodomy Law on the Books." *The Times-Picayune*, April 15, 2014.

Oliver, Michael. *The Politics of Disablement.* London: Macmillan, 1990.

On Air Money Melissa Francis. "New Law Requires Sex Offenders to List Their Status on Facebook." *Fox Business*, July 5, 2012. Video, 3:13. http://video.foxbusiness.com /v/1721708504001/new-law-requires-sexoffenders-to-list-their-status-on-facebook/.

Osmundson, Joseph. *Virology: Essays for the Living, the Dead, and the Small Things in Between.* New York: W.W. Norton & Company, 2022.

Owens, Emily A. *Consent in the Presence of Force: Sexual Violence and Black Women's Survival in Antebellum New Orleans.* Chapel Hill: University of North Carolina Press, 2023.

Pacelle, Wayne. "Deliver Us from the Evils of Bestiality." *A Humane World*, May 15, 2017. https://blog.humanesociety.org/2017/05/deliver-us-evils-bestiality.html.

Painter, George. "The Sensibilities of Our Forefathers: The History of Sodomy Laws in the United States." *Gay & Lesbian Archives of the Pacific Northwest*. www.glapn.org /sodomylaws/sensibilities/introduction.html.

Palmer, Clare, Sandra Corr, and Peter Sandøe. "Inconvenient Desires: Should We Routinely Neuter Companion Animals?" *Anthrozoös* 25, Supplement 1 (2012): S153–S172.

Parreñas, Juno Salazar. *Decolonizing Extinction: The Work of Care in Orangutan Rehabilitation*. Durham: Duke University Press, 2018.

Pateman, Carole. *The Sexual Contract*. Cambridge: Polity, 1988.

Pateman, Carole, and Charles W. Mills. *Contract and Domination*. Cambridge: Polity, 2007.

Perea, Juan F. "The Echoes of Slavery: Recognizing the Racist Origins of the Agricultural and Domestic Worker Exclusion from the National Labor Relations Act." *Ohio State Law Journal* 72, no. 1 (2011): 95–138.

Piazza, Tom. *Why New Orleans Matters*. New York: HarperCollins Publishers, 2005.

Picket, Malik, Emily Satifka, and Riya Saha Shah with Vic Wiener. "Labeled for Life: A Review of Youth Sex Offender Registration Laws." *Juvenile Law Center*, August 13, 2020. https://jlc.org/resources/labeled-life-review-youth-sex-offender-registration-laws.

Platt, Lucy, Pippa Grenfell, Rebecca Meiksin, Jocelyn Elmes, Susan G. Sherman, Teela Sanders, Peninah Mwangi, and Anna-Louise Crago. "Associations Between Sex Work Laws and Sex Workers' Health: A Systematic Review and Meta-analysis of Quantitative and Qualitative Studies." *PLOS Medicine* 15, no. 12 (2018): 1–54.

Poche, Kaylee. "Bill to Decriminalize Sex Work in Louisiana Fails to Make it Out of Committee." *Gambit*, May 4, 2021. www.nola.com/gambit/news/the_latest/bill-to-decriminalize-sex-work-in-louisiana-fails-to-make-it-out-of-committee/article_5 33f35da-ad22-11eb-8018-9ff9cf06337b.html.

"Police Reports [4631 W. Napoleon Ave.]" *The Times-Picayune*, December 6, 1980.

Pollan, Michael. *The Omnivore's Dilemma: A Natural History of Four Meals*. New York: Penguin, 2007.

Pollvogt, Susannah W. "Unconstitutional Animus." *Fordham Law Review* 81, no. 2 (2012): 887–937.

Posner, Richard A. *Sex and Reason*. Cambridge, MA: Harvard University Press, 1992.

Posner, Richard A. "The Uncertain Protection of Privacy by the Supreme Court." *Supreme Court Review* 1979 (1979): 173–216.

Posner, Richard A., and Katharine B. Silbaugh. *A Guide to America's Sex Laws*. Chicago: University of Chicago Press, 1996.

Powell, Anastasia, and Nicola Henry. *Sexual Violence in a Digital Age*. London: Palgrave MacMillan, 2017.

Puar, Jasbir K. "The Cost of Getting Better: Suicide, Sensation, Switchpoints." *GLQ* 18, no. 1 (2011): 149–158.

Puar, Jasbir K. "Prognosis Time: Towards a Geopolitics of Affect, Debility, and Capacity." *Women and Performance: A Journal of Feminist Theory* 19, no. 2 (2009): 161–172.

Puar, Jasbir K. *The Right to Maim: Debility, Capacity, Disability*. Durham: Duke University Press, 2017.

Puar, Jasbir K. *Terrorist Assemblages: Homonationalism in Queer Times*. Durham: Duke University Press, 2007.

Purdy, Chase. *Billion Dollar Burger: Inside Big Tech's Race for the Future of Food*. New York: Portfolio, 2020.

Ramachandran, Gowri. "Against the Right to Bodily Integrity: Of Cyborgs and Human Right." *Denver University Law Review* 87, no. 1 (2009): 1–57.

Range, Friederike, Lisa Horn, Zsófia Viranyi, and Ludwig Huber. "The Absence of Reward Induces Inequity Aversion in Dogs." *PNAS* 106, no. 1 (2009): 340–345.

Rape, Abuse & Incest National Network. "Perpetrators of Sexual Violence: Statistics." www.rainn.org/statistics/perpetrators-sexual-violence.

Rasmussen, Claire E. *The Autonomous Animal: Self-Governance and the Modern Subject.* Minnesota: University of Minnesota Press, 2011.

Rawls, John. *Justice as Fairness: A Restatements.* Cambridge, MA: Harvard University Press, 2001.

Rawls, John. *Political Liberalism.* New York: Columbia University Press, [1993] 2005.

Rawls, John. *A Theory of Justice.* Cambridge, MA: Harvard University Press, [1971] 1999.

Reddy, Chandan. *Freedom with Violence: Race, Sexuality and the US State.* Durham: Duke University Press, 2011.

Reddy, Gayatri. *With Respect to Sex: Negotiating Hijra Identity in South India.* Chicago: University of Chicago Press, 2005.

Renfro, Paul M. "Sex Offender Registries Are Fueling Mass Incarceration—And They Aren't Helping Survivors." *Jacobin*, June 22, 2020. https://jacobin.com/2020/06/sex-offender-registries-mass-incarceration.

Renfro, Paul M. *Stranger Danger: Family Values, Childhood, and the American Carceral State.* Oxford: Oxford University Press, 2020.

Richards, Gary. "Queering Katrina: Gay Discourses of the Disaster in New Orleans." *Journal of American Studies* 44, no. 3 (2010): 519–534.

Ritchie, Andrea J. "Crimes against Nature: Challenging Criminalization of Queerness and Black Women's Sexuality." *Loyola Journal of Public Interest Law* 14, no. 1 (2013): 355–374.

Roach, Joseph. *Cities of the Dead: Circum-Atlantic Performance.* New York: Columbia University Press, 1996.

Roach, Shoniqua. "Black Sex in the Quiet." *differences: A Journal of Feminist Cultural Studies* 30, no. 1 (2019): 126–147.

Roach, Tom. *Friendship as a Way of Life: Foucault, AIDS, and the Politics of Shared Estrangement.* Albany: SUNY Press, 2012.

Roach, Tom. *Screen Love: Queer Intimacies in the Grindr Era.* Albany: SUNY Press, 2021.

Roberts, Dorothy E. *Killing the Black Body: Race, Reproduction, and the Meaning of Liberty.* New York: Pantheon Books, 1997.

Robertson, Stephen. "Shifting the Scene of the Crime: Sodomy and the American History of Sexual Violence." *Journal of the History of Sexuality* 19, no. 2 (May 2010): 223–242.

Rocke, Michael. *Forbidden Friendships: Homosexuality and Male Culture in Renaissance Florence.* New York: Oxford University Press, 1996.

Rollins, Joe. *AIDS and the Sexuality of Law: Ironic Jurisprudence.* New York: Palgrave Macmillan, 2004.

Rosenberg, Gabriel N. "Animals." In *The Routledge History of American Sexuality*, edited by Kevin P. Murphy, Jason Ruiz, and David Serlin, 32–41. New York: Routledge, 2020.

Rosenberg, Gabriel N. "Fetishizing Family Farms." *Boston Globe*, April 16, 2016. www.bostonglobe.com/ideas/2016/04/09/fetishizing-family-farms/NJszoKdCSQWaq2XBw7kvIL/story.html.

Rosenberg, Gabriel N. *The 4-H Harvest: Sexuality and the State in Rural America.* Philadelphia: University of Pennsylvania Press, 2016.

Rosenberg, Gabriel N. "How Meat Changed Sex: The Law of Interspecies Intimacy after Industrial Reproduction." *GLQ: A Journal of Lesbian and Gay Studies* 23, no. 4 (2017): 473–507.

Rosenberg, Gabriel N. "No Scrubs: Livestock Breeding, Eugenics, and the State in the Early Twentieth-Century United States." *Journal of American History* 107, no. 2 (2020): 362–387.

Rosenberg, Gabriel N. "On the Scene of Zoonotic Intimacies: Jungle, Market, Pork Plant." *Transgender Studies Quarterly* 7, no. 4 (2020): 646–656.

Rosenberg, Gabriel N. "A Race Suicide among the Hogs: The Biopolitics of Pork in the United States, 1865–1930." *American Quarterly* 68, no. 1 (March 2016): 49–73.

Rosenfeld, David L., and Anthony L. Burrow. "The Unified Model of Vegetarian Identity: A Conceptual Framework for Understanding Plant-based Food Choices." *Appetite* 112 (2017): 78–95.

Rosky, Clifford J. "Fear of the Queer Child." *Buffalo Law Review* 61, no. 3 (2013): 607–697.

Ross, Andrew Israel. *Public City/Public Sex: Homosexuality, Prostitution, and Urban Culture in Nineteenth-Century Paris.* Philadelphia: Temple University Press, 2019.

Ross, Loretta J., and Rickie Solinger. *Reproductive Justice: An Introduction.* Oakland: University of California Press, 2017.

Rothgerber, Hank. "A Comparison of Attitudes toward Meat and Animals among Strict and Semi-Vegetarians." *Appetite* 72 (2014): 98–105.

Roughgarden, Joan. *Evolution's Rainbow: Diversity, Gender, and Sexuality in Nature and People.* Berkeley: University of California Press, 2013.

Rubenfeld, Jed. "The Right of Privacy." *Harvard Law Review* 102, no. 4 (February 1989): 737–807.

Rubin, Gayle S. "Thinking Sex: Notes for a Radical Theory of the Politics of Sexuality." In *Deviations: A Gayle Rubin Reader,* edited by Gayle S. Rubin, 137–181. Durham: Duke University Press, [1984] 2011.

Rudy, Kathy. "LGBTQ . . . Z?" *Hypatia* 27, no. 3 (Summer 2012): 601–615.

Rudy, Kathy. *Loving Animals: Toward a New Animal Advocacy.* Minneapolis: University of Minnesota Press, 2013.

Saketopoulou, Avgi, and Ann Pellegrini. *Gender Without Identity.* New York: The Unconscious in Translation, 2023.

Sakha, Sarah, Emily Greytak, and Mya Haynes. *Is Sex Work Decriminalization the Answer?* ACLU, 2020. www.aclu.org/report/sex-work-decriminalization-answer -what-research-tells-us

Sandler, Jeffrey C., Naomi J. Freeman, and Kelly Michael Socia. "Does a Watched Pot Boil? A Time-Series Analysis of New York State's Sex Offender Registration and Notification Law." *Psychology Public Policy and Law* 14, no. 4 (2008): 284–302.

Sankofa, Jasmine. "From Margin to Center: Sex Work Decriminalization Is a Racial Justice Issue." *Amnesty International,* December 12, 2016. www.bostonreview.net /articles/pornographys-contradictions.

Satz, Ani B. "Disability, Vulnerability, and the Limits of Antidiscrimination." *Washington Law Review* 83, no. 4 (2008): 513–568.

Savci, Evren. *Queer in Translation: Sexual Politics under Neoliberalism.* Durham: Duke University Press, 2021.

Savin-Williams, Ritch C. *The New Gay Teenager.* Cambridge, MA: Harvard University Press, 2006.

Sawyer, Wendy. "BJS Fuels Myths about Sex Offense Recidivism, Contradicting its Own New Data." *Policy Prison Initiative,* June 6, 2019. www.prisonpolicy.org/blog/2019 /06/06/sexoffenses/.

Schulhofer, Stephen J. *Unwanted Sex: The Culture of Intimidation and the Failure of Law.* Cambridge, MA: Harvard University Press, 2000.

Schulman, Sarah. *Israel/Palestine and the Queer International.* Durham: Duke University, 2012.

Scott, Darieck. *Extravagant Abjection: Blackness, Power, and Sexuality in the African American Literary Imagination*. New York: New York University Press, 2010.

Sedgwick, Eve Kosofksy. *Epistemology of the Closet*. Berkeley, CA: University of California Press, 1990.

Sedgwick, Eve Kosofsky. "How to Bring Your Kids Up Gay." *Social Text* 29 (1991): 18–27.

Shah, Nayan. *Stranger Intimacy: Contesting Race, Sexuality, and the Law in the North American West*. Berkeley: University of California Press, 2011.

Shah, Svati P. *Street Corner Secrets: Sex, Work, and Migration in the City of Mumbai*. Durham, NC: Duke University Press, 2014.

Shakespeare, Tom, ed. *The Disability Studies Reader: Social Science Perspectives*. London: Cassell, 1998.

Shakespeare, Tom, Kath Gillespie-Sells, and Dominic Davies, eds. *The Sexual Politics of Disability: Untold Stories*. London: Cassell, 1996.

Shamir, Hila. "Feminist Approaches to the Regulation of Sex Work: Patterns in Transnational Governance Feminist Law Making." *Cornell International Law Journal* 52 (2019): 177–233.

Sharpe, Christina. *Monstrous Intimacies: Making Post-Slavery Subjects*. Durham: Duke University Press, 2010.

Sheldrake, Rupert, and Pamela Smart. "A Dog that Seems to Know When His Owner Is Coming Home: Videotaped Experiments and Observations." *Journal of Scientific Exploration* 14, no. 2 (2000): 233–255.

Siebers, Tony. "A Sexual Culture for Disabled People." In *Sex and Disability*, edited by Robert McRuer and Anna Mollow, 37–53. Durham: Duke University Press, 2012.

Simoneaux, Marie. "Bestiality Bill Is Not an Attempt to Strike Unconstitutional Sodomy Laws, Senator Says." *The Times-Picayune*, April 10, 2018. www.nola.com/news/crime _police/article_67fa6c79-5d0d-5202-bc60-33a96cacfa3c.html

Simoneaux, Marie. "John Bel Edwards Signs Tougher Bestiality Bill into Law." *The Times-Picayune*, May 31, 2018. www.nola.com/news/crime_police/john-bel-edwards -signs-tougher-bestiality-bill-into-law/article_1a432925-1107-56b6-8a71-e34b9 b1a350b.html.

Simoneaux, Marie. "Stricter Bestiality Law Passes in House Committee." *The Times-Picayune*, April 25, 2018. www.nola.com/news/crime_police/article_08fd563a-65c9 -5878-929a-c8a64077d636.html.

Singer, Peter. *Animal Liberation*. New York: Harper Perennial, [1975] 2009.

Singer, Peter. "Heavy Petting." *Prospect*, April 20, 2001. www.prospectmagazine.co.uk /magazine/heavypetting.

Smith, Molly, and Juno Mac. *Revolting Prostitutes: The Fight for Sex Workers' Rights*. Verso: London, 2020.

Smyth, Clelia, and Yolanda Estes. "The Myth of the Happy Hooker: Kantian Moral Reflections on a Phenomenology of Prostitution." In *Analyzing Violence against Women*, edited by Wanda Teays, 257–264. Switzerland: Springer, 2019.

Snorton, C. Riley. *Black on Both Sides: A Racial History of Trans Identity*. Minneapolis: University of Minnesota Press, 2017.

Snyder, Sharon L., Brenda Jo Brueggemann, and Rosemarie Garland-Thomson, eds. *Disability Studies: Enabling the Humanities*. New York: Modern Language Association of America, 2002.

Solis, Marie. "Sex Workers Will Finally Be Able to Carry Condoms Without Fear of Arrest in California." *Vice*, July 29, 2019. www.vice.com/en/article/j5wymd/sex-workers -condoms-abuse-california-law.

Sosin, Kate. "Against Backdrop of Anti-Trans Bills, Transgender Homicides Double." *The 19th*, April 16, 2021. https://19thnews.org/2021/04/against-backdrop-anti-trans-bills-transgender-homicides-double/.

Spear, Jennifer M. *Race, Sex, and Social Order in Early New Orleans*. Baltimore: Johns Hopkins University Press, 2008.

Spector, Jessica, ed. *Prostitution and Pornography: Philosophical Debate about the Sex Industry*. Stanford: Stanford University Press, 2006.

Spillers, Hortense J. "Mama's Baby, Papa's Maybe: An American Grammar Book." *Diacritics* 17, no. 2 (1987): 64–81.

Spindelman, Marc. "Surviving *Lawrence v. Texas*." *Michigan Law Review* 102, no. 7 (2004): 1615–1667.

Srikanth, Anagha. "Florida's New Ban on Transgender Sports Would Allow Schools to Subject Minors to Genital Inspections." *The Hill*, April 15, 2021. https://thehill.com/changing-america/respect/equality/548534-floridas-new-ban-on-transgender-students-in-sports-would/.

Srinivasan, Amia. *The Right to Sex: Feminism in the Twenty-First Century*. New York: Farrar, Straus, and Giroux, 2021.

Stallings, L. H. *A Dirty South Manifesto: Sexual Resistance and Imagination in the New South*. Oakland: University of California Press, 2020.

Stanley, Eric A. *Atmospheres of Violence: Structuring Antagonism and the Trans/Queer Ungovernable*. Durham: Duke University Press, 2021.

Stanley, Eric A., and Nat Smith, eds. *Captive Genders: Trans Embodiment and the Prison Industrial Complex*. Oakland: AK Press, 2011.

Stanonis, Anthony J. *Creating the Big Easy: New Orleans and the Emergence of Modern Tourism, 1918–1945*. Athens, GA: University of Georgia Press, 2006.

Stern, Mark Joseph. "You Can Still Be Arrested for Being Gay in Red-State America." *Slate*, August 5, 2013. https://slate.com/human-interest/2013/08/gay-people-are-still-being-arrested-for-having-consensual-sex-in-some-red-states-like-louisiana.html.

Stockton, Kathryn Bond. *The Queer Child, or Growing Sideways in the Twentieth Century*. Durham: Duke University Press, 2009.

Stop It Now! "About Us." www.stopitnow.org/about-us/who-we-are.

Stryker, Susan. "Transgender History, Homonormativity, and Disciplinarity." *Radical History Review* 100 (2008): 145–157.

Stryker, Susan, Paisley Currah, and Lisa Jean Moore. "Introduction: Trans-, Trans, or Transgender?" *Women's Studies Quarterly* 36, no. 3/4 (2008): 11–22.

Stryker, Susan, and Jim Van Buskirk. *Gay by the Bay: A History of Queer Culture in the San Francisco Bay Area*. San Francisco: Chronicle Books, 1996.

Sunstein, Cass R. "Liberty after *Lawrence*." *Ohio State Law Journal* 65, no. 5 (2004): 1059–1079.

Swift, Taylor. "You Need to Calm Down," *Lover*. Republic Records, 2019.

Taylor, Sunaura. *Beasts of Burden: Animal and Disability Liberation*. New York: The New Press, 2017.

Tewksbury, Richard. "Collateral Consequences of Sex Offender Registration." *Journal of Contemporary Criminal Justice* 21, no. 1 (2005): 67–81.

Thomas, Kendall. "Corpus Juris (Hetero)sexualis: Doctrine, Discourse, and Desire in *Bowers v. Hardwick*." *GLQ: A Journal of Lesbian & Gay Studies* 1, no. 1 (1993): 33–51.

Thomas, Lynnell L. *Desire and Disaster in New Orleans: Tourism, Race, and Historical Memory*. Durham: Duke University Press, 2014.

Threadcraft, Shatema. "North American Necropolitics and Gender: On #BlackLives-Matter and Black Femicide." *South Atlantic Quarterly* 116, no. 3 (2017): 553–579.

Thusi, I. India. "Harm, Sex, and Consequences." *Utah Law Review* 2019, no. 1 (2019): 159–213.

Thusi, I. India. "Ne Nya Sexpuritanerna." *Yale Journal of Law and Feminism* 34, no. 2 (2023): 66–73.

Thusi, I. India. *Policies Bodies: Law, Sex Work, and Desire in Johannesburg.* Stanford: Stanford University Press, 2022.

Thusi, I. India. "Radical Feminist Harms on Sex Workers." *Lewis and Clark Law Review* 22, no. 1 (2018): 185–229.

Tortorici, Zeb. "Against Nature: Sodomy and Homosexuality in Colonial Latin America." *History Compass* 10 (2012): 161–178.

Tower, Rev. Philo. *Slavery Unmasked: Being a Truthful Narrative.* Rochester: E. Darrow & Brother, 1856.

Tremain, Shelley. "On the Subject of Impairment." In *Disability/Postmodernity: Embodying Disability Theory*, edited by Mairian Corker and Tom Shakespeare, 32–47. London: Continuum, 2002.

Turner, Bryan S. *Vulnerability and Human Rights.* University Park: Penn State University Press, 2006.

Umbers, Lachlan Montgomery. "Enfranchising the Youth." *Critical Review of International Social and Political Philosophy* 23, no. 6 (2020): 732–755.

United States Department of Justice, Civil Rights Division. "Investigation of the New Orleans Police Department." Washington, D.C., 2017. www.justice.gov/crt/about/spl/nopd_report.pdf.

University of Chicago. "Trafficking, Prostitution and Inequality: A Public Lecture by Catharine MacKinnon." Video, 1:27:34. *YouTube*, December 14, 2011. www.youtube.com/watch?v=zpYegz1OqHA.

Upchurch, Charles. *"Beyond the Law": The Politics of Ending the Death Penalty for Sodomy in Britain.* Philadelphia: Temple University Press, 2021.

Vargas, Deb. "Ruminations on *Lo Sucio* as a Latino Queer Analytic." *American Quarterly* 66, no. 3 (2014): 715–726.

Vásquez, Bob Edward, Sean Maddan, and Jeffery T. Walker. "The Influence of Sex Offender Registration and Notification Laws in the United States: A Time-Series Analysis." *Crime & Delinquency* 54, no. 2 (2008): 175–192.

Vaught, Jeannette. "How to Make a Horse Have an Orgasm." In *Living with Animals: Bonds across Species*, edited by Natalie Porter and Ilana Gershon, 157–168. Ithaca: Cornell University Press, 2018.

Vaught, Jeannette. "Is It Sex if the Veterinarian Does the Work? The Problem of Pleasure in Multispecies Sexual Labor." In *The Relational Horse*, edited by Gala Argent and Jeannette Vaught, 135–146. Leiden: Brill, 2022.

Visé, Daniel de. "Vegetarianism Is on the Rise—Especially the Part-Time Kind." *The Hill*, November 3, 2022. https://thehill.com/changing-america/sustainability/3747206-vegetarianism-is-on-the-rise-especially-the-part-time-kind/.

Vogler, Stefan. *Sorting Sexualities: Expertise and the Politics of Legal Classification.* Chicago: University of Chicago Press, 2021.

Vrangalova, Zhana, and Joe Pardavila. "Sex Work in America." *The Science of Sex*, March 12, 2019. Podcast, 1:02:00.

Wall, John. *Children's Rights: Today's Global Challenge.* Lanham, MD: Rowman & Littlefield, 2017.

Wall, John. *Give Children the Vote: On Democratizing Democracy*. London: Bloomsbury Academic, 2022.

Ward, Jane. *Not Gay: Sex Between Straight White Men*. New York: New York University Press, 2015.

Ward, Jane. "Radical Experiments Involving Innocent Children: Locating Parenthood in Queer Utopia." In *A Critical Inquiry into Queer Utopias*, edited by Angela Jones, 231–243. New York: Palgrave Macmillan, 2013.

Warner, Michael. "New English Sodom." *American Literature* 64, no. 1 (1992): 19–47.

Weaver, Harlan. *Bad Dog: Pit Bull Politics and Multispecies Justice*. Seattle: University of Washington Press, 2021.

Weheliye, Alexander G. *Habeas Viscus: Racializing Assemblages, Biopolitics, and Black Feminist Theories of the Human*. Durham: Duke University Press, 2014.

Weheliye, Alexander G. "Pornotropes." *Journal of Visual Culture* 7, no. 1 (2008): 65–81.

Wiegman, Robyn. *Object Lessons*. Durham: Duke University Press, 2014.

Wilderson, Frank B., III. *Afropessimism*. Liveright: New York, 2020.

Withers, A.J. *Disability Politics and Theory*. Halifax: Fernwood, 2012.

Wolak, Janis, David Finkelhor, and Kimberly Mitchell. "Internet-Initiated Sex Crimes against Minors: Implications for Prevention Based on Findings from a National Study." *Journal of Adolescent Health* 35, no. 5 (2004): 424e11–e20.

Women With A Vision. "Constitutional Challenge Launched." NO Justice Project. https://wwav-no.org/no-justice-project/.

Wooten, Terrance. "Keyword 4: Sex Offender." *differences: A Journal of Feminist Cultural Studies* 30, no. 1 (2019): 82–90.

Wooten, Terrance. "'The Streets Are My Home': Black Male Sex Offenders, Hypersurveillance, and the Liminality of Home." *Feminist Formations* 33, no. 1 (Spring 2021): 33–55.

WPMI Web Staff. "Ten Louisiana Lawmakers Vote against 'Sex with Animals' Ban." *NBC*, April 11, 2018. Video, 0:27. https://mynbc15.com/news/local/ten-louisiana-lawmakers-vote-against-sex-with-animals-ban.

Wright, Richard G., ed. *Sex Offender Laws: Failed Policies, New Directions, 2nd Edition*. New York: Springer, 2015.

Wurgraft, Benjamin Aldes. *Meat Planet: Artificial Flesh and the Future of Food*. Berkeley: University of California Press, 2019.

Wynter, Sylvia. "On How We Mistook the Map for the Territory and Re-imprisoned Ourselves in Our Unbearable Wrongness of Being, of Desêtre: Black Studies Toward the Human Project." In *Not Only the Master's Tools: African-American Studies in Theory and Practice*, edited by Lewis R. Gordon and Jane Anna Gordon, 107–169. New York: Routledge, 2006.

Wynter, Sylvia. "Unsettling the Coloniality of Being/Power/Truth/Freedom: Towards the Human, after Man, Its Overrepresentation—An Argument." *CR: The New Centennial Review* 3, no. 3 (Fall 2003): 257–337.

Young, Amy M., Carol Boyd, and Amy Hubbell. "Prostitution, Drug Use, and Coping with Psychological Distress." *Journal of Drug Issues* 30, no. 4 (2000): 789–800.

Young, Damon R. *Making Sex Public and Other Cinematic Fantasies*. Durham: Duke University Press, 2018.

Zelizer, Viviana A. *The Purchase of Intimacy*. Princeton: Princeton University Press, 2007.

Zevits, Richard G., and Mary Ann Farkas. "Sex Offender Community Notification: Managing High Risk Criminals or Exacting Further Vengeance?" *Behavioral Sciences and the Law* 18, no. 2–3 (2000): 375–391.

Index

Joseph J. Fischel is Professor of Women's, Gender, and Sexuality Studies at Yale University. He is the author of *Screw Consent: A Better Politics of Sexual Justice* and *Sex and Harm in the Age of Consent.*

www.ingramcontent.com/pod-product-compliance
Lightning Source LLC
Chambersburg PA
CBHW030643270326
41929CB00007B/189